LEARNING TO TEACH USING ICT IN THE SECONDARY SCHOOL

Learning to Teach Using ICT in the Secondary School offers teachers of all subjects a comprehensive, practical introduction to the extensive possibilities that ICT offers pupils, teachers and schools. Underpinned by the latest theory and research, it provides practical advice and guidance, tried-and-tested examples, and covers a range of issues and topics essential for teachers using ICT to improve teaching and learning in their subject.

The third edition has been fully updated in light of rapid changes in the field of both ICT and education and includes five brand new chapters. Key topics covered include:

- theories of learning and ICT
- effective pedagogy for effective ICT
- using the interactive whiteboard to support whole class dialogue
- special needs and e-inclusion
- literacy and new literacies*NEW*
- multi-play digital games and on-line virtual worlds*NEW*

- mobile learning*NEW*
- e-safety
- supporting international citizenship through ICT*NEW*
- linking home and school
- ICT tools for administration and monitoring pupil progress*NEW*
- tools for professional development.

Including case studies and tasks to support your own learning, as well as ideas and activities to use with all your students, *Learning to Teach Using ICT in the Secondary School* is a vital source of support and inspiration for all training teachers as well as those looking to improve their knowledge. If you need a guide to using ICT in the classroom or for professional support, start with this book.

Marilyn Leask is Professor of Educational Knowledge Management, University of Bedfordshire, UK.

Norbert Pachler is Professor of Education at the Institute of Education, University of London, UK.

LEARNING TO TEACH SUBJECTS IN THE SECONDARY SCHOOL SERIES

Series Editors: Susan Capel and Marilyn Leask

Designed for all students learning to teach in secondary schools, and particularly those on school-based initial teacher training courses, the books in this series complement *Learning to Teach in the Secondary School* and its companion, *Starting to Teach in the Secondary School*. Each book in the series applies underpinning theory and addresses practical issues to support student teachers in school and in the training institution in learning how to teach a particular subject.

Learning to Teach in the Secondary School, 6th edition
Edited by Susan Capel, Marilyn Leask and Tony Turner

Learning to Teach Art and Design in the Secondary School, 2nd edition
Edited by Nicholas Addison and Lesley Burgess

Learning to Teach Citizenship in the Secondary School, 2nd edition
Edited by Liam Gearon

Learning to Teach Design and Technology in the Secondary School, 2nd edition
Edited by Gwyneth Owen-Jackson

Learning to Teach English in the Secondary School, 3rd edition
Edited by Jon Davison and Jane Dowson

Learning to Teach Geography in the Secondary School, 2nd edition
David Lambert and David Balderstone

Learning to Teach History in the Secondary School, 3rd edition
Edited by Terry Haydn, James Arthur, Martin Hunt and Alison Stephen

Learning to Teach ICT in the Secondary School
Edited by Steve Kennewell, John Parkinson and Howard Tanner

Learning to Teach Mathematics in the Secondary School, 3rd edition
Edited by Sue Johnston-Wilder, Peter Johnston-Wilder, David Pimm and Clare Lee

Learning to Teach Foreign Languages in the Secondary School, 4th edition
Norbert Pachler, Michael Evans, Ana Redondo and Linda Fisher

Learning to Teach Music in the Secondary School, 2nd edition
Edited by Chris Philpott and Gary Spruce

Learning to Teach Physical Education in the Secondary School, 3rd edition
Edited by Susan Capel

Learning to Teach Religious Education in the Secondary School, 2nd edition
Edited by L. Philip Barnes, Andrew Wright and Ann-Marie Brandom

Learning to Teach Science in the Secondary School, 3rd edition
Edited by Jenny Frost

Learning to Teach Using ICT in the Secondary School, 3rd edition
Edited by Marilyn Leask and Norbert Pachler

Starting to Teach in the Secondary School, 2nd edition
Edited by Susan Capel, Ruth Heilbronn, Marilyn Leask and Tony Turner

LEARNING TO TEACH USING ICT IN THE SECONDARY SCHOOL

A companion to school experience

3rd Edition

Edited by
**Marilyn Leask and
Norbert Pachler**

Routledge
Taylor & Francis Group

LONDON AND NEW YORK

Third edition published 2014
by Routledge
2 Park Square, Milton Park, Abingdon, Oxon OX14 4RN

and by Routledge
711 Third Avenue, New York, NY 10017

Routledge is an imprint of the Taylor & Francis Group, an informa business

First edition published by Routledge 1999
Second edition published by Routledge 2006

British Library Cataloguing in Publication Data
A catalogue record for this book is available from the British Library

Library of Congress Cataloging in Publication Data
Learning to teach using ICT in the secondary school : a companion to school experience / edited by Marilyn Leask and Norbert Pachler. -- Third edition.
pages ; cm
ISBN 978-0-415-51651-8 (hb) -- ISBN 978-0-415-51652-5 (pb) -- ISBN 978-0-203-12420-8 (eb) 1. Computer-assisted instruction--Great Britain--Case studies. 2. Information technology--Great Britain--Case studies. 3. Education, Secondary--Great Britain--Data processing--Case studies. 4. Education--Great Britain--Computer network resources--Case studies. I. Leask, Marilyn, 1950- II. Pachler, Norbert.
LB1028.5.L3884 2005
371.33'4--dc23
2013012889

ISBN: 978-0-415-51651-8 (hbk)
ISBN: 978-0-415-51652-5 (pbk)
ISBN: 978-0-203-12420-8 (ebk)

Typeset in Times New Roman
by Saxon Graphics Ltd, Derby

Printed and bound in Great Britain by
TJ International Ltd, Padstow, Cornwall

CONTENTS

INTRODUCTION   xix

NORBERT PACHLER AND MARILYN LEASK

■ References

1 PERSPECTIVES ON AND THEORIES OF LEARNING WITH DIGITAL TECHNOLOGIES   1

NORBERT PACHLER

■ introduction ■ what is the potential of digital technologies for learning? ■ what is learning and how can it be enhanced? ■ the centrality of the role of the teacher ■ the impact of technology on classroom practice ■ summary ■ references

2 THE IMPACT OF TECHNOLOGY ON TEACHING AND LEARNING: LESSONS FROM RESEARCH   18

MARGARET J. COX

■ introduction ■ the development of ICT technologies and focus of the research ■ uptake of ICT by schools and teachers ■ evidence of the impact of ICT on learning ■ attitudes towards ICT in education ■ the gender differences ■ contribution of ICT to enhance access and learning for special needs ■ the role and practices of the teachers ■ notes ■ summary ■ references

TASKS

TASKS ■ ■ ■ ■

TABLES

FIGURES

FIGURES ▪ ▪ ▪ ▪

LIST OF CONTRIBUTORS

Elisabetta Adami teaches and researches in Facoltà di Lingue e Letterature Straniere of the Universita degli studi Gabriele D'Annunzio Chieti Pescara; she is an associate member of the London Mobile Learning Group.

Ben Bachmair is Visiting Professor at the Institute of Education, University of London; he is a founding member of the London Mobile Learning Group.

Margit Böck is Professor of Language Teaching and Learning at the Institut für Deutschdidaktik at the Alpen-Adria-Universität Klagenfurt, Austria.

Kevin Burden, Course Leader for the Advanced Certificate in Sustained Professional Development, University of Hull (http://www2.hull.ac.uk/ifl/ces/staff-in-ces/kevin-burden.aspx).

Andrew Burn is Professor of Media Education at the London Knowledge Lab, Institute of Education, University of London and director of the DARE Centre (http://darecollaborative.net/).

Michele Burns is Deputy Headteacher at The Sandon School, Chelmsford.

Margaret J. Cox is Emeritus Professor of Information Technology in Education at King's College, London.

Nic Crowe is a specialist in online games. He is a Senior Lecturer and Course Leader (Contemporary Education), School of Sport and Education at Brunel University http://www.brunel.ac.uk/sse/education/staff/dr-nic-crowe.

Beat Döbeli Honegger is Professor at the Institut für Medien und Schule at the Pädagogische Hochschule Schwyz, Goldau, Switzerland; he is an associate member of the London Mobile Learning Group.

James Durran is part of the English team of the North Yorkshire Learning Zone.

Sara Flynn is a teacher undertaking a PhD at Brunel University with a focus on digital technologies and learning.

Sara Hennessy is Senior Lecturer in Teacher Development and Pedagogical Innovation in the Faculty of Education at the University of Cambridge.

Sarah Jones is a specialist in online learning and online professional development. She is director of Core Education UK. http://www.core-ed.org.uk/contact/Sarah.jpg/view.

Core Education is a founder member of the Education Futures Collaboration www. edfuturescollaboration.org.

Lorraine Kaye is an early years specialist and a senior lecturer at Middlesex University. http://www.mdx.ac.uk/aboutus/staffdirectory/Lorraine_Kaye.aspx.

Christina Kuegel's specialism is in special educational needs. She is a senior lecturer at the University of Bedfordshire which is a founder member of the Education Futures Collaboration.

Marilyn Leask is Professor of Educational Knowledge Management at the University of Bedfordshire, UK. She has been researching the use of digital technologies for educational uses for more than thirty years. http://www.beds.ac.uk/research/ired/groups/marilyn-leask. The University of Bedfordshire is a founder member of the Education Futures Collaboration www.edfuturescollaboration.org and she is Chief Editor of the Mapping Educational Specialist knowhow editorial board and a MirandaNet Fellow.

Lloyd Mead is a lecturer in special educational needs at Lambeth College.

Lorian Mead is an occupational therapist and she works for the National Health Service.

David Morris is a Senior Lecturer at the Cass School of Education and Communities at the University of East London.

Norbert Pachler is Professor of Education at the Institute of Education, University of London and the convenor of the London Mobile Learning Group (http://www.londonmobilelearning.net).

Ana Redondo is Senior Lecturer in Education and Subject Leader of a Secondary PGCE in Modern Languages. She has co-authored 'Learning to teach foreign languages in the Secondary school' (London: Routledge, 2013) and co-edited 'Teaching foreign languages in the Secondary School: a practical guide' (London: Routledge, 2014).

Judith Seipold is a professional in the field of media education specializing in mobile learning; she is an associate member of the London Mobile Learning Group.

Michelle Selinger is Director of Education Practice, Cisco Systems (http://www.cisco.com/web/about/ac79/edu/ourpractice.html).

James Shea is an English and ICT specialist and a senior lecturer in English education at the University of Bedfordshire. the University is a founder member of the Education Futures Collaboration. http://www.beds.ac.uk/howtoapply/departments/teacher-education/staff/james-shea.

Mary E. Webb is Senior Lecturer in IT and Education in the Department of Education and Professional Studies at King's College London.

Gareth Whyte is a trained ICT teacher and PhD student. He also runs a Hassle Free Computing, a computing and education business http://www.linkedin.com/pub/gareth-whyte/39/a67/286.

Lawrence Williams is an experienced teacher at the forefront of innovations in ICET and Computer Science in education. He is a teaching fellow at Brunel University School of Sport and Education and a long term MirandaNet Fellow.

Sarah Younie is a principal lecturer in education at De Montfort University with specialisms in digital technologies, learning and change. De Montfort University is a founder member of the Education Futures Collaboration www.edfuturescollaboration.org.

INTRODUCTION

Norbert Pachler and Marilyn Leask

The approaches to teaching and learning used in classrooms in innovative schools where digital technologies or ICTs are integrated across the curriculum can be considerably different to those that student teachers and current teachers experienced themselves at school. Practice in teaching and learning in UK schools has changed radically in schools whose staff have embraced the opportunities offered to learners and teachers by digital technologies and ICTs. All children are entitled to leave school fully equipped to use digital technologies in their work and in their everyday lives and, to achieve this, schools need to ensure pupils develop appropriate problem-solving capabilities and are familiar with the wide variety of technological tools and how they can be used. Indeed, schools increasingly face the challenge of adequately reflecting the 'cultural practices' (Pachler *et al.*, 2010) and 'genres of participation' (Ito *et al.*, 2008) around digital technologies young people have developed in their everyday lives.

In this text, we are not talking about moving to teacherless classrooms but about schools where it is natural for pupils to choose from a wide range of technologies in order to engage in work of high quality, satisfying a range of learning outcomes.

The contributors to this book come from a variety of backgrounds – schools, universities, LAs, industry and government agencies. Each addresses the issues from their perspective based on their experience and the research relevant to their field. All have a long history of being involved in developing and testing out innovative practice in the use of ICTs in education and for teachers' professional development. All are involved in international exchanges of ideas either through international collaborations between their pupils and others, through collaborative research and development projects and through international conferences. It is this experience that leads us to feel confident in sharing the ideas expressed in the book.

We believe that there is enough evidence that the appropriate integration of ICT into the curriculum enhances pupil learning, and the contributions to this text acknowledge the evidence for practice where it exists. However, teachers need to work and learn together to establish new and high-quality professional practice in their own schools. This has to include assessment methods as well as teaching methods and different learning environments. Research into innovative schools shows that schools where staff are mutually supportive of each other's developing knowledge and skills are more likely to be successful in tackling these challenges than those where knowledge about computers and computing is seen to be the province of a select few.

As a profession, teachers need to find solutions to issues related to wider use of ICT such as ensuring the availability and reliability of equipment, resourcing, training and the development of new pedagogic skills as well as ethical and health issues. Different schools are finding different ways of solving these problems. But the challenge of changing practice must be faced if children are to be prepared adequately to face life in the twenty-first century and not ghettoised from an early age into the 'information rich' and the 'information poor' sectors of society.

The ideas that are discussed in this book reflect what some teachers are doing now. New ways of teaching pupils are continually developing and all involved in education need to be prepared to regularly review and adapt new practice. Digital technologies for example offer considerable opportunities for personalising learning and assessment but both these approaches to focusing teaching on the individual's needs are relatively underdeveloped in the school system.

The book is of course just a starting point for exploring the possibilities that ICTs offer to schools and teachers and pupils alike, but we hope we have provided enough ideas and thorough enough justification of these ideas to encourage those who are new to this area to embark on experimentation in their classrooms and schools with some confidence.

The ideas in this book have been tried and tested in innovative schools around the UK and abroad. The school in which you teach may not be able to offer you all of the opportunities that you read about here. However, you may find that working through online communities of colleagues provides opportunities to extend your skills and knowledge. We are committed to the notion of lifelong learning and hope this book provides you with opportunities for continuing professional development, which we think is a professional responsibility we all need to undertake for the benefit of the education of our pupils.

The focus of this book is on pedagogy, on the application of new technologies in the classroom, not on how to use the technology. It aims to present a framework for ICT use in subject teaching based on an understanding of theoretical issues, possible approaches, strategies and examples from practice. We include activities that are intended to act as an 'interface' between the experience of the authors of individual chapters and your own personal circumstances.

We believe that changes in the world around us present us with the moral obligation to prepare young people for an adult life which increasingly requires knowledge, skills and understanding other than those traditionally covered by school curricula, such as the capability to work effectively with technologies in order to be able to make a full contribution to society or critical media literacy to ensure that they are able to take part in social and entertainment activities not as passive recipients but as active and empowered participants.

We hope you share our vision.

Marilyn Leask and Norbert Pachler, June 2013

REFERENCES

Ito, M., Horst, H., Bittanti, M., Boyd, D., Herr-Stephenson, B., Lange, P., Pascoe, C. and Robinson, L. (2008) *Living and learning with new media: summary of findings from the digital youth project*, Chicago: MacArthur Foundation. Available at: http://www.itofisher.com/mito/weblog/2008/11/living_and_learning_with_new_m.html.

Pachler, N., Bachmair, B. and Cook, J. (2010) *Mobile learning: structures, agency, practices*, New York: Springer.

PERSPECTIVES ON AND THEORIES OF LEARNING WITH DIGITAL TECHNOLOGIES

Norbert Pachler

INTRODUCTION

This chapter starts from the premise that any teaching, be it enhanced by digital technologies or not, in order to be effective, i.e. maximise student learning, needs to be based on a principled understanding of learning and on insights from (educational) psychology and learning theory. The aim of this chapter, therefore, is to explore the potential of digital technologies in relation to some of what is known about how we learn as a basis for informed decisions about whether, when and how best to use digital technologies for pedagogical purposes.

In view of the quick pace of change in the world of technologies, their use in educational settings is often predicated on a certain degree of faith in the potential of a particular tool, application or service by 'early adopters', at times with little or no empirical evidence being available and often with too little thought being given to a proper conceptualisation of their affordances in relation to intended learning outcomes. The introduction of interactive whiteboards in recent years in UK schools is a case in point. And there exists a danger that the new wave of mobile technologies will suffer a similar fate. Only after enough schools had purchased and installed interactive whiteboards, often with the expectation that they would increase standards in teaching and learning and improve, develop and enhance effective pedagogy, was and could research aiming to identify and disseminate leading practice in their use be carried out.

The history of technology-enhanced learning is littered with unfulfilled, unrealistic promises and technological fetishisation, a trend Larry Cuban (2001) memorably termed 'oversold and underused'. There are many reasons for this: the allure of technology as panacea coupled with a persuasive business and industry lobby is one; the level of confidence in using digital technologies on the part of teachers is another, as are access to hardware and the lack of availability of professional development focusing on pedagogical issues. For a detailed discussion of possible barriers, see e.g. Jones, 2004.

Another reason affecting the effectiveness of digital technologies in teaching and learning relates to the limitations of available research. Frequently, given the complexity of variables governing technology use in education, research and evaluation paradigms tend to be 'macrostructural' (Cox and Marshall, 2007, p. 60) rather than large-scale and longitudinal.

Cuban, rightly, makes the point that frequently new technologies are introduced into schools without giving enough thought to how best to use them. This is also borne out by research in the UK. Cox and Marshall (2007, p. 65), for example, note that a lack of knowledge of technologies and a lack of confidence are important factors impacting on the effectiveness of technology use in teaching and learning. As a result, technology use often does not bring about significant pedagogical innovation and improvement in the learning experience and outcomes of students. The presence of technology does not in and of itself empower learners; schools and teachers have a crucial role to play. Arguably, use of digital technologies as productivity tools, as opposed to creativity tools, for example the use of interactive whiteboards simply as display technology, is missing the point. Instead of doing new things, it promotes doing old things in new ways (see Noss and Pachler, 1999).

Reflecting on what is known about how pupils learn, coupled with acquiring an in-depth understanding of the affordances of different technologies, are useful strategies when introducing the variable 'digital technologies' into already complex processes of teaching and learning, in order to maximise positive impact:

> While a study may be able to demonstrate an improvement in a pupil over time, it is very difficult (and sometimes impossible) to determine whether the use of ICT was critical, or played a role in improved attainment because so many other factors will have played a part. ... Additionally, ICT provision and use is likely to be very closely related to factors like quality of teaching and learning more generally, pupil characteristics, and quality of school leadership. For these reasons, isolating 'ICT' as a separate factor is often not meaningful or desirable, and understanding its links with other factors is a key facet of studying its impact.
>
> (Pittard *el al.*, 2003, p. 4)

As its title suggests, this chapter focuses on a discussion of theories of and perspectives on learning; the affordances of technology can only be sketched out here in an indicative manner due to a lack of space.

Conole and Dyke (2004), for example, list the following features: accessibility; speed of change; diversity; communication and collaboration; reflection; multimodality and nonlinearity; risk, fragility and uncertainty; immediacy; monopolisation; surveillance – all of which, they argue, can help to inform practitioners in their use of specific technologies. Fisher, Higgins and Loveless (2006, pp. 20–1) articulate the affordances of technology in the context of teacher learning as clusters of purposeful activities (see Table 1.1), which appear to have great transfer value to student learning.

■ **Table 1.1** Clusters of purposeful activities with digital technologies

Knowledge building	■ adapting and developing ideas ■ modelling ■ representing understanding in multimodal and dynamic ways
Distributed cognition	■ accessing resources ■ finding things out ■ writing, composing and presenting with mediating artefacts and tools
Community and communication	■ exchanging and sharing communication ■ extending the context of activity ■ extending the participating community at local and global levels
Engagement	■ exploring and playing ■ acknowledging risk and uncertainty ■ working with different dimensions of interactivity ■ responding to immediacy

Source: Fisher, Higgins and Loveless, 2006, pp. 20–1.

Note: The terms Information and Communication Technologies (ICT), new technologies and digital technologies will be used more or less interchangeably in this chapter.

OBJECTIVES

By the end of this chapter you should have an awareness of:

■ some of the claims made about the potential of digital technologies for learning;
■ dominant theories and conceptualisations of learning and their implications for the use of digital technologies;
■ criteria for the selection and effective use of technological tools and services in teaching and learning.

WHAT IS THE POTENTIAL OF DIGITAL TECHNOLOGIES FOR LEARNING?

Technology can be seen to possess potential, for example, to liberate users from routine tasks and empower them to focus on creative and cognitive, rather than procedural, aspects of tasks such as writing. It also makes available vast amounts of information, the ability to produce and disseminate such information and not just use and consume it. It enables networking and immersion in virtual worlds and much more.

These and other possibilities are, however, not unproblematic, as they can be seen, potentially at least, to deprive learners of real, first-hand (multi-sensory) experiences at the cost of simulations and models. Also, the quality of an artefact can easily become more important than the processes involved in creating it or the quantity of information can easily be misconstrued for quality of experience (see Bonnett, 1997).

In short, the potential of digital technologies and their affordances for learning in formal contexts frequently need to be harnessed by teachers, as often, and the work of Charles Crook (2012) exemplifies this clearly, tensions exist between the cultural and media practices of young people in everyday life and those valorised by the socio-cultural settings of schools.

Angela McFarlane (2001, p. 230) provides a number of reasons why a systematic engagement with technology is valuable and important. She abstracts the following generic traits and specific educational benefits of technologies from research such as:

■ learner enthusiasm;
■ learner confidence;
■ cognitive processing speed;
■ concentration;
■ range of writing forms used;
■ quality of revisions to writing;
■ spelling, and presentation in writing;
■ speed of learning;
■ information handling skill;
■ critical thinking;
■ ability to organise and classify information;
■ improved reading and comprehension;
■ learner autonomy, leading to improved motivation and improved learning;
■ transformed power relationships in learning, leading to benefits for the learner.

One of the key claims normally made in similar lists is that of technology promoting 'interactivity'. Beauchamp and Kennewell (2010, p. 760) define interactivity as 'the ability to respond contingently to the learner's actions' and view it in terms of 'the orchestration of features of the classroom to provide potential and structure for action towards learning goals'. Interestingly, in their research they found that the nature of interactivity in whole-class teaching, i.e. the types of student–teacher interactions (e.g. exposition, types of questioning [funnelling, probing, uptake], collective reflection, etc.), appeared to be more important in bringing about learning than the use of technology. They ascribe this to a lack of dialogic interaction, which – with reference to Robin Alexander (2004) – they characterise as collective, reciprocal, supportive, cumulative, purposeful and as developing meaning through voicing multiple perspectives around educational uses of technologies, which – for them – leads to greater understanding of ideas. They focused in particular on interactive whiteboards in their work and conclude that expertise in the orchestration of resources such as digital technologies is key. Specifically, they argue for a shift from educational uses of technologies as 'objects of participation' to 'tools for conducting interaction'.

Task 1.1 **Using technology to foster interactivity**

With reference to an aspect of your subject specialism, how can digital technologies be used as a 'tool for conducting interaction'? Then, consider some of the tools you have used in your own learning or in your teaching and evaluate them in terms of their potential for fostering interaction.

However, a tendency to perceive the value of digital technologies in terms of a transmission and delivery model still prevails rather widely. The fields of e-learning and mobile learning are cases in point. E-learning discourses can be dominated by discussions about often static learning resources as an embodiment of content to be taught and learnt, of the storage of, and access to content in online repositories; in relatively emancipated perspectives on e-learning such content is user-generated but the focus is still on content. For a critical discussion of e-learning, see Pachler and Daly, 2011. Mobile learning, the emerging sub-domain of technology-enhanced learning, is often plagued by similarly reductive approaches (see e.g. Pimmer and Pachler, forthcoming). In this view, learners are seen as 'empty vessels' to be filled by education with the help of technology. For a socio-cultural ecological approach to mobile learning which focuses on mobile devices as cultural resources and foregrounds user-generated *contexts* for learning, see Pachler, Bachmair and Cook, 2010.

Increasingly, though, there have been attempts to explore the potential contribution of digital technologies to the social qualities of our lives and there has been a considerable growth in the significance of technologies as agents in interaction and collaboration rather than more narrowly as productivity tools. To this is linked the centrality of technology in a digital age for how we communicate with each other, how we use language, how we socialise, spend our leisure time, shop, entertain ourselves as well as work and learn in and about the world. In short, technology has become an integral part of everyday life and it has made possible new human practices, such as social networking.

Lee Rainie, Director of the Pew Research Center's Internet and American Life Project, a 'non-profit, non-partisan fact tank' that studies the social impact of the internet, in a presentation at the University of Florida in 2007 (http://www.pewinternet.org/Presentations/2007/The-impact-of-technology-on-peoples-everyday-lives.aspx), stresses that the connectivity inherent in new digital eco-systems changes our relationship to information and media as well as to each other in ten important ways:

- volume of information grows;
- velocity of information increases: 'smart mobs';
- venues of intersecting with information and people multiply: place shifting, time shifting, 'absent presence' and 'present absence';
- venturing for information changes: new search strategies and search expectations;
- vigilance for information transforms: it is truncated and elongated;
- valence of information improves and variety increases;
- vetting of information becomes more social;
- viewing of information is disaggregated and becomes more horizontal;
- voting and ventilating about information proliferates;
- invention of information and the visibility of new creators is made easier.

In short, digital technologies are having a significant impact on social life and media habits, which is sometimes called 'participatory turn' (see also Pachler, Bachmair and Cook, 2010). For a detailed discussion of the implications of these fundamental changes, see Crook (2012), whose work suggests they cause a range of tensions and challenges requiring carefully considered pedagogical responses.

Mitchel Resnik (2002, pp. 32–3) concludes that in order to take full advantage of new technologies 'we need to fundamentally rethink our approaches to learning and education – and our ideas of how technology can support them'. In particular, he advances the view that there prevails the fallacy that learning is about information, which – according to him – is limiting and distorting. Resnik posits that learning is not about information transmission but an active process of construction of new understandings through active exploration, experimentation, discussion and reflection. 'In short: people *don't get* ideas, they *make* them.' He promotes the view that the best learning experiences involve designing and creating things – with the help of new technologies. From this, it follows for Resnik that we need to fundamentally reorganise classrooms and replace what he calls a 'centralised-control model' with a more 'entrepreneurial' approach to learning (p. 36). Key features of this approach are learner agency and autonomy/independence and interdisciplinary topic- and project-based approaches. In addition, he argues for an updating of curricula for the digital age from a focus on 'things to know' to a focus on 'strategies for learning things you don't know' (p. 36).

However, there are also cautionary voices in relation to technology use for and in education. Emma Haughton (1999), in a book review of Jane Healy's *Failure to connect* (1999), discusses Healy's view that '[just] because children ... are performing tasks that look technologically sophisticated does not mean they are learning anything important'. Haughton goes on to report Healy's opinion that much of 'educational' software is 'crowded with extraneous and time-consuming effects that accomplish little beyond distracting children and distancing them from real learning'. Among other things, Healy mentions dangers such as impulsive clicking, trial-and-error use or guessing. In Healy's view, computer time can subtract from talking, socialising, playing, imagining or learning to focus the mind internally, leading to a loss of ground.

In summary, whilst there are strong claims to be made for educational uses of technologies, they cannot be viewed as a panacea, as *the* solution to the educational challenges we face by virtue of their sheer existence.

WHAT IS LEARNING AND HOW CAN IT BE ENHANCED?

In the absence of a very strong evidence base about the impact of technologies on and in education, and in view of the complexity of schools and classrooms as well as of the 'disruptive' force ascribed to technologies in relation to the ecology of classrooms (see e.g. Sharples, 2003), this chapter will now explore the notion of learning in some detail with a view to identifying key features and processes the affordances of digital technologies can be used to support and maximise.

Alex Moore (2000, p. 1) makes the pertinent point that every teacher operates according to a theory of learning and within a certain philosophical context be they explicit/conscious or implicit/unconscious. He goes on to note (p. 2) that the presence of explicit theory in educational policy has been conspicuous by its absence. This is also true for education technology policy where very often financial exigencies, in particular the hope for making savings, or the desire to bring about innovation and change as well as an increase in the attainment levels of learners, are key drivers. Similarly, it needs to be remembered that software and app designers also have their own mental models of what learning is and how it best be fostered; these models tend to feed into product design.

In the literature frequently three different learning paradigms are distinguished: behaviourism, cognitive theories and social interactionism. They will be discussed here briefly in turn and with reference to the affordances of digital technologies.

Behaviourism is a perspective on learning in which the notion of *conditioning is central*, i.e. the idea that it is possible to explain human behaviour in terms of responses to stimuli and that, dependent on the nature of the stimulus, varying kinds of human responses can be provoked. This principle was subsequently extended by the idea that human behaviour can be accounted for through what is observable, that environmental rather than genetic factors result in learning, that there exists a range of behaviours that are possible and that reinforcement is imperative:

> [behaviourist] theory thus came to explain learning in terms of *operant conditioning*: an individual responds to a stimulus by behaving in a particular way. Whatever happens subsequently will affect the likelihood of that behaviour recurring. If the behaviour is reinforced (i.e. rewarded or punished) then the likelihood of that behaviour occurring on a subsequent occasion will be increased or decreased.
>
> (Williams and Burden, 1997, p. 9)

In its application in educational technologies, the behaviourist tradition is characterised by an instructional pattern characterised by a sequential series of small steps each covering a piece of the subject domain or a particular skill in focus. The technological device or application models the role of the tutor by offering some input or paradigm, which the learner can 'drill and practise' followed by the provision of feedback.

Mark Warschauer (1996) identifies the following rationale behind these programs, which he considers to have value:

■ Repeated exposure to the same material is beneficial or even essential to learning.
■ A computer is ideal for carrying out repeated drills, since the machine does not get bored with presenting the same material and since it can provide non-judgemental feedback.
■ A computer can present such material on an individualised basis, allowing students to proceed at their own pace and freeing up class time for other activities.

One of the particular problems with 'drill and practice' software is that it can potentially create 'a passive mentality which seeks only the "right" answers, thus stifling children's motivation to seek out underlying reasons or to produce answers that are in any way divergent' (Bonnett, 1997, pp. 157–8). More advanced hybrids of the computer-as-tutor software tradition, such as artificial intelligence, intelligent tutoring or integrated learning systems, preoccupied with '(1) individualisation [of] problems and questions tailored to the [changing] needs of particular learners, and (2) the delivery of constructive feedback' (Crook, 1994, p. 12), have proved very difficult to develop. One of the important arguments Crook (1994) advances in his critical evaluation of the tutor model of educational computing is that,

> 'tutoring' talk is something that is organised at levels superordinate to that of the current moment. In other words, effective tutoring dialogues are embedded in more extensive contexts of shared experience. Such dialogues are normally made possible by the history of this experience.
>
> (Crook, 1994, p. 15)

The value, therefore, of interactions with human tutors lies in the fact that, unlike computational devices, they are able to draw on their knowledge of the learner gained through previous interactions in similar and different contexts. Given the complexity of the processes involved, it is very difficult to program it through mathematical algorithms.

Cognitive theories of learning move beyond a focus on observable behaviour and, instead, focus on what goes on inside people's heads, i.e. on mental processes. Knowledge is no longer seen as a passively absorbed behavioural repertoire. As a result, the learner is framed as a mentally active participant in the learning process.

Two main schools of thought can be distinguished, *information processing* and *constructivism*. The former tries to explain the workings of the brain in terms of rules and models of information intake, storage and processing and how this helps to explain human behaviour. The latter sees knowledge as made up of symbolic mental representations and something that learners actively construct on the basis of their existing cognitive structures and learning as a process of active discovery. This, importantly, means that knowledge is relative to learners' stage of development and existing mental representations (see Perry, 1999).

> [The developmental psychologist Jean] Piaget saw cognitive development as essentially a process *of maturation*, within which genetics and experience interact. The developing mind is viewed as constantly seeking *equilibration*, i.e. a balance between what is known and what is currently being experienced. This is accomplished by the complementary processes *of assimilation* and *accommodation*. Put simply, assimilation is the process by which incoming information is changed or modified in our minds so that we can fit it in with what we already know. Accommodation, on the other hand, is the process by which we modify what we already know to take into account new information. Working in conjunction, these two processes contribute to what Piaget terms the central process of cognitive *adaptation*.
>
> (Williams and Burden, 1997, p. 22)

Research on intelligence or intelligent behaviour, which can be seen as 'the appropriate use of cognitive skills and strategies within specific contexts' (Williams and Burden, 1997, p. 20), can be seen to have been significantly informed by the information processing model of cognitive psychology. Aptitude and capacity to learn are one important aspect; another is the proposition that people learn in different ways, which has given rise to interest in so-called 'learning styles', i.e. in the notion that students have different learning preferences such as visual, aural and/or kinaesthetic (VAK). This has been keenly debated in the educational literature and after a phase of relatively uncritical acceptance of the existence and benefits of distinct, if not neurologically determined learning styles, by many schools and practitioners, currently a more nuanced and critical perspective prevails (see e.g. Coffield *et al.*, 2004).

In terms of educational technologies, the theories of cognitive psychologists can be seen to inform software following the 'revelatory' paradigm of discovery-based and problem-solving oriented learning and simulation (see Collins *et al.*, 1987, p. 16). The most notable proponent of using the potential of new technologies to help learners 'construct new understandings through their exploratory activity' (Crook, 1994, p. 16) is Seymour Papert with his notion of a 'microworld':

> Papert's proposal is driven by a compelling image. If you wish to learn to speak French, he argues, you go to France. This surely makes good sense to us. But if

> France is where you go to command French, where do you 'go' to command, say, mathematics? What must be discovered in that case is a sort of 'Mathsland'.
>
> (Crook, 1994, p. 16)

Multimedia, combining and integrating the written and the spoken word as well as various kinds of still and moving images, as well as virtual worlds, such as Second Life, can be seen to have considerable potential for presenting to learners near-to-life microworlds modelling and (re)creating diverse aspects of subjects. There remain, of course, problems, which should guard us against over-reliance on technology-based approaches. True representations of reality are often – if not always – impossible, there exists the danger of (over)simplification as well as of working in isolation and at one stage removed from reality itself. There is also the question whether technology-based activities add or subtract authenticity to classroom-based learning activities.

Theories of cognitive psychology also allow us to understand the impact of applications and tools, which help users process information, engage them in abstract thinking, allow them to make the knowledge-construction processes transparent and help them to build classificatory systems. Generic software, such as word processors, databases, spreadsheets, etc., fall into this category. There is some consensus amongst commentators that these applications are liberating and empower the user to engage in cognitive and creative thinking.

Social interactionism, the third school of thought of (educational) psychology discussed here briefly, adds the importance of the location of human learning within a socio-cultural environment to the idea of learners constructing their own knowledge and understanding.

The best-known proponent is the Russian Lev Vygotsky, whose work, whilst conceived in the 1930s, did not become available in the West in translation until the 1960s and 1970s. Put simply, the premise of his work revolves around the importance of interaction with others as part of the learning process:

> Vygotsky took issue with the Piagetian view that from the time of their birth children learn independently by exploring their environment, and with the behaviourist view that adults are entirely responsible for shaping children's learning by the judicious use of rewards and punishment.
>
> (Williams and Burden, 1997, p. 39)

Vygotsky afforded great importance to the role of language in the interaction of learners with one another: '[it] is by means of language that culture is transmitted, thinking develops and learning occurs' (Williams and Burden, 1997, p. 40). According to social interactionism, learning takes place through engagement with contextualised and situationalised socio-cultural environments and through 'contact with a culture of material and social resources that everywhere supports cognitive activity' (Crook, 1994, p. 32). A crucial part is played by other significant people in learners' lives, be they parents, teachers or peers, who enhance the learning of others by 'selecting and shaping the learning experiences presented to them' and who help them 'to move into and through the next layer of knowledge or understanding' which Vygotsky called the *zone of proximal development* (Williams and Burden, 1997, p. 40).

Digital technologies can be seen to have mediatory potential in the Vygotskyan sense as the idea of social negotiation includes the internalisation of the pre-given world of cultural resources, which, in a digital age, are fundamentally bound up with technology. For a detailed discussion, see Pachler, Bachmair and Cook, 2010 and Pachler, Cook and Bachmair, 2010. Furthermore, technology enables the sharing of cognitive resources among people in order to extend the cognitive resources of an individual, a phenomenon called distributed cognition in the specialist literature. One frequently cited example of such 'culturally constituted functional groups' in the literature is the airline cockpit (Hutchins and Klausen, 1996); others are consultations amongst doctors in hospitals. For a more detailed discussion of distributed cognition in the context of e-learning, see e.g. Pachler and Daly, 2011.

There is, of course, a large body of literature dealing with the notion of learning, which is applied and builds on the ideas derived from (educational) psychology and which focuses on areas such as pedagogy, didactics, learning design or technology-enhanced learning. In the following a few carefully selected **perspectives on learning** are discussed as they offer useful food for thought about how to try to maximise the affordances of technology in teaching and learning.

Let us start with a paper by Mary Kalantzis and Bill Cope (2004), who explore the dynamics of education, the curriculum and pedagogy as *'designs for learning'*. They make the simple but important point that, at one level, learning can be understood as making meaning in and of the world. Education for them – and that is where the role of the school and teachers come in – 'is the conscious nurturing of learning in a community which has been designed primarily for that purpose' (p. 39). 'Conscious nurturing' is, therefore, about fostering learning by design, normally with the following features: conscious, systematic, explicit, goal-orientated, for and about the real world (p. 39). Kalantzis and Cope (2004, p. 40) go on to stress that learning is determined by the conditions in which it occurs; in other words, it is always situated. 'Situated learning' is a term popularised by Lave and Wenger (1991), who are also well known for the notion of communities of practice, and refers to the fact that meaning is not just a result of the interrelationship of signs (words, images, sounds, acts, objects, etc.) and the user of signs but that it also depends on situations. The focus for Kalantzis and Cope is more on conditions (Table 1.2):

> And some conditions are more favourable than others. Two conditions, particularly, impact on learning: first, whether a person's identity, subjectivity or sense of themselves has been engaged; and second, whether the engagement is such that it can broaden their horizons of knowledge and capability.
>
> (Kalantzis and Cope, 2004, p. 40)

■ **Table 1.2** Conditions of learning

Condition 1: BELONGING – effective learning engages the learner's identity. It builds on the learner's knowledge, experiences, interests and motivation. In any learning community, there is a broad range of difference, and this is because the everyday life-worlds from which students come are always varied.

Condition 2: TRANSFORMATION – effective learning takes the learner on a journey into new and unfamiliar terrains. However, for learning to occur the journey into the unfamiliar needs to stay with a zone of intelligibility and safety. At each step, it needs to travel just the right distance from the learner's life-world starting point.

Source: Kalantzis and Cope, 2004, p. 46.

Kalantzis and Cope (2004, p. 61) go on to discuss their understanding of knowledge, which they characterise as 'the process of connecting the stuff in the mind to the stuff of the world' and to define learning in relation to that as '[l]earning is a relationship between the knower and the knowable, in which the learner discovers that the knowable can in fact be known and is perhaps worth knowing'.

Task 1.2 **Effective technology-enhanced pedagogy**

With reference to an aspect of your subject specialism, how can digital technologies be used to draw the knower closer to the knowable ensuring a sense of belonging, for example by relating the work to the learner's life world, whilst at the same time creating an element of transformation by extending the learner's exiting framework? What examples of this can you identify in your department and across your school?

Another perspective is that of *authentic collaborative knowledge building* promoted by Marlene Scardamalia and Carl Bereiter (1999), which re-conceptualises learners from 'clients' of the service provider school to knowledge constructors and collectors and participants in a learning organisation. The concept is similar to problem-based learning and project-based learning but more radial in the sense that the problems are real, not set and the focus is not on artefact creation but on the knowledge itself, not its physical representation (p. 276). The perspective on learning is underpinned by the idea of schools preparing young people for life and work in a knowledge society and an understanding of knowledge as a cultural and economic 'resource' and not only as 'stuff in the head'. Scardamalia and Bereiter liken the role of the learner to that of a contributor to a scientific research team with the aim of the production of new knowledge with the difference that it is most likely not going to be knowledge that is new to the world but knowledge that is derivative rather than original and new to the students. In the process, students are allowed and required to exercise a high level of responsibility and to contribute solutions to and explanations of problems. Digital technologies for the authors come in as a discourse medium and they set out a number of characteristics that would foster authentic collaborative knowledge building such as a problem, rather than a topic focus; a focus on the production of knowledge rather than media objects; on contribution rather than display; on theory improvement rather than answer finding; on sustained versus 'single-pass' knowledge creation and on public rather than person-to-person communication as well as on reflection rather than short wait times (pp. 281–2).

Third, *cognitive apprenticeship* has gathered some traction in the literature and deserves a mention here. It is related to situated learning and socio-cognitive approaches to learning by focusing on the cognitive processes of the individual but locates them in problem-solving in social settings. It combines traditional apprenticeship approaches to learning focusing on the experiential with cognitive elements and recommends to teachers to provide students with the 'opportunity to observe, engage in, and invent or discover expert strategies in context' (Collins *et al.*, 1991, p. 13). Collins *et al.* identify the following related 'teaching methods': modelling, coaching, scaffolding, articulation, reflection and exploration.

And finally, it is instructive to look at the premise behind Paul Kirschner's (2006) research programme on *interactivity and learning* in education, who notes that learning can best take place, when instruction facilitates, stimulates or activates: (1) interaction with others such as peers and experts in pairs, teams, or communities through different forms of external dialogue, (2) interaction with oneself on the individual cognitive and metacognitive level via internal dialogue, (3) the confrontation between internal and external dialogue including the social relationships that arise as a result of this, and (4) the interaction between the individuals and others with the learning, training, and social environment in which learning and instruction is taking place, including the environment's physical, temporal and emotional attributes (i.e., its affordances, constraints, and conventions).

(Kirschner, 2006, p. 11)

Task 1.3 **Using digital technologies to foster learning**

Consider how digital technologies could be used to support one or more of the 'teaching methods' of cognitive apprenticeship or one or more of the interactions discussed by Kirschner (2006). Draw up a list with the methods and types of interaction on the left-hand side and map examples of technology use that is relevant to the learners you teach against the individual items.

For a discussion from a socio-cultural ecological perspective around structures, agency and cultural practices, see Chapter 13 by Seipold *et al.* in this volume or Pachler, Bachmair and Cook, 2010.

From the above it can be concluded that it is vitally important for teachers to be aware how the use of digital technologies in the classroom impacts on teacher–learner, learner–teacher and learner–learner interactions as well as on the social context surrounding the use of technology and how it is shaped by them. Also, there are the issues of the impact of educational technologies on the status of the teacher and the role of digital technologies as mediators of learning. Given the importance of interpersonal interaction, questions need to be asked as to whether educational technologies do, indeed, have this mediatory potential or whether their use will undermine the social quality of education and deprive learners of vital 'scaffolded social encounters' (see Crook 1994, pp. 61, 80). Charles Crook, in his 1994 book *Computers and the collaborative experience of learning,* repeatedly points out the need to employ computer-mediation very carefully and deliberately and to ask searching questions as to its potential to provide interactions that are actually significant in bringing about learning.

The discussion of theories of learning in this section, then, suggests that learning is as – if not more – likely to take place via the interactions of learners with peers and the teacher whilst using educational technologies as it is via the interactions with technology itself.

THE CENTRALITY OF THE ROLE OF THE TEACHER

One thing research shows is that teachers' pedagogical actions have a large impact on students' uses of new technologies. In their review of the research, Cox and Webb (2004) identify a range of factors, such as

teachers' beliefs about how their students learn; and the types of ICT resources teachers choose to use; their knowledge about their own subject and the potential for ICT to enhance their pupils' learning.

(Cox and Marshall, 2007, p. 65)

Whilst acknowledging the fundamental impact on traditional pedagogical modes, it is important to emphasise how the effectiveness of new technologies in the learning process depends on the 'centrality' of the role of the teacher in rendering pupils' experiences and work at and with the computer – and other digital devices – coherent by embedding them in a context of interpersonal support (see Crook, 1994, p. 101). The role of the teacher remains pivotal, such as, for example, in identifying appropriate learning outcomes, choosing appropriate software and activities and structuring and sequencing the learning process or in facilitating moderating online discussions. Nevertheless, fundamental changes to the role of the teacher continue to take place, in John Higgins' terms, from 'magister' (instructor) to 'pedagogue' (facilitator of pupil learning) (see Higgins, 1988). Mauri Collins and Zane Berge (1996) characterise the changes not just in the role of the teacher but also that of the learner, as summarised in Table 1.3.

■ **Table 1.3** Changes in the roles of teacher and learner

Changing instructor roles	*Changing student roles*
From oracle and lecturer to consultant, guide, and resource provider	From passive receptacles for hand-me-down knowledge to constructors of their own language
Teachers become expert questioners, rather than providers of answers	Students become complex problem-solvers rather than just memorisers of facts
Teachers become designers of student learning experiences rather than just providers of content	Students see topics from multiple perspectives
Teachers provide only the initial structure to student work, encouraging increasing self-direction	Students refine their own questions and search for their own answers
Teacher presents multiple perspectives on topics, emphasising the salient points	Students work as group members on more collaborative/cooperative assignments; group interaction significantly increased
From a solitary teacher to a member of a learning team (reduces isolation sometimes experienced by teachers)	Increased multicultural awareness
From teacher having total autonomy to activities that can be broadly assessed	Students work toward fluency with the same tools as professionals in their field
From total control of the teaching environment to sharing with the student as a fellow learner	More emphasis on students as autonomous, independent, self-motivated managers of their own time and learning process
More emphasis on sensitivity to student learning styles	Discussion of students' own work in the classroom
Teacher–learner power structures erode observation of the teacher's expert performance or just learning to 'pass the test'	Emphasis on knowledge use rather than only emphasis on acquiring learning strategies (both individually and collaboratively)
	Access to resources is significantly expanded

Source: Collins and Berge, 1996.

In their research, John and Sutherland (2004, p. 102) stress that what they call 'subject subculture', the traditions and antecedents of which often influence how innovative educational technology practices are developed: 'teachers only tend to adopt new practices if the assumptions inherent in the innovation are consistent with their epistemological beliefs and personal theories'. Subsequently they also point to the importance of established school subject subcultures and that there can be a juxtaposition of a teacher's personal style and subject cultural factors (p. 105).

THE IMPACT OF TECHNOLOGY ON CLASSROOM PRACTICE

Based on research in nine UK secondary schools and data collected in and around 85 lessons in which Information and Communication Technologies for learning were well embedded, Crook *et al.* (2010, p. 4) conclude that new technologies can reconfigure classroom practice in the following, important ways:

- ICT makes possible new forms of classroom practice. This is apparent in three particular respects: (1) the reconfiguration of space such that new patterns of mobility, flexible working and activity management can occur; (2) new ways in which class activities can be triggered, orchestrated and monitored; (3) new experiences associated with the virtualisation of established and routine practices – such as using multiple documents in parallel or manipulating spatial representations.
- ICT creates the possibility of a wide variety of learning practices. Overarching this variety are three central activities which are significantly enriched by the increasingly ubiquitous availability of technologies: (1) exposition, which is animated by the opportunity to invoke rich shared images, video and plans; (2) independent research, which is extended by the availability of internet search opportunities; (3) construction, which is made possible by ready-to-hand ICT-based tools.

The report, which makes for very interesting reading, goes on to discuss emerging themes and to analyse conditions under which ICT has an impact on learning.

The impact of technology in the classroom is also linked to our earlier discussion of learning and knowledge. Kalantzis and Cope (2004, pp. 62–3) distinguish four fundamental ways of knowing or 'knowledge movements' as they call them: experiencing the known and the new, conceptualising by naming and theorising, analysing functionally and critically, and applying appropriately and creatively.

Task 1.4 **Using digital technology to support 'knowledge movements'**

Again with reference to an aspect of your subject specialism, how can digital technologies be used to support Kalantzis and Cope's four 'knowledge movements'? First, relate the knowledge movements to activities from your schemes of work and then map technology uses against them.

Finally, for the purposes of this chapter, in her discussion of pedagogical forms for mobile learning, Diana Laurillard (2007, pp. 157–8) lists the following activities, which illustrate that digital technologies offer new opportunities for engaging learners that are all linked to key processes of learning and coming to know; at the same time, the list clearly shows how these activities are fundamentally routed in more traditional pedagogical approaches:

- exploring;
- investigating;
- discussing;
- recording, capturing data;
- building, making, modelling;
- sharing;
- testing;
- adapting;
- reflecting.

As teachers, we should give careful consideration to how best to engage learners with the help of digital technologies.

SUMMARY

This chapter tried to show the importance of an understanding of theories of learning for effective technology-enhanced pedagogy. This includes awareness on the part of the teacher of the assumptions made by devices and applications and their creators about how learning takes place. This is, of course, not to argue technological determinism, i.e. to suggest that technology determines human behaviour, social relations and organisation. Instead, it recognises that technologies do not operate in a contextual vacuum and that the effect of a particular medium is never intrinsic in a medium but instead mediated by type of use and contexts (see Luke, 2000, p. 74). Careful selection of devices and applications and types of uses on the basis of knowledge about learning are key to effective technology use in education.

REFERENCES

Alexander, R. (2004) *Dialogic teaching*, York: Dialogos.

Beauchamp, G. and Kennewell, S. (2010) 'Interactivity in the classroom and its impact on learning', *Computers and Education* 54(3), pp. 759–66.

Bonnett, M. (1997) 'Computers in the classroom: some values issues' in A. McFarlane (ed.) *Information technology and authentic learning: realising the potential of computers in the primary classroom*, London: Routledge.

Coffield, F., Moseley, D., Hall, E. and Ecclestone, K. (2004) *Learning styles and pedagogy in post-16 learning: a systematic and critical review*, London: Learning and Skills Research Centre. Available at: http://www.leerbeleving.nl/wp-content/uploads/2011/09/learning-styles.pdf (accessed 7 May 2013).

Collins, A., Brown, J. and Newman, S. (1987) 'Cognitive apprenticeship: teaching the craft of reading, writing, and mathematics', Technical Report No. 403, Illinois University, Urbana,

Center for the Study of Reading, Bolt, Beranek and Newman, Inc., Cambridge, MA. Available at: http://ocw.metu.edu.tr/pluginfile.php/9107/mod_resource/content/1/Collins%20report.pdf (accessed 23 May 2013).

Collins, A., Brown, J.S. and Holum, A. (1991) 'Cognitive apprenticeship: making thinking visible', *American Educator* 15(3), pp. 6–11. Available at: http://www.academia.edu/281205/Cognitive_Apprenticeship_Making_Thinking_Visible (accessed 7 May 2013).

Collins, M. and Berge, Z. (1996) 'Facilitating interaction in computer mediated online courses', background information paper for a presentation at the FSU/AECT Distance Education Conference, Tallahassee, Florida.

Conole, G. and Dyke, M. (2004) 'What are the affordances of information and communication technologies?' *ALT-J* 12(2), pp. 113–24.

Cox, M. and Webb, M. (2004) *ICT and pedagogy: a review of the research literature*, Coventry: Becta.

Cox, M. and Marshall, G. (2007) 'Effects of ICT: do we know what we should know?', *Education and Information Technologies* 12(2), pp. 59–70.

Crook, C. (1994) *Computers and the collaborative experience of learning*, London: Routledge.

——(2012) 'The "digital native" in context: tensions associated with importing Web 2.0 practices into the school setting', *Oxford Review of Education* 38(1), pp. 63–80.

Crook, C., Harrison, C., Farrington-Flint, L., Tomas, C. and Underwood, J. (2010) *The impact of technology: value-added classroom practice*, Coventry: Becta. Available at: http://dera.ioe.ac.uk/1771/1/upload-dir/downloads/page_documents/research/reports/the_impact_of_technology.pdf (accessed 7 May 2013).

Cuban, L. (2001) *Oversold and underused: computers in the classroom*, Cambridge, MA: Harvard University Press.

Fisher, T., Higgins, C. and Loveless, A. (2006) *Teachers learning with digital technologies: a review of research and projects*, Bristol: Futurelab. Available at: http://archive.futurelab.org.uk/resources/documents/lit_reviews/Teachers_Review.pdf (accessed 7 May 2013).

Haughton, E. (1999) 'Look what they've done to my brain, ma', *The Independent Education*, 3 June, p. 2.

Higgins, J. (1988) *Language, learners and computers: human intelligence and artificial unintelligence*, London: Longman.

Hutchins, E. and Klausen, T. (1996) 'Distributed cognition in an airline cockpit' in D. Middleton and Y. Engeström (eds), *Communication and cognition at work*, Cambridge, UK: Cambridge University Press.

John, P. and Sutherland, R. (2004) 'Teaching and learning with ICT: new technology, new learning?' *Education, Communication and Information* 4(1), pp. 101–7.

Jones, A. (2004) *A review of the research literature on barriers to the uptake of ICT by teachers*, Coventry: Becta. Available at: http://dera.ioe.ac.uk/1603/1/becta_2004_barrierstouptake_litrev.pdf (accessed 7 May 2013).

Kalantzis, M. and Cope, B. (2004) 'Designs for learning', *E-learning* 1(1), pp. 38–93.

Kirschner, P. (2006) '(Inter)dependent learning: learning is interaction', inaugural address, Utrecht University. Available at: http://www.ou.nl/Docs/Expertise/NELLL/publicaties/(Inter)dependent%20learning%20-%20Learning%20is%20interaction%20-%20Inaugural%20address%20Utrecht%20University.pdf (accessed 7 May 2013).

Laurillard, D. (2007) 'Pedagogical forms of mobile learning: framing research questions', in N. Pachler (ed.) *Mobile learning: towards a research agenda*, London: WLE Centre, Institute of Education. Available at: http://www.wlecentre.ac.uk/cms/files/occasionalpapers/mobilelearning_pachler_2007.pdf (accessed 7 May 2013).

Lave, J. and Wenger, E. (1991) *Situated learning: legitimate peripheral participation*, Cambridge: Cambridge University Press.

Luke, C. (2000) 'Cyber-schooling and technological change: multiliteracies for new times' in B. Cope and M. Kalantzis (eds), *Multiliteracies*, London: Routledge.

McFarlane, A. (2001) 'Perspectives on the relationships between ICT and assessment', *Journal of Computer Assisted Learning*, 17(3): pp. 227–34.

Moore, A. (2000) *Teaching and learning: pedagogy, curriculum and culture*, London: Routledge Falmer.

Noss, R. and Pachler, N. (1999) 'Building new pedagogies: the ICT challenge' in R. Mortimore (ed.) *Understanding pedagogy and its impact on learning*, London: Paul Chapman.

Pachler, N. and Daly, C. (2011) *Key issues in e-learning: research and practice*, London: Continuum.

Pachler, N., Bachmair, B. and Cook, J. (2010) *Mobile learning: structures, agency, practices*, New York: Springer.

Pachler, N., Cook, J. and Bachmair, B. (2010) 'Appropriation of mobile cultural resources for learning', *International Journal of Mobile and Blended Learning* 2(1), pp. 1–21, reprinted in D. Parsons (2012) (ed.) *Refining current practices in mobile and blended learning: new applications*, Hershey, PA: IGI Global, pp. 10–30.

Perry, W. (1999) *Forms of ethical and intellectual development in the college years*, San Francisco: Jossey-Bass Publishers.

Pimmer, C. and Pachler, N. (forthcoming) 'Mobile learning in the workplace: unlocking the value of mobile technology for work-based education' in M. Ally and A. Tsinakos (eds), *Mobile learning development for flexible learning*, Edmonton: Athabasca University Press.

Pittard, V., Bannister, R. and Dunn, J. (2003) *The big pICTure: the impact of ICT on attainment, motivation and learning*, London: DfES.

Resnick, M. (2002) 'Rethinking learning in the digital age' in G. Kirkman (ed.) *The global information technology report 2001–02: readiness for the networked world*, Oxford: Oxford University Press.

Scardamalia, M. and Bereiter, C. (1999) 'Schools as knowledge-building organizations' in D. Keating and C. Hertzman (eds), *Today's children, tomorrow's society: the developmental health and wealth of nations*, New York: Guilford. Available at: http://www.ikit.org/fulltext/1999schoolsaskb.pdf (accessed 7 May 2013).

Sharples, M. (2003) 'Disruptive devices: mobile technology for conversational learning', *International Journal of Continuing Engineering Education and Lifelong Learning*, 12(5/6), pp. 504–20.

Warschauer, M. (1996) 'Computer-assisted language learning: an introduction' in S. Fotos (ed.) *Multimedia language teaching*, Tokyo: Logos International.

Williams, M. and Burden, R. (1997) *Psychology for language teachers: a social constructivist approach*, Cambridge: Cambridge University Press.

THE IMPACT OF TECHNOLOGY ON TEACHING AND LEARNING: LESSONS FROM RESEARCH

Margaret J. Cox

INTRODUCTION

This chapter draws on the many years of research into the uses of ICT for teaching and learning, telling the story of how technologies have changed and how, along with the focus of research, these have affected our teaching. A large part of this evidence has been on the impact of different types of software and hardware uses on the learning of the individual student. The focus here is on what kinds of learner challenges and interactions are promoted and enabled by specific styles of educational software environments. No uses of technologies in mainstream education will, however, be successful without the appropriate choices and guidance by the teachers themselves. The chapter discusses the range of research lessons about what kinds of practices by teachers have been successful and how teacher-training strategies have or have not been effective.

As the technologies have evolved and diversified, examples are given as to how to cope with these advances by both taking advantage of the evidence about the impact on learning as well as the impact on the curriculum and how these can be applied to today's ICT technologies. What the extensive research has shown is that to be able to integrate ICT into your teaching you need to consider the specific features of various ICT resources and how they relate to the knowledge, skills and processes that you are aiming to teach. Finally, as new technologies emerge there is no static situation, students are gaining experience and expertise outside of formal education and we need to harness this to make best uses of ICT in the curriculum.

This chapter presents evidence from more than 40 years of research into the impact of ICT in secondary schools on teaching and learning. Even in the twenty-first century we read media reports and even government reports questioning whether the use of ICT is really beneficial to teaching and learning. The problem we all have in keeping up with this research evidence is that it is extensive and irrefutable and therefore extremely time consuming to read and difficult for teachers to see which evidence is valuable to their teaching. This chapter could be peppered with many reliable international references to back up the evidence but I have limited these mostly to well-known substantial reviews and books and a few academic papers to which you can turn for more details of the impact of technologies on teaching and learning. This impact has been profound where there has been an *appropriate* and *sustained* use of ICT within the curriculum but because as we know ICT is forever changing, the success in achieving an integration of technology within a subject over a period of time has been limited by shifting challenges for teachers and schools. On the one hand there has been a steady growth of technology in schools and an explosion of personal access to technologies; on the other hand, because the teaching and learning opportunities change with every new device or technological enhancement, it has been and continues to be time-consuming and often daunting for teachers to embrace the full facilities and features of ICT technologies within the curriculum.

To make things even more difficult for teachers, since 1988 we have had the introduction of a national curriculum followed by numerous versions of it with changing priorities and examples of how to use technology in your teaching. This has been made even more complicated by the recent government decision to scrap the existing ICT curriculum and replace it with a computer science curriculum with a stronger emphasis on computational thinking and the fundamentals of computer science.[1] As a result it has been very difficult for teachers to keep up with which aspect of ICT might help enhance their teaching and when they can fit it into the already very full curriculum. This chapter therefore presents the research evidence, which is now well known to show what impact different technologies have had on students' learning and how these have contributed to teachers' knowledge and practices. It will therefore also enable you to think about what potential the most recent ICT technologies might have on your students' learning and your teaching drawing on lessons from the past. The intention is to convince you that using ICT can greatly enhance your teaching and students' learning in the sure knowledge that there are years and years of positive reliable evidence to back it up.

OBJECTIVES

By the end of this chapter you should:
■ have gained a diachronic overview of research into ICT for teaching and learning;
■ understand some of the learner challenges and interactions promoted by educational software; and
■ have learned about successful teacher practices in the use of ICT.

THE DEVELOPMENT OF ICT TECHNOLOGIES AND FOCUS OF THE RESEARCH

As early as the mid-1960s, when technologies were mainly in the form of standard computers, these were being used by mathematics and science educators to enhance students' learning, but the opportunities were limited by the types of machines available and the computer programs that would run on them. The types of programs were mainly 'drill and practice' followed by simulations. The primary purpose of those teachers using IT resources then was to enhance teaching and learning of specific topics but without the later distractions of commercial software primarily developed for the workplace. In other words, ICT resources were specifically designed in collaboration with teachers for educational purposes, not for commercial and personal use as is the case for most technologies today. The research and development of ICT in education was therefore often intertwined with the design of the ICT tools themselves and provided feedback to developers for improving the software and educational design. The limitations of the early technology resources were not the only constraints on their educational use in those early days, as we shall see later in the chapter, but there were many difficulties that teachers had in first obtaining any ICT resources and second, having sufficient knowledge and experience to be able to use them effectively in their teaching.

During that early period there were many research studies investigating the impact on students' learning which showed, for example, that using science simulations could enhance students' understanding of complex concepts and relationships, and geography and history role-playing decision-making games could help students develop an understanding of conflicting roles and decisions and the consequences of these on specific outcomes. Most software developed and used between the 1960s to the late 1980s, before the widespread use of the internet in education, was designed to try to remedy the difficulties which teachers perceived learners to have in learning, and which they, themselves, had in teaching.

However, even though by the 1990s there was strong evidence of the benefits of using ICT in schools (Watson, 1993; Cox and Abbott, 2004; Leask and Pachler, 2005), pressure from national governments brought about a dilemma for schools that were on the one hand being required to obtain ICT resources to teach all learners ICT and computing skills, and on the other hand wanting to expand the use of ICT within other curriculum subjects. These two approaches continue to the present day but are now much more complex, with the expansion and diversification of new technologies which include online communications, personalised learning, social software and mobile devices; and with the recent proposed fundamental change in the United Kingdom to the ICT curriculum in schools. Table 2.1 shows the key technological developments over the last 50 years since the invention of the internet and the changing focus of researching their impact in education.

The topics chosen for educational software programs drew upon learners' misconceptions and alternative frameworks identified from the large body of knowledge about what kinds of misconceptions learners have and what kinds of teaching methods and resources have been found to help address such misconceptions. This body of educational research enabled developers and researchers to produce educational software, which addressed these learning difficulties. What is also evident from the research results published over decades is that the types of ICT use for teaching are closely related to specific concepts and skills and tend to be topic specific. It was during the earlier subject specific uses of ICT that significant government investments were made into technology resources for education, teacher training and curriculum development. Now, in the twenty-first century, more than 40 years later, the most significant evidence confirming that ICT can have a positive impact on students' learning in secondary education still comes from the use of these styles of subject-based software, but with modern interfaces and graphical features, specifically designed for education or of the uses of more generic software primarily developed for commercial and private sectors such as spreadsheets, databases, and web-based courses (Cox and Abbott, 2004; Plomp *et al.*, 2009).

However, whereas the early uses of technology were mainly either on a one-to-one basis, students working in pairs or whole class demonstrations; more recent developments and much greater levels of ICT resources in schools have resulted in networks of

■ **Table 2.1** Technological developments for education and the focus of research into teaching and learning

Dates/era	Technological developments	Development of IT in education and focus of research
1950–67	Large-scale mainframe valve-based analogue computers. Miniaturisation of electronic components (transistors and diodes) and circuitry leading to the large-scale digital computer. Increase in memory and processing capacity.	Subject-based drill and practice programs for use with small groups of students. The impact on students' learning and evaluating educational software.
1968–70	The introduction of the internet – ARPANET* seeding the international networks of computers.	Remote access to schools and universities to widen the use of subject specific software, comparing learning with subject specific software to learning with traditional resources.
1970–74	Creation of JANET**, a UK network of computers, and real-time interactive computers. User graphics online computer terminals. Internet connections for some schools. Remote access to computers from different locations. Forerunners of desktop computers: e.g. Hewlett Packard, Horizon.	Remote access to educational software programs from universities to schools and colleges. Individual computer workstations. The impact on learning and evaluating educational software.
1975–79	Miniaturisation of computers. Production of small desktop computers with 32k of memory and graphics. Move from tape-based storage to disk-based storage of large computer programs. Prestel/Teletext: commercial and educational information provided online.	Educational graphic simulations, expanding range of educational software. Changes in the IT subject curricula. The impact on learning and the requirements for teacher training.
1980–84	Fibre optics facilitating fast and large-scale communication. Modems in schools providing wider remote access. Range of input and output devices for education, e.g. concept keyboard/graphics tablets, touch screens, speech input and output.	Large range of drill and practice and simulation software available to schools. The impact on students' learning, attitudes and uptake by teachers and schools. Effectiveness of teacher training.

Dates/era	Technological developments	Development of IT in education and focus of research
1985–89	Microsoft windows launched. More powerful cheaper personal microcomputers. Invention of the World Wide Web by Tim Berners-Lee (http://en.wikipedia.org/wiki/Tim_Berners-Lee). New external storage devices: CD-ROM; interactive video; plug-in memory cards.	More diverse range of educational software, including modelling software and some access to the internet and Http://www. International school collaborations. The impact on learning, uptake by teachers and schools, and collaboration amongst learners. International comparisons.
1990–95	Laptop computers. Spread of wireless computer technologies: networks; air-mouse; video conferencing. Mobile phones.	School/home uses of IT. Pressure on IT resources for teaching IT as a subject and teaching with IT. Organisation of learning with IT and online. School priorities and level of integration. Theories underpinning educational change.
1996–99	Interactive whiteboards. Personal Digital Assistants (PDAs).	Whole class teaching with IT. Individualised learning. Informal education.
2000–04	Further increases in processing and storage of personal computers. Wide, cheap access to the internet and the World Wide Web. Virtual learning environments (VLEs).	More powerful educational software. Conflict between office software and educational bespoke software. Online courses and assessment. Networked learning.
2005–09	Web2, Wikis, VLEs. Thin clients. Thin client technologies in schools and colleges. Haptic devices for use in education. Development of molecular computing technology. Widespread access to wireless networks. Web2 technology – social software environments: e.g. Wikipedia, Second Life.	Digital literacies and agendas, relative benefits of different IT resources in school and home. New representations. Changing focus of human computer interactions. Impact on formal/informal learning. Changing teacher–learner–external expert relationships.
2010–13	Graphics portable devices: iPhone; Blackberry; iPad; Satnav; MP3-players; e-books. Social software: Facebook; blogs; Twitter; social bookmarking; One World TV. Integration of mobile technologies with social software.	Mobile learning. Levels of immersion in technologies. Impact of social software on learning scope and agendas. Impact of informal learning with ICT on formal learning and vice versa.

Notes: * ARPANET (Advanced Research Projects Agency Network), created in 1969.
      ** JANET (Joint Academic Network).

computers in rooms, online 24 hour access and students with personal computers, leading to a change in focus of researching technology impact in schools as more influential factors were identified. The types of uses were dependent upon the priorities of the school, the way the curriculum was delivered and the types of ICT tools developed at the time. These changing goals, shown in Table 2.1 and discussed below, which have expanded the opportunities for effective use of ICT in schools, were as a consequence of the growth of technology in education and the outcomes of previous research studies.

UPTAKE OF ICT BY SCHOOLS AND TEACHERS

A major change in the impact of ICT on students' learning was of course brought about by a gradual and substantial increase in the level of resources in schools. Until there was a reasonable level of resources in schools it was impossible for the majority of teachers to take advantage of the potential benefits of the technology for students' learning. Once ICT resources became cheap enough to be able to be purchased in large numbers, schools purchased networks of computers, clusters of stand-alone ones and some for administrative purposes, and eventually access to the internet. In the late 1980s, as is shown in Table 2.1, four major changes took place that changed the whole educational research agenda for technology in education and its impact on teaching and learning (Cox, 2005):

1   The cost of computing reduced sufficiently for schools in many countries to be able to afford networks of computers and display monitors.
2   The computer manufacturers provided bundled 'educational' generic software when the networks were purchased, mainly chosen for the wider software market in commerce and industry; i.e. word-processing, spreadsheets, database software and graphics applications, which mostly displaced the educational software being used.
3   The complex design of the 'new' software environments required a greater understanding of human–computer interfaces, curriculum potential and the wider learning context.
4   It was recognised that schools and teachers needed to have a great deal more training beyond how to use the technology, in order to be able to take up and integrate the use of ICT in their teaching.

ICT in education was no longer seen by governments as an optional extra – it was a very large investment that required ongoing justification and substantial research to show what impact it was having across all sectors of education, especially schools. National policies on ICT in education became closely linked to government-led research agendas (Pelgrum and Plomp, 1993; Plomp *et al.*, 2009) and a large element of this was to measure the uptake of technology in schools by teachers, students, types of computers and so on, which, as we all know, resulted in the erroneous conclusion that nearly all teachers were using ICT regularly in their lessons. This conclusion has been frequently based on the assumption that if most teachers report using ICT in their teaching then they must be using a wide range of software and resources in a variety of lessons and subjects on a regular basis. However, more in-depth research over the years has shown that this isn't often the case.

More than ten years ago in a questionnaire survey of 100 British IT teachers whose main responsibility was to teach the ICT curriculum, conducted by Preston, Cox and Cox (2000), the frequency of use of ICT, as reported by these teachers, was for every lesson and every day of the week, as one might expect. However, in response to more probing questions about the *frequency of specific types* of ICT resources used, i.e. word-processing, spreadsheets, educational simulations, modelling etc., 96 per cent of the teachers reported only using *word-processing* more than once a month. All the other software resources they were expected to use were actually only being used very infrequently. This shows that had the researchers relied on questions that only asked about uses of ICT (as has been the case in many national and international surveys) without specifying what *types* of ICT, then the results would have been very misleading. Therefore, if we are to learn from previous research we need to examine the research evidence which specifies what kinds of technology the teachers were using, in what curriculum areas and what kinds of uses actually occurred with the students.

EVIDENCE OF THE IMPACT OF ICT ON LEARNING

Since the mid-1960s one of the major goals of researching ICT in education has been to examine an intervention ('What was the treatment?') and examine the impact ('What was the impact?'). The original research design for measuring the effects of an intervention was to expose a select group of students to using a technology tool specifically designed for educational purposes, sometimes in a school setting, sometimes in a laboratory, and to measure improvements in learning through pre- and post-testing. Many examples of this type of research can be found in the early editions of the *Computers and Education Journal*, the *Journal for Computer Assisted Learning* and other similar journals. The various limitations of this type of research design included the researchers often assuming that the tests could be based on those that measured traditional learning gains. The intervention was often an additional extra to the students' learning programme and the results could not be generalised to other schools and settings. However, what this kind of study showed was that when a specific subject-based software program was used within a relevant curriculum area and where the results identified were measurable accurately, then there was often a positive impact on the students' learning (Watson, 1993; Cox and Abbott, 2004).

An important word of warning for teachers and researchers that came from many of the earlier studies between 1975 and 1995 is that what the students learned was often not what the teachers and researchers had anticipated them learning. As we shall see later in this chapter, the interactions between the learners and ICT are not the same, for example, as between learners and the teacher, or learners and a book.

A literature review of ICT and attainment by Cox and Abbott (2004) showed that the most robust evidence of technology use enhancing students' learning was from studies that focused on specific uses of technology. Where the research aim has been to investigate the effects of technology on attainment without clearly identifying the range and type of technology use then unclear results have been obtained, making it difficult to conclude any repeatable impact of a type of technology use on students' learning. What has often provided more detailed information about the actual learning activities and processes is action research (e.g. Somekh, 1995; Ziegler, 2001). This research approach involves researching the implementation of an innovation, usually from multiple points of view, which usually involves the researchers also taking part in the teaching where the innovation is occurring using an evaluation strategy to document, within and across school, changes in practice. The evidence collected then forms the basis of the discussions amongst teachers and researchers, which gives more in-depth information about how ICT has been used, what specific contribution it has made to students' learning and what kinds of changes in teaching practices were required to use ICT effectively.

Effects of ICT on learning strategies and processes

Once there were sufficient ICT resources in many schools and classrooms, there was an increase in research projects to measure in more detail how specific technology uses impacted upon learning strategies and processes, requiring different research methods including audio-visual recordings of students' technology uses, human computer interactions, and the devising of specific tasks that students had to complete relating to specific ICT uses. As is explained in other chapters of this book, learning processes include learners' interactions with the teacher, their fellow students whether present in reality or present through social networking, and the interactions with the ICT technology itself. It can also be experienced synchronously or asynchronously in relation to the learning resource that the student is using. Three broad examples are given below of what kinds of interactions the learner might be experiencing in relation to the type of software environment they might be using followed by evidence of the impact on learning and the consequences for teaching.

TUTORIAL STYLE INTERACTIONS

One of the earliest designs of interactive software tasks, which used to be called computer assisted learning drill and practice programs, was based on Skinner's principles of programmed learning. The design of this type of program is shown in Figure 2.1, and can be used for problems in almost any curriculum area, including science, economics or geography problems. The underlying design is based on a concealed mathematical model (fixed model with few variables) created by the developers/teachers resulting in a problem displayed on the screen. The student is required to provide answers, which would be checked by the program, and then a response as to whether the answer is correct or not is provided to the learner.

Many studies have shown that the positive impact on learning of this type of interactive task has been through similar learning gains to those that might be achieved by a non-ICT-based drill and practice exercise but with more challenging tasks. This type of software was widely available in the 1970s, 1980s and 1990s and ranged in scope from simple arithmetic-based problems, to complex tutorial systems developed by Plato. More recent extensive software of this type includes integrated learning systems with video strips and speech but the principles are still based on tutorial-style behaviourist theories of learning. Students using the integrated learning systems evaluated by Underwood and colleagues (Wood, Underwood and Avis, 1999) were found to improve their mathematics knowledge after extensive use of the system. However, the research evidence across a range of different studies does not show consistent benefits to students' learning (Marshall and Cox, 2008). Most recent learning environments of this type include a series of problems with progressively more and more difficult tasks. Research has shown that, basically, if the student knows the answer to the problem then no new challenge is presented; on the other hand, if the student is unable to answer the first problem then the contribution to the students' learning will be dependent upon the feedback information provided to help progress the students' understanding. It is now known that the tasks that

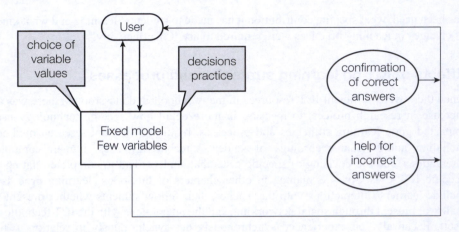

■ **Figure 2.1** Tutorial style learner interactions

can be incorporated into this type of software are often not challenging enough for the learner (Voogt and Knezek, 2008). What the research has shown is that these kinds of technology resources can show the student and the teachers what level of understanding regarding specific concepts has already been reached.

SIMULATIONS

The second type of interactive software environment involves simulations that have been developed and used over the last 50 or more years, the interaction model of which is shown in Figure 2.2.

In the case of simulation software, the design is based on a model of a process that the learner can investigate, trying out hypotheses, studying relationships and investigating theories. This type of software, as explained earlier, was originally based on real experiments or scenarios and situations previously beyond the scope of the school setting. For example, science simulations include predator–prey systems, satellite motion, chemical processes; geography simulations include global warming, river flows, farming, traffic flow; economic simulations include manufacturing, export, balance of payments, etc. (e.g. see Cox, 1992, 1996; Webb, 2008). In addition to allowing learners to investigate complex processes without the need for advanced mathematical skills, the way in which the simulation is designed and presented has been shown to influence the nature of the knowledge presented to and understood by the learners (Laurillard, 1992; Sakonidis, 1994).

The interactive dynamic graphical displays produced by computer simulations has been shown to assist learners who have difficulty in visualising multi-dimensional relationships, a familiar problem to many science and humanities teachers. For example, the propagation of waves showing reflection or interference reveals maxima and minima and resulting wave patterns that are very difficult for learners to understand from the theory alone. 'Three' dimensional drawings can be produced on the screen to provide a clear image of an electric or magnetic field, for example, the location of poles and pole strengths being controlled by the learners. Visual displays can therefore play a significant role in providing a picture that demonstrates the relative importance of the parameters governing a particular relationship. There are many examples described in the literature in many languages which have shown enhancements to learning through enabling learners

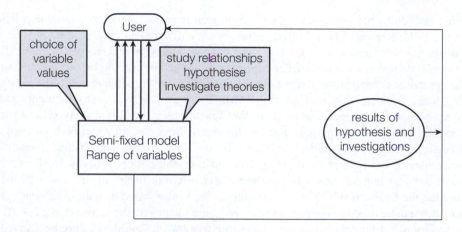

■ **Figure 2.2** Simulations – learner interactions

to test hypotheses, investigate behaviours of models of scientific and other systems, interpret experimental data, and contrast simulations with experiments (Cox and Abbott, 2004; Voogt and Knezek, 2008). Therefore, if you, as a teacher or teacher-trainer are using or considering using this type of technology, be it in a stand alone format (CD) or an online activity, you can examine what kinds of processes the students would be able to investigate and thereby what the students might learn.

Until recently, the development of subject-based simulations has been based on the assumption (for the reasons described earlier) that the problems that learners appear to have in understanding particular processes might be overcome through investigating a simulated experiment. However, simulations are based on fixed models embedded within the software and therefore restrict the learner from hypothesising new models or adding variables to the existing model. These constraints are ideal for the teacher wanting the student to focus on learning-specific relationships and understanding specific variables. However, these limitations identified by many earlier research studies also showed that as the ICT technologies became more powerful and faster, as is shown in Table 2.1, educational simulations need not be restricted to the fixed embedded model within them. These findings led to the development of modelling software that would enable the learner(s) to extend the simulations to hypothesise and investigate their own models of scientific or other processes (Mellar *et al.*, 1994) as is explained below.

FRAMEWORK SOFTWARE

The third style of software originally developed for teaching and learning can be categorised as modelling or framework software, the learning processes for which are shown in Figure 2.3. This type of software has no in-built model but has a designed interface enabling the learner to construct his or her models and then investigate them in relation to his or her theories or real life experiments. Examples of such software include Logo (Papert, 1980), and both quantitative and qualitative learning environments (Cox, 1996). Current examples include, of course, spreadsheets and databases, which became a core part of the ICT provision to all schools when they purchased networks in the early 1990s and which are used widely in schools and elsewhere today.

The power of this type of software has been shown by numerous research studies over many years to enable learners to challenge their own ideas about topics, hypothesise the effects of adding new variables and develop models to extend their understanding (Mellar *et al.*, 1994; Reeves, 2008). Different framework software can challenge the learner to investigate the same processes but may have totally different representations. For example, an investigation of energy consumption in the home could be carried out using the spreadsheet application Excel or an earlier educational modelling environment such as Model Builder (Cox and Webb, 1994). These two software environments have completely different representations in the way the user sees the display on a screen, controls the inputs and outputs and can interact with it, but they can both be used to investigate and solve similar problems. In the case of the spreadsheet modelling environment, the learner needs to understand the relationship between mathematical equations and tabular means of presenting and inserting these. In the case of Model Builder, the learner needs to learn a new modelling syntax based on natural language and how this can be used in conjunction with icons and images on the screen (Cox, 2008).

In Figure 2.3 the 'choice of model learning framework' could therefore be a specific program like logo, a spreadsheet program, a data analysis package or even an investigative learning environment into which the learner might enter data through sensors monitoring the environment (Sharples *et al.*, 2011). The difference between simulation and modelling software is that the latter is designed with few or no assumptions about the learner's prior knowledge of a topic but there are assumptions that the teachers and learners will be able to operate the software and understand how it works. There is no inbuilt teacher control except for the constraints imposed by the modelling framework, although you can always, of course, construct the activity for a particular topic, lesson or ability level. The subject and level of difficulty of the activities can both be determined by you, the teacher, and/or the learners themselves. Unlike with tutorial or simulation style software, the outcomes are unknown and cannot be predicted. There is now evidence from many previous research studies (e.g. Cox and Marshall, 2007; Reeves, 2008), which show that in building and investigating their own scientific, mathematical, geographical, economic, etc. models, learners gain a greater understanding of the concepts and processes involved than using more conventional learning tools. There is now wide support for the development of off-line and online tools to enable learners to explore their own personal ideas and theories, and to compare those with scientists', geographers', economists' or other professional theories.

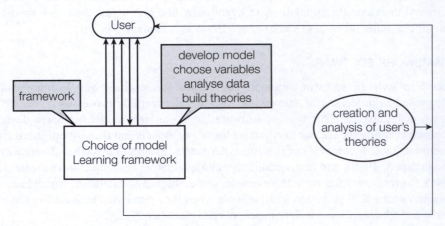

Figure 2.3 Framework – learner interactions

Although specific modelling software developed for education, such as Model Builder, Logo, and the Dynamic Modeling System, are no longer widely used in schools, every teacher knows about spreadsheets, which are widely accessible in schools. However, recent research has shown that the use of spreadsheets or data analysis software is still often limited to very basic models in the secondary curriculum. What we know from many previous research studies is that first, if you consider the specific processes that you want your students to understand and then get them to construct these with your help in, for example, a spreadsheet environment and then test them out, adding new variables as their understanding grows, this experience should greatly enhance their understanding beyond what can be achieved by more traditional teaching methods. Second, there are ICT modelling environments available to teachers today with many sample models which can be used as a foundation on which to build increasingly challenging tasks. This does require an initial investment of time in studying the different types of framework software available for education and also creating activities which on the one hand will help your students construct and investigate relevant and useful models and on the other hand will complement their other curriculum activities.

Data analysis packages, which enable data to be recorded and analysed, can also be included in the category of modelling or framework software where the focus is on analysing sets of experimental, geographical, historical or other data rather than on building models to perform the calculations; for example, comparing data between different rows or columns of a spreadsheet. An early example of a three-dimensional database is BIOVIEW (Squires and McDougall, 1994), which was designed to be used by learners studying environmental science. Archived data collected from a Devon reservoir (Slapton Lea) over many years was entered into the computer and could be displayed on the screen as cubes of data for the abundance of different species of grasses (x-axis), each sample collected (y-axis), and the year of collection (z-axis). Students could compare the abundance of a particular species for different locations (samples) in a particular year, or the abundance of the same species for different years, or the types of species in the different locations. The same software environment or other similar data analysis software could be used for a whole range of different subjects and curriculum activities: e.g. investigating relationships between: (a) the spread of AIDS, the regions of the world and the years over which it has developed; (b) the balance of payment in the UK, the year this was calculated and import tariffs; (c) maximum and minimum river levels, average yearly temperatures, years recorded and so on.

The range of possibilities for using data analysis investigations in the curriculum is endless and previous research into its effectiveness has shown that it can enhance students' learning and help develop their investigative skills (Voogt and Knezek, 2008). What has changed since those earlier studies has been the limitless access to online data sets that you can download and use in the classroom or get your students to find and download for you. Your students can study the relationships between sets of experimental data and can perform simple statistical analyses without having to make assumptions about the scientific models or theories relating to the data. By plotting graphs or drawing pie charts students can then develop their own theories by studying the patterns and relationships in the data they have collected or downloaded. Learning to use and analyse data sets is a very important skill for all your students and there are many large data sets online in almost any subject, teaching activities and different types of data investigation activities for all ages of learners.[2,3] What is important to remember regarding what the research evidence has told us is that the most beneficial way of using online data is to design learning tasks for your students that require them to analyse the relationships between data sets themselves, not just download a report on previously conducted analyses.

The same framework style of software can be designed to form the basis of a sensing and control learning environment which enables the user to enter values for data they have collected and then analyse those to investigate specific relationships as mentioned earlier (Sharples *et al.*, 2011). Previous research literature in science education that spans more than 35 years has examples of many science experiments that can be done more accurately and reliably using computers linked to sensors and switches than using other apparatus (e.g. Rogers, 1987, Frost[4]). In the simulations described earlier, researchers have found that time is a significant constraint in many laboratory experiments and environmental investigations. Just as with simulations, where time can be contracted or extended, using the computer for control and data collection enables learners to run experiments for 24 hours, a week, month, or longer, while they are attending to other activities. It also enables them to study very fast reactions and very small changes in properties that they could not otherwise perform in the laboratory. Laboratory or other environmental data can be collected and analysed using short-targeted programs or compared with large sets of data obtained over the internet.

The three broad categories of educational software environments explained in this section are equally relevant to today's technologies even though the research evidence goes back much further than some of the specific ICT technologies we have at our finger tips today. As teachers, it is easy to become overwhelmed by the resources now available online via the computers in schools or through mobile devices and to struggle to know how to use these effectively in one's teaching. However, what the research evidence here has reliably shown is that by focusing on the concepts, skills, processes and knowledge we are trying to teach, and understanding the kinds of learning interactions the students will experience with these technologies, we can select and harness technological resources to challenge and excite our students at the same time as enriching the curriculum and learning experiences.

INTEGRATED AND CONNECTED TECHNOLOGIES

The research evidence of the range of uses of technologies reported above was drawn from investigations into the effects of their educational uses on individual learners or learners working in pairs with mostly curriculum activities led by the teacher or suggested by the researchers. Yet, the earlier subject-based tutorial and simulations software specifically designed for education was mostly superseded in schools by the early 1990s, as is shown in Table 2.1. This was brought about by the advent of commercial hardware and software purchased on massive scales for schools and colleges followed by widespread access via the internet to limitless subject knowledge and resources. When schools purchased large networks of desktop computers, they included Office software bundled with it but with few educational activities and little guidance for the teachers on how to use it to teach mathematics or geography or any other subject. It took a long time for teachers to know what to do with this software in their curricula and even now there is little evidence of widespread use of framework software for investigations or hypothesising relationships. Furthermore, when the students themselves gained access to online resources at home as well as in school and were able to communicate with each other online this resulted in some loss of control of the teacher within formal educational settings.

New ICT technologies have changed the ways in which the learner (and teacher) can interact with them; which means that as teachers we can no longer assume what our students might be understanding, as we could with reasonable confidence when using more traditional and familiar educational resources such as books, whiteboards, films and experiments. New technologies have brought new representations and consequently a recodifying of knowledge, i.e. how subject information, relationships, etc. might be displayed on a large or small (mobile phone) screen and how this relates to learners' mental models. Previous research has shown that learners develop new ways of reasoning and hypothesising their own and new knowledge. How different these ways are, is influenced by the nature of the representation system and the ability of the learner to interpret new images and new literacies. Research into this area ranges from the artificial intelligence research into the interpretation of diagrammatic representations (Cheng *et al.*, 2001) to research into the learner's causal reasoning using modelling environments (Bliss, 1994). All the evidence from 50 years of research in this field points to a fundamental change in the representations and therefore boundaries of knowledge within a particular knowledge domain that is constantly changing and therefore very difficult for us as teachers to know how to manage.

As a consequence of a large number of studies of students using computers in different class settings and the growing awareness of researchers about the importance of teamwork amongst students, research in ICT in education expanded to include the goal of measuring what effects students collaborating had on their learning and teamwork skills. Furthermore, when students are using different ICT technologies, what effects might these have on those collaborative skills? Since the rapid growth in the use of online learning, in order to find out about these effects more sophisticated research tools have been developed, including online monitoring of students' computer use, online assessment techniques and the need to take account of the different knowledge representations that such complex environments provide.

Research into students' learning through online communication of computer-supported collaborative learning (CSCL) have shown that, in order to take advantage of new learning opportunities provided by social networking technologies, users also need different social and emotional skills in addition to those used in face-to-face communication. These include the ability not only to share knowledge, but also to share emotions by means of digital communication and to develop knowledge in collaboration with others. Although the potential for developing thinking and knowledge construction through CSCL needs further research, published studies have shown that online learning has the potential to expand and transform the learning opportunities for students towards more autonomy in learning. Yet how learning and collaborating through social networking, both in formal and informal educational settings, are influencing students' learning strategies and practices is not yet clearly understood (Cox, 2012).

Student autonomy is an important part of learning to learn and can be developed through assessment for learning where students are supported to develop self-awareness and metacognitive skills (Webb, 2010). Recent research has shown that young people's digital repertoires (technology skills) enhances students' autonomy in learning but there are still uncertainties about how such skills and experiences will affect their 'school learning' activities. Further research is needed to characterise the pedagogical approaches evident in activities involving the use of technologies and to explore their synergy with young people's technology skills and understanding. Therefore a growing challenge that faces the teaching profession is to be able to take account of each and every student's digital repertoires when planning and using technology in the curriculum.

As explained above, it is known that many school students use their technological skills outside school even more than in school; and learning outside school is equally important in young people's development. Passey (2000) found that effective home–school links can also enhance learning, especially of young children. There is a long history of teachers setting homework to extend school work and evidence that effective homework can improve attainment (Hallam, 2004). Therefore, increasing access to 'school learning' resources at home through portable computers or virtual learning environments can support these links between class work and homework (Pachler and Redondo, 2005; Underwood *et al.*, 2007). Furthermore, the distinction between leisure activity and school work may become more blurred as teachers make use of web-based video material or podcasts to support students' homework (Pachler, 2007). Pachler found that students who used computers more at home also tended to make more use of them at school (2007). The use of computers by young people in their homes has encouraged them to interact with each other to share expertise about their computer use, e.g. about the relative merit of different games, how to solve problems in gaming environments, etc. Thus, opportunities have increased dramatically for consolidating links between classroom-based work, homework and other educational activities in young people's leisure time but the extent and nature of these relationships are not yet fully understood. What has been known for a long time from previous studies is that the extent of student use of ICT in school and home is also influenced by their attitudes towards ICT technologies and whether they perceive their use to be a valuable and an achievable goal (Sakamoto *et al.*, 1993).

ATTITUDES TOWARDS ICT IN EDUCATION

In spite of a large increase in ICT resources in schools and informal educational settings, recent research into the uptake by teachers and students in many schools still shows that this is disappointingly low. It has been known for some time that the attitudes of teachers and learners significantly affect their willingness and abilities to use ICT tools and thereby the level of benefit which could be achieved. A large number of research studies into attitudinal and personality factors towards technology in education (e.g. see Knezek and Christensen, 2008) have shown that a fear of computers, liking of ICT, liking using them in schools, etc., have strong links between students' and teachers' attitudes and the effects on ICT use and learning.

The use of ICT is also known to influence and be influenced by students' motivation in and outside school settings (Cox, 1997) and to help build their self-confidence (Passey, 2000). Evidence is building of ways in which social interaction outside of school associated with the use of technologies can influence the development of dispositions towards learning (Barron, 2007). 'Disposition' refers to characteristics of people that 'dispose them to act' in particular ways. Some learning dispositions, e.g. resilience, have been investigated and explained by theories of motivational goals (Ames, 1992; Dweck, 2000). Attitudes and their relationship to behaviour including using ICT have been defined by several well-tested theories, e.g. the Theory of Planned Behaviour (TPB) (Ajzen, 1991) and have been found to be a significant factor in students' abilities to use ICT. Therefore, in order to understand how learners acquire technological skills and what is often called 'digital repertoires', and the variation of the extent of these among different learners, it is necessary to have some idea about your students' attitudes towards learning and using ICT for learning, and their dispositions, which may support or hinder their development.

The earlier discussion in this chapter has explained how challenging interactive uses of ICT can enhance your students' learning, but the attitudinal research discussed above also shows that each of your students will have a unique attitude and motivation to using new technologies as well as having specific motivations to study diligently in your lessons and towards learning more generally. A positive attitude and good motivation will be partly influenced by how confident and skilled the student is in using ICT especially when applied to learning. Popular media reports often give the impression that students are more knowledgeable about using ICT than their teachers. It may be the case that your students are familiar with particular technologies and be highly motivated to use them. However, they are not as knowledgeable about the subject you are teaching and therefore how ICT might best enhance the learning of that subject. This will depend upon your role and expertise as a teacher and how you select, organise and use ICT to enhance your teaching, which is explained later in the chapter.

THE GENDER DIFFERENCES

In the early days of ICT uses in schools, many researchers reported that, especially with teaching IT or Computer Science as a subject, many more boys were making regular use of ICT compared with girls, resulting in a range of studies into the rate of access to computer use by girls and boys and types of ICT use etc. (Meelissen, 2008). What many of these studies showed was that girls in general used computers in different ways to boys. Some studies reported a difference between the attitudes of girls and boys to using computers, whereas others showed no difference at all. A good explanation for this inconsistency of results is that when measuring, for example, computer attitudes, some of the questionnaires were specifically biased to more technical aspects of computers while others were broader, considering the social aspects as well. The range and type of questions will make a difference to the conclusions about males' and females' positive and negative attitudes to technology.

There is very reliable evidence of the lower participating rates of girls in computer science and IT professions generally, which is partly attributable to the role models they have within the family and amongst their friends. Yet in the early years of computing (1960s) females were just as involved in computer science as males, with many computer programmers being female. Furthermore, there are more positive attitudes found amongst girls in single sex schools compared with co-educational schools, as there is with science education research studies. This suggests that female students can be equally engaged with using ICT in learning their subjects as male students. However, previous research has also shown that 'students' computer attitudes are partly determined by the attitudes, confidence and abilities of the teacher to integrate ICT in a meaningful way in the lessons'. (Meelissen, 2008, p. 389). It is therefore up to you to help dismiss the myth that boys are better than girls at ICT and many good examples of excellent uses in schools by girls can be found on the web to help overcome what is considered by some as a 'gender digital divide'.

CONTRIBUTION OF ICT TO ENHANCE ACCESS AND LEARNING FOR SPECIAL NEEDS

One important goal, which is sometimes overlooked by governments and local authorities, is to harness the important contribution technology use can make to students with special needs (Abbott, 2002). This continues to be a very complex research area because of the contribution that technology can make to both physically and mentally disadvantaged pupils. Some technology devices may consist of hand-held manipulative toys, which provide sound feedback when a task is performed correctly; others may involve sound output for blind pupils typing email messages on a computer; and others may involve providing safe technology environments for pupils who emotionally find it difficult to relate directly to humans.

The evidence from research regarding technology helping those with special needs, like with other learners, goes back more than 30 years (Cox, 1981) but the opportunities are much greater now, with many devices and additional inputs available to assist learning. An important development in this area is the use of symbols for those students who need assistance with hand manipulation, as discussed by Abbott and Detheridge (2010). What previous research has shown is that not only are there many ways of assisting learners to have the same opportunities as those without special needs, there are also specific devices which were originally used primarily for students with special needs now being used for many other purposes as well. For example, the Concept Keyboard, which has a touch screen input, was first designed for education in 1984 with overlays enabling students to touch pictures or words in response to specific tasks instead of having to use a qwerty keyboard. Now the most widespread use of concept keyboards is in restaurants, bank ATMs, airports, supermarkets and for many other commercial purposes.

Very recent research by the SynergyNet project[5] has developed and researched the use of multi-touch screens (concept keyboards) formed as table tops to enable children to perform mathematics and other tasks in groups of four and to collaborate with the children on other tables by passing their displays across from one table to the next. The technology is basically the same as the earlier concept keyboards but with many more features, which could provide challenging learning environments for any student who has difficulties in using the traditional keyboard.

In mainstream education the large range of devices available to schools can enable teachers to meet the learning needs of all their pupils more effectively. How successful the incorporation of technology into the curriculum will ultimately depend upon the role and practices of the teachers, as has been mentioned earlier in this chapter.

THE ROLE AND PRACTICES OF THE TEACHERS

Even though there has been a steady growth in ICT use by teachers and students reported in many countries, years of research evidence has shown that the ways in which ICT has been used have been very dependent upon teachers themselves, what they believe to be important, how they select the technology tools for their curriculum, how they organise the lessons and so on. The relatively recent international research volume on policies and practices in education in 37 countries (Plomp et al., 2009) has shown that although in most countries the number of students per computer in schools has declined steadily over the last 25 years, the actual uses by teachers has mostly moved from simulations and modelling to focus on internet searches, email and online courses. Large-scale studies have shown that although the uptake of ICT resources in schools varies across countries, the overriding factor which influences the use in schools by students is the role of the teacher and the conflicting requirements of national curricula (Voogt and Knezek, 2008; Plomp et al., 2009). Therefore, in spite of the many years of research evidence showing that using simulations and modelling can significantly enhance students' learning, this use in recent years has mostly been replaced by commercially led technologies.

Evidence from earlier case studies and an extensive literature review (Cox and Webb, 2004) showed that pedagogical practices of teachers who use technology ranged from only small enhancements of more traditional methods to fundamental changes in their philosophy of teaching. The most effective uses of new technologies as evidenced above were those in which the teacher and the software could challenge students' understanding and thinking. However, these studies and many others have shown that there is only limited understanding of teachers' pedagogical practices with a range of technology uses and in different subjects, and there was still a need for further substantial research to develop an in-depth understanding of the ways in which teachers select and use technology resources to enhance their teaching.

For many years teachers' professional development has been known to be an important influence on teachers' beliefs and their consequent uses of technology (Desforges, 1995; Rhodes, 1999). Professional development in ICT use over the last 20 years has taken many forms, such as out of school courses, in school courses, informal peer teaching and online courses and individual support (cf. Preston *et al.*, 2000). In the previous decade the UK government spent well over £250m on the professional development of teachers in the uses of ICT. Detailed studies of teachers' professional development in relation to pedagogical innovations of assessment showed that teachers explored theory and developed their own personal philosophies alongside changes in their pedagogical practices.

Over the years computers have been in schools, teachers have been offered whole school one-day awareness courses, short out of school courses, longer postgraduate courses and online courses to develop the skills, expertise and knowledge of how to use ICT in their teaching. The professional development that has been found to be the most useful has been a combination of longer part-time postgraduate courses augmented by sustained in-school support. Although online courses and support have their place the overriding barrier to the successful uptake and integration of technology in teaching is lack of time – lack of time to try out and learn about new ICT resources, lack of time to revise the existing curriculum practices and lack of time to update one's ICT skills to keep up with the ever changing IT technologies.

SUMMARY

If we reflect back on the evidence and implications for your uses of ICT in teaching as discussed in this chapter, then a useful way of considering how these all link together is shown in Figure 2.4. From research we now know that your teaching practices and therefore how you might adopt and use ICT in your teaching are influenced by your attitudes towards ICT technologies and your epistemologies, i.e. your knowledge of education, ICT and the ways in which these communicate and receive information from learners. Both of these are influenced by the training you first received and then subsequent training whether delivered by experts, colleagues, face-to-face or remotely.

In parallel with these factors and the changes induced by using ICT are those of the learner. The attitudes of your students will affect how they perceive using ICT in their learning. This in turn might affect the way you organise and conduct your teaching.

What you relied on in the past may need to be revised when getting immersed in using ICT for teaching.

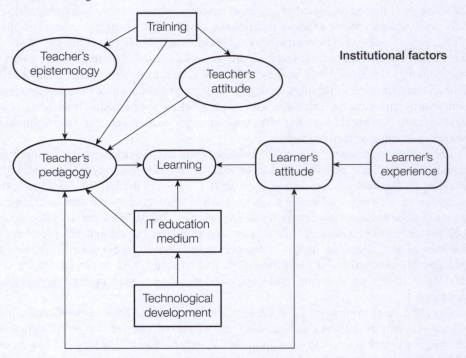

Figure 2.4 The main factors affecting the impact of using technology in students' learning

All of these factors, which research has shown are intertwined, are constantly perturbed by the ever-changing technologies and how your school or college makes them available in education. What is changing outside this diagram is the uncontrollable and relentless march of technological change. No longer can we feel secure in our teaching, which we could once control, because the outside world is now integrated in our students' 'formal' education. Even though research has shown that there are many challenges for teachers to adopt and integrate ICT into the curriculum, the evidence presented here, which is just the tip of the iceberg, shows that using ICT effectively and appropriately can expand and enhance our students' learning in ways that could never have been achieved without these revolutionary IT technologies.

NOTES

1 The draft proposed programme of study for this new Computer Science school curriculum has been produced by the British Computer Society. See http://academy.bcs.org/upload/pdf/ict-pos.pdf (accessed 7 May 2013).
2 Examples of how data analysis can be used for GCSE level can be found on the BBC Bitesize website; for example, http://www.bbc.co.uk/schools/gcsebitesize/ict/databases/2databases.shtml (accessed 7 May 2013).

3 United States AIDS statistics. See http://www.avert.org/usa-statistics.htm (accessed 7 May 2013).
4 Roger Frost has produced many data logging ICT activities. See http://rogerfrost.com/ (accessed 7 May 2013).
5 SynergyNet has been one of the TLRP-TEL projects. See http://tel.dur.ac.uk/synergynet/ (accessed 7 May 2013).

REFERENCES

Abbott, C. (ed.) (2002) *Special Educational Needs and the Internet: Issues in Inclusive Education*, London: Routledge-Falmer.

Abbott, C. and Detheridge, C. (2010) 'Access all areas: the use of symbols in public spaces' in J. Seale and M. Nind (eds), *Understanding and Promoting Access for People with Learning Difficulties*, London: Routledge, pp. 57–68.

Ajzen, I. (1991) 'The theory of planned behavior', *Organizational Behavior and Human Decision Processes* 50: 179–211.

Ames, C. (1992) 'Classroom: goals, structures and student motivation', *Journal of Educational Psychology* 84(3): 261–71.

Barron, B.J.S. (2007) 'The development of dispositions to create with new technologies: a learning-ecologies perspective', *American Educational Research Association 2007 Annual Meeting: The World of Educational Quality*, Chicago, Illinois.

Bliss, J. (1994) 'Causality and common sense reasoning' in H. Mellar, J. Bliss, R. Boohan, J. Ogborn and C. Tompsett (eds), *Learning with Artificial Worlds: Computer Based Modelling in the Curriculum*, London: The Falmer Press.

Cheng, P.C-H., Lowe, R.K. and Scaife, M. (2001) 'Cognitive science approaches to diagrammatic representations', *Artificial Intelligence Review* 15(1/2): 79–94.

Cox, M.J. (1981) *Microcomputers as an Aid to Learning*, London: Orchard Lodge Studies of Deviancy, Orchard Lodge Regional Resource Centre.

——(1992) 'The computer in the science curriculum' T.J. Plomb and J. Moonen (eds), *The International Journal for Educational Research*, 17(1): 19–35.

——(1996) 'Computer simulations and modelling' in T. Plomp and D.L. Ely (eds), *The International Encyclopaedia of Educational Technology*, second edition, Oxford: Elsevier Science (Pergamon), September, pp. 411–14.

——(1997) *The Effects of Information Technology on Students' Motivation: Final Report*, London: NCET/King's College.

——(2005) 'Educational conflict: the problems in institutionalizing new technologies in education', in G. Kouzelis, M. Pournari, M. Stoeppler and V. Tselfes (eds), *Knowledge in the New Technologies*, Frankfurt, Berlin, Bern, Bruxelles, New York, Oxford, Vienna: Peter Lang, pp. 139–65.

——(ed.) (2008) '10 methods for researching IT in education' in J. Voogt and G. Knezek (eds), *International Handbook of Information Technology in Primary and Secondary Education*, Berlin, Heidelberg, New York: Springer, pp. 947–64.

——(2012) 'Formal to informal learning with IT: research challenges and issues for e-learning', *Journal for Computer Assisted Learning*, Early View, March.

Cox, M.J. and Abbott, C. (2004) *ICT and Attainment: A Review of the Research Literature*, Coventry and London: British Educational Communications and Technology Agency/ Department for Education and Skills.

Cox, M.J. and Webb, M.E. (2004) *ICT and Pedagogy: A Review of the Research Literature*, Coventry and London: British Educational Communications and Technology Agency/ Department for Education and Skills.

Cox, M.J. and Marshall, G. (2007) 'Effects of ICT: do we know what we should know?', *Education and Information Technologies*, 12: 59–70.

Desforges, C. (1995) 'How does experience affect theoretical knowledge for teaching?', *Learning and Instruction*, 5: 385–400.

Dweck, C.S. (2000) *Self-Theories: Their Role in Motivation, Personality and Development*, London: Taylor and Francis.

Hallam, S. (2004) *Homework: The Evidence*, Bedford Way Papers, London: The Institute of Education, University of London.

Knezek, G. and Christensen, R. (eds) (2008) 'IT competencies and attitudes' in J. Voogt and G. Knezek (eds), *International Handbook of Information Technology in Primary and Secondary Education*, New York: Springer, pp. 319–420.

Laurillard, D. (1992), 'Phenomemographic research and the design of diagnostic strategies for adaptive tutoring systems' in M. Jones and P. Winne, *Adaptive Learning Environments: Foundations and Frontiers*, Berlin: Springer-Verlag, pp. 233–48.

Leask, M. and Pachler, N. (2005) *Learning to Teach using ICT in Secondary School: A Companion to School Experience*, Abingdon: Routledge.

Marshall, G. and Cox, M.J. (2008) 'Research methods: their design, applicability and reliability', in J. Voogt and G. Knezek (eds), *International Handbook of Information Technology in Primary and Secondary Education*, Berlin, Heidelberg, New York: Springer, pp. 983–1002.

Meelissen, M. (2008) 'Computer attitudes and competencies among primary and secondary school students' in J. Voogt and G. Knezek (eds), *International Handbook of Information Technology in Primary and Secondary Education*, New York: Springer, pp. 381–95.

Mellar, H., Bliss, J., Boohan, R., Ogborn, J. and Tompsett, C. (eds) (1994) *Learning with Artificial Worlds: Computer Based Modelling in the Curriculum*, London: The Falmer Press.

Pachler, N. (ed.) (2007) 'Mobile learning: towards a research agenda', London: WLE Centre Occasional Papers in Work-based Learning 1, Institute of Education, London. Available at: http://www.wlecentre.ac.uk/cms/files/occasionalpapers/mobilelearning_pachler_2007.pdf (accessed 25 May 2013).

Pachler, N. and Redondo, A. (2005) 'Linking school with home use' in M. Leask and N. Pachler (eds), *Learning To Teach Using ICT In The Secondary School: A Companion To School*, Abingdon: Routledge.

Papert, S. (1980) *Mindstorms: Children, Computers and Powerful Ideas*, New York: Basic Books.

Passey, D. (2000) 'Developing teaching strategies for distance (out of school) learning in primary and secondary schools', *Educational Media International*, 37(1): 45–57.

Pelgrum, W. and Plomp, T. (1993) 'The use of computers in education in 18 countries', *Studies in Educational Evaluation* 19: 101–25.

Plomp, T., Andersen, R., Law, N. and Quale, A. (eds) (2009) *Cross-National Information and Communication Technology: Policies and Practices in Education*, second edition, Charlotte, NC: Information Age Publishing.

Preston, C., Cox, M.J. and Cox, K.M.J. (2000) *Teachers as Innovators: An Evaluation of the Motivation of Teachers to Use Information and Communications Technologies*, Croydon: Teacher Training Agency/Mirandanet.

Reeves, T.C. (2008) 'Evaluation of the design and development of IT tools in education' in J. Voogt and G. Knezek (eds), *International Handbook of Information Technology in Primary and Secondary Education*, New York: Springer, pp. 1037–52.

Rhodes, V. (1999) *IT in Primary Schools: The Rhetoric and the Reality, Supporting Teachers in the Process of Implementation*, London: King's College, University of London.

Rogers, L.T. (1987) 'The computer-assisted laboratory', *Phys. Educ.* 22: 219.

Sakamoto, T., Zhao, L.J. and Sakamoto, A. (1993) *Psychological IMPACT of Computers on Children*, The ITEC Project: Information Technology in Education of Children, Final Report of Phase 1, New York: United Nations Educational Scientific and Cultural Organization.

Sakonidis, H. (1994) 'Representations and representation systems' in H. Mellar, J. Bliss, R. Boohan, J. Ogborn and C. Tompsett (eds), *Learning with Artificial Worlds: Computer Based Modelling in the Curriculum*, London: Falmer Press, pp. 39–46.

Sharples, M., Collins, T., Feißt, M., Gaved, M., Mulholland, P., Paxton, M. and Wright, M. (2011) 'A "laboratory of knowledge-making" for personal inquiry learning' in G. Biswas, S. Bull, J. Kay and A. Mitrovic (eds), *Artificial Intelligence in Education: Proceedings of 15th The International Conference, AIED 2011, Auckland, New Zealand, June/July 2011*. Springer Lecture Notes in Artificial Intelligence 6738, Berlin: Springer-Verlag, pp. 312–19.

Somekh, B. (1995) 'The contribution of action research to development in social endeavours: a position paper on action research methodology', *British Educational Research Journal* 21(3): 339–55.

Squires, D. and McDougall, A. (1994) *Choosing and Using Educational Software*, London: Falmer Press.

Underwood, J., Baguley, T., Banyard, P., Coyne, E., Farrington Flint, L. and Selwood, I. (2007) *Impact 2007: Personalising Learning with Technology*, Nottingham: Nottingham Trent University for Becta. Available at: http://dera.ioe.ac.uk/1439/ (accessed 25 May 2013).

Voogt, J. and Knezek, G. (eds) (2008) *International Handbook of Information Technology in Primary and Secondary Education*, Berlin, Heidelberg, New York: Springer.

Watson, D.M. (ed.) (1993) *The Impact Report: An Evaluation of the Impact of Information Technology on Children's Achievement in Primary and Secondary Schools*, London: King's College.

Webb, M.E. (2008) 'Impact of IT on science education' in J. Voogt and G. Knezek (eds), *International Handbook of Information Technology in Primary and Secondary Education*, Berlin, Heidelberg, New York: Springer, pp. 133–44.

——(2010) 'Beginning teacher education and collaborative formative e-assessment', *Assessment and Evaluation In Higher Education* 34(5): 597–618.

Wood, D., Underwood, J. and Avis, P. (1999) 'Integrated learning systems in the classroom', *Computers and Education* 33(2–3): 91–108.

Ziegler, M. (2001) 'Improving practice through action research', *Adult Learning* 12(1): 3–4.

3

ICT TOOLS FOR PROFESSIONAL DEVELOPMENT

Sarah Jones and Sarah Younie

INTRODUCTION

This chapter covers key considerations in the use of ICT tools for the continual professional development of teachers. Both professional development and ICT tools are first defined before looking at specific tools. The use of ePortfolios is discussed, as a way of drawing together various resources, evidence and new knowledge for practice. The chapter then pays specific attention to reflective practice, an essential process to be used in conjunction with ICT tools for professional development. Following on from this section, strategies for accessing and assessing evidence, new knowledge and researching practice are explained before exploring open educational resources, open online courses, networks and communities. Finally, the important and sometimes controversial area of online professional identity is discussed. Throughout the chapter there are tasks for you to complete after each section, so that you might consolidate your learning and, where possible, references have been made to literature and useful websites.

> ### OBJECTIVES
>
> At the end of this chapter you should be able to:
>
> - create and maintain your own professional development ePortfolio;
> - engage in critical reflective practice;
> - access and assess new kinds of knowledge and evidence for professional practice;
> - develop an appropriate professional online identity.
>
> Check the requirements for your course to see which relate to this unit.

WHAT IS CONTINUING PROFESSIONAL DEVELOPMENT?

Learning and developing the craft of teaching is an ongoing process throughout your teaching career. What you are learning today, may become out of date in the years that follow, so how do you ensure that you have the necessary knowledge and skills to support your practice? Some of your new understanding comes from the experiences you get by doing the job itself. However, some of it comes from what is called continuing professional development, or CPD for short. CPD can be informal, for example talking to your colleagues about teaching and learning issues over a coffee in the staffroom, or formal, for example going on a course.

The UK Teacher Development Agency (2008) suggests that 'Continuing professional development (CPD) consists of reflective activity designed to improve an individual's attributes, knowledge, understanding and skills. It supports individual needs and improves professional practice'.

With the fast rate of technological changes occurring in our society today, one area of development that employers will be expecting to see in your practice is up-to-date use of and knowledge about ICT tools (i.e. your digital literacy) in your teaching and management of your students' learning. You will need to address this in your own professional development throughout your teaching career. The focus of this chapter is to look specifically at how a selection of ICT tools themselves can support your professional development. One such tool is an ePortfolio, which provides a way of you planning and recording your learning.

WHAT ARE ICT TOOLS?

The term 'ICT tools', or alternatively 'digital tools', covers a wide and varied domain. On the one hand we could be talking about a digital camera, on the other we could be talking about the internet and Google Hangouts. Likewise there are different ways to categorise ICT tools – some might suggest a distinction between those that are more collaborative (e.g. blogs) and those that are less collaborative (e.g. rss feeds); some that are more synchronous (e.g. Skype) and those that are more asynchronous (e.g. LinkedIn). However, no categorisation is definitive. The edges are often blurred, with many tools having multiple applications, depending on how they are woven into the context in which they are being used. With regards to professional development, some tools may be more useful than others. The limit or extent of the ICT tools can also be determined by the particular learning style and creativity of the person using the tool. The key question to ask yourself, when considering using ICT tools is, does the use of this tool add value in some way? The answer to this question could be about saving time, being better organised, having access to a wider variety of resources, courses or people or it might be about working more efficiently and having everything to do with professional development in one place.

CREATING A PROFESSIONAL DEVELOPMENT EPORTFOLIO

What is a portfolio?

A portfolio is literally a type of briefcase and, as such, is a place to keep items that are of importance to you. As a teacher, you would be expected to develop a career portfolio. This involves selecting items that are important to your professional identity and development, such as artefacts, evidence, critical reflections on your practice – in short, those artefacts that demonstrate your development in your teaching career with a view to providing evidence of your skills and abilities. An ePortfolio is a collection of electronic artefacts (e.g. documents, podcasts, links to resources) which can be web based, annotated, updated and enable you to track and record your professional development over time, and, in this sense, is dynamic in that it can change.

ePortfolios

Advances in technology have enabled dynamic platforms that integrate a myriad of ICT tools that support your constantly emerging professional development needs. Accessing suitable courses, taking part in learning events, recording evidence, linking with professional standards, collaborating and sharing your work can now all be done at the touch of a button and with these advancements has come the ability to create a living online portfolio, or ePortfolio, which you can update throughout your career. Of course, you may already be familiar with the concept of portfolios as these are being increasingly used in teacher education courses (Strudler and Wetzel, 2005). Some institutions use them for accreditation purposes. However, a word of caution – clarity is needed regarding the purpose of your portfolio. If it is trying to achieve too many goals, it may end up missing them all!

Lygo-Baker and Hatzipanagos (2012) suggest that ePortfolios 'offer staff a digital technology that can be both a personalised learning space, owned and controlled by the learner, and a presentation tool, which can be used for formal assessment purposes' (p. 37). Key features might include a Personal Development Plan (also know as a PDP), links to useful websites, record of attendance certificates, lesson evaluations, a learning journal, a place to upload useful documents, your CV, a copy of your professional standards. Some ePortfolios might have a private area where only you can see the contents and a public area, where others can view what you allow them to see or even leave a comment.

There is a range of different software options in which you might create your ePortfolio. Some people use blogging software (e.g. Word Press), others might create a website but many will turn to bespoke software (e.g. http://www.e-portfolios.net/, http://www.pebblepad.co.uk/) because it is also used in their institution or school. However, you should remember that wherever you decide to create it, you must be able to take it with you when you leave an institution or move to a new place of employment.

A patchwork ePortfolio: using different genre and ICT tools

Patchwork Text (Winter and Scoggins, 1999) was originally developed for learners in higher education, as a technique to enable 'critical understanding'. Specifically, it uses a combination of genres in conjunction with reflection to explore topics that are then presented for assessment. This technique can also be used in professional development for extending your learning, with the added dimension of incorporating different ICT tools such as podcasts or blogs or video to build up your ePortfolio.

Creating your own ePortfolio

The points in Table 3.1 should be taken into consideration before setting up your ePortfolio.

Task 3.1 **Using ePortfolios to support your professional development**

A. Some countries are developing a national ePortfolio framework and some schools already have a set format. Find out if this is the case either in your country or in the schools where you are doing your school experience and then ask if you can look at it.

B. Carry out a web search to find other ePortfolio tools, comparing the strengths and weaknesses of each, then, using the table above, consider what kind of ePortfolio you would like to create and, if possible, set up your own ePortfolio.

■ **Table 3.1** Creating an ePortfolio for professional development

Consider the following:	Some key questions to help you:
Be clear about the ePortfolio purpose	What do you need it for? What sorts of things will you include in it? What activities will you want to undertake? Can you set something up that is flexible in design so that if your purpose changes, you can adapt the tool?
Select a tool that is fit for this purpose	Will you create an offline version on your computer or a version, which is hosted on the web? Will you use a weblog? Will you buy a purpose-made tool or use open source software?
The audience	Is this a private document, just for you? Who will you share it with? What parts of it will you share? Do they want to be involved? Will you want them to participate in the ePortfolio, assess any work you present in there or just be able to view things you have posted up?
Functionality	What tools will you need in your ePortfolio? Will you need a place for collaboration? Will you need a place for showcasing your new learning, ideas, artefacts? Will you want to upload documents, link to useful websites and resources or keep a learning journal?

CRITICAL REFLECTION

Creating an ePortfolio is not just about collecting information; it is about creating a process that will enable you to continually transform your practice. Thus an essential skill that goes alongside the creation of an ePortfolio is the ability to critically reflect and self-audit. In this section, we encourage you to develop your reflective thinking skills, which must relate to your teaching experience, the exact focus and emphasis is for you to determine and record in your ePortfolio. There is much literature on the subject of critical reflection. A quick Google search will yield you enough responses to last you a month or more. However, the following section gives you a brief overview and suggests some tasks to help get you started.

The basics of reflection

Schon (1983) identifies two different types of reflection – 'reflection-in-action' and 'reflection-on-action'. The former is often referred to as 'thinking on your feet'. For example, it is the process of small checks you might make during a lesson which alter the way you run the lesson. Perhaps a task you have set your pupils is demotivating them and they are beginning to mess about. As this is happening, you stop the task and introduce something else to re-engage them. The new task might ultimately result in the same learning outcome, but it was adapted and changed during the lesson as a result of 'thinking on your feet' or as Schon would say, because of 'reflecting-in-action'. Reflection-on-action, is what you might do after the lesson is over, perhaps informally during the lunch break with a colleague or on your own as you are driving home. Moon (1999: 23) writes that this kind of reflection is 'a form of mental processing with a purpose and/or anticipated outcome that is applied to relatively complex or unstructured ideas for which there is not an obvious solution'.

Moon (1999: 23) goes on to outline the purposes of reflection thus:

We reflect in order to:

- consider the process of our own learning – a process of metacognition;
- critically review something – our own behaviour, that of others or the product of behaviour (e.g. an essay, book, painting, etc.);
- build theory from observations: we draw theory from generalisations – sometimes in practical situations, sometimes in thoughts or a mixture of the two;
- engage in personal or self-development;
- make decisions or resolve uncertainty;
- empower or emancipate ourselves as individuals (and then it is close to self-development) or to empower/emancipate ourselves within the context of our social groups.

However, this more critical form of reflection and the resultant learning can often be lost if it is not done in a structured manner. Using a reflective model and recording 'reflection-on-action' can be invaluable in refining your teaching skills. In the rest of this section we are going to concentrate on this latter type of critical reflection.

Critical reflection

Stripped to the essential ingredients, critical reflection is a process that allows us to learn from something that has happened. In particular, we look at 'critical incidents' perhaps a 'eureka!' moment or a puzzling one or a moment when things 'went wrong' and try to analyse why this was so. Tripp (1993: 8) suggests that 'critical incidents are produced by the way we look at a situation: a critical incident is an interpretation of the significance of an event'. In your professional context, a critical incident might be a confrontation you have with a student or a lesson that went particularly well. To help recall the critical incident, it is often useful to have an 'artefact'. An artefact is something that reminds you of the critical incident. This could be a lesson plan, a video of the way a room was left after class or a picture of an entrance hall display. As you cannot always know when a critical incident is going to happen, you might find it useful to ask others who were present, to talk about what happened and if possible, record what they say. This recording then becomes an artefact. These artefacts can then be uploaded into your ePortfolio and the critical incident can be reflected upon.

Reflective models

Once you have your critical incident and an artefact, you then need to apply a reflective model and there are many to choose from. Commonly, they all have several steps to follow which are associated with first describing what happened and then thinking about what you have learned from that and finally articulating what, if anything, you might do differently next time. Figures 3.1, 3.2 and 3.3 are three examples. Model 1 (Figure 3.1) comes from Burton (1970); model 2 (Figure 3.2) comes from Kolb (1984); and model 3 (Figure 3.3) comes from Boud *et al.* (1985).

To understand the value of critical reflection, Gibbs (1988: 9) asserts that,

> It is not sufficient simply to have an experience in order to learn. Without reflecting upon this experience it may quickly be forgotten, or its learning potential lost. It is from the feelings and thoughts emerging from this reflection that generalisations or concepts can be generated. And it is generalisations that allow new situations to be tackled effectively.

To this end, Gibbs (1988) wants to encourage deeper reflection and he develops stages for a 'Structured Debriefing' that are based on Kolb's (1984) Experiential Learning Cycle (Table 3.2).

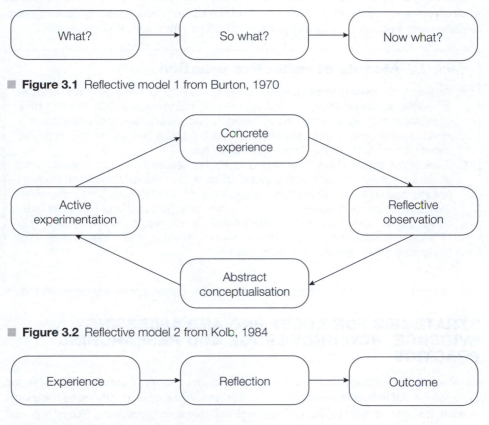

■ **Figure 3.1** Reflective model 1 from Burton, 1970

■ **Figure 3.2** Reflective model 2 from Kolb, 1984

■ **Figure 3.3** Reflective model 3 from Boud *et al.*, 1985

■ **Table 3.2** Encouraging deeper reflection (adapted from Watton *et al.*, 2009)

Description:	What is the stimulant for reflection? (critical incident) What do you want to reflect on?
Feelings:	What were your reactions and feelings to this incident?
Evaluation:	What was positive and negative about the incident?
Analysis:	What are you to understand from the incident? Or, what sense can you make of the situation?
Conclusions:	What can you conclude from these reflections and the analyses you have undertaken?
Action plan:	What are you going to do differently from now on? What have you learnt?

In trying to reflect deeply, there is some merit in referring to Bloom's taxonomy of learning.

Bloom (1964) outlined differing levels of learning or thinking processes. Bloom presented these in his famous taxonomy and hierarchy, which can be used as a framework for your reflection.

Not everything in an ePortfolio needs to be critically reflected upon. Some things that you reflect upon, you might wish others to read and add their reflections. Reflective pieces are often best written in a 'learning journal', which can form part of your ePortfolio.

Task 3.2 **Models of reflective practice**

A. Research the three reflective models above (Burton, 1970, Kolb, 1984 and Boud *et al.*, 1985), copying the diagrams into your ePortfolio and annotating them with further information, then explore the relative strengths and weaknesses of each model.

B. Find out what other authors say about reflective practice and critical reflection. You can do this by going to the library or looking online.

C. Think of two critical incidents relating to your school experience – one that was more positive in nature and one that highlighted an issue or challenge. Collect two artefacts to remind you of these incidents and upload these in your ePortfolio. Then, using either the guidance above or another model you have come across in your search, critically reflect on the incidents using two different models and record the outcomes in your ePortfolio. As well as reflecting on the critical incidents themselves, reflect on the use of the models. Which one did you prefer and why?

STRATEGIES FOR ACCESSING AND ASSESSING EVIDENCE, NEW KNOWLEDGE AND RESEARCHING PRACTICE

Evidence and knowledge about professional practice can vary, from the informal to the more formal. Knowledge might be based on peer reviewed evidence, it might be contextual or decontextualised, only be available through collaborative endeavours, free or accessed via a subscription or fee. There is a growing movement to make evidence and knowledge about practice more accessible to those at the chalk face. This can be seen in the large number of open online courses now available and in the open educational resources that can be found online.

Accessing evidence, resources and knowledge

Open educational resources, or OERs as they are often called, refers to online resources that teachers can access and reuse as befits their needs. The term 'open educational resources' appears to have been first coined by UNESCO (2002: 1). They define them as 'technology-enabled, open provision of educational resources for consultation, use and adaptation by a community of users for non-commercial purposes'. OERs provide a wide range of teaching resources, which research shows can enhance and support teaching and learning (Younie and Jones, 2012). However, this knowledge about OERs and the ways in which they can be re-purposed is not uniformly known across the wider teaching workforce. OERs can be used by teachers in the classroom, applied in an online context and stored in your ePortfolio.

Open online courses are also growing in popularity. Some are related to subject specialties and others are related to the practice of teaching and learning. Open online courses are sometimes referred to as MOOCs (massive open online courses). Networks are another very good way to both hear about professional development opportunities and to engage in informal learning through collaboration within that network. There are a wide variety of networks to get involved in, which will help you to research practice such as those provided by your subject association, CEBE (http://www.cebenetwork.org/) or the Education Futures Collaboration (http://www.edfuturescollaboration.org), for example, which build professional knowledge from evidence-based practice. Some teachers use micro-blogging software such as Twitter to build up a list of people who are leaders or experts in their field, whom they can follow to learn about new ideas, knowledge. There is more information about online networks and communities on pages 48–49.

Once you have found useful websites or networks, make life simpler for yourself by subscribing to newsletters or setting up email alerts so that you do not have to continually visit different places. Some websites and online communities/networks allow you to syndicate their pages through rich site summary (RSS) feeds. If this is possible, you then need to download a RSS reader or aggregator where all the summaries of those places you are interested in, are collected. Many of these readers are open source (free). Once downloaded, this reader sits on your computer and automatically downloads a summary of any new items that appear on the websites in which you are interested, to save you from visiting them all individually, which can be very time consuming.

Assessing what you find

Accessing evidence and new knowledge, however, is only part of the journey. The next step is to evaluate it for quality and relevance. In other words, when you use textbooks to access information, you assess the quality and relevance of what you have found, making critical judgements about the value of the information. Likewise, the same processes of critical evaluation must be applied to information found online. Criticality is also required when learning from other people involved in online networks, when you visit lively forums and discussion areas. For example, if you are engaging in dialogue with a group of people in an online network or community, try to locate the home page or profile of the group members to see the context in which they are making their comments. Some people are very good at speaking with conviction without having any qualification, experience or evidence to support their claims. Likewise, don't believe everything you read on the internet, trace resources to find out more about the host, editor or author using 'the breadcrumb trail' or by cross referencing information you have found to check for validity or bias.

BUILDING AND PARTICIPATING IN ONLINE PROFESSIONAL NETWORKS AND COMMUNITIES

Constructivist theory (Vygotsky, 1978; Bruner, 1986) sees learning as a social act. Knowledge is 'constructed' through reflective dialogue rather than through the passive receipt of information. Therefore, keeping in touch with colleagues across your profession, not just in your immediate school, can provide a vital source of professional development. Meeting up with them, however, is not realistic on a regular basis, which is why there has been a growth in online networks and communities.

There are different kinds of online community. One stems from Wenger's (1998) work on communities of practice. Wenger defines a community of practice as a place where membership is made up of people who already have some commonality resulting from 'shared histories of learning', for example, they are all nurses or they are all fishermen. Someone can move into a community of practice from outside. From a starting point of 'apprenticeship', Lave and Wenger (1991) suggest that new members refine their practice through their participation within that community. The primary focus of the community is their sameness with the obvious ability to learn from each other's practice. Secondarily, however, they can collectively change the nature of their common practice through their participation with each other. Wenger (1998: 55) states that: 'Participation refers to the process of taking part and also to the relations with others to reflect this process. It suggests both action and connection'. It is a complex process, combining various actions and involving the whole being. Although his definition does not proceed to the online world, there is some resonance with his work and the philosophy that underpins some online learning communities. An example of an online community of practice might be an online forum within Education Communities (http://www.educationcommunities.org) or an area on your subject association website.

Another type of community is a community of inquiry. There is much literature (Garrison et al., 2004; Slye and Williamson, 2004; Lushyn and Kennedy, 2000) touching on aspects of communities of inquiry, looking at assessment in them, or how to facilitate them. In his work on 'The fixation of belief', Peirce (1877) looked at the relationship between doubt and belief, defining the struggle between the two as 'inquiry'. Dewey (1938) believed that the opportunity for inquiry learning could be enhanced if the individual married their interests with the society surrounding them. Lipman (1991) does not see inquiry as separate from community and he sees all communities of inquiry as 'the methodology for the teaching of critical thinking'. Garrison and Anderson (2003: 23) attempt to define communities of inquiry by suggesting that they are a place where both teachers and pupils collaborate 'with the specific purpose of facilitating, constructing and validating understanding, and of developing capabilities that will lead to further learning'. Thus it can be seen that learning as a collaborative process is at the heart of communities of inquiry and that they contain both learners and teachers. This is a fundamental difference to online communities of practice, where teachers might not be present yet learning still takes place.

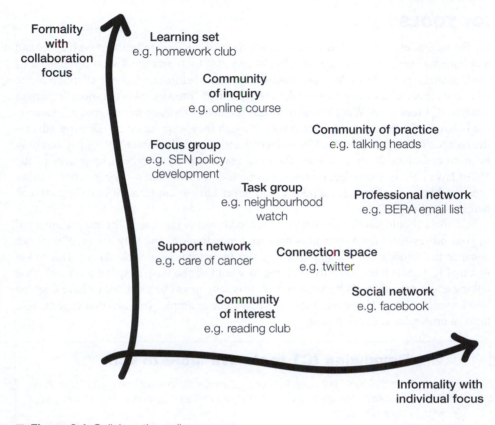

■ **Figure 3.4** Collaborative online spaces
Source: Jones 2009.

Online networks differ from online communities in that their focus is on connecting individuals rather than building a culture of learning, but this makes them no less valuable, just that they have a different kind of value when it comes to professional development. Figure 3.4 shows a variety of different online collaborative spaces. Some are more formal, where the focus is on collaboration within the group, and others are less formal, where the focus is on two-way interactions.

Task 3.3 **Finding online communities in your subject specialism**

Find out whether you have a subject association for the area in which you teach. If you do, are there any online collaborative spaces that you can join? Ask the teachers in your placement school if they participate in any professional online networks and communities.

ICT TOOLS

So far in this chapter we have spent much time discussing reflection, evaluation and assessment. These are what we would call 'process' tools and are a vital component of professional development. We have focused on these before turning our attention to the ICT tools themselves in order to make the point that 'process' is often more important than the ICT tool itself. What we mean by this is that ICT tools come and go. For example, iPads have only been around since 2009 (although they were based on the early tablet – the Newton MessagePad 100 in 1993). Twitter and the trend of 'micro-blogging' has only been around since 2006. Likewise, the once commonplace overhead projectors of the 1980s have been in sharp decline since the mid to late 1990s and no one in schools today uses the Magic Lantern – most people will never have even heard of one (http://www.magiclantern.org.uk).

ICT tools should not be used for their own sake, rather the reason for integrating them in your professional development is because depending on how they are used, they can enhance the 'process' of learning in a way that more traditional tools do not. Due to the fact that ICT tools are constantly evolving, it would not be wise to spend too much time talking about specific tools because very shortly they might be outdated or have evolved into something new. However, Table 3.3 lists three example websites that explore ICT tools in professional development.

Task 3.4 **Reviewing ICT tools available to you**

A. Find out what ICT tools are used in your placement school and do a web search on how other teachers are using ICT tools for professional development. Record your findings in your ePortfolio.

B. Create an action plan, listing tools that you have found interesting or useful for professional development and plot times when you will begin experimenting with them.

■ **Table 3.3** Examples of websites that explore ICT tools in professional development

Title	Web address	Purpose
Teacher Training Videos	http://www.teachertrainingvideos.com	Although some of the ICT tools covered here are specifically about using ICT tools in your teaching, many of them can be used in similar ways for your own professional development. For example, you might use Wall Wisher to develop your thinking about a certain topic with your peers.
Twitter	http://www.edutopia.org/digital-generation-new-media-classroom-tips-video	Susie Boss talks about how micro-blogging (with Twitter) is helping keep her professional knowledge up to date.
CPD 23	http://cpd23.blogspot.co.uk/2011/05/all-about-23-things.html	Although aimed at librarians, this website lists a range of tools that can also be useful for you as a teacher interested in continual professional development. Take some time to go through the blog archive and read about the tools.

ONLINE PROFESSIONAL IDENTITY

Each of us has multiple identities within our lives. One person can at the same time be a son, a father, a student, a teacher, a friend, a political activist, a morris dancer. The internet allows us to portray these different identities in a variety of social media from micro-blogging software such as Twitter, to online forums found on hobby websites. However, the way that you choose to be seen by your family and friends may often be different to the way you wish your employer, your pupils and their parents to see you.

The notion of 'online identity' comes in two forms, digital footprints and digital identities. Digital footprint refers to the trail you leave behind when online. Imagine if you wanted to find out some information on a person – perhaps a new colleague you are about to meet or a keynote speaker you are about to hear. You might go into a search engine such as Google or Yahoo and type in that person's name. What comes up is a list of everything that has been attributed to that person. This could be the latest book they have written, but it could also be a photo tagged in Facebook.

Digital identities are related to digital footprints. Some would say they are the same thing; however, we might make a distinction between the two. Digital footprints represent the past. Digital identities might include the past, but will also include a conscious step to create and project the type of identity that you wish others to see when they search for you online. It might mean deleting part of the footprint that currently exists, created before you realised that others can view your holiday snaps.

You might of course decide that you want to create multiple digital identities. The notion of multiple identities comes from the idea that we have multiple logins to a variety of online services, tools and communities, which collect different data from us. For example, information we submit on our Facebook page might be different to what we submit on our online bank account, which will thus lead to 'different identities' for the same person. In the context of our professional lives, we might find we have multiple identities if we move into the realm of virtual worlds such as SecondLife, where we use avatars that can hide the real self from the online world, something that might be done in role play exercises. For example, you might remember on pages 45–46 we talked about using different genres to reflect upon critical incidents. In SecondLife, you might take on another identity such as a news reporter or poet, which might project your identity in a different way to the 'normal self'.

Task 3.5 **School policies about social networking and blogging**

A. Find out what the policy is in your placement school about staff using social networking sites such as Facebook or micro-blogging software such as Twitter.
B. Do a web search on your name and critically reflect upon what you find. You should also do a web search on the names of colleagues or academics in your field. How do they present their identity online? What tools do they use to do this? What does it tell you about them?
C. Create an action plan, along with a timeline, of the things you need to do to create a digital identity that is appropriate for your role as an educator.

SUMMARY

In this chapter you have learned about using ICT tools for your professional development. Specifically you have explored the use of ePortfolios as a way of documenting and recording artefacts, which enable you to reflect on your practice. To this end you have learned about the value of ePortfolios as an ICT tool and how these can be an effective mechanism for collating and providing evidence of your professional growth. To make the most of ePortfolios we have suggested that the value lies in your ability to reflect on your teaching experiences and to critically develop your own reflectivity.

In addition to using ICT tools and developing your reflective practice, the chapter explored strategies for accessing and assessing evidence from educational research. This research evidence should be referred to as it provides a way for you to keep up-to-date with developments in the field, any new knowledge or insights should then inform your practice, thereby enabling you to develop professionally. Using ICT tools, such as online communities, professional networks, your subject association website, etc. provide you with ways to access new knowledge, which combined with researching your own practice, through critical reflection, can lead to improvements in practice. Finally, this chapter examined the important and sometimes controversial area of online professional identity.

If you are a student teacher check which requirements for your course you have addressed through this chapter.

FURTHER READING

Bolton, G. (2001) *Reflective Practice: Writing and Professional Development*, London: Sage Publications.

This book outlines the process of reflective practice and covers a variety of models. Throughout the book there is reference to the theories and principles of reflective practice.

Moon, J.A. (2005) *Reflection in Learning and Professional Development*, London: RoutledgeFalmer.

Moon provides an overview of what is meant by reflection, from the literature as well as its common meanings, and explores the value of reflection as a way of improving professional practice.

Strudler, N. and Wetzel, K. (2011) 'Electronic portfolios in teacher education: forging a middle ground', *Journal of Research on Technology in Education* 44(2): 161–73.

This outlines the use of ePortfolios by exploring theoretical perspectives, analysing policy implications and challenges, and provides recommendations regarding adoption and implementation decisions.

ADDITIONAL RESOURCES AND WEBSITES

Atherton, J. 'A critical review of the process of "reflection"'. Available online at: http://blogs.gre. ac.uk/ed/2012/03/26/james-atherton-the-limits-of-reflection/ (accessed 22 September 2012).

This website has a variety of resources linked to teaching and learning and links to further readings.

GESCI 'ICT Teacher Professional Development Framework Tool'. Available online at: http://www.gesci.org/knowledge-tools.html#planning-tpd (accessed 22 September 2012).

This toolkit is funded by the UN ICT Task Force. If you download the ICT Competency Standards for Teachers, you will see that the last section covers professional development.

JISC 'ePortfolios – An overview'. Available online at: http://www.jisc.ac.uk/eportfolio (accessed 21 September 2012).

This provides an overveiw and explores why ePortfolios are so important. There is an ePortfolios infokit, providing guidance from JISC; a wiki-based 'Implementation Toolkit' and further links to effective practice with ePortfolios and related projects funded by JISC. Although aimed at the HEI sector, this is an informative site regarding the use of ePortfolios.

ACKNOWLEDGEMENTS

This chapter significantly develops and updates an earlier chapter by Younie, S. and Moore, T. (2005) 'Supporting teachers' professional practice with ICT' in M. Leask and N. Pachler (eds), *Learning to Teach in the Secondary School Using ICT*, London: Routledge.

Research from a range of projects funded by the EU, HEA, JISC, BECTA and TDA underpins this chapter. You will find materials from an HEA/JISC project that have been designed to develop your own digital literacy at http://www.educationcommunities.org/c/75979/home.do.

Google 'educationcommunities', register if you have not already done so and then click 'Digital literacy and creativity community'.

REFERENCES

Atherton, J. (2012) 'A critical review of the process of "reflection"'. Available online at: http://blogs.gre.ac.uk/ed/2012/03/26/james-atherton-the-limits-of-reflection/ (accessed 22 September 2012).

Bloom, B. (1964) *Taxonomy of Educational Objectives: Handbook 1: Cognitive Domain*, New York: Longman.

Boud, D., Keogh, R. and Walker, D. (eds) (1985) *Reflection: Turning Experience into Learning*, London: Kogan Page.

Bruner, J. (1986) *Actual Minds, Possible Worlds*, Cambridge, MA: Harvard University Press.

Burton, T. (1970) *Reach, Touch, and Teach: Student Concerns and Process Education*, St Louis, MO: McGraw-Hill.

Dewey, J. (1938) *Experience and Education*, New York: Simon and Schuster.

Garrison, R. and Anderson, T. (2003) *E-Learning in the 21st Century: A Framework for Research and Practice*, London: RoutledgeFalmer.

Garrison, R., Kanuka, H. and Hawes, D. (2004) *Communities of Inquiry.* Available online at: http://www.commons.ucalgary.ca (accessed 22 September 2012).

GESCI (n.d.) 'ICT Teacher Professional Development Framework Tool'. Available online at: http://www.gesci.org/knowledge-tools.html#planning-tpd (accessed 22 September 2012).

Gibbs, G. (1988) *Learning by Doing: A Guide to Teaching and Learning Methods*, London: Further Education Unit.

Hatton, N. and Smith, D. (1995) 'Reflection in teacher education', *Teaching and Teacher Education*, 11: 33–49.

JISC (n.d.) 'ePortfolios: an overview'. Available online at: http://www.jisc.ac.uk/eportfolio (accessed 21 September 2012).

Jones, S. (2009) *Collaborative Spaces – the Nature of Dialogue (Part I)*, Presented at ULearn09 Christchurch, New Zealand. Available online at: http://www.sarahjones.biz/collaborative-spaces-the-nature-of-dialogue/ (accessed 22 September 2012).

Kolb, D. (1984) *Experiential Learning: Experience as the Source of Learning and Development*, New Jersey, USA: Prentice Hall.

Lave, J. and Wenger, E. (1991) *Situated Learning*, Cambridge, UK: Cambridge University Press.

Lipman, M. (1991) *Thinking in Education*, Cambridge, UK: Cambridge University Press.

Lushyn, P. and Kennedy, D. (2000) *Community of Inquiry from a Psychodynamic Perspective.* Available online at: www2.kspu.kr.ua/blogs/lushin/en-1.html (accessed 22 September 2012).

Lygo-Baker, S. and Hatzipanagos, S. (2012) 'Enabling professional development with e-Portfolios: creating a space for the private and public self', *International Journal of Online Pedagogy and Course Design* 2(1): 37–52.

Moon, J. (1999) *Learning Journals: A Handbook for Academics, Students and Professional Development*, London: Kogan Page.

Peirce, C. (1877) 'The fixation of belief', *Popular Science Monthly* 12 November: 1–15.

Schon, D. (1983) *The Reflective Practitioner: How Professionals Think in Action*, New York, USA: Basic Books.

Slye, G. and Williamson, E. (2004) 'Supporting education programs through the Electronic Reserve System' (ERes), paper presented at the New Learning Technologies Orlando 2004 Conference, Orlando, USA.

Strudler, N. and Wetzel, K. (2005) 'The diffusion of electronic portfolios in teacher education: issues of initiation and implementation', *Journal of Research on Technology in Education* 37: 411–33.

Teacher Development Agency (2008) *Continuing Professional Development Guidance.* Available at: http://webarchive.nationalarchives.gov.uk/20120203163341/tda.gov.uk/training-provider/serving-teachers/cpd.aspx.

Tripp, D. (1993) *Critical Incidents in Teaching: Developing Professional Judgement*, London: Routledge.

UNESCO (2002) 'UNESCO promotes new initiative for free educational resources on the internet', United Nations Educational, Scientific and Cultural Organization, New York. Available online at: http://www.unesco.org/education/news_en/080702_free_edu_ress.shtml (accessed 24 May 2012).

Vygotsky, L.S. (1978) *Mind in Society*, Cambridge, MA: Harvard University Press.

Watton, P., Colling, J. and Moon, J. (2009) *Reflective Writing: Guidance Notes to Students*, Library Learning Support, Leicester: De Montfort University.

Wenger, E. (1998) *Communities of Practice: Learning Meaning and Identity,* Cambridge, UK: Cambridge University Press.

Winter, R. and Scoggins, J. (1999) 'The patchwork text: a coursework format for education as critical understanding', *Teaching in Higher Education* 4(4): 485–99.

Younie, S. and Jones, S. (2012) *Digital Literacy and Creativity: Open Educational Resources Project*, Final Report to Higher Education Academy and JISC, UK, Bedford: University of Bedfordshire.

4

LITERACY IN A DIGITAL AGE

Norbert Pachler, Margit Böck and Elisabetta Adami

INTRODUCTION

In this chapter we discuss the impact of digital technologies on notions of literacy and critically explore literacy as normally understood by school curricula (as developing reading, writing and spelling) in relation to 'new literacies' (relating to the production and reception of digital and multimodal artefacts and representations as social and situated practices). The chapter also explores related cultural practices of learners in everyday life and their relationship to school-based learning.

OBJECTIVES

By the end of this chapter you will:

- be able to critically reflect on the efficacy of traditional approaches to literacy in educational settings in the context of the normalisation of media practices in students' everyday life;
- understand literacy as a cultural practice that extends beyond traditional texts to – often technology-mediated – other modes of communication;
- have started to consider the pedagogical implications of how digital technologies are impacting both on the types of texts that we exchange and the way we produce and share them.

'TRADITIONAL' AND 'NEW' LITERACIES

One important recent publication in the field of traditional literacy is the US National Early Literacy Panel report (2009, pp. vii–viii), which uses the term 'conventional literacy' in relation to skills such as decoding, oral reading fluency, reading comprehension, writing and spelling. It distinguishes it from what it calls precursor, 'early literacy' skills characterised by:

- knowledge of the names and sounds associated with printed letters;
- the ability to detect, manipulate, or analyse the auditory aspects of spoken language;
- the ability to rapidly name a sequence of random letters or digits;
- the ability to rapidly name a sequence of repeated random sets of pictures of objects;
- the ability to write letters in isolation on request or to write one's own name;
- the ability to remember spoken information for a short period of time;
- the ability to produce or comprehend spoken language;
- the ability to match or discriminate visually presented symbols.

School-based approaches to the teaching of reading, certainly in the UK, have been highly influenced by political and policy debate since the so-called Bullock Report, entitled *A language for life*, published in 1975 (http://www.educationengland.org.uk/documents/bullock/), and have tended to focus on narrowly technical aspects of literacy, in particular the relationship of phonemes, graphemes and pronunciation rather than on language in the curriculum and language and communication (see for example the 2009 Rose Report, http://www.education.gov.uk/publications/eOrderingDownload/Primary_curriculum_Report.pdf).

Scholars such as Gunther Kress (2010) argue for the importance of a focus on the social dimension of reading and writing and their role in meaning making in communication, which in turn are bound up in changing forms and functions of texts. Kress (2010, p. 6) enumerates the following four factors:

1   Texts are becoming intensely multimodal, that is, image is ever-increasingly appearing with writing, and, in many domains of communication, displacing writing where it had previously been dominant.
2   Screens (of the digital media) are replacing the page and the book as the dominant media.
3   Social structures and social relations are undergoing fundamental changes, as far as writing is concerned, predominantly in changes of structures of authority, and in the effects of changing genre formations.
4   Constellations of mode and medium are being transformed. The medium of the book and the mode of writing had formed a centuries-long symbiotic constellation; this is being displaced by a new constellation of medium of the screen and mode of image.

Kress argues that the consequences of these factors are profound and lead to multimodality, which requires us to think in new ways about reading and writing, new dispositions towards the making of meaning with and of texts. Despite the normalisation of new literacy practices in young people's everyday life worlds, school still tends to focus on the reading and writing of traditional texts.

In the Digital Youth Project, Mimi Ito and colleagues (2008) identify a number of different so-called genres of participation. Ito and her colleagues stress the importance of new media use by young people for participation in shared culture and sociability and distinguish day-to-day negotiations with friends and peers and specialised activities around personal interests (pp. 9–10) and delineate the following genres: hanging out, messing around and geeking out (pp. 13–34).

They draw the following conclusion from their attempt to understand 'learning and participation in contemporary networked publics':

■ Participation in the digital age means more than being able to access 'serious' online information and culture; it also means the ability to participate in social and recreational activities online (p. 35).

■ In addition to economic barriers, youth encounter institutional, social, and cultural constraints to online participation (p. 36).

■ Networked publics provide a context for youth to develop social norms in negotiation with their peers (p. 36).

■ Youth are developing new forms of media literacy that are keyed to new media and youth-centred social and cultural worlds (p. 36).

■ Peer-based learning has unique properties that suggest alternatives to formal instruction (p. 36).

The last point in particular is echoed strongly in the work of James Paul Gee, who coined the term 'passionate affinity-based learning' which, according to him, occurs 'when people organise themselves to learn something connected to a shared endeavor, interest or passion' (http://www.jamespaulgee.com/node/50).

Important questions arise about the literacy practices prevailing in the context of such technology-mediated and media-orientated activities, and the extent to which traditional approaches to the teaching of reading and writing in school are helpful and relevant in relation to them. For a detailed discussion, see Pachler and Bachmair, forthcoming.

One very popular literacy practice of young people with new media is text messaging, but it is one which, according to a number of commentators in the popular press, is 'ruining our language': 'they are destroying it: pillaging our punctuation; savaging our sentences; raping our vocabulary' (John Humphrys, 2007, in the *Daily Mail,* http://www.dailymail.co.uk/news/article-483511/I-h8-txt-msgs-How-texting-wrecking-language.html). It is interesting to note that academic research actually found 'repeated positive relationships between use of text register language and traditional literacy skills, as measured through standardized tests and assessments' (Plester and Wood, 2009, p. 1108; see also Wood *et al.*, 2011).

In his research, Charles Crook (2012) shows that the relationship between traditional and new literacies is far from straight forward and that they pose considerable challenges for teachers and schools. He argues that the social and cognitive practices young people develop around Web 2.0 use, including text production and reception, are contingent and that tensions exist between the ambitions and expectations between cultures of media use in and out of school. Crook's data suggests that the strongly 'textual bias' of academic disciplines is misaligned with 'multi-modal literacies' of Web 2.0. And Crook highlights three issues that cause tension: service blocking by schools; technology as reward; and differential in the 'Web 2.0 readiness' of students (p. 75).

Task 4.1 **Mobile literacy practices**

Consider the implications of the headline findings of the research by Plester and Wood (2009) as well as Crook (2012): based on your observations of students' literacy practices around the use of mobile devices and social media, what scope is there for transformational change in educational practice to take on board young people's literacy practices in everyday life? And, what are the barriers and how might they be overcome?

NORBERT PACHLER, MARGIT BÖCK, ELISABETTA ADAMI ■ ■ ■ ■

LITERACY: 'GEOLOGICAL LAYERS' OF A COMPLEX FIELD

In this chapter, we take 'literacy' to refer to the semiotic potentials and resources of (alphabetic) writing which are available in a culture for the production of written (parts of) texts of all kinds. The reference to *alphabetic* writing draws attention to the particular relation between speech and writing in societies with alphabetic script cultures and those in which the script system is not in any (significant or major) way seen as a means of transcription of speech – ideographic scripts, for instance. The presence or absence of that relationship has major social and semiotic consequences for both speech and writing, and for the interrelations of each with the range of media, which are available in a society. Even in 'alphabetic cultures' the social as much as the semiotic relations of speech, alphabet and writing are not at all the same. The assumption that the alphabet facilitates the 'transcription' of speech to writing, and, conversely, acts as a bridge from writing to speech, is easier to maintain in some European languages than in others – easier in Spanish, Italian, German or Finnish for instance, and far less so in others, among which English is a particularly problematic case.

The question of different languages and different script-systems – of the relation between spoken and written language – becomes ever more important in a time when multilingualism is the normal condition of most classrooms. It points to the fact that debates around literacy are too frequently conducted at a level that is too general to attend to important differences. This is particularly so in pedagogic contexts where a default position is 'everybody knows what is meant by "literacy"'. This reductive simplification contradicts the fact that 'literacy' itself changes in line with constant, ongoing changes in social and medial environments (Kress, 2003).

Both for pedagogic and for semiotic reasons it is crucial to realise that the transition from writing (seen) as the central or major 'mode' of representation, to writing as one among a number of other modes is now far advanced. A generational 'gap' has opened, in which those below the ages of 20 to 25 have an increasingly 'distant' relation to 'traditional' forms of writing, to its modes of production and dissemination (e.g. 'letters'), and its genres. As one consequence, the majority of those who teach in schools 'inhabit' a different representational world to those who are there to learn – even if not to be taught. That gap – at times more like a chasm – of course exists also in relation to employers and new employees, etc. The consequences go beyond the pedagogic to the world of public, economic, social life. There the traditional forms of writing lead an increasingly precarious and contradictory life. In 'elite environments', writing in its traditional forms remains most highly valued even though it may not be the most commonly used. In other parts of the public world – on websites, in PR materials, in advertising, in materials designed for information – the newer non-traditional forms dominate, by and large. There, writing is increasingly displaced from a formerly central place to filling an increasing number of increasingly different kinds of function.

One can see the present situation akin to the metaphor of geological layers: a layering of forms and practices, produced over time, continued by age-as-generation, and existing together – differentiated by social groupings (education and the older notion of 'class' still are relevant; e.g. Böck, 2012), by generation, and by function, among others. That differentiation is accompanied by one of the kinds of genres available and in use, in the means of producing texts and in the media of dissemination, with an increasing blurring of boundaries here too. The traditional genre of the narrative (whether as novel or as shorter texts of various kinds) or of the letter remain linked more with paper-based media such as the book; newer genres such as email, blog, tweet are linked with screen-based media.

It seems clear that in pedagogic settings both traditional and new forms of 'writing' need to be taught. The forms used by the social and economic elites need to be fully available to all those who go to school, so that for them access to all areas of social and economic life remain open; or if anything, are taught much more effectively than hitherto. At the same time, the new forms, which are by now normal, and 'naturalised' even, for the younger generation will need to become part of the normal literacy curriculum. That of course is a much more difficult demand to meet: not enough is as yet securely known about these forms. We do not know what genres exist and what their affordances are nor what their epistemological effect will be on the various curricular entities of the overall school curriculum. At the same time the new forms of representation, the media, as much as social conditions, are in a constant process of change. It is not possible, in reality, to focus on writing alone in the way it has been done for many decades. Nevertheless, here we make some comments on writing as it is and is developing.

The 'monomodal' text, as noted, has a precarious existence. It lives on as handwritten notes, as simple instructions or notices – e.g. 'no smoking please' – right up to complex narratives; though as pointed out earlier and in the next section, increasingly, as the written elements/components of multimodal texts of various kinds and in a variety of media. In schools a protected 'biotope' exists, still: here conceptions of writing, and with them writing tasks, often continue, much as they might have been some three or four decades ago. Here are two examples for university entrance level examinations. These give what are in fact quite specific instructions for the generic form of the texts to be produced.

Example 1
Provide a summary of the core statements of the attached text [a newspaper-article] and *state your position* in regard to the several claims [...].

Example 2
Analyse the following extract from the speech of [...]. *Make* detailed *comments* on the content, the linguistic-rhetorical and argumentative shaping and the intentions of the author. *Discuss*, starting from a definition of the concept 'culture' [...].

What has changed within the traditional pedagogic approach is that more attention is being given to the teaching of formal aspects of texts – forms of genre, for instance. In part this is a response to the result of tests comparing performance in 'literacy' internationally. In part it is a response – though not usually recognised as such – to the profound changes in the interest of young people in the different forms of representing, which becomes evident in their lesser interests in 'schooled literacy'.

(TRADITIONAL FORMS OF) WRITING IN A TIME OF TRANSITION

As far as 'traditional literacy' is concerned, the pedagogic task is to make the benefits of traditional forms evident to the younger generations, and in doing so provide some counterweight to the attractions of the newer forms. What are the benefits of traditional forms of writing? The emergence of multimodal ways of looking at representation not only shows the attractions of, say, image over writing. It also asks of academics to answer the question of the affordances of the various modes: what can image do that writing cannot? Or, conversely, what can writing do that image cannot? In the era of the dominance of writing that question simply had not emerged: (alphabetic) writing was thought, quite simply, to be the (or one of the) highest achievements of some human cultures, and was capable of representing all one would want to communicate.

So the question now is: do we actually know what writing can do, when put, for example, against the potentials of moving image? Can we express these potentials clearly and simply enough to show their attractions convincingly to young people in schools?

The digital media and their potentials for text-production, -shaping, -mediation, and use have had their effects in changing texts and the social uses of texts in fundamental ways. The term 'literacy' – or more frequently its plural, 'literacies' – is applied to the texts that result, whatever the role of writing in such texts. The emergence of such texts has given rise to quite a new question, appearing usually in the form of outrage, for instance: 'this is just cutting and pasting', or at times, especially given the ubiquity of 'plagiarism detection' programs, the accusation of 'plagiarism' – a topic we deal with in more detail below. The actual, underlying, issue is that with new forms of text-production, the digital media, and changed forms of social relations (fostered by, e.g. the so-called 'social media') giving rise to new genres, a radical rethinking both of compositional principles and of the entities of compositions is required.

That will require profound thinking about these same questions and principles in relation to traditional forms of literacy. Was it the case that letters are or were the basic building blocks of written texts? Were sentence types constantly newly made? Or genres? Or was there in fact a massive amount of legitimated recycling of existing materials – words, turns of phrase, 'sayings', clichés, ways of structuring genres appropriately? Answering that question for compositions of all kinds will permit a more soundly based approach to both traditional and new forms of composition.

The compositional entities which are proving to be the bane of teachers at all levels of education are building blocks which include letters and words, phrases cut from somewhere or lifted from a remembered snatch of conversation, larger pieces of text regarded as relevant right here, and of course images from many sources. Some of the entities are ready made, some are newly made according to traditional notions of 'new making' – i.e. 'state, using your own words, your sense of Holger Brow's aesthetic conception of formal gardens'.

In the meantime, the most frequently used medium for (producing) (new forms of) writing or for reading is what was until very recently called the mobile 'phone' – ineptly named for some time and now rapidly displaced by 'smart phones' or other mobile devices. Its (former) technical constraints – length of text, the conditions of writing with a numerical pad – were leading, until overtaken by newer devices, to the development of a new script and of expressive 'systems'. These, as well as other out-of-school (writing and reading) practices, offer many possibilities of networking and connecting with other 'literacy practices' in the context of the school. In order to make these available for 'schoolish practices' and to support young people in using these for extending their competencies in the contexts of the school and to recognise their relevance and advantages in shaping their own lives, teachers must have the resources to 'recognise' these 'literacy practices' as forms of using writing and give them full valuation.

The 'New Literacies' (e.g. Lankshear and Knobel, 2006, 2008; Coiro *et al.*, 2008) attempt to describe these changes at the level of texts as much as at the level of the agents and their making and uses of these texts. In the process, the concept of 'literacy' – initially applied to (the mode of) writing – is being extended to other modes of communication. This leads to a situation where it is becoming even less clear what the term can usefully be taken to mean (e.g. Böck and Kress, 2010).

Task 4.2 **Traditional and contemporary genres**

Reading and writing practices are differentiated by education, gender, class, 'culture' and age-as-generation. Think about the environments of reading and writing in your own childhood and adolescent life and your habits of reading and writing. What was 'common', what was 'special' compared to your friends? Talk to your parents or people of your parents' and grandparents' generation and try to find out what reading and writing meant to them in their childhood and what sort of reading media and forms of writing they grew up with. Talk to students in your class or ask them to produce a 'diary of reading and writing' during two or three days. Compare the different literacy environments and practices of these three generations, by taking gender and educational differences into account. How can you connect contemporary literacy practices of students and texts they use and produce with literacy practices they do not integrate into their everyday lives? How can you use contemporary genres (e.g. text messages) and (more) traditional genres (e.g. emails, formal letters) to allow students to experience the situatedness of these genres and texts in general? Do they have usefulness in relation to the curriculum that you are teaching? What advantages for students' writing and learning do they offer?

DIGITAL AFFORDANCES: MULTIMODALITY AND COPY-AND-PASTE

The wide availability of digital technologies for everyday representation and communication is impacting on both the types of texts that we exchange and the way we produce and share them. As for the types of texts, digital technologies of any kind allow multimodal texts (combining, e.g. videos, pictures, writing, music and/or speech) to be produced and shared as easily as written texts. As for the production of texts, digital technologies enable texts to be created through the reuse of texts produced previously; thanks to copy-and-paste, it is now easier to forward an existing text into new contexts and for new communication purposes than to produce *ad hoc* text 'from scratch'. A characteristic affordance of digital media, the copy-and-paste functionality enables also the assemblage of selected sections of texts, combined together to create a new, remixed text.

The first affordance of digital sign-making – multimodality – is undermining the dominance of writing for recorded and distance communication; indeed writing is now only one of the many modes composing digitally-produced texts. One cannot say that we are writing less; on the contrary, we are probably writing more, and more often (Blommaert and Velghe, 2013), yet our writing is rather likely to be coupled by images (even when in the mere case of emoticons) and other modally constituted signs. The second aspect – copied-and-pasted text production – is changing the ways in which we conceive of and experience texts. Manipulated as objects, displaced and recombined as building blocks, texts are now reused to produce new meanings in new contexts.

Anyone who uses a word processor knows only too well the usefulness of copy-and-paste to his/her writing needs; yet students' use of the affordance is giving rise to major concerns in educational contexts, where issues of plagiarism intersect problems in assessing students' actual learning (Villano, 2006; Hartley, 2007; Haviland and Mullins, 2009; Hobbs, 2009). The extant changes in our media landscape have produced a rather conflicting situation. Technologies enable certain textual practices; these are becoming increasingly frequent, adapting to and influencing sign-making conventions in all contexts; yet while both practices and conventions are praised or considered as the norm in certain contexts, they are stigmatised in others, especially when produced by the weakest participants. The question hence is how education can face changes and prepare students to be successful sign-makers in all contexts; in this light, a thorough consideration of the effects of the use of copy-and-paste in everyday sign-making can be useful to assess gains and losses and how they could be addressed in educational contexts.

SIGN-MAKING EFFECTS OF MULTIMODAL COPY-AND-PASTE

The frequent use of multimodal copy-and-paste in everyday online communication is producing a series of consequences. First, it is giving rise to texts characterised by absence of cohesion and marked implicitness (Adami, 2012a). Implicit communication can be highly successful in certain contexts and genres – humour uses it extensively, for example – but not that effective in others (Adami, 2012b). The fact that so-called 'digital natives' are accustomed to sign-making characterised by implicitness and fragmentation needs to be taken into consideration when designing activities in literacy classes, especially when introducing students to linear and explicit genres such as academic essay writing, for example.

Second, and related to the previous aspect, multimodal (copied-and-pasted) sign-making is redefining the functions of writing, which, combined with other modally constituted signs, is more likely to follow the modular logics of multimodally composed texts, rather than the linear and sequential logics of writing. While the trend is attested in both informal and formal texts as Bezemer and Kress' (2010) analysis of English textbooks shows, contexts and genres differ in respect to the ways in which content is distributed across different modes. For instance, writing–image juxtaposition is generally acceptable in, for example, Facebook posts, whereas explicit interlinking is required in academic writing, where images, graphs and tables need to be referred to in the written text when relevant content is discussed. In this sense, it is crucial for digital natives to be aware of the different ongoing image–writing conventions in every context.

Third, the use of copy-and-paste is producing different conventions in different contexts as to the need of making sources explicit. On the one hand, as teachers know only too well when they 'google' their students' texts to detect possibly copied excerpts, many different pages on the web often exist reporting the same wording without bothering to acknowledge the text's initial author and with no apparent concern for plagiarism. On the other hand, copy-and-paste in educational and academic contexts has long been actualised in the practice of direct quotation, while any unacknowledged reuse of previously existing text has been considered inappropriate (however, until recently, this had been mainly confined to Western academic tradition, cf. Bennett, 2011). Yet again, in literary and artistic contexts, reuse is considered as a sort of homage to the source, which does not need to be referenced; here it is understood that intertextuality (Kristeva, 1980) activates readers' background knowledge, while readers' recognition of the implicit intertextual reference is part of their enjoyment of the text.

Finally, sign making through reuse foregrounds abilities such as pragmatic meaning making and editing rather than semantic meaning making and design from scratch. Every text reused in another context undergoes inevitably a shift in meaning; hence, rather than making meaning of the text as is, at a solely semantic level, communication through recontextualisation requires sign makers to be able to foresee the pragmatic effects of the copied text as will be resignified by virtue of its relation with the new context. Besides, and also in consequence of that, sign makers need to be able to adjust and refine the selected text, possibly together with further co-text, according to the new communicative purposes for which it is reused (Adami, 2011).

Such a changed semiotic landscape opens compelling questions to educational contexts, such as:

■ How can students' awareness of different conventions and literacy practices be raised to enable them to select the proper ones on the basis of assessment of what is needed in each context and genre?

■ How can learning, creativity, reflection and re-elaboration of contents be assessed when texts are produced through copy-and-paste?

■ Should teaching priorities be redefined, given that *ad hoc* pragmatic meta-reflection (rather than 'competence'), and editing for cohesive re-adjustment (more than morpho-syntactic production) become the abilities needed to communicate successfully?

Here it is argued that the above questions can find some initial answers by problematising copy-and-paste in the curriculum, instead of seeking to ban it.

MULTIMODAL COPY-AND-PASTE: POTENTIAL LEARNING OUTCOMES

Learning activities promoting the explicit use of copy-and-paste can complement the curriculum to respond to the changing semiotic landscape (Adami, 2011).

In any subject of the curriculum, the explicit use of copy-and-paste in learning activities can foster, as suggested by Moody (2007), a dialogic approach to pre-existing knowledge, conceiving of one's contribution as a self-positioning against, an addition to and a refinement of prior knowledge, rather than as individual creation 'out of the blue'. Writing activities that promote an explicit use of copy-and-paste can be a useful introduction to the academic conventions of referencing and quoting and, if accompanied by proper discussion, they can be a pre-emptive strategy that pre-empts students from presenting copied-and-pasted text as their own productions. When, as in remixes, creativity is assessed and rewarded for the way in which other texts are selected, assembled and transformed, rather than for creation from scratch, the fact that one's original contribution can exist only on the basis of knowledge built by previous ones becomes apparent. Not only does this foster a more dialogic conception of knowledge, but also nullifies any motive for 'cheating'.

In the writing classroom, activities can be designed to facilitate students' awareness of the construction mechanisms of linear writing, comparing them to compositional patterns of recontextualised and assembled texts. For example, constructing the thematic structure of an essay by using copied-and-pasted excerpts can firstly promote students' summarising skills, in finding a topic for each copied paragraph – a learning objective still unachieved by a significant number of students (OECD, 2004, 2009). It can further train them to construct coherent argumentation, by working with each copied paragraph as a sub-topic, manipulating paragraphs on the screen and logically sequencing them one after another, considering various possible topic structures and choosing the most coherent and effective argumentative structure. A subsequent editing activity can familiarise students with reporting verbs, thus introducing them to crucial linguistic expressions of stance. Editing can also involve students' use of cohesive devices such as discourse markers, to make the logical connections among concepts explicit and have the text adhere to a linear structure. Practicing cohesive devices is particularly needed for 'digital natives' whose experience of recontextualised texts frequently involves implicit types of communication, as mentioned above, while, the text refining activity as a whole trains also students' editing skills, which are rarely included within the curriculum but are increasingly required in contemporary sign making.

As regards students' multimodal literacy, the copy-and-paste activity of essay composition introduced above should ask students to combine writing and visuals, given that the latter are increasingly frequent in academic papers in all fields. This can promote students' meta-reflection on different conventions of multimodal sign making. Students can be made aware of the fact that copied-and-pasted images too have to be referenced. Besides, the activity can trigger a reflection on how content can be differently distributed among modes and students can be introduced to the specific conventions for writing–image relations in each genre, when asked to apply the proper one to their 'patchwork' paper during the editing activity.

Finally, in the foreign language classroom, all the above learning activities can be aimed at familiarising students with the foreign culture- and language-specific conventions and textual practices, such as referencing and structuring arguments, for example. In this regard, crucial lexico-discursive areas of foreign language learning such as reporting verbs and cohesive devices can be introduced and practiced through the editing activity illustrated above, especially if accompanied by discussion in class triggering students' meta-reflection on their choices. Moreover, selecting and manipulating native writing to structure an argument practices students' reading comprehension, while assembling it with students' own productions can be preparatory for autonomous writing and, when properly directed, can trigger further meta-reflection on features such as texture, register and morpho-syntactic structure of the language. The latter is particularly called into question in editing activities when, for example, the copied excerpt's syntactic structure requires a morpho-syntactic adjustment of the micro-context in which it is pasted. This can produce particularly useful learning outcomes especially for specialised languages and text types with which students are not yet familiar, such as scientific writing.

Task 4.3 **Multimodal essay composition**

Consider the activity of essay composition through multimodal copy-and-paste suggested in this section: if you were implementing it for your class, could you envisage any learning objectives it could serve? What kind of changes in the activity tasks would be needed for it to serve them? What kind of changes would the activity imply, in terms of students' and teachers' attitudes towards and understanding of 'literacy', 'learning' and 'knowledge'?

The authors would be happy to receive feedback on such copy-and-paste learning activities in your class. Please email e.adami@unich.it.

SUMMARY

In this chapter we have tried to show how literacy practices are changing in everyday life as a consequence of technological transformations and the normalisation of powerful handheld computing devices and attendant applications and services. We have also considered some of the implications of these developments for teaching and learning.

REFERENCES

Adami, E. (2011) 'In defence of multimodal re-signification: a response to Håvard Skaar's "In defence of writing"', *Literacy* 45(1): 44–50.

——(2012a) 'The rhetoric of the implicit and the politics of representation in the age of copy-and-paste', *Learning, Media and Technology* 37(2): 131–44.

——(2012b) 'Mashing genres up, breaking them down: literacy in the age of copy-and-paste', *Linguagem em Foco/Language in Focus*, 2011/1, pp. 25–42.

Bennett, K. (2011) 'Plagiarism reassessed: a culturalist take on academia's cardinal sin', *The European Messenger* 20(1): 74–7.

Bezemer, J. and Kress, G. (2010) 'Changing text: a social semiotic analysis of textbooks', *Designs for Learning* 3(1–2): 10–29. Available at: http://jeffbezemer.files.wordpress.com/2011/11/dfl_0102_10_bezemer_kress.pdf (accessed 10 May 2013).

Blommaert, J. and Velghe, F. (2013) 'Learning a supervernacular: textspeak in a South African township', in A. Creese and A. Blackledge (eds), *Heteroglossia as Practice and Pedagogy*, New York: Springer.

Böck, M. (2012) 'Lesen und Schreiben als soziale Praxis. Jugendliche und Schriftlichkeit' in F. Eder (ed.), *PISA 2000. Nationale Zusatzanalysen für Österreich*. Münster: Waxmann, pp. 9–58.

Böck, M. and Kress, G. (2010) 'Soziale Kontexte der digitalen Kommunikation und Probleme der Begrifflichkeiten: "New Literacy Studies", "Multiliteracies" und "Multimodality" als Beispiele', *Medienimpulse* 4. Available at: http://ww.medienimpulse.at/articles/view/271.pdf (accessed 10 May 2013).

Coiro, J., Knobel, M., Lankshear, C. and Leu, D. (eds) (2008) *Handbook of Research on New Literacies*, New York: Routledge.

Crook, C. (2012) 'The "digital native" in context: tensions associated with importing Web 2.0 practices into the school setting', *Oxford Review of Education* 38(1): 63–80.

Hartley, J. (2007) 'There are other ways of being in the truth: the uses of multimedia literacy', *International Journal of Cultural Studies* 10(1): 135–44.

Haviland, C. and Mullins, J. (eds) (2009) *Who Owns This Text? Plagiarism, Authorship and Disciplinary Cultures*, Logan: Utah State University Press.

Hobbs, R. (2009) 'The power of fair use for media literacy education', *Afterimage* 37(2): 15–18.

Howard, R. (2004) 'Mapping the territory of plagiarism'. Available at: http://wrt-howard.syr.edu/Papers/WashingtonState/Address/WSU.htm (accessed 10 May 2013).

Ito, M., Horst, H., Bittanti, M., Boyd, D., Herr-Stephenson, B., Lange, P., Pascoe, C. and Robinson, L. (2008) *Living and Learning with New Media: Summary of Findings from the Digital Youth Project*, The John D. and Catherine T. MacArthur Foundation Reports on Digital Media and Learning, Chicago: The MacArthur Foundation. Available at: http://digitalyouth.ischool.berkeley.edu/files/report/digitalyouth-WhitePaper.pdf (accessed 10 May 2013).

Kress, G. (2003) *Literacy in the New Media Age*, London: Routledge.

——(2010) 'The profound shift of digital literacies', in J. Gillen and D. Barton (eds), *Digital Literacies: A Research Briefing*, Technology Enhanced Learning phase of the Teaching and Learning Research Programme. London Knowledge Lab. Available at: http://www.tlrp.org/docs/DigitalLiteracies.pdf (accessed 10 May 2013).

Kristeva, J. (1980) *Desire in Language: A Semiotic Approach to Literature and Art* (L. S. Roudiez, trans.), Oxford: Blackwell.

Lankshear, C. and Knobel, M. (2006) *New Literacies: Everyday Practices and Classroom Learning*, 2nd edition, Maidenhead: Open University Press.

——(eds) (2008) *Digital Literacies: Concepts, Policies and Practices*, New York: Peter Lang.

Moody, J. (2007) 'Plagiarism or intertextuality? Approaches to teaching EFL academic writing', *Asian EFL Journal 9*(2): 195–210.

National Early Literacy Panel (2009) *Developing Early Literacy: Report of the National Early Literacy Panel*, Washington, DC: National Institute for Literacy. Available at: http://www.nichd.nih.gov/publications/pubs/upload/NELPReport09.pdf (accessed 10 May 2013).

OECD (2004) *Messages from PISA 2000*, Paris: OECD Publications. Available at: http://www.oecd.org/dataoecd/31/19/34107978.pdf (accessed 10 May 2013).

——(2009) *PISA 2009 Results: What Students Know and Can Do: Student Performance in Reading, Mathematics and Science*, Vol. I. Available at: http://www.pisa.oecd.org/dataoecd/10/61/48852548.pdf (accessed 10 May 2013).

Pachler, N. and Bachmair, B. (forthcoming) 'What is happening to literacy?', *International Journal of Learning and Media*. Special Issue on 'New media, new literacies, and new forms of learning'.

Plester, B. and Wood, C. (2009) 'Exploring relationships between traditional and new media literacies: British preteen texters at school', *Journal of Computer-mediated Communication* 14(4): 1108–29.

Share, P. (2004) 'Managing intertextuality: meaning, plagiarism and power', AISHE Inaugural Conference, Trinity College, Dublin. Available at: http://www.aishe.org/conf2004/proceedings/paper23doc (accessed 10 May 2013).

Villano, M. (2006) 'Taking the work out of homework', *THE* 33(15): 24–30.

Wolff, J. (2006) 'Does plagiarism matter? Answer in your own words', *Guardian Weekly*, 3–9 March.

Wood, C., Jackson, E., Hart, L., Plester, B. and Wilde, L. (2011) 'The effect of text messaging on 9- and 10-year-old children's reading, spelling and phonological processing skills', *Journal of Computer Assisted Learning* 27(1): 28–36.

PEDAGOGY WITH ICT

Mary Webb

INTRODUCTION

How should teachers make decisions about how to teach and how to organise their pupils? These are key issues that pedagogy as the science or theory of teaching seeks to address. The aim in this chapter is to examine pedagogy in relation to information and communications technology (ICT). There are two interrelated aspects of this endeavour: 1) the use of ICT to support, enhance or transform learning and teaching; 2) the more general effect that ICT, especially the internet and mobile technologies, is having on the modern world and how this affects pedagogy.

For you as student teachers, learning how to plan lessons and how to incorporate specific uses of ICT to provide appropriate learning experiences for your pupils is challenging. Making minute by minute decisions while your pupils are learning, about when to intervene, what questions to ask, how to respond to pupils' questions and answers is even more challenging and depends on developing your professional knowledge and expertise as you review theory, observe other teachers and reflect on your practice. In order to help to make sense of these decision-making processes this chapter explores pedagogy with ICT by: 1) reviewing theoretical frameworks that have emerged over recent years as our understanding of the use of ICT for learning has developed; and 2) examining examples of pedagogical practices as they relate to these theoretical ideas.

OBJECTIVES

At the end of this chapter you should be able to:

- explain how the changing world mediated by the internet and mobile technologies is affecting pedagogy;
- approach pedagogical decision-making in relation to ICT use more confidently;
- consider where to start with developing your pedagogical practices with ICT.

WHAT IS PEDAGOGY?

The term pedagogy has been defined in various ways including: the art of teaching, the science of teaching, the craft of teaching, the profession of teaching or just as another word for the practice of teaching. Part of this variation is due to different traditions of education in different cultures. Part is due to a belief that teaching is an art not a science. Certainly when you identify a good teacher their expertise may best be described as an art. However, much is known about teaching from research and making sense of the evidence and theorising about it is essential for the continuing development of the profession. Therefore in this chapter pedagogy has been defined, within a European tradition, as the science or theory of teaching and it is about the analysis of the body of knowledge that is accumulating about teaching in order to explain how teaching operates and to establish principles.

According to Alexander (1992) the two facets of pedagogy are teaching methods and pupil organisation, which exist within a framework of educational practice containing seven interrelated aspects: content, context, pedagogy, management, children, society, and knowledge. This implies that pedagogy incorporating ICT exists in a broad framework and what you observe in the classroom is only part of educational practice. Thus, understanding teachers' ICT-related pedagogical practices requires examining teachers' ideas, values, beliefs, and the thinking that leads to observable elements in practice.

Pedagogy is frequently depicted as being in a dynamic triangular causal relationship with the curriculum and assessment all of which are moderated by theories of learning. Thus pedagogy is not static but changes to reflect our understanding of how learning occurs. During the twentieth century, for example, pedagogy changed as constructivist theories of learning and socio-cultural theory gained acceptance and the importance of metacognition was recognised (Watkins and Mortimore, 1999). Furthermore, the prevailing ideas in pedagogy are influenced by curriculum and assessment regimes. High-stakes assessments tend to dominate pedagogy leading to a constricted curriculum and discouraging the development of creativity and the social and cultural aspects of learning (Harlen and Deakin Crick, 2002).

FROM THEORIES OF LEARNING TO PEDAGOGY

There are many different theories of learning, and no unifying theory as yet because we have no complete social and biological explanation of how people learn. Therefore theories are based predominantly on observations of the visible signs of learning or computer models of the mind. Developments in neuroscience are gradually unravelling the complexity of brain function and it is possible that within the next 10 to 20 years we may have a much better understanding of how people learn. In a future scenario for the practical use of neuroscience techniques outlined by Geake and Cooper (2003), students wear neuro-imaging headsets while they do assessment tasks. Their individual images are statistically analysed by a computer, and teachers use their pedagogical knowledge to review the reports. Where teachers identify specific difficulties associated with brain development they recommend courses using real-time biofeedback to strengthen specific memory circuits for individual learners. These possibilities may not be realised for many years and will raise a range of ethical issues but they do suggest that as pedagogy continues to adapt to our changing understanding of learning, incorporating findings from neuroscience and determining directions in the newer field of educational neuroscience may be important (Fischer *et al.*, 2010). For teachers, gaining a general understanding of neuroscience is advisable in order to be able to distinguish innovations based on neuromythologies from those based on real science (see for example Geake, 2008).

Understanding how people learn is only a first step in thinking about pedagogy. There is still a significant leap from understanding how people learn to deciding how they should be taught. For example, development of constructivist pedagogical practices in science have taken place since the 1980s but Harlen (1999) reported from a review of research studies of effective teaching of science: 'There is no firm evidence as to the effectiveness of different approaches to developing students' ideas within a constructivist framework' (p. 40). Similarly, research on mathematics education found no clear characteristics defining effective teachers of mathematics (Brown *et al.*, 2001). Instead, evidence in this and other studies suggests a complex model for pedagogy in which much depends on how teachers and pupils relate to each other and interact. There are, however, some signposts towards excellence in education developed by Hattie (2009), based on meta-analyses of innovations in education. These are presented in Table 5.1 and you may want to reflect on your own experience about whether this seems to be a comprehensive list.

■ **Table 5.1** Signposts towards excellence in education

1 Teachers are among the most powerful influences in learning.

2 Teachers need to be directive, influential, caring, and actively engaged in the passion of teaching and learning.

3 Teachers need to be aware of what each and every student is thinking and knowing, to construct meaning and meaningful experiences in light of this knowledge, and have proficient knowledge and understanding of their content to provide meaningful and appropriate feedback such that each student moves progressively through the curriculum levels.

4 Teachers need to know the learning intentions and success criteria of the lessons, know how well they are attaining these criteria for all students, and know where to go next in light of the gap between students' current knowledge and understanding and the success criteria of: 'Where are you going?', 'How are you going?', 'Where to next?'

5 Teachers need to move from the single idea to multiple ideas, and to relate and then extend these ideas such that learners construct and reconstruct knowledge and ideas. It is not the knowledge or ideas, but the learner's construction of this knowledge and these ideas that is critical.

6 School leaders and teachers need to create school, staffroom and classroom environments where error is welcomed as a learning opportunity, where discarding incorrect knowledge and understandings is welcomed, and where participants can feel safe to learn, re-learn, and explore knowledge and understanding.

Source: Hattie, 2009, p. 238.

Task 5.1 **Articulating your theories of learning**

Try to define and write down how you think people learn. In this endeavour you need to go beyond just stating 'people learn by doing XYZ' and think about what goes on in their heads, and perhaps other parts of their bodies, while they are doing XYZ or perhaps after they have finished. Don't worry if you find this difficult: most teachers find it difficult to explain their theories of learning but all teachers do hold their own ideas about how people learn and they use these to make pedagogical decisions in their lesson planning and interaction with their pupils. So it is useful to spend some time reflecting on your own experience and trying to come up with a description of your theory. You may want to outline several aspects of theory that suit different contexts or topics.

When you have written a paragraph that you feel reflects what you think, record it in your personal development plan (PDP) so that you can refer to it from time to time to see whether it needs updating to reflect changes in your thinking.

If possible share your theories of learning with other student teachers and identify differences and similarities.

CHANGING PEDAGOGY AND EVIDENCE OF INNOVATIONS WITH ICT

Ideally we would always ensure that pedagogical practices are based on evidence. However, identifying which types of ICT to use and how to deploy them, based on evidence, is difficult because meta-analyses of effect sizes have shown much variation and no clear patterns with regard to the value of different types of ICT (Hattie, 2009). Instead, these analyses confirmed those of other studies (Cox *et al.*, 2004; Cox and Webb, 2004) that the value of the ICT use depends on the specific learning intentions and how the ICT resources are deployed alongside other elements of the learning environment.

The analyses of effect-sizes of interventions (Hattie, 2009, p. 221) did suggest that key attributes leading to the highest effects of the use of ICT were:

1   There is a diversity of teaching strategies.
2   There are multiple opportunities for learning.
3   The pupils rather than the teacher are in control of the learning.
4   Peer learning is optimised.
5   The tasks are challenging.
6   There is well-explained and focused feedback.

This list provides some useful pointers but needs to be interpreted with caution. Hattie's findings are based on a synthesis of meta-analyses. Each separate meta-analysis would have derived from studies that met certain criteria so many studies would have been excluded (see Hattie, 2009, Chapter 2 for an explanation of effect sizes and the limitations of meta-analysis). In particular, many qualitative studies that examined practice in depth as well as most practitioner-based research will not have been incorporated. In addition, it is important to remember that all such evidence is based on history, and ICT is changing all the time so to understand the full story it is important to continually examine the pedagogical potential of new technological innovations, to think forward and to try out new approaches as well as to learn from the findings of previous research.

CHANGING SOCIETY AND CHANGING PEDAGOGY

Rapid technological developments have brought about major changes in our understanding of the nature of learning, as illustrated by the following set of terms that are becoming commonplace in educational discourse: lifelong learning, informal learning, virtual schooling, online learning, blended learning, social networking and M-learning (mobile learning). Internet and mobile technologies in particular, together with the explosion in online social networking, have led to radical changes in the ways that young people socialise and learn (Ito *et al.,* 2008; Livingstone and Haddon, 2009; Bavelier *et al.*, 2010). Furthermore, studies in the UK (Crook and Harrison, 2008), across Europe (Livingstone and Haddon, 2009) and in the US (Rideout *et al.*, 2010) have shown that young people spend much more time using the web outside of school than in school indicating the growing importance of informal learning. Therefore, substantial shifts in our view of learning have been identified. For example, a shift to mobility in learning is characterised by Kress and Pachler as a constant state of contingency, provisionality and knowledge creation brought about by an expectation of immediate access to a world of resources, materials and social interaction (Kress and Pachler, 2007). Thus there is a shift in emphasis from teaching to learning (Bauman 2005; Kress and Pachler 2007) in which responsibility is transferred to individual students to manage their learning trajectories (Bauman, 2005).

Changes in our conceptions of learning are thus a reflection of broader social change characterised by the Polish philosopher and sociologist Zygmunt Bauman as a passage from the 'solid' to 'liquid' phase of modernity (Bauman, 2000). In this new environment, change is too rapid for social forms to solidify, the future is unpredictable and people are expected to be flexible rather than following rules or using established knowledge (Bauman, 2000). For education the changing nature of knowledge is particularly significant:

> Like everything else in the world, all knowledge cannot but age quickly and so it is the refusal to accept established knowledge, to go by precedents and to recognize the wisdom of the lessons of accumulated experience that are now seen as the precepts of effectiveness and productivity.
>
> (Bauman, 2000, p. 154)

Therefore, Bauman argued that this need for continual knowledge creation through interaction in socio-cultural settings militates against an education that focuses on gradually building young people's knowledge through a pre-determined sequence of learning as specified in most curricula (Bauman, 2005). Furthermore, survival in liquid modernity depends on 'individualisation' as people are continually forced to make choices through lives consisting of many separate episodes in frail and volatile settings (Bauman, 2000). How pedagogy, and education more generally, changes in response to this and other changes in our world is likely to continue to be a matter of debate for some time to come (see for example Mioduser *et al.*, 2008).

It has long been recognised that pupils' learning and experiences outside of school are important in their overall learning and development, but access to the internet has given massively increased opportunities. At the very least teachers need to be aware that much of pupils' learning takes place outside of school. Furthermore, they need to plan ways of taking account of these prior experiences of pupils in order to build and develop their understanding. Such considerations are essential for schooling to appear relevant to pupils as well as to be successful in enabling learning in school. In addition, the education system has a responsibility to help pupils to make sense of their informal learning opportunities as well as to learn from their more formal experiences in school. Therefore enabling pupils to use ICT to support their learning is necessary for them to take advantage of their lifelong learning opportunities. The knowledge society is stimulating us to define new literacies. For example, Mioduser *et al.* (2008) have identified seven literacies that relate to ICT knowledge, skills and understanding and will need to be developed in cross curricular contexts as: multimodal information processing, navigating the infospace, interpersonal communication, visual literacy, hyper-literacy (hyperacy), personal information management (PIM), and coping with complexity.

TEACHERS' ICT KNOWLEDGE, SKILLS AND UNDERSTANDING

In a review of research into ICT and pedagogy (Cox and Webb, 2004, p. 7) we identified the following ICT skills and understanding that are needed by teachers in order to make effective use of ICT.

■ Teachers need to understand the relationship between a range of ICT resources and the concepts, processes and skills in their subject.
■ Teachers need to use their subject expertise to obtain and select appropriate ICT resources that will help them meet the learning objectives of a particular lesson. Resources include subject-specific software as well as more generic resources.
■ Teachers need knowledge of the potential of ICT resources, not only in terms of their contribution to pupils' presentation skills but also in terms of their facilities for challenging pupils' thinking and extending pupils' learning in a subject.
■ Teachers need confidence in using a range of ICT resources, which can only be achieved through frequent practice with more than one or two uses of ICT.
■ Teachers need to understand that some uses of ICT will change the nature and representations of knowledge and the way the subject is presented to and engages the pupils.

The list may seem daunting, but the way to start is to try out one approach focusing on your learning intentions for your pupils with one piece of software. Then you can gradually expand your experience through observing other teachers, finding out about good practice, e.g. through online fora, and experimenting in your own lessons. You will also be developing elements of the seven literacies (Mioduser *et al.*, 2008) mentioned earlier.

TEACHERS' DECISION-MAKING

In order to take account of the decision-making underlying interactions that enable learning and how they are designed, Lee Shulman developed a model of pedagogical reasoning based on his many years of experience of teaching and teacher education (Shulman, 1987). Shulman's model, which was seminal in understanding teachers' decision-making, included both generic and subject-specific knowledge. However, the model focused predominantly on teachers and underplayed both the opportunities for pupil involvement in planning and managing their learning as well as the importance of interactions in learning. Therefore the processes and knowledge types that Shulman proposed have been incorporated into a model of knowledge and reasoning that recognises the potential involvement of pupils in pedagogical decision-making as shown in Figure 5.1 (Cox and Webb, 2004; Webb and Cox, 2004; Webb, 2005).

Figure 5.1 provides an overview that indicates some of the complexity of a system that comprises of processes and sub-processes that may be external or internal to teachers or pupils. These processes take place in learning environments where the behaviours of pupils, teachers and ICT interact together to provide affordances for learning. The pedagogical reasoning of teachers consists of a familiar cycle: planning, teaching,

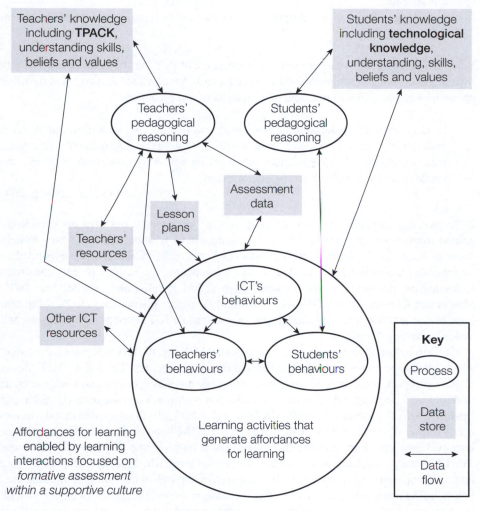

Adapted from Webb and Cox, 2004

■ **Figure 5.1** Framework for pedagogical practices relating to IT use
Source: Adapted from Webb and Cox, 2004.

assessing and evaluating. These can be further deconstructed into sub-processes that include 'transformation' as key to enabling learning, i.e. the teacher must transform the ideas required by the curriculum so that the pupils can learn them (Shulman, 1987) by providing examples, analogies, opportunities to build ideas, etc. Shulman identified a range of types of knowledge that are used by teachers:

■ content knowledge;
■ general pedagogical knowledge;
■ curriculum knowledge;
■ pedagogical content knowledge (PCK);
■ knowledge of learners and their characteristics;
■ knowledge of educational contexts: groups, classes, the school and the wider community;
■ knowledge of educational purpose and values, and their philosophical and historical grounds.

Since Shulman's (1987) earlier work the importance of PCK has been recognised widely by researchers and practitioners and has more recently been defined as a complex dynamic phenomenon that arises from teachers' reflection in and on action:

> PCK is teachers' understanding and enactment of how to help a group of students understand specific subject matter using multiple instructional strategies, representations, and assessments while working within the contextual, cultural, and social limitations in the learning environment.
>
> (Park and Oliver, 2008, p. 264)

PCK therefore depends not only on deep subject knowledge, but also on knowledge gained from experience of the difficulties learners have with concepts and how to help them to learn. In the framework presented in Figure 5.1, PCK has been expanded to incorporate technological knowledge by introducing the more recent construct: technological pedagogical content knowledge (TPACK) (Koehler and Mishra, 2005; Mishra and Koehler, 2006). TPACK is a similarly complex phenomenon to PCK but also implies that teachers need to integrate use of appropriate ICT when planning lessons and making teaching decisions.

The framework shown in Figure 5.1 captures TPACK and the technological knowledge, with which some pupils may be more familiar than their teachers. The full TPACK Model is more complex and comprehensive containing several new types of knowledge such as technological pedagogical knowledge represented within a Venn diagram (Koehler and Mishra, 2005). A critique of the TPACK Model (Graham, 2011) concluded that the model needs further development to create clarity in the TPACK construct definitions and their inter-relationships. Furthermore, the model has a high degree of parsimony, because TPACK is easy to understand at a surface conceptual level, while hiding a deep underlying level of complexity (Graham, 2011). If you search on the web or in bibliographic databases you will find many references to TPACK, because much research and development with teachers across the world is making use of this model, so it is worth reviewing these developing ideas.

The transformation sub-process of pedagogical reasoning, as described by Shulman, requires the teacher to: prepare and structure curriculum content; think of examples, analogies, etc. to represent the content; select teaching approaches; adapt the approaches to the age and ability of pupils and tailor or differentiate the resulting plans for specific groups of pupils. This is an iterative process that takes place while teachers are interacting with pupils as well as when they are planning lessons. This view mirrors Perrenoud's (1998, p. 92) two facets of interactive regulation of learning processes, in which teachers regulate learning through two levels of management:

1 The setting up of situations that favour the interactive regulation of learning processes.
2 Interactive regulation of these situations.

Thus a range of factors contributes to the affordances for learning as summarised in Figure 5.1 and expert teachers use a wide range of knowledge and expertise to create learning situations that provide affordances for learning and to make decisions when interacting with their students.

PROVIDING AFFORDANCES FOR LEARNING WITH ICT

Affordances for learning are dependent on a combination of the whole environment for learning together with the characteristic of the learner (Cox and Webb, 2004; Webb, 2005). Table 5.2, which is adapted from previous findings of how specific affordances were enabled by teachers (Cox and Webb, 2004; Webb and Cox, 2004), categorises affordances in order to identify the main types of ICT involved. The table also shows whether the types of ICT are generic, implying that similar knowledge and skills are needed to deploy these types of ICT across a range of subjects, or whether subject-specific pedagogical knowledge is essential in order to choose and use the ICT resource. This categorisation shows that generic ICT types can provide many affordances for learning, suggesting that developing capabilities in using these could support much learning. Nevertheless, there is a fairly long list of generic ICT types and each has a range of features.

Task 5.2 **Key affordances for learning with ICT in your subject area**

Make a copy of Table 5.2 and highlight the three or four categories of affordances that are most useful in your subject area.

Look at the types of ICT (in column 3) that can support these categories of affordances and tick those that you are familiar with using. You may be able to think of other types of ICT that are equally useful to support these categories of affordances – the list is not comprehensive; it was created from actual examples observed or reported by teachers.

You should now have a set of three or four categories of affordances together with a general indication of the learning supported and the ICT used.

Think about whether you need to develop your technological knowledge or skills in relation to any of these types of ICT in order to make use of them in your teaching.

File your notes in your PDP.

Table 5.2 Categories of affordances for learning supported by ICT

1 Categories of affordances	2 Learning supported	3 Type of ICT used	4 Generic or subject specific ICTs
Researching information	Acquiring knowledge, consolidating understanding	Internet, web browsers, web cams, video conferencing, content specific databases	Generic/subject specific
Preparing presentations and producing materials	Organising ideas, reflecting, reviewing, evaluating, consolidating understanding	PowerPoint, wikis, blogs word processors	Generic
Presenting	Presentation skills, organising ideas, reflecting, reviewing, evaluating	PowerPoint, interactive whiteboard	Generic
Visually representing processes/ideas	Understanding dynamic processes, reflecting, reviewing, comparing, evaluating, consolidating understanding	Simulations, animations, virtual worlds	Subject specific
Feedback	Knowing what aspects need more learning, thinking, predicting, self-assessment	Simulations, mind mapping software, interactive whiteboard, shared blogs, microblogging, discussion boards, content specific tutorial systems	Generic/subject specific
Making a drawing	Thinking about what they already know about composition	Drawing package	Subject specific
Taking turns	Social skills, sharing	Roamer, shared computer	Generic
Broadening experience	Generalising from examples, extending their ideas, clarifying, generating new ideas	Internet, web browsers, web cams, video conferencing, shared blots, microblogging, discussion boards	Generic
Drawing graphs	Thinking about relationships between variables	Spreadsheets, data-logging packages	Generic
Investigating relationships, testing hypotheses	Thinking about relationships between variables, reflecting, reviewing, comparing, evaluating, consolidating understanding	Simulations, spreadsheets, data-logging packages, specific modelling packages, virtual worlds with haptics	Generic/subject specific

Source: Adapted from Cox and Webb ,2004; Webb, 2005.

PLANNING FOR THE DEPLOYMENT OF ICT TO SUPPORT AFL

The analyses of effect-sizes of interventions (Hattie, 2009) discussed above suggested that key attributes leading to highest effects were learner control, peer learning and challenging tasks with well-explained and focused feedback. These attributes are consistent with assessment for learning (AfL), for which effect sizes for innovations are particularly large (ranging from 0.4 to 0.8) (Wiliam, 2011). One way, therefore, of considering how to deploy ICT effectively is to identify how ICT use can support AfL in pedagogy. A framework for AfL (Wiliam and Thompson, 2007), based on empirical research in classrooms, specifies five strategies for AfL as:

1   Clarifying and negotiating learning intentions and criteria for success.
2   Engineering effective discussions and other learning tasks that elicit evidence of student understanding.
3   Providing feedback that moves learners forward.
4   Activating students as instructional resources for one another – peer support, peer feedback.
5   Activating students as the owners of their own learning.

In Figure 5.2 this framework has been modified to incorporate ICT-use based on discussions with practitioners, researchers and policy-makers at EdusummIT 2011 (Webb *et al.*, 2012) and overlaid with potential key uses of specific types of ICT.

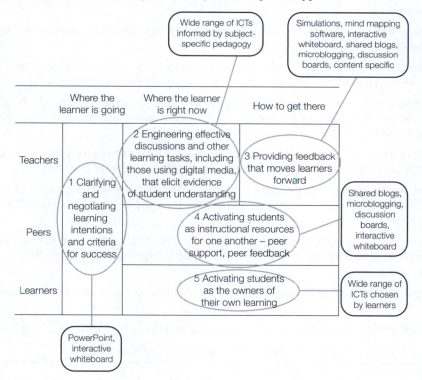

■ **Figure 5.2** Framework for AfL incorporating ICT use

Task 5.3 **Using ICT to support AfL**

Think about a lesson you have observed or taught where the elements of AfL, included in the framework above, were in evidence. (N.B. you need to think carefully: many teachers claim they are using AfL when the actual practice falls far short of that indicated in this framework.)

If ICT was used in the lesson reflect on whether and how it supported AfL.

If ICT was not used in the lesson reflect on whether and how ICT could have been used to support AfL and, if you think ICT could support AfL, outline one possible use of ICT for this purpose.

Make a copy of Figure 5.2, annotate it in relation to the example you have been reflecting on and then file it in your PDP.

BROADENING THE RANGE OF ICT USES

Table 5.3 shows brief outlines of scenarios for different types of ICT use that were created from examples explained by teachers.

■ **Table 5.3** Scenarios for different types of ICT use

---

1 In small groups pupils role-play a story or episode from fact or fiction which they video. They then edit the video to produce a film or multimedia presentation, for a particular audience.

2 The whole class brainstorms about a topic to produce a mind-map on the interactive whiteboard.

3 The teacher leads a question and answer session with the whole class based on a simulation, animation or problem-solving activity on the interactive whiteboard.

4 Pupils work at a cluster of computers in the classroom on an art, design data-logging or problem-solving task that focuses on some specific learning intentions for the current topic while the rest of the class work on other activities.

5 Pupils work collaboratively in groups during lessons to research a topic from the web, obtain material and develop a multimedia presentation, poster, or newspaper.

6 The teacher develops a web-based multimedia resource that functions as a set of notes and learning activities. The teacher refers to it in the lesson and sets homework based on the resource.

7 Pupils work individually to research a topic from an internet or intranet-based resource prepared or selected by the teacher and produce notes or answers to specific questions.

8 Pupils research a topic individually by conducting their own web searches and making notes.

9 Pupils construct models to investigate the relationship between variables in a process.

10 Pupils search a specialised database to find answers to questions.

Source: Cox and Webb, 2004, pp. 122–3.

Task 5.4 **Planning for using ICT**

■ Choose one of the scenarios from Table 5.3 that you think might be useful in your own subject.

■ If you used this approach what might it enable pupils to learn?

■ How might it add value to what you would do without technology?

■ What epistemological assumptions would you be making?

■ What would be the learning intentions and success criteria?

■ What technological knowledge would you need?

■ How would you incorporate AfL?

■ How would you organise the learning environment and the pupils?

■ If possible discuss and compare your ideas with other student teachers.

■ Record your notes in your PDP.

BUILDING ON THE GLOBAL KNOWLEDGE BASE FOR PEDAGOGY WITH ICT

There are many examples on the web of how teachers have used ICT to support their pedagogical practices so one of the best ways of developing your own practice is through some web-based research to identify possible approaches, perhaps engaging in discussions online with other teachers, and then evaluating the ideas that you find in the context of your own teaching situation.

Task 5.5 **Finding and evaluating a case study**

First you need to find a case study, by searching online, that looks promising as an approach for using ICT in your teaching (see 'Researching pedagogical approaches on the web', page 81, if you need help).

Then review the case study and consider the following questions:

■ What epistemological assumptions are being made?

■ What are the learning intentions and success criteria?

■ What does the teacher do?

■ What do the students do? Is peer learning evident?

■ What opportunities are there for the students to develop deep understanding?

■ Is AfL evident? If not, could AfL be incorporated?

■ What resources are needed and how are they used?

■ How might this approach add value to teaching this topic beyond approaches that do not use ICT?

■ What technological knowledge and skills does the teacher need?

■ What technological knowledge and skills do the students need?

■ In summary, what would be the benefits and limitations of using this approach for one of your classes?

Store your evaluation either in your own developing database or in your PDP.

You can maintain a database of web-based ideas using a bibliographic database system (e.g. Endnote or Mendeley), your browser-based bookmarking system or a social bookmarking system (e.g. Delicious).

Task 5.6 **Deciding whether to use ICT for a specific learning intention**

Review an element of the curriculum that you need to teach and think about a lesson you are planning. Choose something that is challenging for students to learn and requires development of deep understanding because this is where ICT has much to offer and its potential is often under-used.

- What are the learning intentions and success criteria?
- What possible activities can you think of for pupils to learn these things? Create a list. Even if one particular activity springs to mind and seems to be the right one, spend some time thinking of as many alternatives as possible. Also consider any web-based examples you have found.
- What types of ICT do you know that might support these activities?
- Now consider what added value the ICT would provide.
- Also consider whether there is potential for the ICT to aid the development of deep understanding by supporting different ways of organising or constructing knowledge, e.g. creating an animation; a 3D graph; an interactive picture; some hypertext.

N.B. You may decide that the use of ICT would add no value for your learning intention: there is nothing to be gained in using ICT on every occasion if other approaches are more effective.

ONLINE PEDAGOGICAL PRACTICES

Increasingly, teachers are being expected to interact with their pupils online as well as in face-to-face teaching situations and also to set up individual and group activities that can be completed by pupils working together online outside of the classroom. For most schools these activities constitute useful extensions to existing teaching approaches but for some there is a move towards virtual schooling where some teachers interact predominantly online with their pupils (see Jopling, 2012 for a review). The key ideas discussed in this chapter about teachers' decision-making, the types of knowledge that are needed, categories of affordances and strategies for AfL are equally important for online learning and teaching. The particular ways in which these are implemented do depend on the nature of the online learning space and the types of communication facilities available. Furthermore, the nature of assessment information may be very different, for example, opportunities to observe pupils while they are working and to gain information from non-verbal cues may be limited. Instead there may be more opportunities to review computer-based analyses of pupils' performances or to replay key parts of their interactions. Therefore teachers need to develop new skills and knowledge as opportunities for online learning develop.

SUMMARY

In this chapter pedagogy was discussed first in its broader educational context, particularly in relation to theories of learning. Then ways in which pedagogical practices can be developed, based on evidence, as well as how pedagogy is affected by broader changes in society, was discussed. A key point here is that whether or not we have evidence that using ICT for learning is more effective than other teaching approaches, young people need to be developing new literacies to support them in the knowledge society. Most of these literacies are expected to be developed through learning across the curriculum, therefore teachers need to use ICT where appropriate to help pupils to develop new literacies. The knowledge, skills and understanding of ICT that teachers need and how they use these to make decisions were examined in some depth. Then types of affordances for learning that can be provided by deploying a range of types of ICT were reviewed. A way of deciding how to deploy ICT resources based on AfL strategies was examined because evidence suggests that innovations based on AfL are particularly effective. You were encouraged to reflect on these approaches and think about planning some activities relevant for your particular subject as well as evaluating web-based examples. Finally, online pedagogical practices were discussed briefly in relation to the theoretical ideas developed in this chapter. Check which requirements for your course you have addressed through this unit.

FURTHER READING

Researching pedagogical approaches on the web

There is a plethora of useful free material and ideas on the web but the web addresses change fairly often because much of the innovative work is associated with particular projects that don't always maintain their websites once they are completed. Therefore rather than listing specific websites I suggest the following strategies for your web-based research on pedagogy:

■ Search Google using subsets of the following keywords: {your subject} (ICT or technology or digital media or digital technology) case-study school TPACK webquest.

■ Browse through any ideas that look interesting and identify whether they are of interest and whether they contain sufficient detail to be evaluated.

■ Evaluate each activity using the approach suggested in Task 5.5.

In addition, the websites of the following organisations are worth browsing for innovative ideas: MIT Media Lab: Futurelab, MirandaNet.

Cox, M.J. and Webb, M.E. (2004) *ICT and Pedagogy: A Review of the Research Literature*, Coventry and London: British Educational Communications and Technology Agency/ Department for Education and Skills.

This report is some years old now but it contains evidence of best pedagogical practice with ICT at that time and since teachers' pedagogical practices are changing relatively slowly the examples are still of interest. Furthermore it explains some of the theoretical ideas discussed in the current chapter in more depth.

Webb, M.E. (2013) 'Changing models for researching pedagogy with information and communications technologies', *Journal of Computer Assisted Learning* **29(1): 53–67, doi: 10.1111/j.1365-2729.2011.00465.x.**

> This paper examines some of the models for pedagogy that have been outlined here in more depth as well as presenting some others for which there was not enough space in this chapter.

Webb, M.E., Gibson, D. and Forkosh-Baruch, A. (2013 in press) 'Challenges for information and communications technology supporting educational assessment', *Journal of Computer Assisted Learning.*

> This paper examines the potential for the use of ICT in assessment playing a major role in transforming assessment practices to support the needs of learners in the twenty-first century. Such changes could have significant impacts on pedagogy. In particular the paper examines the nature of evidence that can be used to support decisions about pupils' learning.

Mioduser, D., Nachmias, R. and Forkosh-Baruch, A. (2008) 'New literacies for the knowledge society', in J. Voogt and G. Knezek (eds), *International Handbook of Information Technology in Primary and Secondary Education,* **London: Springer.**

> This paper discusses what it means to be literate in the knowledge age and explains the basis of the seven literacies that were mentioned in the current chapter. The paper makes clear that these ideas are still developing as the knowledge society develops and that as yet they are barely recognised in current pedagogy. As you read this paper, reflect on how you might develop your pupils' literacies through your teaching.

Jopling, M. (2012) '1:1 online tuition: a review of the literature from a pedagogical perspective', *Journal of Computer Assisted Learning* **28(4): 310–21, doi: 10.1111/j.1365-2729.2011.00441.x.**

> This paper outlines the findings of a review that examined the literature around current practice in online tuition in schools and higher education. It is focused predominantly on one-to-one tutoring and discusses a range of issues about pedagogy for online tuition.

REFERENCES

Alexander, R. (1992) *Policy and Practice in Primary Education*, London: Routledge.

Bauman, Z. (2000) *Liquid Modernity*, Cambridge, UK and Malden, MA: Polity Press.

——(2005) 'Education in liquid modernity', *Review of Education, Pedagogy, and Cultural Studies* 27(4): 303–17.

Bavelier, D.C., Green, S. and Dye, M.W.G. (2010) 'Children, wired: for better and for worse', *Neuron, 67*.

Brown, M., Askew, M., Rhodes, V., Denvir, H., Ranson, E. and Wiliam, D. (2001) 'Magic bullets or chimeras? Searching for factors characterising effective teachers and effective teaching in numeracy', paper presented at the British Educational Research Association Annual Conference Symposium on Pedagogy and Educational Policy: Modernising Teaching or Narrowing the Agenda?, University of Leeds, 13–15 September .

Cox, M.J. and Webb, M.E. (2004) *ICT and Pedagogy: A Review of the Research Literature*, Coventry and London: British Educational Communications and Technology Agency/ Department for Education and Skills.

Cox, M.J., Abbott, C., Webb, M.E., Blakeley, B., Beauchamp, T. and Rhodes, V. (2004) *ICT and Attainment: A Review of the Research Literature*, Coventry and London: British Educational Communications and Technology Agency/Department for Education and Skills.

Crook, C. and Harrison, C. (2008) *Web 2.0 Technologies for Learning at Key Stages 3 and 4: Summary Report*, Coventry: Becta.

Fischer, K.W., Goswami, U., Geake, J. and the Taskforce on the Future of Educational Neuroscience (2010) 'The future of educational neuroscience', *Mind, Brain, and Education* 4(2): 68–80.

Geake, J. (2008) 'Neuromythologies in education', *Educational Research*, 50(2): 123–33.

Geake, J. and Cooper, P. (2003) 'Cognitive neuroscience: implications for education?', *Westminster Studies in Education* 26(1): 7–20.

Graham, C.R. (2011) 'Theoretical considerations for understanding technological pedagogical content knowledge (TPACK)', *Computers and Education* 57(3): 1953–60.

Harlen, W. (1999) *Effective Teaching of Science: A Review of Research*, Edinburgh: Scottish Council for Research in Education.

Harlen, W. and Deakin Crick, R. (2002) *A Systematic Review of the Impact of Summative Assessment and Tests on Students' Motivation for Learning*, London: EPPI-Centre, Social Science Research Unit, Institute of Education, University of London.

Hattie, J.A.C. (2009) *Visible Learning: A Synthesis of Over 800 Meta-Analyses Relating to Achievement*, Abingdon: Routledge.

Ito, M., Horst, H.A., Bittanti, M., Boyd, D., Herr-Stephenson, B., Lange, P.G., Pascoe, C.J., Robinson, L. (with Sonja Baumer, Rachel Cody, Dilan Mahendran, Katynka Martínez, Dan Perkel, Christo Sims, and Lisa Tripp.) (2008) *Living and Learning with New Media: Summary of Findings from the Digital Youth Project*, Chicago, IL: The John D. and Catherine T. MacArthur Foundation.

Jopling, M. (2012) '1:1 online tuition: a review of the literature from a pedagogical perspective', *Journal of Computer Assisted Learning* 28(4): 310–21, doi: 10.1111/j.1365-2729. 2011.00441.x.

Koehler, M.J. and Mishra, P. (2005) 'What happens when teachers design educational technology? The development of technological pedagogical content knowledge', *Journal of Educational Computing Research* 32(2): 131–52.

Kress, G. and Pachler, N. (2007) 'Thinking about the "m" in m-learning', in N. Pachler (ed.), *Mobile Learning: Towards a Research Agenda*, London: WLE Centre, Institute of Education, pp. 7–32.

Livingstone, S. and Haddon, L. (2009) *EU Kids Online: Final Report*, London: LSE.

Mioduser, D., Nachmias, R. and Forkosh-Baruch, A. (2008) 'New literacies for the knowledge society', in J. Voogt and G. Knezek (eds), *International Handbook of Information Technology in Primary and Secondary Education*, London: Springer.

Mishra, P. and Koehler, M.J. (2006) 'Technological pedagogical content knowledge: A framework for teacher knowledge', *Teachers College Record Volume* 108(6): 1017–54.

Park, S.and Oliver, J.S. (2008) 'Revisiting the conceptualisation of pedagogical content knowledge (PCK): PCK as a conceptual tool to understand teachers as professionals', *Research in Science Education* 38(3): 261–84.

Perrenoud, P. (1998) 'From formative assessment to a controlled regulation of learning processes: towards a wider conceptual field', *Assessment in Education* 5(1): 85–102.

Rideout, V.J., Foehr, U.G. and Roberts, D.F. (2010) *Generation M2: Media in the Lives of 8- to 18-year-olds*, Kenlo Park, CA: Henry J. Kaiser Family Foundation.

Shulman, L. (1987) 'Knowledge and teaching: foundations of the new reform', *Harvard Educational Review* 57(1): 1–22.

Watkins, C. and Mortimore, P. (1999) 'Pedagogy: What do we know?', in P. Mortimore (ed.), *Understanding Pedagogy and its Impact on Learning*, London: Chapman, pp. 1–19.

Webb, M.E. (2005) 'Affordances of ICT in science learning: implications for an integrated pedagogy', *International Journal of Science Education* 27(6), 705–735.

——(2013) 'Changing models for researching pedagogy with information and communications technologies', *Journal of Computer Assisted Learning* 29(1): 53–67, doi: 10.1111/j.1365-2729.2011.00465.x.

Webb, M.E. and Cox, M.J. (2004) 'A review of pedagogy related to ICT', *Technology, Pedagogy and Education* 13(3): 235–86.

Webb, M.E., Gibson, D. and Forkosh-Baruch, A. (2013, in press) 'Challenges for information and communications technology supporting educational assessment', *Journal of Computer Assisted Learning*.

Wiliam, D. (2011) 'What is assessment for learning?', *Studies In Educational Evaluation* 37(1): 3–14.

Wiliam, D. and Thompson, M. (2007) 'Integrating assessment with instruction: what will it take to make it work?', in C.A. Dwyer (ed.), *The Future of Assessment: Shaping Teaching and Learning*, Mahwah, NJ: Lawrence Erlbaum Associates, pp. 53–82.

6 ICT TOOLS AND APPLICATIONS

Michelle Selinger and Lorraine Kaye

INTRODUCTION

The whole landscape of tools and applications for learning is changing rapidly. Games have emerged as productive and effective learning tools; mobile learning has come of age, and any new developments are expected to run on multiple devices from desktop PCs to smart phones. Internet connectivity is now taken for granted in the UK and we are close to ubiquitous access to technology. We no longer have to justify the use of ICT in education: it is taken as given. We now have to think carefully about the selection of tools and applications we use as the range to choose from has increased dramatically.

Vast arrays of tools and applications have been developed that help teachers to make effective use of ICT for learning and teaching. Some have been specifically developed for the education market, while others are generic but directly applicable. We hope to illustrate, through a range of ideas and examples, how teachers can make choices about which tools and applications to use in their teaching, and where learners can use these tools themselves to advance their learning in ways that are more robust and engaging.

We thought long and hard about how to position this chapter, and eventually decided to consider the tools and applications available from two equally valid perspectives: (i) learners as consumers; and (ii) learners as producers. We added this second focus for four reasons:

1   Students learn by doing – by being actively engaged in their learning – and when learning is made more relevant and authentic. Technology makes this increasingly possible.
2   Learners are adept at using social networks. They post videos, blogs and images onto multiple sites such as YouTube and Facebook.
3   More and more software encourages learners to be either creators of content or interact with software, and even content that was previously one way has become interactive.
4   Classrooms can be far more open through voice, video and text based collaboration.

We also had to make decisions about what to leave out in the vast and ever growing landscape of tools and applications. We have covered a smorgasbord of ideas and not specified the platforms on which they sit. This is because we see every application being available now or in the not too distant future, on any device, whether it be desktop computers, laptops, mobile devices or smart phones, and in a world where most people will have two, if not more, of these devices to hand.

OBJECTIVES

By the end of this chapter you will be more confident to:

- select resources and applications that are appropriate to your students' learning needs and the subject(s) you teach;
- understand more about how social networking can be used effectively in the classroom;
- know which type of collaboration tools to use when and where;
- understand how ICT can help teaching and learning beyond the classroom.

THE TEACHER'S ROLE IN A CONNECTED ENVIRONMENT

Broadband connectivity has dramatically altered the role of teachers: they now have to support and guide learners through the myriad of information available in a variety of guises online and in multiple formats. Before computers were available in schools the learner drew on information from their teachers, TV, radio, museums and galleries and print media in the form of books, newspapers, journals and magazines. The school selected the books in the school library. Access to wide sources of information was far more limited than it is today. Consider a post-16 pupil studying chemistry in 2012: Figure 6.1 shows the extent of resources to which they now have access.

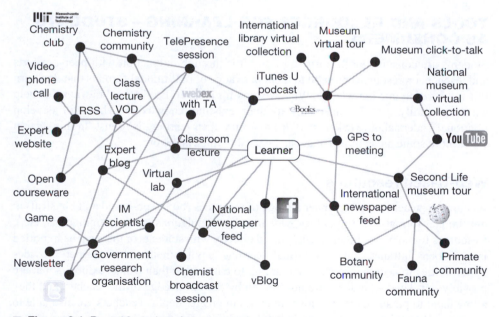

■ **Figure 6.1** Post-16 students' access to chemistry resources
Source: Cisco.

How *do* students make decisions about which resource to use, which datasets are valid, or which forum has real experts? It is teachers as experts in their domain of study who help students to make more informed choices and decisions about which paths to follow. A teacher's role has become more like that of a museum curator as they have to make decisions about what to put on 'display', and what to keep aside for detailed exploration should an individual want to delve deeper and feed their curiosity. The artefacts on show have to be displayed in such a way as to guide learners through the learning process in order to help them become more knowledgeable by developing a robust understanding of new concepts and building on and deepening their understanding of existing ones. The abundance of resources on the internet means there can be less reliance on the teacher for sources of information on the subject being studied. But information is not knowledge, as Hilton (2006) explains:

■ Knowledge is what you do with information.
■ Knowledge is how you make meaning out of information.
■ You often gain knowledge through an interactive process.
■ Achieving knowledge requires a richer, more complex environment than gaining information.

As the expert in the domain of study, the teacher is able to help learners to make sense of contradicting sources of evidence and information, and help them to understand and question the validity of each resource. Couple this with theories of learning such as social constructivism (Bruner, 1986) and connectivism (Siemens, 2004), then the world of technology opens up substantial opportunities through a networked world to broaden and deepen learning opportunities in ways that make collaboration a necessity, while exploiting individual learning styles, preferences and aptitudes.

TOOLS AND RESOURCES FOR LEARNING – STUDENTS AS CONSUMERS

Students are consumers of information, and it is through interaction with peers, experts and teachers on resources brought to them in a range of multimodal formats that they turn this information into knowledge. What we look for is for ICT to be used in ways that help students readily make connections to their existing knowledge. This will develop relational understanding (Skemp, 1976) to ensure their learning is robust. In this section we explore some areas of ICT that can be used in this endeavour.

Web-based resources

As curators, teachers pull together a range of resources (both web-based and physical) in multimodal formats (text, graphics, video, audio, simulations, games, animations, etc.). Resources found on the internet can be used directly with students or they can be imported into a local intranet and/or a virtual learning environment. The internet provides opportunities to access resources that are up to date rather than using textbooks that are possibly out-dated – students are not limited by the knowledge of the teacher, and they allow them to pursue their individual interests in greater depth. Teachers are also able to work together (either virtually or locally) to design and adapt resources and produce relevant web-based learning experiences for students that are suitable for local needs and are culturally sensitive and pedagogically relevant.

Over the last ten years online learning resources have developed and grown to provide a vast range of tools and applications that can be used in the classroom across all areas of the curriculum. See the Amazing Web 2.0 Projects 2 (http://www.ictineducation.org/amazing-web-2-projects) for some examples of how these tools have been used.

ICT can also bring conceptual understanding to learners more quickly and make it more robust. The contents of a biology book with images of different body parts and systems are significantly enhanced through digitisation by offering virtual models and simulations of the blood and nervous systems and 3D models of the human body that can be rotated and manipulated virtually (see for example http://www.spongelab.com). Such enhancements also provide students with relational understanding. Task 6.1 asks you to identify tools relevant to your subject area.

Task 6.1 **Visit Cool Tools for Schools**

Visit Cool Tools for Schools (http://cooltoolsforschools.wikispaces.com/Home) and search for some resources to use within a topic you have to teach. Find out more about one resource. Now find out if your department uses any particular software/online resource to teach that topic and either review the software, if they do, or discuss with them the reasons why they do not use any software.

Interactive whiteboards

Resources projected through an interactive whiteboard (IWB) can be most effective: 'using the IWB as a "digital hub" can effectively draw together different technologies for dialogic teaching and learning; sound and images in particular' (Hennessey *et al.*, 2010). Additionally, the IWB supports the full range of learning styles and because there is greater participation by the class, there is greater reinforcement through kinaesthetic input. When students generate input to the process – by moving an image into a sequence; by activating a routine; or by conventional methods using a keyboard or a mouse – learning is more powerful, and reinforced for the whole group. A range of possibilities can be tried, with immediate outcomes generated, promoting discussion and scaffolding learning. 'Children do not learn as effectively when they are passive. Active engagement with things and ideas promotes mental activity that helps students retain new learning and integrate it with what they already know' (Bureau of Elementary Education, Department of Education, Culture, and Sports, the Philippines, in cooperation with UNICEF, 1994, http://www.unicef.org/teachers/learner/exp.htm). By using the interactive whiteboard, teachers are also able to adapt and annotate the resource. Annotations can be saved and re-visited providing an assessment tool and a resource, which can be shared and adapted for use by colleagues. Additionally voting technologies used with the IWBs ensure engagement and involvement and allow the teacher to do quick formative assessments of class understanding before proceeding with a lesson. Both mobile phones and dedicated handheld devices can be used for this purpose.

Virtual classroom tools and video conferencing

A range of collaboration tools making use of video, voice and messaging technologies now provide the learner with instant access to their peers, their teachers, and experts in their field of study. Both video and audio conferencing provide opportunities for authentic and new learning opportunities. The European Schoolnet eTwinning initiative (http://www.etwinning.net) is testament to the myriad of ways students engage beyond the classroom over video conferencing, Skype and virtual classroom links. Students who are unable to attend a lesson for any reason can join virtually through virtual classroom technologies such as Skype (http://www.skype.com), Cisco WebEx (webex.co.uk), Adobe Connect (http://www.adobe.com/uk/products/adobeconnect.html) or Blackboard Collaborate (http://www.blackboard.com/Platforms/Collaborate/Overview.aspx). Alternatively students can catch up later or review a lesson by listening to a podcast or watching a video replay of the lesson – along with all the discussion, questions asked and responses given. Sophisticated and secure video replay technologies allow students and teachers to add their own responses by tagging the recording and ask further questions, and point to resources that refute or validate any theory a teacher has proposed, and generally catch up with, and maybe go beyond the content their teacher or external expert has presented to develop a unique understanding of the subject which they then share back with the class (see for example Show and Share http://www.cisco.com/en/US/prod/video/ps9339/ps6681/show_and_share.html).

Virtual classrooms and video conferencing have both proved to be invaluable around the world to provide economies of scale and offer more curriculum choice for shortage and minority subjects, as these can be taught to small groups across a number of schools. Group work is easily facilitated through these tools, and with virtual classrooms teacher set group tasks, allocate students to rooms either in the same location or geographically distributed, and check progress by joining any group virtually. They can then bring the whole class back together for feedback and lesson summary. Virtual classroom support is also facilitated: Sugata Mitra (2010) for example, employs retired English speakers, often on a voluntary basis, to listen to children in India learning to read in English using Skype, over what he calls the 'Granny Cloud'.

These technologies, however, require a new way of thinking about teaching and learning since they depend on students interacting either locally, nationally or internationally with peers, remote teachers and subject experts in new ways and entering into constructive debate. The tools allow students to have more control over their learning and provide opportunities and the wherewithal for them to test out new theories and go beyond the curriculum through online interaction with a wide range of people and with relevant and adjacent multimodal resources.

Multimodal resources

Large databases of images, slides enlarged via an electronic microscope, as well as digitised artefacts including images, sound and video, are now stored electronically so they are easily searchable and accessible. One example, seen at a conference organised by Microsoft for their Innovative Teachers programme in Europe, was demonstrated by a Swedish teacher: he combined horrific images with video and sounds from the First World War to provide the atmosphere and setting for students to empathise with soldiers. After observing the video and images, and hearing the digitised sounds of war, the teacher told his students to imagine they were a soldier in the trenches about to go 'over the top'.

He then asked them to write a letter home to their mothers. The quality of the writing and the emotion displayed in the letters illustrated the power of digital media in motivating students and providing them with the empathy necessary to write such moving letters. This example also demonstrates that resources do not have to be pre-packaged into complete courses to be of value or involve high levels of sophistication, but they must be easily accessible and teachers must know such resources exist and know where to find them, if they are to put it to good use. You can work with a colleague or a group of colleagues to identify an area of your curriculum which would benefit from a multimodal approach, and then find film clips, images and sound recordings from sites such as the British Film Institute (http://www.bfi.org.uk), Pathe News (http://www.britishpathe.com), museum websites (e.g. http://www.britishmuseum.org and http://www.vam.ac.uk), or through your subject association. Details of the location of useful resources are listed at the end of the chapter. Once you have developed a bank of resources there are numerous sites where you can share your ideas with other teachers, such as TES (http://www.tes.co.uk/teaching-resources/).

Sharing such 'home made' resources together with some description of how they were used, and the impact they had on learning, also means that other teachers can take what someone else has produced, use it as is, or disassemble the materials and add their own flavour to them. They then post the adapted product for other teachers to use. Technologies that allow users to review and recommend them, such as seen on YouTube and Amazon, will ensure the very best resources surface to the top. Other 'recommender' systems such as Heystaks (http://www.heystaks.com) are valuable time-saving, social search tools that enable groups to tag resources so they are easy to find when group members search for resources.

Geographical Information Systems

In geography, geographical information systems (GIS) are used to analyse global statistics, investigate coastal erosion, and design and map infrastructure improvements in a local area. GIS is a way of displaying and analysing spatially referenced information. The three main components of GIS are a map, spatially referenced data, and software that display the data. Online maps and online applications such as Google Earth enable classroom-based virtual field trips. Developments in mobile phone and Global Positioning System (GPS) technology now offer the potential for rich multimedia experiences and for location-specific resources (for example, see the *Juicy Geography* website http://www.juicygeography.co.uk/index.htm).

Simulations

In science lessons, students need to both observe and undertake experiments in order to understand the potential inaccuracy of results, and to develop an understanding of experimentation. This includes the need to keep all except one factor constant so as to observe the effects of increasing or decreasing one variable at a time. Computer simulations can augment and enhance students' understanding of experimentation. Through these media, students are able to observe experiments that are either too dangerous or too expensive to carry out in class, would take too long, or perhaps have ethical implications. However, it is not to say that these should replace all practical work because simulations can reflect a simplified version of reality and mask the complexities of experimentation. It is the teacher's role to consider which experiments will be attempted in class and which will be simulations in the same way that they decide to demonstrate an experiment or let the class undertake it themselves. Presentation of procedures and results can be further enhanced by the use of collaborative tools, presentation tools and spreadsheets.

Virtual labs are now available such as the Virtual Bacterial Identification Lab (http://www.hhmi.org/biointeractive). The purpose of the lab is to familiarise students with the science and techniques used to identify different types of bacteria based on their DNA sequence. As such processes are time consuming as well as expensive to perform, the opportunity to undertake a simulation in a virtual lab means that time can be 'sped up'. What is important, however, is that a teacher is available to ensure the students are not just clicking their way through without taking any note of the procedures. Instead a whole class demonstration on an interactive whiteboard is used, which involves students more actively, or by a teacher setting tasks on the way, so that students really engage fully with the simulation.

Games

Research suggests that UK learners are some of the unhappiest in Europe and performance suggests that they may be some of the least engaged too (Bradshaw *et al.*, 2007). New learning technologies hold the potential to bring back playfulness and engagement in the classroom. Interactive games, characterised by players making choices, are becoming eclipsed by participative games, characterised by players making contributions. 'The strategies for successful game playing are increasingly complex, sophisticated, challenging and cerebral. This edges games towards the very heart of where learning is headed' (Heppell, 2006). Some commercially available games such as *The Sims* and *Myst III* provide rich, immersive environments to centre learning around. Others provide learners with one-to-one interaction and feedback on a specific subject. Research by Paul Howard-Jones (2008) cites an example at Ralph Allen Comprehensive in Bath. Students in Year 9 were allowed to play *Wipe Out*, a game designed by researchers at the Neuroeducational Network (NEnet) at the University of Bristol. Students played in pairs against the computer in a quiz game about science concepts, winning points when they gave the answer correctly, or otherwise being offered another chance to learn that concept.

In contrast to conventional ideas about reward consistency, the points available for a correct answer depended on the throw of a dice. In each turn, the pupils, or the computer, continue answering questions until their one is incorrect. To add more uncertainty, if they rolled a '1' they would forfeit all points for that turn, and a double '1' meant they lost all points accrued so far in the game – a complete 'Wipe Out'. Surprisingly, there were no objections of unfairness when pupils lost all their points on the throw of the dice. Instead, the room filled with the excitement of an amusement arcade. Victories were celebrated as achievements of intellect and ability, while losses were attributed to bad luck. Post-test scores revealed significant gains in scientific knowledge.

Games can encourage self-reliance and self-determination in terms of a learner's ability to make progress within a demanding but incrementally staged environment, and help them to appreciate that the skills necessary for success in games, such as problem solving and critical thinking, can have relevance in other curricular areas and other social contexts like study or work. They also create an implicit and explicit understanding that as a learner on our own we can be good, but as a learner in a connected team we can be much better (Education Scotland, http://www.educationscotland.gov.uk) so aligning with a social constructivist perspective on learning. However, in order for game-based learning projects to be successful, they require pedagogical practices that align with such practice as well as support from the school leadership.

TOOLS AND RESOURCES FOR LEARNING: STUDENTS AS PRODUCERS

In recent years, the nature of the internet has changed. The web is no longer just a medium for transmitting information, but also a platform on which content is created, mixed, remixed and distributed. This evolving web is widely referred to as 'Web 2.0' and defines a trend in the use of World Wide Web technology and web design that aims to facilitate creativity, information sharing, and, most notably, collaboration among users. These concepts have led to the development and evolution of web-based communities and hosted services, such as social networking sites, wikis, blogs, collaborative tagging, social classification, social indexing, and social tagging.

Although social networking is most commonly attributed to non-educational activity such as Facebook or YouTube, these applications have educational uses with dedicated education channels that help to make learning more authentic and engaging. As noted earlier, social networking software supports both a social constructivist and a connectivist view of learning. For an overview of learning theories see Burton (2013) and Younie and Leask (2013). The term 'social software' came into use in 2002 and is generally attributed to Clay Shirky. Shirky, a writer and teacher on the social implications of internet technology, defines social software simply as 'software that supports group interaction' (Shirky, 2003).

This use of the internet has turned students and teachers from mere readers into writers to the web as well, and facilitated the tracking and filtering of the ever-growing sources of information coming online each day.

> Web 2.0 technologies have the ability to transcend the walls of the classroom, to enable children to reach out to other audiences and be able to work with other pupils around the world, using collaborative tools that allow several users to develop and enrich the online content.
>
> (Simpson and Toyn, 2011: 78)

People use video on channels like YouTube to learn how to do things by observing amateurs and experts alike. In fact serious providers of information now use YouTube to ensure the public receives correct public safety messages.

By making use of these tools in the classroom, students can be trained on important issues regarding access, privacy, security, and free expression. Local authorities and schools have guidelines and acceptable use policies (AUP) regarding the use of school computers and networks and the internet, but students need to be taught explicitly about what is acceptable and what is not. AUPs set out terms and conditions to identify acceptable online behaviour and access privileges. Policies regarding the displaying of any pupils' work must be strictly adhered to. The argument about what should be filtered in schools will rage for many years, but schools have a duty of care not just to protect their students, but also to teach them about appropriate and safe use of the internet, and not leave the latter to chance. The following guidelines are suggested:

■   Inform parents of procedures and secure parental permission.
■   Teach students safe, acceptable, and sensible behaviour as online authors and readers.
■   Review policies and guidelines pertaining to pupil access.
■   Teach the non-posting rules of no complete names, e-mail accounts, or references to reveal location.
■   Set clear expectations regarding tone, respect and consequences.
      (http://www.glencoe.com/sec/teachingtoday/educationupclose.phtml/print/47)

Having set the context for students as creators, here are some ideas about how collaboration tools can be used in schools.

Co-production

The development of 'cloud' based services, i.e. remote storage and retrieval applications, supports collaborative online applications such as bubbl.us, a group mind mapping tool, and Google docs which allows you to share and edit many types of files – documents, spreadsheets, presentations and more – in real time with others using an online word processor, spreadsheet and presentation editor. This enables you and your students to create, store and share instantly and securely, and collaborate online in real time. You can create new documents from scratch or upload existing documents, spreadsheets and presentations. There is no software to download, and all your work is stored safely online and accessible from any computer. Other applications like *Dropbox* (http://www.dropbox.com) allow safe file sharing between pupils and between pupils and teachers.

Blogs and wikis

Perhaps one of the most effective self-publication tools that have emerged from the developments of Web 2.0 applications is the 'blog'. A shortening of the term 'Web log', the blog is an online publishing tool that is written rather like a diary, with comments and reflections on what has happened to the writer on a regular basis. It may be supported with photos and other digital graphics. Teachers have discovered the value of classroom blogging, both as an avenue for their communications and as a tool for giving voice to what their students are learning and how they are learning. Blogs are highly motivating to students, especially those who otherwise might not become participants in classrooms, and offer authentic opportunities for students to read and write. As readers of blogs are allowed to comment on other people's blogs, they also act as effective forums for collaboration and discussion and provide a platform for scaffolded learning or mentoring. Additionally, blogs can be worked on any time, in any place, using any internet-enabled device to create an environment that extends beyond the boundaries of the classroom.

At the Evelina Hospital School in London, where pupils in the secondary classroom write most of the posts on the classroom blog, staff have seen pupils becoming more self-critical, willing to draft and redraft work, and use dictionaries to check spellings, as they know it might be seen by a worldwide audience. News stories feature prominently, with pupils suggesting ideas and choosing what to write about in a class editorial meeting. The stories about celebrities and violent crime reflect teenage pre-occupations.

Pupils learn their writing has to gain readers' attention quickly. By encouraging them to explore other blogs, staff help children understand how great the competition is, and how they probably have less than ten words to impress before the mouse is clicked to another page. Although short pieces predominate, children also have the opportunity to write longer features, as well as take part in creative writing and photography challenges, and to suggest YouTube videos to post that have amused or impressed them (SecEd, http://www.sec-ed. co.uk/).

Other examples of the use of blogs include:

■ Students conducting original interviews with local senior citizens, placing text, images, video and audio clips on their blog as a digital archive of local history.

■ In science lessons, students share lab data and collaborate in writing up lab reports on a class blog. This also allows students to see the variety of data collected from the class and to comment and critique reports.

■ Inviting students to submit a question about course content, related ideas, or 'what they want to find out' in advance of starting a new unit. This provides a focus point and makes the content more meaningful to them.

There are a number of blogging websites that are free (typically advertising based), the most popular of which are *Blogger* (http://www.blogger.com/) and *Edublogs* (http://edublogs.org/). These are simple to set up and use by students. Alternatively there are teacher or community websites which are also free and allow a teacher to set up a number of individual blogs under a single website such as *Classblogmeister* (http://www. classblogmeister.com/), *Gaggle* (http://www.gaggle.net) and *21 Publish* (http://www.21publish.com). These may be a little more difficult to set up, but one of the advantages of these community sites is that there are often controls or restrictions for the administrator, from restricting the viewing of the blogs to specific groups or individuals, to having to preview blogs or comments before they are posted.

Whilst a blog is a type of personal, online journal that is updated whenever the author desires, a 'wiki' is a website that allows users to add and update content on the site using their own web browser. A wiki allows multiple users to create, modify and organise web page content in a collaborative manner. *Wikipedia* is probably the most famous of all wikis and has become the de facto starting point for many students when researching a topic. This is because there are many links to other resources that help update the information on an item, but caution is advised. Most Wikipedia pages are moderated for truth and certainty, but even this can be biased. It is important to ensure students look at other resources not linked through Wikipedia when undertaking their research in order to validate or refute the information they find.

The main educational wiki providers are *Wikispaces* (http://www.wikispaces.com), *PBWorks* (pbworks.com/) and *Wetpaint for Educators* (http://wikisineducation.wetpaint. com/). Wikis are also quick and easy to set up and are ideal for small collaborative writing projects as well as showcasing students' multimedia creations to the wider community. They can be moderated or password-protected and used for storing downloadable files or embedding video and audio clips for students to access outside the classroom.

Wikis can be used for a variety of project work, especially collaborative group projects. This could include a travel brochure wiki on different literary, historical, or cultural locations and time periods: Dickens' London, fourteenth-century Italy in Verona and Mantua (Romeo and Juliet) or a virtual art gallery with ongoing criticism and responses regarding artwork found online or originals from your art classroom. See *Educational Wikis* (http://educationalwikis.wikispaces.com) for ideas and links to a wide variety of school wikis. Task 6.2 asks you to review some blogs and set up a class blog of your own.

Task 6.2 **Blogging in the classroom**

Review some blog posts and identify features that could support your pupils in learning. You could start with blogs on the sites listed above or at http://www. guardian.co.uk/teacher-network. Start a class blog, a personal blog or get each pupil to start his or her own in the subject you teach. Encourage comments and debates from others.

Podcasts and vodcasts

A podcast is an audio programme that may be distributed on the internet and can be downloaded from a website or a school server and listened to on a computer or a portable MP4 player. It can also be a recording created by a teacher to enhance the learning and teaching process within and beyond the classroom, or a podcast or radio programme created by pupils. Increasingly the term is also being applied to video (vodcast), which provides a full visual and audio experience for the user.

To create a podcast you need a microphone, a PC and audio editing software. *Audacity* is free, open source software for recording and editing sounds. It is available for Mac OS X, Microsoft Windows, GNU/Linux, and other operating systems and can be downloaded from http://audacity.sourceforge.net. The resulting MP4 audio file is uploaded to a website from where it can be downloaded and then listened to 'on demand' via a portable MP4 player or a computer. An increasing number of websites are dedicated to providing a listing service for podcasts such as *Radiowaves* (http://www.radiowaves.co.uk) and the *Education Podcast Network* (http://www.epnweb.org) that provide carefully selected quality podcasts from schools covering a wide range of subject areas and age ranges.

To create a vodcast all that is needed is a webcam and the recording feature that comes with the camera software. If the vodcast or podcast is embedded in a web page then text can be added to link the resources together. The UK Open University has produced a large number of interactive books that do this too. These are available on iBooks2 and herald the future of online textbooks. Podcasting and vodcasting are both powerful mediums to support teaching and learning:

■ They provide another way of sharing and transmitting resources for teaching and learning in schools and at home.
■ Students are able to record, produce and publish on the internet in secure environments that can be reviewed before posting to a wider audience.
■ They can be tailored to enhance any curriculum area.
■ The can provide bespoke materials to support any learning situation where text or images are not as meaningful, e.g. music recitals, drama productions, science experiments, cookery demonstrations.
■ They can be produced by both students and teachers, as well as experts outside the school environment (e.g. museum curators, nurses) for further instructional content to reinforce learning.
■ Excellent for homework tasks – either for describing them or undertaking them.

■ They have the potential to support or extend the work of any pupil with special needs.

■ An excellent vehicle for community/school links and for disseminating school, local and national information.

■ A very powerful motivator for children who miss sessions through illness, etc., if real time virtual classrooms described above are not available.

■ They provide a variation in modality for those with a reading difficulty or with English as a second or third language, or for those who just prefer to learn visually and orally.

■ They promote a concept of ownership of materials.

■ They accentuate and promote sustained effort in publishing for specific audiences.

■ They are a vehicle for personalised learning.

(Adapted from Doug Dickinson
http://www.dougdickinson.co.uk/blog/2007/01/why-educational-podcasting.html)

The following are just some ideas for creating podcasts:

■ talk and music shows;

■ jingles – use software such as *eJay* (PC) or *Garageband* (Mac) to create jingles, which can be used to introduce particular features to the show;

■ an outside broadcast – use an MP4 player with recording facilities to record a feature 'on location' around the school, or on a school field trip. You can then download this to your computer and add it to your show;

■ interviews;

■ storytelling and audio books;

■ tutorials and instructions;

■ giving directions and sharing information;

■ providing commentaries on events.

See *Podcasting in Education Resources* compiled by Gary S. Stager (http://www.stager. org/podcasting.html) for a comprehensive directory of resources.

Ideas for students creating video include not just demonstrating practical skills, but also working in groups to develop a documentary. In Australia Mitzi Goldman, an award winning documentary filmmaker, works with young people on the skills of making a documentary. There are considerable twenty-first century skills involved in this process, including collaboration, decision-making, problem solving and critical thinking. Students have to agree the themes for the documentary, decide how to present an argument, storyboard it, film the content, edit it using editing software, and join clips together with a scripted commentary. The shorter the end product the better, and students have to work hard to convey their meaning as precisely and as vividly as possible. In her work, Goldman observed:

■ a growth in visual literacy and engagement in school;

■ excited and passionate students working as teams;

■ increased focus, concentration and listening skills;

■ greater awareness of social issues;

■ development of empathy and understanding the perspective of others;

■   critical thinkers with tools for independent social enquiry;
■   increased confidence and self-esteem;
■   assistance to teachers;
■   a fun way to learn.

(http://www.sproutmediabykids.com.au/outcomes.php)

Task 6.3 asks you to review, subscribe to and consider the use of a podcast or vodcast in your subject.

Task 6.3 **Using a podcast or vodcast in your teaching**

Locate a podcast or vodcast related to your subject and subscribe to it. Consider how this could be used in your teaching.

Coding and programming

In January 2012 Minister for Education Michael Gove announced that the ICT curriculum for England was to be scrapped at the end of the 2011/2012 academic year and instead replaced with a new 'flexible curriculum in computer science'. He announced a consultation on the new computing curriculum, effective immediately although, at the time of writing, there are no published findings of the consultation.

A number of bodies such as the Royal Society, the Association for Learning Technology, Computing at School and the British Computer Society, have published reports and discussion documents about the relevance of ICT in the curriculum. There has been a significant decline in applicants for computer science courses, particularly from female candidates, and gaming companies report difficulties with recruiting programmers. Next Gen Skills is an alliance between the biggest names from the UK digital, creative and hi-tech industries and the UK's leading skills and educational bodies to improve the computer programming skills needed for the future growth of the UK's economy (http://www.nextgenskills.com/). Google, Microsoft and other leading technology names have registered their support for a greater emphasis on programming, arguing that the UK could be a global hub for the video games and special effects industries.

All programming languages are tools for modelling reality and an example of discovery learning or constructivism (Papert, 1980). Seymour Papert developed the Logo programming language to support constructivist learning in which children actively construct new knowledge for ourselves as they learn. New knowledge is constructed through interaction with sensory data on the backdrop of past experiences. The essence of Logo involves *thinking about processes*; about how you are doing what you are doing and the process of creating your product is more important than the finished product (constructionism).

However, in recent years the teaching of information technology in schools has left behind programming such as Logo and HTML as developments in computing have simplified the interface and design of websites. Instead the focus has been on using software for clerical skills such as researching websites, using Word and PowerPoint, rather than understanding systems, according to those campaigning for change. 'Learning about computing is like learning to drive a car, and since a knowledge of the internal combustion technology is not essential for becoming a proficient driver, it followed that an understanding of how computers work was not important for our children' (Naughton,

2012). Naughton considers a set of key concepts that are essential if schoolchildren are to understand the networked world in which they are growing up:

> Computer science involves a new way of thinking about problem-solving: it's called computational thinking, and it's about understanding the difference between human and artificial intelligence, as well as about thinking recursively, being alert to the need for prevention, detection and protection against risks, using abstraction and decomposition when tackling large tasks, and deploying heuristic reasoning, iteration and search to discover solutions to complex problems.

One initiative in response has been the setting up of *Code Clubs* (http://codeclub.org.uk/), which will aim to instil the basics of computer programming into children aged 10–11. The clubs are built around practical hands-on tasks using Scratch programming language that includes children making games and controlling robots (http://scratch.mit.edu/). Scratch is a programming language designed for 8- to 16-year-olds to create interactive art, stories, simulations and games and share those creations online. At the core of Scratch is a graphical programming language that lets you control the actions and interactions among different media. To create a script, you snap together graphical blocks, much like LEGO bricks or puzzle pieces.

Further developments include the introduction of the Raspberry Pi which is a single-board computer developed in the UK by the Raspberry Pi Foundation with the intention of stimulating the teaching of basic computer science in schools – the impact of which is yet to be seen. Task 6.4 asks you to consider development in the ICT curriculum in the light of government changes, and how it relates to your context.

Task 6.4 **Review of developments in the ICT curriculum**

Find out about the ICT curriculum relevant to the context in which you are working and find out what has been developed and how it relates to or will relate to you either as an ICT coordinator, or as a subject specialist.

SUMMARY

ICT is integral to every area of life including education. However, in countries like Australia and Singapore where ICT is used extensively in the classroom, the focus is generally on pupils as consumers of online resources. There is little collaboration between schools or use of external experts. Additionally, summative assessment rarely has a technology component, so we are still nowhere near a situation in which ICT is truly embedded in every facet of school life. We hope that the ideas presented here, especially in the section on pupil as producer, are adopted or adapted and then explored in schools.

In the seven years since the second edition of this book was published, the proliferation of new and sophisticated tools and applications have opened up untold opportunities for new and exciting ways to engage students both within and outside the classroom. The next seven years will bring even more significant changes and a review of the way we teach and learn with ICT is long overdue. We must act now to prepare our students and ourselves for the future.

FURTHER READING

Thomas, D. and Brown, J.S. (2011) *A New Culture of Learning.* **Published on demand from Amazon.**

> This concise and jargon-free text explores the premise that old ways of learning cannot keep up with our rapidly changing world, and that new media forms are making peer-to-peer learning easier and more natural.

Zagal, J.P. (2011) *Ludoliteracy: Defining, Understanding and Supporting Games Education*, **ETC Press.**

> This book explores ludoliteracy, or the question of what it means to understand games, by looking at the challenges and problems faced by students taking games-related classes. In response to these challenges, this book then describes how online learning environments can be used to support learning about games by helping students get more from their experiences with games, and helping students use what they know to establish deeper understanding. Based on the findings from a series of research studies, Ludoliteracy examines the broader implications for supporting games education.

Messenger Davies, M. (2010) *Children, Media and Culture*, **Open University Press.**

> This book discusses the ongoing debate about the role of popular media in children's lives including anxieties relating to the effects of rapid technological change and outlines some interesting case studies.

Richardson, W. (2006) *Blogs, Wikis, Podcasts and Other Powerful Web Tools for Classrooms*, **Corwen Press.**

> A guide to using web tools in the classroom with specific teaching applications which provides easy to follow instructions and ideas to get you started.

ADDITIONAL RESOURCES AND WEBSITES

In addition to the websites listed in the text above you might also like to review:

http://www.nen.gov.uk

> The Education Network is a learning and teaching resource providing schools with a secure network designed and maintained by experts within the educational community.

http://www.london-galleries.co.uk
   An A–Z listing of London museum and gallery links.

http://www.bbc.co.uk/archive
   BBC archives with themed collections of radio and TV programmes, documents and photographs from as far back as the 1930s.

http://botw.org.uk/Education/Teaching/Organisations/Subject_Associations
   Provides links to the different subject association websites.

REFERENCES

Bradshaw, J., Hoelscher, P. and Richardson, D. (2007) 'An index of child well-being in the European Union 25', *Journal of Social Indicators Research* 80: 133–77.

Bruner, J. (1996) *The Culture of Education*, Cambridge, MA: Harvard University Press.

Bureau of Elementary Education, Department of Education, Culture, and Sports, the Philippines (1994) *The Multigrade Teachers' Handbook*, Philippines: Bureau of Elementary Education, Department of Education, Culture, and Sports, the Philippines, in cooperation with UNICEF.

Burton, D. (2013) 'Ways pupils learn', in S. Capel, M. Leask and T. Turner (eds), *Learning to Teach in the Secondary School: A Companion to School Experience*, Abingdon: Routledge/ TaylorFrancis.

Durrant, I. (2012) 'Classroom blogging'. Available at: http://www.sec-ed.co.uk/cgi-bin/go.pl/ article/article.html?uid=90061;type_uid=2;section=Features (accessed 1 March 2012).

Education Scotland (undated) *Games Based Learning*. Available at: http://www.educationscotland. gov.uk/usinggglowandict/gamesbasedlearning/about/aboutgamebasedlearning.asp (accessed 1 May 2012).

Freedman, T. (ed.) (2010) *Amazing Web 2.0 Projects Book*. Available at: http://www.terry-freedman.org.uk (accessed 13 May 2013).

Hennessy, S., Warwick, P. and Mercer, N. (2010) *Using the Interactive Whiteboard to Support Classroom Dialogue*. Available at: http://dialogueiwb.educ.cam.ac.uk/ (accessed 13 May 2013).

Heppell, S. (2006) *Play to Learn, Learn to Play*. Available at: http://www.heppell.net/weblog/ stephen/otherwriting/2006/10/20/Playtolearnlearntoplay.html (accessed 1 September 2012).

Hilton, J. (2006) 'The future for higher education: sunrise or perfect storm?', *Educause*, March–April.

Howard-Jones, P. (2008) *Play a Smart Game*. Available at: http://www.tes.co.uk/article. aspx?storycode=6000946 (accessed 1 September 2012).

Mitra, S. (2010) 'The child-drive education' (video). Available at: http://www.ted.com/talks/ sugata_mitra_the_child_driven_education.html (accessed 13 May 2013).

Naughton, J, (2012) 'Why all our kids should be taught how to code', *Guardian*, 31 March. Available at: http://www.guardian.co.uk/education/2012/mar/31/why-kids-should-be-taught-code (accessed 1 September 2012).

Papert, S. (1980) *Mindstorms: Children, Computers and Powerful Ideas*, New York: Basic Books.

Shirky, C. (2003) *Social Software and the Politics of Groups*. Available at: http://www.shirky.com/ writings/group_politics.html (accessed 1 September 2012).

Siemens, G. (2004) 'Connectivism: a learning theory for the digital age'. Available at: http://www. elearnspace.org/Articles/connectivism.htm (accessed 13 May 2013).

Simpson, D. and Toyn, M. (eds) (2011) *Primary ICT Across the Curriculum*, Exeter: Learning Matters.

Skemp, R.R. (1976) 'Relational understanding and instrumental understanding', *Mathematics Teaching* 77: 20–6.

Younie, S. and Leask, M. (2013) *Teaching with Technologies*, Maidenhead: Open University Press.

7 USING THE INTERACTIVE WHITEBOARD TO SUPPORT DIALOGUE IN THE WHOLE CLASS CONTEXT

Sara Hennessy

INTRODUCTION

'Classroom dialogue' refers to the ways that teachers and learners explore and generate ideas and questions together, make their reasoning clear, and most importantly, build on and critique others' ideas as well as their own. It is now widely recognised that such 'dialogic' communication between teachers and pupils is educationally valuable. However, research shows that 'interactive whole class teaching' is in practice often dominated by fast, closed questioning led by the teacher (Moyles *et al.*, 2003) – with little opportunity for dialogue in which learners contribute their own ideas. This chapter illustrates how the interactive whiteboard (IWB)[1] can help teachers offer this opportunity, presenting a space for children to communicate their ideas visually and for a class to build up knowledge together. It leads the way for both teachers and pupils to use this powerful and increasingly prevalent tool more interactively.

The chapter draws on recent research carried out by a team at Cambridge University. We investigated how teachers can use the IWB purposefully to help get pupils talking and thinking in more depth, testing out ideas, and learning from their classmates. This case study research involved collaboration with teachers who developed their practice to exploit the IWB in new ways. They used it to support rich new forms of dialogue – between teachers and pupils and between pupils – in a variety of subject areas. These new kinds of dialogue went beyond the notion of 'talk' since participants used different kinds of media to communicate ideas and to share their viewpoints. These included video, audio, text, photographs, diagrams and drawings. The chapter illustrates some of the resulting classroom practices with varied, concrete examples backed up by a freely accessible collection of video clips (http://sms.cam.ac.uk/collection/1085164). The examples offer a stimulus for discussion, reflection and trialling of new ideas in the classroom.

OBJECTIVES

At the end of this chapter you should:

■ have extended your understanding of 'dialogue';
■ be able to plan activities that exploit the IWB to support new, multimodal forms of dialogue;
■ be able to engage a class of learners in joint knowledge building using the IWB as a communication space for sharing and critiquing ideas;
■ realise that thinking about the learning purpose is more important than developing 'whizzy' uses of the board!

Check the requirements for your course to see how they might relate to this unit.

WHAT IS DIALOGUE?

The term dialogue is defined as 'discussion directed towards exploration of a subject or resolution of a problem' (Oxford English Dictionary). The notion of dialogue developed here builds on the writings of Bakhtin (1981) who similarly defines dialogue as shared enquiry (as opposed to conversation). His account and subsequent related work by Wegerif (2007) describe 'dialogic' as the gap between two or more perspectives held together in the tension of a dialogue. New meaning arises within that gap. Opening up a dialogic space is considered fruitful at least in topic areas where ideas are likely to differ. Classroom dialogue is thus more than just 'talk'. It means learners exchanging ideas and negotiating new meanings through *responding to and taking into account others' perspectives* (Rogoff, 1990). It means teachers soliciting and building on pupils' prior knowledge. An underpinning assumption is that we know more collectively than we do individually and that we benefit from sharing our diverse understandings.

In practice, dialogue:

■ involves teachers and learners commenting and cumulatively building on each other's ideas, posing questions and constructing interpretations together (Alexander, 2008; Mercer and Littleton, 2007; Mortimer and Scott, 2003);
■ is characterised by chains of (open) questions and answers and chained lines of thinking and enquiry (Alexander, 2008);
■ may be sustained over the course of a single lesson or across lessons;
■ depends on cultivating a supportive classroom ethos – and devoting time – for exploring, sharing and challenging ideas;
■ builds on the notion of 'exploratory talk' in which reasoning is visible – learners justify their views, construct shared knowledge and are willing to change their minds and critique their own ideas (Mercer, 2000);
■ but in the context of IWB use, learners do not always articulate their reasoning verbally – they might instead represent their thinking through drawing or manipulating objects on the board. Dialogue can be non-verbal too!

Here is an excerpt of classroom dialogue (edited for brevity) from a secondary school (boys-only) history lesson during a discussion of the question 'Is it possible for us to imagine the experience of trench warfare?'

RICKY: It's like when you imagine winning the lottery ... it wouldn't necessarily be like what you think.

ROBERT: You can imagine what it would look like, but you can't imagine what it would feel like or how you would be feeling.

T: Ok. What do you think about that Owen? You could imagine what it would look like, but not actually what it would feel like. I quite like that.

OWEN: Yes, because on the DVDs or on the films and the poems and stuff [displayed earlier on the IWB], it explains and you can see what it looks like, in wasteland, and you're both in trenches, but you wouldn't know what it was like to go ages without food or water.

RICKY: That's partially true, but you wouldn't know what it would be like to be shot by a bullet or be bombed or something. You wouldn't see what it looked like either.

FELIX: Every single person's experience with it would be different. Everybody's got different feelings towards the war, and you wouldn't know what anyone would have felt like, even if we were there, you would only know what you felt like.

T: Yes, can we ever achieve a common understanding of anything?

Dialogue can take up more lesson time than other forms of classroom communication. Yet research confirms its long-term *value for pupil learning*, especially reasoning skills but also literacy and subject attainment scores. Drawing learners into extended and thought-provoking question-and-answer exchanges is associated with improved learning outcomes (Rojas-Drummond and Mercer, 2004). A series of studies has shown that exploratory talk training as in the 'Thinking Together' approach (Dawes *et al.*, 2004) promotes both (individual and group) reasoning skills plus learning gains in mathematics and science (Mercer *et al.*, 2004; Mercer and Sams, 2006; Rojas-Drummond *et al.*, 2010; Wegerif *et al.*, 1999). Scott *et al.* (2010) have further illustrated how a dialogic approach supports the meaningful learning of scientific concepts. Importantly, it can lead to longer term change well after the interaction as pupils reflect further on how ideas are different (Howe *et al.*, 2005).

Recent incarnations of national examinations and policy strategies in the UK have moved increasingly towards an emphasis on classroom discussion of controversial topics and development of dialogue skills in subjects such as history, geography, science and citizenship. Yet a conflicting policy (and school inspection) emphasis on rapid lesson pace (disregarding the desired *pace of learning*) and soliciting correct answers, coupled with many teachers' and policymakers' lack of understanding of dialogic pedagogy, mean that a dialogic approach is not yet commonly observed (Galton, 2007; Mercer and Littleton, 2007).

WHAT ROLE CAN THE INTERACTIVE WHITEBOARD PLAY?

The IWB is typically used for whole class teaching. In many countries, there has been substantial government investment and policymakers' interest in it as a classroom tool (Thomas and Cutrim-Schmid, 2010) and an exponential increase in its prevalence in schools. The IWB is now found in 85 per cent of UK classrooms, in 60 per cent of classrooms in Denmark and the Netherlands, 53 per cent of classrooms in Australia, 47 per cent of classrooms in the United States of America, and 34–38 per cent of classrooms in Canada and Spain (Futuresource Consulting, 2012). An astounding one in eight classrooms (34 million teaching spaces) across the world now have an IWB, and by 2015, one in five will have one (Futuresource Consulting, 2012). However, its use has been associated with superficial collaboration, motivation and participation at the expense of uptake questioning (Higgins *et al.*, 2005), pupil talk and reflection (Becta, 2003; Gillen *et al.*, 2007; Kennewell and Beauchamp, 2007; Smith *et al.*, 2006). Government-funded research shows that pressure to 'get through' curriculum content means that IWB use may decrease thinking time and opportunity for learner input, resulting in teacher-only operation (Moss *et al.*, 2007). In our earlier studies of IWB use in secondary science, pupils' physical use of the board was desired by teachers but constrained by subject cultures, curriculum and assessment frameworks (Hennessy *et al.*, 2007). Nevertheless the large-scale SWEEP study of primary teachers (Somekh *et al.*, 2007) indicated that IWB use became embedded after a period of two years and new or improved pedagogical practices then began to emerge. Around a quarter of teachers reported more interactive lessons with greater active pupil involvement, made possible by the functionality of the board.

Unlike most other current forms of educational technology and software, the IWB is a *generic* classroom tool. It provides an unrestricted portal for interaction with an infinitely wide range of secondary digital resources, especially when linked to a computer with internet acess. This offers teachers tremendous ease and flexibility in sourcing materials to stimulate dialogue. The IWB additionally allows *multimodal* interaction with a wide range of digital media. In particular, using graphical and dynamic representations and audio or video helps to make complex concepts and processes more explicit, concrete and transparent. Such representations can in fact communicate meaning less abstractly than oral texts (Wells, 1999, Chapter 4) because interaction with them is usually mediated through both teachers' and pupils' interpretative talk, gaze and gesture at certain points during the course of activity. This offers opportunities to check understanding and supply clarification.

In addition IWB use can support collaborative knowledge building by a class through constructing texts and objects within its proprietary software environments (eg. SMART Notebook or ActivInspire). This knowledge-building process is aided by its specialised tools for directly manipulating digital objects and for focusing attention through highlighting, annotating and hide-and-reveal; these facilities contribute to its 'value added' beyond other technology uses. IWB use helps to make differences between perspectives more explicit while understanding is developing (Hennessy, 2011). It supports dialogue because different ideas can more easily be juxtaposed, highlighted, explored, connected and contrasted, and their strengths and weaknesses become more salient. It opens up new opportunities for learners and teachers publicly to express, explain, justify, evaluate and reformulate ideas – both orally and using other rich representations. These external, dynamic representations of knowledge within objects constructed and manipulated on the board offer support for the creative process of collective knowledge building. They also provide interim records of that process, evolving to become rich resources for a group later on.

Research carried out during three projects[2] at Cambridge University in recent years has investigated how teachers can exploit the IWB to support pupils' learning by using its more interactive features in whole class contexts. Ten in-depth case studies of 8 teachers using IWBs in a variety of subject areas were carried out in (mainly secondary) schools in the East Anglia region of the UK between 2002–2010. The examples extracted from two of the projects, *T-MEDIA* (Deaney and Hennessy, 2011; Hennessy and Deaney, 2009a, 2009b; Hennessy *et al.*, 2010) and *IWBs and Dialogic Teaching* (Hennessy, 2011; Mercer *et al.*, 2010; Warwick *et al.*, 2011), are elaborated using digital video in the resulting multimedia professional development resources.[3]

Some of the emerging *key examples of IWB use that potentially support dialogic interaction* are now outlined. Note that while many of these dialogic uses do not actually require an IWB, they are often much more cumbersome without, and since so many classrooms now have IWBs, the examples offer some guidance about how to use them interactively. They are not models to copy, but may offer some ideas for developing your own practice if you have access to an IWB. If not, many of them can be carried out with imaginative use of a data projector or other resources.

EXAMPLES OF DIALOGIC USE OF THE IWB

Supporting dialogue within a lesson by building in learners' responsiveness to others' ideas

A single rich resource can be progressively manipulated and interacted with in different ways for different purposes, often within the relatively short time period of a lesson. In particular, highlighting and annotating images and texts by hand in real time during discussion is a simple but powerful technique. Examples of *responding being built into the activity itself* are as follows:

(a) ***The progressive building up of a food chain or web.*** A set of photographs of organisms was provided and each pupil used drag-and-drop to add a link in turn and communicated their reasoning to the class (Hennessy *et al.*, 2007).

(b) ***Drawing a collective picture of a trench through learners adding elements in turn.*** Learners built on each other's ideas, and also on their knowledge and experiences from previous lessons. A class product was thereby created through a nonverbal form of dialogue. The resulting diagram (Figure 7.1) depicted an imaginative range of elements perceived by learners to be typically present in a trench during a sequence of history lessons on trench warfare. It succinctly portrayed more than pupils actually said while drawing. It 'built on their informed speculation from some of the things that they had seen' (teacher) on the IWB during their previous two lessons and contained elements arising from pair/class dialogue. See video clips of the drawing in action at http://sms.cam.ac.uk/media/1095570 and a compilation of some of the preceding activities at http://sms.cam.ac.uk/media/1085205.

(c) ***Annotating a portrait of Queen Elizabeth I.*** Pupils in turn graphically annotated a portrait of a digital photograph of the young Queen Elizabeth I projected onto the IWB during a secondary school history lesson (see video clip at http://sms.cam.ac.uk/media/1085166). Here learners subsequently interpreted their peers' thinking by drawing links to labels that others had written around the image without comment: for example, 'rich', 'religious', 'intelligent'. This activity developed a collective, enhanced understanding of the 'Golden Age' of Elizabeth (Deaney *et al.*, 2009). It also maximised the number of pupils that could interact directly with the portrait. The teacher built upon the learners' interpretations in the plenary by subtly helping

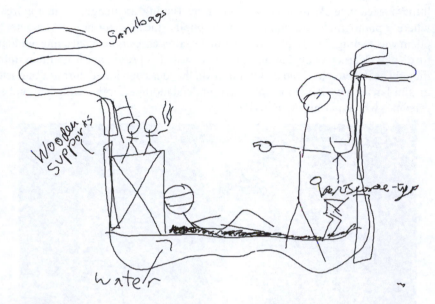

■ **Figure 7.1** Diagram of a World War I trench collectively drawn by learners in history

them to understand Elizabeth's motives and subsequent events. He created continuity by comparing the portrait with a previously displayed one of the older Elizabeth. He questioned the 'reality' portrayed by any historical artefact, concluding both that pictures only tell a partial story and that his own ideas had been changed by the activity. In this democratic classroom, the teacher was also a learner.

Task 7.1 **Devise and try out your own IWB activity**

How did the teachers portrayed in these examples support classroom dialogue?

How useful and feasible are these kinds of activities and strategies in your own setting?

Devise and try out your own IWB-based activity that requires learners to respond to peers' ideas.

Think about your own role *during* the activity too – what questions will you pose and how will you elaborate and perhaps record pupils' contributions?

Technical versus pedagogical skill

Notice that quite straightforward uses of the IWB can be remarkably effective in supporting the process of active co-construction of knowledge; you don't need to be a technical whiz! (This is confirmed by other research too: Gillen *et al.*, 2008; Kennewell and Beauchamp, 2007). In example (c), for instance, the teacher simply projected a carefully chosen image and then pupils annotated it graphically and with text. The sophistication was evident in planning and managing the activity rather than in technical use of the IWB.

(d) *Brainstorming.* Another simple technique that novice IWB users can try is a class brainstorm. This might be either in response to a single projected question or prompt (see video clip of brainstorming ideas under the heading 'causes of war' at http://sms.cam.ac.uk/media/1097431) or overlaying an image, as in Figure 7.2, where a photograph was annotated with pupils' ideas about how a character in a poem was feeling. The English teacher in the latter case argued that using annotation to display learner contributions offers 'a visual representation of their train of thought as it develops', and that building on the ideas generated during a brainstorm or similar activity develops collective understanding, pupil confidence and self-esteem – whilst permitting individuality.

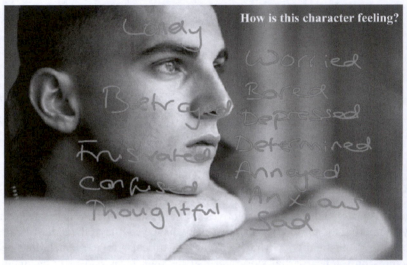

Male teenager

■ **Figure 7.2** Image linked to the poem 'Education for Leisure' by Carol Ann Duffy, annotated to describe a teenager's feelings

Stimulating dialogue using a 'square of truth' or 'magic box/window'

This activity creates suspense and stimulates discussion by allowing learners to sort objects, words or text phrases according to their properties. For example, correct answers to a question, true/false, or prime numbers, metaphors or addictive substances will be correctly categorised when dropped into a box/other shape or a window is dragged over them. Typically pupils are asked in turn to predict whether – and to explain why – a set of given statements will be true/false or fit the given category, then to drag the statements (or the teacher does so on their behalf) over a central square or other opaque object to receive immediate physical feedback about correctness. Statements deemed false by the teacher are previously formatted to disappear behind the box using the object layering feature of the proprietary IWB software; those that are true stay visible. They can also make predictions about what is concealed behind an object, or which objects have a particular property. This kind of activity can either develop or test pupils' understanding.

(e) *'Moon of truth'.* This example displays a number of controversial statements for learners to discuss in groups; having tried this out with adults at a conference, I know that it generates a great deal of animated debate. The screenshots shows the statements before (Figure 7.3) and during (Figure 7.4) the activity of dragging them onto the object (the moon in this case) to see which are actually true.

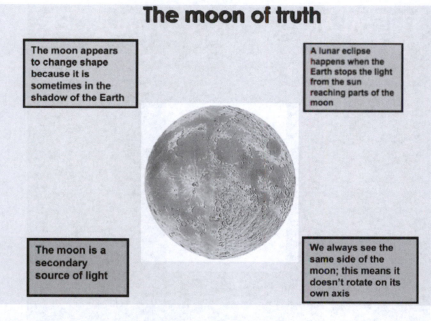

Figure 7.3 'Moon of truth' before manipulation

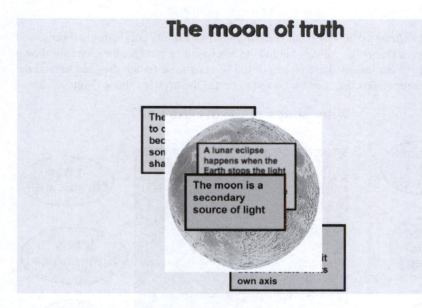

Figure 7.4 'Moon of truth' during manipulation

(f) ***Preparing for writing a crime story.*** In this example from a series of middle school English lessons focusing on elements of the crime-writing genre, pupils dragged the statements onto the badge. The aim was to consolidate their understanding of the plot of a real-life crime, developing both crime vocabulary and ideas for their own crime story (Figure 7.5).

THE ALMOST PERFECT MURDER

Roger Harrington was framed for Donnah's murder.

Deann Schultz could have faced prosecution.

Winger's bail was set at $5 million.

Winger's crime was pre-meditated.

Winger could have got away with it.

Donnah was dead by the time the paramedics arrived.

The police didn't make any mistakes when investigating the case.

Mark Winger didn't have an alibi.

Winger didn't have any opportunity to commit the crime.

The police know why Winger committed the crime.

■ **Figure 7.5** 'Badge of truth': evidence for a fictitious murder

(g) ***Guess the shape or 'box of truth' activity.*** In this example pupils might discuss and predict what shape they think is behind the box based on whether the clues are shown to be true (when dragged are on top of the box) or false (when dragged behind the box). The green box can then be moved to reveal the mystery shape (Figure 7.6).

What shape is behind the box?

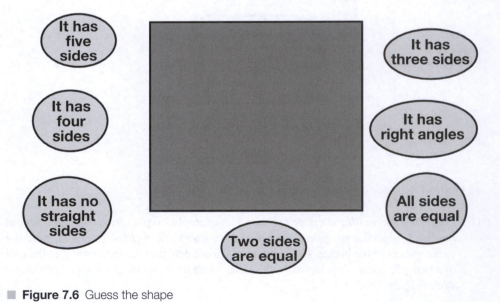

It has five sides

It has three sides

It has four sides

It has right angles

It has no straight sides

All sides are equal

Two sides are equal

■ **Figure 7.6** Guess the shape

Task 7.2 **Create your own magic box**

Follow the steps below to create your own magic box or window (ask a more experienced IWB user to help you if you are uncertain how to perform these actions on your particular system). Plan an activity that challenges pupils to think and stimulates discussion as they make predictions about what is concealed, which statements are true or which objects have a particular property. Try it out in the classroom.

■ Draw or pull into the centre of the flipchart a rectangle shape or other simple image. Or for 'What's behind the box?' insert a shape behind a box and lock it in place. Fill it in a light colour, outline it in another colour if using a rectangle.
■ Create objects (pictures or text boxes) to be categorised; you may want to group the text in each text box with a background shape.
■ Send to the front the objects to be revealed when dropped into the box or when the window is dragged over them. Send to the back the objects to be concealed.

Selecting, manipulating and discussing own words/pictures/scenarios from a given set

(h) *Group annotation of images.* In this example (Figure 7.7) each group of four to five pupils selected a slightly different combination of images pertaining to personal safety issues, arranged them on the IWB as they desired and annotated them during group discussion (generating advice 'as a team working for Childline' and recording this on large sheets of paper). In the video clip one group talks through their ideas to the class, annotating the images; the teacher encourages other students to comment. See http://sms.cam.ac.uk/media/1085308. One group product is shown. This can also be done with paper replicas at tables (see Matched Resources page 000) with one pair showing their work on the board afterwards.

■ **Figure 7.7** Collective representation of a small group's advice on personal safety

(i) *Model mapping/mind mapping.* Pupils use key terms from a set and drag and drop words/draw arrows/add text to make connections and explain key ideas about a topic (Figure 7.8). Results can be saved and added to throughout a lesson/topic of work. Learners could make a mind map at their desks before or during the class activity. They could also do the activity at the beginning and end of a lesson or lesson sequence to illustrate what they have learned. Model mapping is especially useful for children with literacy difficulties.

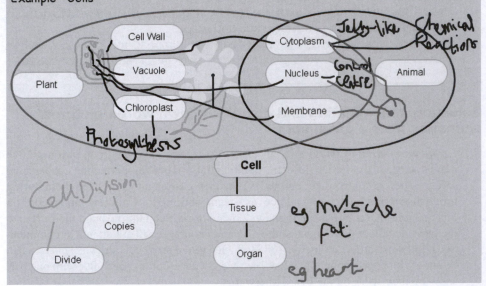

Mind Mapping -
Pupils use the key terms and drag and drop words/draw arrows/add text to make connections and explain key ideas about a topic.
Example - Cells

■ **Figure 7.8** An annotated model map of photosynthesis

(j) *Critiquing peer ideas or model answers.* The IWB can be used to display model answers, which students can highlight and critique. Dialogue may also be promoted when pupils' own ideas or representations are displayed on the IWB and peer assessed.

Use of a visualiser with the IWB

The IWB can be very effectively used with peripherals such as the visualiser or a standard digital camera. The visualiser (also known as a document camera) can be used to display, critique (see (i) above) or compare pupils' work (Figure 7.9) or experimental results, or to project an image as a stimulus for a task.

See a video clip of use in a science lesson at http://sms.cam.ac.uk/media/1090403, playing it from 41.05 to the end. In this example, low-attaining pupils aged 14–15 who are learning about photosynthesis generated their own personal representations illustrating how the plant cell wall protects and supports. Some of these ideas were then drawn freehand by pupils onto the IWB or projected there from their books using a flexible camera (iCam or form of visualiser) and publicly explained by the pupils.

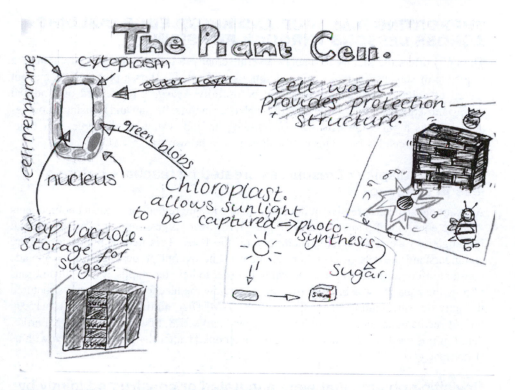

■ **Figure 7.9** Megan's personal representation of sugar storage displayed using visualiser

Further examples of visualiser use by teachers in other contexts are described in these videoed presentations: rtsp://svl.ioe.ac.uk:554/basevideo/StevenandJulie_med.rm; rtsp://svl.ioe.ac.uk:554/basevideo/DougalMcCormick_med.rm; rtsp://svl.ioe.ac.uk:554/basevideo/DianeMavers_med.rm. You may need to download Real Player to view them. They mostly depict primary school uses but they will give you an idea of the tool's versatility. They include rolling a dice for a class to see, showing equipment (ruler/syringe), scrutinising the structure of bread going mouldy, projecting children's work and a photostory. You can also freeze an image, then remove the object from the visualiser and manipulate it, and compare it with the original.

Task 7.3 **Lesson planning to support dialogue**

Plan and teach a lesson containing – or centred around – a new activity that aims to support classroom dialogue. You might try something you have seen above or a related idea of your own. Start by thinking about addressing your learners' particular needs. You might want to focus on engagement or learning of a couple of particular pupils when you evaluate it.

SUPPORTING DIALOGUE AND KNOWLEDGE BUILDING ACROSS LESSONS THROUGH REVISITING

The IWB offers the facility to display several screens in turn and uniquely to archive a sequence of screens, including any alterations to them. It offers a physical, permanent record of collaborative activity that can be usefully *revisited*, referenced or modified during subsequent activity, soon after or much later in time. Saving and re-using resources and slides is a very powerful way of building up and sustaining dialogue over time, including between lessons. This can be done in several ways.

Repeated display of resources created by teachers before a lesson sequence

An example is the progressive building up – and constant revisiting of earlier components – of the equation of photosynthesis (Figure 7.10) over six lessons (along with practical investigation) using an equation template on the IWB. This helped pupils to explore andunderstand the role of each core element in the overall process. The teacher made constant reference back to earlier learning in order to help the pupils. Video illustrations of how the equation was built up over time and how the teacher managed and structured the activities surrounding it can be seen on the T-MEDIA multimedia science resource at http://t-media.educ.cam.ac.uk (Clips 1.3, second part of 2.3, first part of 4.2, 5.1). Further detail of this teacher's practice is available in a book chapter that he co-authored with us (Hennessy *et al.*, 2010).

Revisiting objects that were annotated or constructed jointly by a class

This includes displaying objects as optional, unobtrusive supports for further activity such as pupils doing their own writing after studying a topic or piece of literature. It

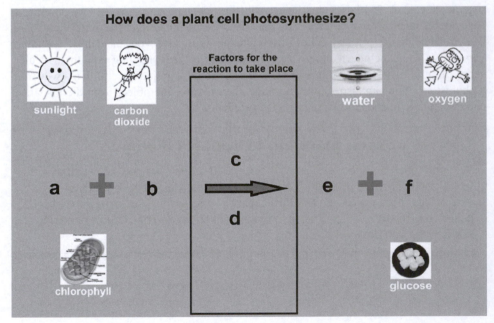

■ **Figure 7.10** Drag-and-drop activity constructing the photosynthesis equation

includes allowing learners to request or access resources or class products by themselves as needed for support.

One English teacher revisited two annotated slides in the subsequent lesson, to bridge between lessons, pulling together ideas from the two poems studied, and refocusing pupils, allowing them constant reference to their earlier ideas and thoughts. These 'aides memoires' reminded learners of what they already knew and provided a springboard for further discussion of the themes depicted (Figure 7.11).

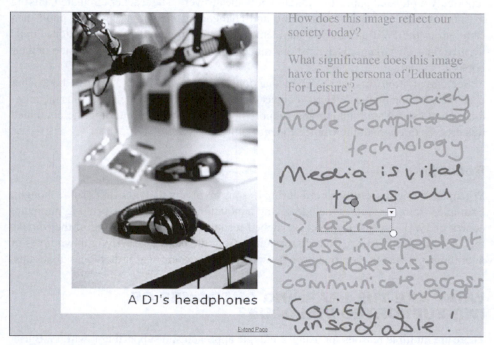

Figure 7.11 Linking an image to a persona in the poem 'Education for Leisure' by Carol Ann Duffy

ENGAGING ALL LEARNERS IN IWB-ENHANCED ACTIVITY

Task 7.4 **Participation in activity at and around the IWB**

Think of as many ways as you can to get all pupils to participate, including those who do not get a chance to come up to the IWB in the lesson.

Is it important do you think for pupils to come up to use the board themselves? If so, what kinds of uses are valuable for them?

Are there opportunities for others to give input or feedback when one pupil is at the board?

Would individual or pair work on mini-whiteboards or in exercise books be useful here?

How can you know what individuals are learning?

Think about your answers and then discuss these questions with other student teachers or colleagues.

Pupils arranging objects on the board and at their desks to show their understanding: matched resources

One science teacher introduced the equation of photosynthesis (Figure 7.10) using colour images of its components and an equation template on the IWB, as mentioned above. The class were given paper mini-diagrams that replicated the IWB images and asked to cut up and order them, justifying their arrangements; this generated quite a lot of discussion and reportedly motivated pupils to 'want to know the answer'. The teacher circulated, talking to small groups of pupils, questioning and challenging their thinking. One pupil then came up to the IWB and moved the elements around to complete the equation. Pupils verified their own diagrams against this model before sticking the correct version in their books.

See clip at http://sms.cam.ac.uk/media/1090412. This clip illustrates how the teacher used the equation on the IWB as an object of reference for the whole class, plus the mini-diagrams to stimulate thinking and support stepwise knowledge building; he continued this process throughout the whole sequence of lessons.

Recording

What pupils might usefully record during lessons involving dialogue takes some thought. Examples from our studies include saving annotations and drawings, printing miniature copies of IWB screens or objects (matched resources), pupils recording in their books their own or peers' ideas (from discussion or from the board), or writing down notes or definitions phrased in their own words. You may have your own further ideas about this.

WHAT ARE THE LEARNING OUTCOMES OF IWB-SUPPORTED DIALOGUE?

There are multiple reasons for using a dialogic approach and supporting it with IWB use. You may want to develop:

1   Dialogue, reasoning and enquiry skills. It is probably necessary for learners to develop these to some extent before being expected to use the IWB in genuinely interactive ways in whole class settings. You might want to do this either explicitly as in the 'Thinking Together' approach (http://www.thinking-together.org.uk/) and as observed in our primary and middle school dialogic classrooms (see videos at http://sms.cam.ac.uk/media/1098208 and http://sms.cam.ac.uk/media/1098087), or implicitly through modelling them yourself.

2   Appreciation of different perspectives on a topic, including those of peers, teacher and sometimes experts (e.g. scientific theories). These may result in either a consensus view, a collection of ideas or an agreement to differ.

3   Fluid forms of subject content and process knowledge that are both individual and shared, internally and externally represented; they may evolve further through dialogue as it continues over time, at least internally if not interpersonally.

These outcomes can all be achieved by a dialogic teacher without an IWB, however teachers who have used the board in the ways detailed earlier have found that these uses can help them and their pupils to achieve such outcomes more easily.

To conclude, classroom dialogue in the context of IWB use is construed as being facilitated by teachers and learners constructing and manipulating digital objects together, in conjunction with talk and gesture. This process of dialogic interaction underpins the learning outcomes listed above. The objects themselves – perhaps embodied in saved IWB 'flipcharts' – may be productively re-used on other occasions, in new contexts and for new purposes. Purposes may include using them as stimuli for discussion with or between pupils about their learning, potentially offering a fruitful form of formative or summative assessment. For example, comparing products such as concept maps created at the beginning and end of a lesson or lesson sequence can powerfully illustrate to learners themselves how their thinking has moved on.

SUMMARY

Using the IWB interactively can support rich new forms of classroom dialogue in which teachers and learners together explore, build on and critique each other's ideas. A continually accessible visual display, interaction with a broad range of digital resources, and jointly creating and directly manipulating objects on the IWB may support collaborative knowledge building in new ways. Teachers' willingness to at least partially relinquish control over the IWB and to take the time to consider pupils' views is critical to developing a productive, dialogic use. In this context, the IWB can be a versatile tool for helping develop classroom dialogue.

A variety of authentic examples of classroom IWB use that potentially support dialogic interaction have been presented. They are based around open-ended activities that aim to stimulate thinking rather than 'right answers'. The examples show that 'whizzy' use of the IWB is not necessary – a single carefully selected image or question can be a powerful springboard for dialogue. They are not models to copy, but may stimulate you to think about developing your own practice in this area. They challenge you to devise ways of building in learners' responsiveness to others' ideas, and to think about how to get all pupils to participate in lesson activities. You may also want to consider how archiving and revisiting earlier work could be useful in continuing a dialogue over time.

Check which requirements for your course you have addressed through this unit.

FURTHER READING AND RESOURCES

We are creating multimedia professional development resources to stimulate teachers' interest in exploring new dialogic approaches and reflecting on their own practice (Hennessy *et al.*, in press). Some of the materials are freely available via our IWBs and Dialogue website at http://dialogueiwb.educ.cam.ac.uk/. The resources are co-authored with teachers participating in our research and they communicate in accessible language the notion of dialogue, along with its preconditions and some strategies to support it. The forthcoming published pack includes a resource bank of video clips and screenshots, each with descriptions of classroom activities, IWB flipchart template activities, and a series of accessible background readings. These include the teachers' own case stories of authentic classroom practice.

Task 7.5 **Does my own teaching support dialogue?**

The 'Dialogue table + guidance' developed by our research team and presented in accessible language by one of our project teachers illustrates what classroom dialogue may be like in the context of IWB use, using headings 'In my classroom, we:', 'You will see us:' and 'So that we can'. You can download it from http://dialogueiwb.educ.cam.ac.uk/resources/.

Column 1 shows how the *classroom climate* needs to support dialogue if it is to happen. Column 2 illustrates *what kinds of things teachers and learners might do in a dialogic classroom*. Column 3 shows the goals – *what dialogic activity could lead to*.

You may wish to audit your own practice (over time) using the table. See which of the statements apply in your classroom. How can you develop a more dialogic approach, where appropriate? Is the ethos in your classroom supportive for dialogue? How could you make it more supportive?

For more guidance about *how* to create a supportive climate, see the free downloadable classroom materials at http://www.thinking-together.org.uk/ and the book by Dawes (2010).

Store the table and the outcome of your audit in your professional development portfolio.

Thomas, M. and Cutrim-Schmid, E. (eds) (2010) *Interactive Whiteboards: Theory, Research and Practice*, **Hershey, PA: IGI-Global.**

> An up-to-date collection of research articles and case studies, including examples from classroom practice in the UK and elsewhere.

Alexander, R.J. (2008) *Towards Dialogic Teaching: Rethinking Classroom Talk* **(fourth ed.), Cambridge: Dialogos UK Ltd.**

> An accessibly written and seminal booklet available at very reasonable cost from http://www.robinalexander.org.uk/dialogos.htm. Highly recommended for anyone wanting to read more about dialogue.

http://iwbcollaboration.educ.cam.ac.uk

> This website contains information about developing dialogue within collaborative pupil groups using the IWB (in science) based on another related research project at Cambridge.

ACKNOWLEDGEMENTS

First and foremost, thanks are due to the dedicated teachers who willingly participated in the various case studies upon which this chapter is based. Likewise, this work would not have been possible without the contributions made by colleagues – Paul Warwick in particular, also Rosemary Deaney, Laura Flitton, Neil Mercer and Kenneth Ruthven. All of the underpinning research was funded by the UK Economic and Social Research Council (see details in Note 2). Some of the material in this chapter derives from a recent article by Hennessy (2011) and is included here by kind permission of the publisher, Wiley-Blackwell. Finally, thank you to Darron Gray who provided helpful comments on an earlier draft of this chapter.

NOTES

1   The IWB is a system comprising a computer linked to a data projector and a large electronic board displaying the projected image. The touch-sensitive board allows direct input via finger or stylus so that objects can be easily manipulated or modified by teacher or pupils.

2   The projects were all funded by the UK Economic and Social Research Council. They included SET-IT ('Situated Expertise in Technology-Integrated Teaching': R000239823) in 2002–2005 (with Kenneth Ruthven and Rosemary Deaney); T-MEDIA ('Teacher Mediation of Subject Learning with Technology: A Multimedia Approach': RES000230825) in 2005–2007 (with Rosemary Deaney), and the 'IWBs and Dialogic Teaching' project undertaken in collaboration with Neil Mercer and Paul Warwick as part of a personal Research Fellowship programme of work carried out in 2007–2010 by the author (ref. RES063270081). Reports and publications from each are available at http://www.educ.cam.ac.uk/research/projects/istl/. The first two projects did not focus on dialogue but the themes emerging encompassed dialogic interaction and this stimulated further investigation.

3   The T-MEDIA multimedia resources (see Hennessy and Deaney, 2007) are all freely available at http://t-media.educ.cam.ac.uk. The 'IWBs and Dialogic Teaching' resources are in press and details are at http://dialogueiwb.educ.cam.ac.uk/resources/.

REFERENCES

Alexander, R.J. (2008) *Towards Dialogic Teaching: Rethinking Classroom Talk* (fourth ed.), Cambridge: Dialogos UK Ltd. Available at: http://www.robinalexander.org.uk/dialogos.htm (accessed 13 May 2013).

Bakhtin, M.N. (1981) *The Dialogic Imagination*, Austin, TX: University of Texas Press.

Becta (2003) *What the Research Says About Interactive Whiteboards*, Coventry: British Educational Communications and Technology Agency.

Dawes, L. (2010) *Creating a Speaking and Listening Classroom*, London: Routledge.

Dawes, L., Mercer, N. and Wegerif, R. (2004) *Thinking Together: A Programme of Activities for Developing Speaking, Listening and Thinking Skills for Children Aged 8–11*, Birmingham: Imaginative Minds.

Deaney, R. and Hennessy, S. (2011) 'Pedagogical issues in embedding ICT in teaching and learning mathematics: a case study of using multiple resources to teach straight line graphs', in A. Oldknow and C. Knights (eds), *Mathematics Education with Digital Technology*, London: Continuum International.

Deaney, R., Chapman, A. and Hennessy, S. (2009) 'A case study of one teacher's use of the interactive whiteboard to support knowledge co-construction in the history classroom', *The Curriculum Journal* 20(4): 365–87. doi: DOI: 10.1080/09585170903424898.

Futuresource Consulting (2012) *Interactive Displays Quarterly Insight: State of the Market Report, Quarter 4*, Dunstable: Futuresource Consulting.

Galton, M. (2007) *Learning and Teaching in the Primary Classroom*, London: Sage.

Gillen, J., Littleton, K., Twiner, A., Staarman, J.K. and Mercer, N. (2008) 'Using the interactive whiteboard to resource continuity and support multimodal teaching in a primary science classroom', *Journal of Computer Assisted Learning* 24(4): 348–58. doi: 10.1111/j.1365-2729.2007.00269.x.

Hennessy, S. (2011) 'The role of digital artefacts on the interactive whiteboard in mediating dialogic teaching and learning', *Journal of Computer Assisted Learning* 27(6): 463–586. doi: 10.1111/j.1365-2729.2011.00416.x.

Hennessy, S. and Deaney, R. (2007) *Teacher Mediation of Subject Learning with ICT: A Multimedia Approach* (RES-000-23-0825), Final Report to ESRC, Cambridge: University of Cambridge.

——(2009a) 'The impact of collaborative video analysis by practitioners and researchers upon pedagogical thinking and practice: a follow-up study', *Teachers and Teaching: Theory and Practice* 15(5): 617–38. doi: 10.1080/13540600903139621.

——(2009b) '"Intermediate theory" building: integrating multiple teacher and researcher perspectives through in-depth video analysis of pedagogic strategies', *Teachers College Record* 111(7): 1753–95. doi: 15305.

Hennessy, S., Deaney, R., Ruthven, K. and Winterbottom, M. (2007) 'Pedagogical strategies for using the interactive whiteboard to foster learner participation in school science', *Learning, Media and Technology, Special issue on Interactive Whiteboards* 32(3): 283–301. doi: 10.1080/17439880701511131.

Hennessy, S., Deaney, R. and Tooley, C. (2010) 'Using the interactive whiteboard to stimulate active learning in school science', in M. Thomas and E. Cutrim-Schmid (eds), *Interactive Whiteboards: Theory, Research and Practice* (pp. 102–17), Hershey, PA: IGI-Global.

Hennessy, S., Warwick, P., Brown, L., Rawlins, D. and Neale, C. (eds) (in press) *Developing Interactive Teaching and Learning Using the IWB: Teacher Resource*: Milton Keynes: Open University Press.

Higgins, S., Falzon, C., Hall, I., Moseley, D., Smith, F., Smith, H. and Wall, K. (2005) *Embedding ICT in the Literacy and Numeracy Strategies: Final Report*, Newcastle upon Tyne: Centre for Learning and Teaching, School of Education, Communication and Language Sciences, University of Newcastle upon Tyne.

Howe, C., McWilliam, D. and Cross, G. (2005) 'Chance favours only the prepared mind: incubation and the delayed effects of peer collaboration', *British Journal of Psychology* 96: 67–93.

Kennewell, S. and Beauchamp, G. (2007) 'The features of interactive whiteboards and their influence on learning', *Learning, Media and Technology* 32(3): 227–41.

Mercer, N. (2000) *Words and Minds: How We Use Language to Think Together*, London: Routledge.

Mercer, N. and Sams, C. (2006) 'Teaching children how to use language to solve maths problems', *Language and Education* 20(6): 507–27.

Mercer, N. and Littleton, K. (2007) *Dialogue and the Development of Children's Thinking*, London: Routledge.

Mercer, N., Dawes, L., Wegerif, R. and Sams, C. (2004) 'Reasoning as a scientist: ways of helping children to use language to learn science', *British Educational Research Journal* 30(3): 367–85.

Mercer, N., Hennessy, S. and Warwick, P. (2010) 'Using interactive whiteboards to orchestrate classroom dialogue', *Themed Issue of Technology, Pedagogy and Education on Interactive Whole Class Technologies (guest edited by Hennessy and Warwick)* 19(2): 195–209. doi: 10.1080/1475939X.2010.491230.

Mortimer, E.F. and Scott, P.H. (2003) *Meaning Making in Secondary Science Classrooms*, Milton Keynes: Open University Press.

Moss, G., Jewitt, C., Levacic, R., Armstrong, V., Cardini, A., Castle, F., Allen, B., Jenkins, A., Hancock, M. and High, S. (2007) *The Interactive Whiteboards, Pedagogy and Pupil Performance Evaluation: An Evaluation of the Schools Whiteboard Expansion (SWE)*, London: DfES.

Moyles, J., Hargreaves, L., Merry, R., Paterson, F. and Esarte-Sarries, V. (2003) *Interactive Teaching in the Primary School: Digging Deeper into Meanings*, Maidenhead: Open University Press.

Rogoff, B. (1990) *Apprenticeship in Thinking: Cognitive Development in Social Context*, Oxford: Oxford University Press.

Rojas-Drummond, S. and Mercer, N. (2004) 'Scaffolding the development of effective collaboration and learning', *International Journal of Educational Research* 39(1–2): 99–111.

Rojas-Drummond, S., Littleton, K., Hernández, F. and Zúñiga, M. (2010) 'Dialogical interactions among peers in collaborative writing contexts', in K. Littleton and C. Howe (eds), *Educational Dialogues: Understanding and Promoting Productive Interaction* (pp. 128–48), Abingdon, Oxon: Routledge.

Scott, P., Ametller, J., Mortimer, E. and Emberton, J. (2010) 'Teaching and learning disciplinary knowledge: developing the dialogic space for an answer when there isn't even a question', in K.

Littleton and C. Howe (eds), *Educational Dialogues: Understanding and Promoting Productive Interaction* (pp. 289–303), Abingdon, Oxon: Routledge.

Smith, F., Hardman, F. and Higgins, S. (2006) 'The impact of interactive whiteboards on teacher-pupil interaction in the National Literacy and Numeracy Strategies', *British Educational Research Journal* 32(3): 443–57.

Somekh, B., Haldane, M., Jones, K., Lewin, C., Steadman, S., Scrimshaw, P., Sing, S., Bird, K., Cummings, J., Downing, B., Harber Stuart, T., Jarvis, J., Mavers, D. and Woodrow, D. (2007) *Evaluation of the Primary Schools Whiteboard Expansion Project (SWEEP): Report to the Department for Education and Skills*, London: Becta.

Thomas, S. and Cutrim-Schmid, E. (2010) *Interactive Whiteboards: Theory, Research and Practice*, Hershey, PA: IGI-Global.

Warwick, P., Hennessy, S. and Mercer, N. (2011) 'Promoting teaching and school development through co-enquiry: developing interactive whiteboard use in a "dialogic classroom"', *Teachers and Teaching: Theory and Practice* 17(3): 303–24. doi: 10.1080/13540602.2011.554704.

Wegerif, R. (2007) *Dialogic, Education and Technology: Expanding the Space of Learning*, New York: Springer.

Wegerif, R., Mercer, N. and Dawes, L. (1999) 'From social interaction to individual reasoning: an empirical investigation of a possible socio-cultural model of cognitive development', *Learning and Instruction* 9(5): 493–516.

Wells, G. (1999) *Dialogic Inquiry: Toward a Sociocultural Practice and Theory of Education*, Cambridge: Cambridge University Press.

SPECIAL EDUCATIONAL NEEDS AND TECHNOLOGY

Christina Kuegel

INTRODUCTION

This chapter aims to demonstrate how new technologies can be used to enable learning and develop inclusive practices and argues the case for a social rather than medical model through which to view learning needs. The chapter begins with a discussion surrounding key terminology and proceeds by examining how technology supports the particular needs of pupils with special needs and disabilities.

OBJECTIVES

At the end of this chapter you should be able to:

- discuss the potential for technology to enable learning for pupils with special educational needs and disability (SEND);
- select appropriate technology-based tools to support the needs of the pupils;
- consider some of the limitations of technology for pupils with SEND;
- identify resources to keep up to date in the field of SEND and technology.

BACKGROUND: DEFINITIONS AND STATUTORY REQUIREMENTS

The term 'inclusive education' or 'inclusion' continues to hold diverse definitions and characteristics throughout government policy and the current research literature.[1] For example, in England, government guidance establishes statutory measures for schools and sets out three principles for developing an inclusive curriculum (DfES, 2001).

1   Setting suitable learning challenges.
2   Responding to pupils' diverse learning needs.
3   Overcoming potential barriers to learning and assessment for individuals and groups of pupils.

However it is evident through school policies, school visits, academic literature, conversations with teachers and government documents that schools, teachers and the government all vary in their understanding of what it means to be an inclusive school.[2] Although the definition of inclusion is often linked to the learning needs of a range of pupils including those with English as an additional language (EAL), gifted and talented (G&T), looked after children (LAC), transient populations and other minority groups, this chapter focuses on pupils with SEND. More specifically,

> pupils have special educational needs and/or disability if they have a learning difficulty which calls for a special educational provision to be made for them. Pupils have a learning difficulty if they:
>
> (a) have a significantly greater difficulty in learning than the majority of children of the same age;
> (b) have a disability which prevents or hinders them from making use of educational facilities of a kind generally provided for children of the same age in schools within the area of the local education authority;
> (c) are under compulsory school age and fall within the definition at (a) or (b) above or would so do if special educational provision was not made for them.
>
> (DfES, 2001, p. 6)

Inclusion, inclusive practice, SEND and learning difficulties can hold different meanings to different people and it is therefore important for you to explore your interpretation of the terms.

Task 8.1 **Defining inclusion**

Ask a range of peers and professionals for their definition of inclusion. Browse some of the government guidance, academic literature and support organisation websites (see: further reading and recommended websites, pp. 129–130) and develop your own personal definition of inclusion.

BREAKING DOWN BARRIERS

In our aim to develop an inclusive education for all children, particularly pupils with a SEND, technology is one tool that can reduce some of the barriers to learning. According to the British Educational Communications and Technology Agency's (BECTA) (2003) analysis of relevant literature, technology can benefit pupils, teachers and parents/carers. Some specific benefits identified by BECTA (2003, 2007, 2009) include greater learner autonomy, communication support, personalised learning opportunities, attainment, motivation, and engagement with learning. This is extended by Florian and Hegarty (2004) who suggest six ways in which technology can be used to meet the needs of pupils with a SEND (Table 8.1).

■ **Table 8.1** Six ways technology can be used to meet the needs of pupils with SEND.

Technology can be:

- used as a tutor;
- used for exploration;
- applied as a tool;
- used to communicate;
- used for assessment purposes;
- used as a management tool.

These can be accomplished through 'specialised assistive technologies or mainstream technologies' (BECTA, 2007, p. 6).

It is possible to promote the inclusion principles through the use of technology for pupils with SEND. The use of technology to meet the wider inclusion agenda is known as e-Inclusion or digital inclusion (European Commission: Ministerial Declaration, Riga, June 2006). This can be accomplished by addressing attitudes and beliefs and clearly addressing the needs of the individual pupils by selecting the appropriate technology to meet the needs of pupils. Furthermore, it is vital to keeping pupils safe online and keep your knowledge on technology and special education up to date.

ATTITUDES AND BELIEFS

The attitudes, beliefs and values surounding inclusion and technology that you, the school and society hold all impact on the success of implementing both inclusion (Glazzard, 2011; Sze, 2009) and also technology in the classroom (Leng, 2011). The combination of attitudes and beliefs regarding SEND and technology can become either a barrier or an asset for both you as the teacher and also for the pupils.

The manner in which inclusion, disability and special educational needs are viewed by individuals is complex and diverse. However, the two main ideological frameworks include the medical and social model of disability. This of course is not to over simplify or suggest these are the only means of viewing disability as it should be noted that consistent debate continues regarding the ways in which SEND is conceptualised.

The medical model of disability (also referred to as individual tragedy, within-child, or deficit model) views disability or persons with a disability as 'faulty' and in need of 'fixing' from their 'limitations' (Barnes *et al.*, 2002). This viewpoint does not see a need to adapt the environment or personal views of practitioners and wider society but implies the problems and responsibilities lie with the person with the disability. This model seeks to return the person to 'normal' on the basis of identification of symptoms, diagnosis and cure (Johnstone, 2001). Key terminology associated with the medical model of disability include, useless, unfortunate, abnormal, unable to enjoy and different (Barnes, 1997).

In the UK, the medical model was originally challenged by the disabled people's movement through the proclamation from the Union of Physically Impaired Against Segregation (UPIAS) in 1976. This document proclaims that 'it is society which disables physically impaired people. Disability is something imposed on top of our impairments by the way we are unnecessarily isolated and excluded from full participation in society'(UPIAS, 1976, p. 14). This counter-argument has grown into what is now known as the social model of disability, as it was coined by the work of Michael Oliver in 1983 (Barton and Oliver, 1997). The social model of disability proposes that disability is constructed by those that are nondisabled, who create environmental barriers, socially stigmatising attitudes and discriminatory behaviour.

Holding a viewpoint akin to that suggested by the social model implies a need to evaluate our views, adopt an enabling outlook and create environments that foster inclusion. Technology has the capacity to enhance these environments but can only be implemented successfully once an enabling viewpoint has been adopted by you, the practitioner. When personal perspectives reflect postive and enabling viewpoints then we begin to focus on the possibilites instead of the problems.

Task 8.2 **Understanding your views**

Reflect on the following questions:

■ What are your personal views on special education and disability?
■ Are your views similar to those around you?
■ Are there advantages and/or disadvantages to differing views?

ADDRESSING THE NEEDS OF THE INDIVIDUAL PUPIL

The use of technology can initially support you and the pupil in identification of their needs. This may include designing assessment materials, researching SEND or computer based assessment (CBA). One example of CBA is Lucid Ability, which is a computerised system for assessing verbal and non-verbal abilities. It must be stated that many of the pre-made CBAs used for the identification of a SEND should not be used independently without a thorough evaluation of the whole pupil. In addition, merely using ready-made online resources or CBAs does not create an enabling environment. The tools must be individualised to assess the needs of the pupil.

Once the initial needs of the pupil have been clearly identified technology can be used to support and create personalised learning opportunities during whole class instruction, independent work, and social activities. However, this way of working must not be interpreted as simply identifying the needs and selecting an appropriate tool. As Bower *et al.* (2010) state, the intricate relationship between technology, content and pedagogical knowledge is complex.[3] The multifaceted relationship must be fully acknowledged in order to meet the needs of pupils and effectively integrate technology into the curriculum.

The SEN Code of Practice for England identifies four principal areas of need: communication and interaction; cognition and learning needs; behaviour, emotional and social development; and sensory and/or physical needs (DfES, 2001, p. 52). Each area of need will now be addressed individually in relation to supporting the pupil's needs with technology. However, this is not to suggest that each area of need is independent of the other as there will indeed be pupils who have additional needs in more than one area or a combination of needs.

COMMUNICATION AND INTERACTION (AUTISTIC SPECTRUM CONDITIONS, SPEECH, LANGUAGE AND COMMUNICATION NEEDS)

Depending on the needs and abilities of the pupil, technology creates opportunities to aid, develop, or teach communication. This can be in the form of augmentative and alternative communication (AAC), which includes all forms of communication except oral speech and provides pupils with a means of communicating or interacting with others. This may be in the form of gestures, signs, symbols, or written words and includes but is not limited to single message devices, static multi-message devices, text-based devices and voice amplifiers (Hodge, 2007). AAC can reduce barriers to and enable learning by providing opportunities for communication.

With the increased availability of mobile technology, the benefits for those who use AAC continue to progress. Mobile technology is becoming less expensive and the ability to adapt personal mobile devices to suit the needs of individuals is expanding. Since the release of Apple's iPad, the number of applications (apps) to support pupils with SEND has flourished and specific programs such as MyChoicePad developed in conjunction with MAKATON (a language program that uses sign and symbols to help communication) can provide the user with the ability to learn signs, make choices and express themselves. The program can save time and energy, aid listening, grab attention, promote sharing, develop vocabulary, help users make requests and aid communication partners (MyChoicePad, 2012). Similar programs to support communication include Proloquo2Go, a text-to-speech program with supporting images. This program claims to 'bring natural sounding text-to-speech voices, close to 8000 up-to-date symbols, powerful automatic conjugations, a large default vocabulary, full expandability and extreme ease of use to the iPhone, iPod touch and iPad' (Proloquo2Go, 2012).

There are limitations to implementing AAC, including the ability of pupils to operate effectively, technical problems, slowness, attitudes from others towards AAC, communication limitation of the equipment, and complexity of the device (Hodge, 2007). When selecting communication tools considerations must be given first to the physical and cognitive abilities of the pupil, the capability of the technology, and the types of communication that will occur (Blackstone *et al.*, 2007). Each selected AAC tool should be easy to operate, require limited training, limited cost, and should be personalised or adaptable. The challenge here is not to replace current methods of communication but to use technology alongside other communication systems (Hodge, 2007). This can reduce or possibly eliminate the communication barriers faced by pupils and begin to place the pupil and not the learning difficulty at the forefront of education.

Furthermore, technology has the potential to teach and aid the development of social skills for pupils that may find it difficult to socialise with peers or adults. This can be done by using software including apps that teach specific social skills, remind students of social behaviours, and encourage or develop social interactions. Apps to teach or reinforce specific social skills can provide independence for learners with learning difficulties. This also limits the singling out of some students who need reminders during social situations. Apps can allow the student to easily use reference material without feeling alienated from their peers and can promote greater inclusion.

It is important to personalise social skills programmes to ensure the needs of the pupil are being met. For example, some applications are preloaded with stories to teach social skills but they may not address the immediate needs of the pupil. However, apps such as

Stories2Learn (http://www.stories2learn.com) allow you or parents to create individualised programmes. There are many apps available to support the social needs of pupils, including Quickcues (http://www.quickcues.com) and Hidden Curriculum for Kids (http://www.aapcpublishing.net).

COGNITION AND LEARNING NEEDS (SPECIFIC LEARNING DIFFICULTIES, MODERATE LEARNING DIFFICULTIES, SEVERE LEARNING DIFFICULTIES, PROFOUND AND MULTIPLE LEARNING DIFFICULTIES)

Cognition and learning refers to a continuum of needs ranging from pupils who occasionally need one to one support to pupils who may need 24-hour one to one support. It would not be possible to explore all of the potential opportunities that technology can provide for this group of pupils, therefore this section briefly examines some key design features that you should consider when using online learning for pupils with cognition and learning needs. In addition, the possibilities of augmented reality (AR) to support this group of pupils are also explored.

Friedman and Bryen (2007, p. 208) explain the importance of design features on websites when they state, 'Well designed web pages based on web design guidelines for users with cognitive disabilities are the equivalent of requiring buildings to have ramps or sidewalk intersections to have curb cuts'. This emphasises the importance of web accessibility knowledge and understanding when creating and using online learning activities for pupils with cognition and learning needs.

The criteria provided by the Web Accessibility Initiative (WAI) provides in-depth guidance on creating and ensuring accessibility for all. These criteria are summarised in Table 8.2.

■ **Table 8.2** Extract from Web Accessibility Initiative (WAI) criteria for web accessibility

---

This section provides a summary of Web Content Accessibility Guidelines WCAG 2.0; however, it is paraphrased and it is not a definitive version.

Perceivable
Provide text alternatives for non-text content.
Provide captions and other alternatives for multimedia.
Create content that can be presented in different ways, including by assistive technologies, without losing meaning.
Make it easier for users to see and hear content.

Operable
Make all functionality available from a keyboard.
Give users enough time to read and use content.
Do not use content that causes seizures.
Help users navigate and find content.

Understandable
Make text readable and understandable.
Make content appear and operate in predictable ways.
Help users avoid and correct mistakes.

Robust
Maximise compatibility with current and future user tools.

Task 8.3 **Web accessibility criteria**

Visit the WAI website and browse the resources. Make certain you review the 'before and after' demonstration (http://www.w3.org/WAI/demos/bad/) to ensure you can identify or create accessible resources for all pupils.

Besides ensuring accessible online learning, augmented reality (AR) is emerging as a tool that can support all pupils in education but which can also contribute to the development of inclusive learning environments for pupils with cognition and learning needs. AR is an experience in which the real world is enhanced by overlaying or mixing reality and computer-generated content (Yuen *et al.*, 2011). AR can connect the pupils' virtual worlds and the real world through the use of a webcam with GPS, compass and object recognition. Although AR itself has been in existence for some time now the possibilities and practicalities of implementation are only just evolving within the field of education. Yuen *et al.* articulate the possibilities as, 'With AR, educators' dream of ubiquitous learning can become a reality' (2011, p. 120).[4]

AR can extend the learning opportunities presented for pupils and create occasions to develop authentic learning focused on the individual learning needs of the pupils within and beyond the classroom. In addition, AR can provide pupils with some control of the pace that their learning occurs at and create possibilities to engage, stimulate and motivate pupils (Yuen *et al.*, 2011). A few tools currently available include StreetMuseum (free iPhone app that allows the user to blend history and reality whilst on the streets of London), and googlesky map (free for android and lets the users interact with the stars in the sky). Furthermore, companies such as String and Magma Studios are continuing to build AR opportunities that can be used to personalise learning for pupils with cognition and learning needs.

Task 8.4 **Exploring augmented reality**

Explore the sites String (http://www.poweredbystring.com) or Magma Studios (http://www.magma-studios.com/augmented-reality-applications) to examine the current projects in augmented reality. Think about the possibilities and barriers to learning created by AR.

BEHAVIOUR, EMOTIONAL AND SOCIAL DIFFICULTIES (BESD)

The SEN Code of Practice defines BESD as 'Children and young people who demonstrate features of emotional and behavioural difficulties, who are withdrawn or isolated, disruptive and disturbing, hyperactive and lack concentration; those with immature social skills; and those presenting challenging behaviours arising from other complex special needs' (DfES, 2001, p. 87). Although this is articulated it is clear that specific characteristics associated with behaviour are well contested amongst the literature (Frederickson and Cline, 2010). With varying interpretations of pupils with BESD it is again important to adopt an enabling outlook by identifying the needs of the pupil to create an environment where the technology is available to support the pupil's needs. This provision can include, but is not limited to, teaching pupil behaviour, positive reinforcement, matching curriculum and ability, ensuring high rates of success, structured transition between activities and self-regulation (Sugai and Horner, 2002).

Self-regulation is an area that can be quickly and inexpensively supported by technology to aid practitioners and/or pupils. Self-regulation or self-management is defined as the 'personal application of behavior change tactics that produce a desired change in behavior' (Cooper *et al.*, 2007, as cited in Joseph and Konrad, 2009, p. 246) and so is about encouraging students to take control of their learning and support academic success.

A few practical technology based methods to support self-regulation include reminder and organisational tools. Many silent reminder/stopwatch/clock functions or specific apps (Motiv®Aider) on a mobile phone can be set to vibrate at given intervals to remind students to complete a self-regulation task. In addition, organisational tools such as Evernote can be used for setting goals, graphing performance or recording written information regarding behaviour. Iprompts, developed by handholdadaptive (http://www.handholdadaptive.com/iprompts.html), which provide picture schedules, visual countdown timers and choices between images, can provide additional organisational opportunities to support self-regulation. Finally, verbal recordings on apps such as Voice Notes or iTalk Recorder can help students to make verbal records of their on task and off task behaviour. This is not an exhaustive list of methods to support self-regulation but is rather a starting point for examining methods to support the specific needs of pupils with BESD.

SENSORY AND/OR PHYSICAL NEEDS (VISUAL IMPAIRMENT, HEARING IMPAIRMENT, MULTI-SENSORY IMPARIMENT AND PHYSICAL DISABILITY)

There is a plethora of assistive technologies to support pupils with additional sensory or physical needs that create enabling environments. A majority are free to download or are built into many websites, PDAs and apps. Examples include large keyboards, a simple-to-operate computer mouse, a virtual magnifying glass, text-to-speech programs and speech-to-text programs. However, with so many different resources available, all of them in a state of constant change and development, there is understandably a limited body of literature evaluating the 'success and performance' of assistive technologies (Jutai *et al.*, 2009, p. 219). A deficit in research surrounding the impact of technology-based tools to support pupils with physical or sensory needs may not necessarily be a negative as this does demonstrate the choice and variation in assistive technologies available (Jutai *et al.*, 2009).

The programs or applications mentioned all provide access to the curriculum; however, teachers must also take into consideration the possibility that technology can also become a barrier to accessing the curriculum and create further tensions. Slobodzian (2009) explains how the use of YouTube in the classroom has been seen as one method to bring the larger world into the classroom; however, teachers must realise that many aspects may not be accessible to students with visual or hearing impairments. YouTube has made closed captioning an option for those creating videos and in the search options teachers can filter results that include videos with closed captioning. For full details see http://www.youtube.com/t/captions_about.

KEEPING UP-TO-DATE

In the complex and rapidly changing areas of SEND and technology keeping up to date in both fields can often be difficult. One method that can support you in this is the use of systems like Twitter.[5] The benefits of Twitter for teachers include short easy to read statements, options to obtain further information, and a large number of contributors in the area of SEND and technology. You can create an account and follow government RSS feeds such as the Department of Education (USA) at https://twitter.com/usedgov or the Department for Education (UK) at https://twitter.com/educationgovuk. You can also follow disability support organisations such as Autism Speaks at https://twitter.com/autismspeaks or British Dyslexia at https://twitter.com/bdadyslexia.

In addition, school, community and international forums such as http://www.tes.co.uk/forums or teachers.net provides opportunities for sharing knowledge and can contribute to your ability to keep up to date. Forums can be used at any time, providing unique opportunities to create extended learning environments suitable to your schedule. Hence professional online spaces such as the special educational needs coordinators (SENCO) or special educational needs information technology (SENIT) forums can provide knowledge from experienced professionals, opportunities to share best practices and a space to obtain resources.[6]

E-SAFETY AND SEND

As technology and exposure to online resources continues to develop so does the dilemma regarding online safety for pupils. The 2007 UK Byron Review (DCSF, 2008) increased political awareness of the potential risks associated with the internet and more recently Spielhofer (2010) suggest knowledge and understanding in the area of online safety has developed. There is still, however, a need for further research. Specifically, more data is needed regarding risks to children with SEND, teachers' knowledge and understanding of methods to safeguard children, and how to teach online safety skills to pupils.

In a survey of over 2,000 secondary schools conducted by BeatBullying, the charity suggests that overall incidents of cyber bullying are not different amongst those with and without statements of SEN. However, pupils with SEN are 16 per cent more likely to be persistently cyberbullied. The charity defines persistent as 'happening day in, day out, over a period of months or sometimes years' (Cross *et al.*, 2009, p. 5). The types of incidents reported included hoax mobile calls, hurtful text or emails, and unkind messages on social networking profiles (Cross *et al.*, 2009). Furthermore, Childnet International describes specific risks for pupils with SEND and these include difficulties with terminology due to language delays, interpretation of content or interactions, understanding of safe and acceptable information to share, or some children may not realise that their behaviour online might be viewed differently by the receiver and therefore may be interpreted as bullying or even sexual harassment.

The awareness that some pupils may encounter additional risks online is not to suggest technology-based resources should be blocked but that enabling environments may need to be created for some pupils with SEND. In the UK the national organisation JISC (originally the UK national Joint Information Systems Committee) suggests vulnerable pupils should be 'empowered to take responsibility for their actions and to manage the risks'. See for example http://www.jisctechdis.ac.uk/techdis/investinyourself/equality/vulnerableusers. You can obtain support and resources regarding online safety from organisations such as Childnet International. For example, the 'Know IT All Secondary Toolkit' provides PowerPoint presentations, films and games to teach online safety topics such as plagiarism, copyright, cyber bullying, grooming, safe use of social networks, digital citizenship and designing safe passwords.

SUMMARY

This chapter has discussed how the use of technology can support the individual needs of pupils with SEND and promote the social model of disability by creating enabling environments. Enabling environments can be created by addressing attitudes, clearly identifying the needs of the individual pupils, and using appropriate tools to meet their needs. A range of pupil needs were explored based on the SEND Code of Practice (COP) (England) and four areas of need and appropriate technology and resources were identified. In addition, online safety and methods to keep up to date in the field were acknowledged. Finally, as the technology market continues to grow and more choices become available you may become overwhelmed with choice. Use your knowledge of pupils' creativity and select the appropriate support tool that creates an enabling environment.

ACKNOWLEDGEMENTS

The contribution of Yota Dimitriadi and Nick Peacey to earlier editions of the SEND chapter for this book are acknowledged.

FURTHER READING

Florian, L. and Hegarty, J. (2004) *ICT and Special Educational Needs*, Maidenhead: Open University Press.

    A key text for anyone seeking further information on the area of technology and special needs. Includes information on staff development, virtual learning environments, computer based assessment, historical information, management of special education and whole school approaches to technology and special education.

Loreman, T., Deppeler, J. and Harvey, D. (2010) *Inclusive Education: Supporting Diversity in the Classroom*, Oxon: Routledge.

    This book provides an overview of practical methods to support inclusive practice in a mainstream setting. The text draws on current research in the field and provides an overview of creating enabling environments.

Hodkinson, A. and Vickerman, P. (2009) *Key Issues in Special Educational Needs and Inclusion*, London: SAGE.

    This book provides a solid foundation for further inquiry in the area of special education. It presents an in-depth discussion on contextualising special education, historical and international perspectives. In addition it provides numerous case study examples to exemplify the content.

RECOMMENDED WEBSITES

http://www.jisctechdis.ac.uk

    The UK advisory service on technology and special education. This site provides information on current research initiatives in the area of special education and technology. It also provides links to online courses, events and current news.

http://www.ed.gov
    The US Department of Education website provides a starting place for further information on best practices in teaching, current news, funding and also government guidelines in education.

http://www.futurelab.org.uk
    Futurelab is an independent not for profit organisation that supports innovative approaches to education with technology. This is accomplished through research, school development projects and continuing professional development opportunities. The site has a wide range of resources to support classroom practices through the use of technology.

http://www.education.gov.uk
    The Department for Education is responsible for education and children's services in England. Resources on current research, policies, and statutory guidance are available.

http://www.disability.gov/technology
    This site provides general information on assistive technologies and funding for each state in the USA. It has an in-depth section on creating accessible documents. The website also presents information on health, housing, benefits, community life and education. This provides you with an overview of services and information regarding disability.

NOTES

1   For further discussion see Hodkinson and Vickerman, 2009, Chapter 5.
2   For further discussion see Armstrong *et al.*, 2011.
3   For further information visit TPACK (Technological Pedagogical and Content Knowledge) at http://www.tpck.org.
4   For further details see Hamilton (2011).
5   For further guidance on setting up a twitter account for education see Anderson (2011) or http://edudemic.com/2010/06/the-ultimate-twitter-guidebook.
6   For further information see the DfE mailing list at http://lists.education.gov.uk/mailman/listinfo.

REFERENCES

Anderson, S. (2011) 'The twitter toolbox for educators', *Teacher Librarian* 39(1): 27–30.

Armstrong, D., Armstrong, A. and Spandagou, I. (2011) 'Inclusion: by choice or by chance?', *International Journal of Inclusive Education* 15(1): 29–39.

Barnes, C. (1997) 'A legacy of oppression: a history of disability in western culture', in L. Barton and M. Oliver, *Disability Studies: Past, Present and Future*, Leeds: The Disability Press.

Barnes, C., Oliver, M. and Barton, L. (2002) *Disability Studies Today*, Cambridge: Polity Press.

Barton, L. and Oliver, M. (1997) *Disability Studies: Past, Present and Future*, Leeds: The Disability Press.

BECTA (2003) *What the Research Says About ICT Supporting Special Educational Needs and Inclusion*. Available at: http://www.mmiweb.org.uk/publications/ict/Research_Barriers_TandL.pdf (accessed 9 September 2010).

——(2007) *The Impact of ICT in Schools: A Landscape Review*. Available at: http://dera.ioe.ac.uk/1627/ (accessed 18 March 2011).

——(2009) *Harnessing Technology Schools Survey: Analysis Report*. Available at: http://dera.ioe.ac.uk/1546/1/becta_2009_htssreport_report.pdf (accessed 4 February 2012).

Blackstone, S., Williams, M. and Wilkins, D. (2007) 'Key principles underlying research and practice in AAC', *AAC: Augmentative and Alternative Communication* 23: 191–203.

Bower, M., Hedberg, J. and Kuswara, A. (2010) 'Framework for Web 2.0 learning design', *Educational Media International* 47(3): 177–98.

Cross, E., Richardson, B., Douglas, T. and Vonkaenel-Flatt, J. (2009) *Virtual Violence: Protecting Children from Bullying*, London: Beatbullying.

DCSF (2008) *Safer Children in a Digital World: The Report of the Byron Review*. Available at: http://www.education.gov.uk/publications/standard/publicationdetail/page1/DCSF-00334-2008 (accessed 2 February 2012).

DES (1978) *Special Educational Needs: Report of the Committee of Enquiry into the Education of Handicapped Children and Young People* ('The Warnock Report'), London: HMSO.

DfE (2011a) 'Support and aspiration: a new approach to special educational needs and disability - a consultation'. Available at: http://www.education.gov.uk/publications/standard/publicationDetail/Page1/CM%208027 (accessed 9 January 2012).

DfE (2011b) *Including all Learners*. Available at: http://www.education.gov.uk/schools/teachingandlearning/curriculum/b00199686/inclusion (accessed 6 February 2012).

DfES (2001) *Special Education Needs: Code of Practice*. Available at: http://www.education.gov.uk/publications/standard/publicationDetail/Page1/DfES%200581%202001 (accessed 10 November 2011).

European Commission: Ministerial Declaration, Riga, Latvia (June 11, 2006) Available at: http://ec.europa.eu/information_society/activities/einclusion/events/riga_2006/index_en.htm (accessed 29 August 2012).

Florian, L. and Hegarty, J. (2004) *ICT and Special Educational Needs*, Maidenhead: Open University Press.

Frederickson, N. and Cline, T. (2009) *Special Educational Needs, Inclusion and Diversity*, Maidenhead: Open University Press.

Friedman, M. and Bryen, D. (2007) 'Web accessibility design recommendations for people with cognitive disabilities', *Technology and Disability* 19: 205–12.

Glazzard, J. (2011) 'Perceptions of the barriers to effective inclusion in one primary school: voices of teachers and teaching assistants', *Support for Learning* 26(2): 56–63.

Hamilton, K. (2011) *Augmented Reality in Education*. Available at: http://wik.ed.uiuc.edu/index.php/Augmented_Reality_in_Education (accessed 4 February 2012).

Hodge, S. (2007) 'Why is the potential of augmentative and alternative communication not being realized? Exploring the experiences of people who use communication aids', *Disability and Society*, 22: 457–71.

Hodkinson, A. and Vickerman, P. (2009) *Key Issues in Special Educational Needs and Inclusion*, London: SAGE.

Iprompts (2012) Available at: http://www.handholdadaptive.com/iprompts.html (accessed 6 February 2012).

JISC (2012) 'Working with vulnerable users'. Available at: http://www.jisctechdis.ac.uk/techdis/investinyourself/equality/vulnerableusers (accessed 3 January 2012).

Johnstone, D. (2001) *An Introduction to Disability Studies*, London: David Fulton.

Joseph, L. and Konrad, M. (2009) 'Help students self-manage their academic performance', *Intervention in School and Clinic* 44(4): 246–9.

Jutai, J.W., Strong, J.G. and Russell-Minda, E. (2009) 'Effectiveness of assistive technologies for low vision rehabilitation: a systematic review', *Journal of Visual Impairment and Blindness* 103(4): 210–22.

Leng, N.W. (2011) 'Reliability and validity of an information and communications technology attitude scale for teachers', *The Asia-Pacific Education Researcher*, 20(1): 162–70.

Magma Studios (2012) Available at: http://www.magma-studios.com/augmented-reality-applications (accessed 9 January 2012).

Motiv®Aider (2012) Available at: http://habitchange.com/motivaider-for-mobile.php (accessed 6 February 2012).

MyChoicePad (2012) Available at: http://www.mychoicepad.com (accessed 9 January 2012).

Proloquo2Go (2012) Available at: http://www.proloquo2go.com (accessed 9 January 2012).

Slobodzian, J.T. (2009) 'Film and video technology: issues of access for hard of hearing and deaf students', *Journal of Special Education Technology* 24(4): 54–9.

Spielhofer, T. (2010) *Children's Online Risks and Safety: A Review of the Available Evidence*, Slough: NFER.

Stories2Learn (2012) Available at: http://www.stories2learn.com/about.php (accessed 6 February 2012).

String (2012) Available at: http://www.poweredbystring.com (accessed 6 February 2012).

Sugai, G. and Horner, R. (2002) 'The evolution of discipline practices: school-wide positive behavior supports', *Child and Family Behavior Therapy* 24(1/2): 23–50.

Sze, S. (2009) 'A literature review: pre-service teachers' attitudes toward students with disabilities', *Education* 130(1): 53–6.

UPIAS (1976) *Fundamental Principles of Disability*, London: Union of the Physically Impaired Against Segregation.

Web Accessibility Initiative (WAI) (2011) Available at: http://www.w3.org/WAI (accessed 6 February 2012).

Yuen, S., Yaoyuneyong, G. and Johnson, E. (2011) 'Augmented reality: an overview and five directions for AR in education', *Journal of Educational Technology Development and Exchange* 4(1): 119–40.

HUNTING DOWN THE MONSTER: USING MULTI-PLAY DIGITAL GAMES AND ONLINE VIRTUAL WORLDS IN SECONDARY SCHOOL TEACHING

Nic Crowe and Sara Flynn

INTRODUCTION

James Paul Gee (2003) observes, somewhat controversially, that whilst much of technology-based learning has a reputation for being dull and ineffective, games have developed a reputation for being fun, engaging, and immersive, requiring deep thinking and complex problem solving. In this chapter we use material drawn from a much wider piece of research about young people's use of digital spaces to explore some of the education possibilities provided by computer/console-based game arenas (such as *Call of Duty Modern Warfare*, *Arkham City* and *The Elder Scrolls*) and digital game worlds (for example *World of Warcraft*, *Eve* and *Runescape*). ICT has traditionally had a role within the curriculum in promoting and facilitating the skills required to develop independent learning. As ICT moves ever-increasingly to an integrated cross-curricula position, one of the challenges for you as a teacher is to explore exciting and innovative ways that new technologies might contribute to teaching and learning.

It has long been recognised that education is more than the mere transfer of information or knowledge (Mezirow, 2000). As you will have read elsewhere in this book, successful learning is often based on how engaged your pupils actually are. This in turn raises questions as to the personalised nature of learning tasks and activities. Arguably some of the most exciting and popular technological forms to emerge in recent years have been the range of virtual social spaces and narratives suggested by Digital Game Worlds. Multi-play gaming (playing alongside other gamers via an internet or LAN connection) is a highly interactive experience incorporating complex layers of cooperative and competitive play and problem solving. It is perhaps surprising then that more hasn't been made of the opportunities offered by these texts to many areas of the curriculum.

OBJECTIVES

By the end of this chapter you should:

■ have an understanding of the educational possibilities offered by digital games and virtual worlds;
■ be able to identify the range of digital gaming spaces that could be used to support teaching and learning;
■ have considered some examples of teaching strategies that could be used or adapted to your own teaching and learning scenarios.

WHY DIGITAL GAMES?

Young people have always been early adopters of this type of technology (Rainie and Horrigan, 2005) and digital games are undeniably popular. By early 2011 the digital games market was estimated to be worth $48.9 billions, exceeding the sales of both books and popular music (PricewaterhouseCoopers, 2010). Digital games are now an important aspect of young people's leisure. The research project *UK Children Go Online* (UKCGO) (Livingstone and Bober, 2005) aimed to offer a rigorous and timely investigation of 9- to 19-year-olds' use of computers and the internet. The authors highlighted that 82 per cent of this age group have at least one games console, and that 70 per cent play digital games online. This survey also acknowledged that most young people spend nearly as much time playing video/computer games as they do engaged with homework (Livingstone and Bober, 2005). By 2010, regular game usage had risen to 91 per cent in the 12–15 year age bracket (OFCOM, 2011).

The UK government-commissioned Byron Review follow up (2010), recognised that engaging with digital technology – including digital gaming – was becoming an ordinary aspect of childhood. Yet despite this apparent 'domesticity', computer games have been largely absent from the curriculum. We find this resistance puzzling. Prensky (2001) accuses teaching professionals of being reluctant to engage with any form of digital technology that is relatively recent and unfamiliar. Of course such fears are not new: popular technology has always been criticised for imposing 'entertainment modality' on learning environments (see Postman, 1985; Greenwald and Rosner, 2003) but, as Taylor (2006) observes, digital worlds provide users with a chance to live differently, and through that living, play. We would further observe that it is through this act of virtual 'play' that opportunities for learning arise (Squire, 2005). Whilst there are a great many 'proprietary' ('educational') games out there, we suggest that more satisfying and effective learning takes place when teachers use 'commercial' (leisure-based) digital games that their pupils are already engaged with. The unique opportunity that this can offer you, as a teacher of ICT, is that the games are so well embedded into the everyday lives of your pupils. As Davies (2005) acknowledges, the most effective education practitioner starts from where young people 'are' – their contemporary experiences – and then seeks to move them beyond this position.

COMPUTER GAMES IN YOUR CLASSROOM?

What we want you to consider in this chapter then is the idea that, as with any other form of 'play', digital gaming can form the basis of effective and purposeful education-based interventions. One of the central themes of curriculum-based ICT is that it encourages problem solving and independent learning. Problem solving is regarded as a key skill for life-long learning (Hoskins and Fredriksson, 2008). Writing in America, both Gee (2007; Gee and Hayes, 2009) and Squire (2005) have been leading exponents of the idea that digital games teach players to become problem solvers. In well-designed games, the player can only advance to a higher level (or unlock more desirable equipment/resources) by testing out a range of different approaches and strategies. So for example in the popular *Tomb Raider* series the next level is only 'unlocked' once a pre-determined set of criteria is met: Lara Croft must 'kill' the monster, solve the code, get to the building on the other side of the ravine. The game requires the player to ask questions such as 'What happens if I do this?', 'Where does this go?', 'What do I need to do next?'. Successful completion of the game requires lateral thinking and the ability to solve increasingly complex problems. Since the game is developmental – it gets harder the further into it you get – players are required to 'learn' the skills and knowledge that they require to solve the next challenge. One of the key aspects of the most complex games is that players need to learn to cope with the rigours of the virtual world, thus one of the functions of digital games is that users are being 'taught' to 'learn'.

In narrative-driven genres such as 'Online Role Playing Games (often termed MMORPG[1] or MMO[2] where the emphasis is on character and skills development rather than special advancement) or popular shooters such as the *Call of Duty: Modern Warfare* series, there are opportunities for you to help your pupils explore and 'test out' a range of alternate narrative and/or character-related issues and problems. So for example in *Fable* or *Hard Rain* each in-game decision (for example choosing whether to be 'good' or 'bad', whether to 'assist' or 'ignore' another character) carries deep significance and real consequence as to how the future narrative unfolded. Games such as *The Sims* series, *HomeFront*, *Arkham City*, even the controversial *Grand Theft Auto* and *Saints Row* series, teach principles of representation, morality, narrative development, interactive skills and aspects of literacy, numeracy and simulation, in situated, experiential ways, that might not be possible – or as accessible – using other texts or forms. As Gee notes, good digital games will teach your pupils 'to solve problems and reflect on the intricacies of the design of imagined worlds and the design of both real and imagined social relationships and identities in the modern world' (2003, p. 48).

Task 9.1 **Identifying pupils' experience of online games**

Take some time to talk to your pupils about the sorts of digital games that they like to play. Can you notice any similarities and differences? Discuss with them the particular pleasures of playing different types of games. Are there different types of enjoyment? Try to include the thoughts of pupils who may not be so familiar or committed to gaming. Are there any pupils who during the process of working with gaming technology have developed new skills they can identify and talk about?

LEARNING AND THE PSYCHOLOGY OF DIGITAL PLAY

In his discussions of child development the psychologist Lev Vygotsky describes play as 'the imaginary, illusory realization of unrealizable desires' (1933, NP). Play is a process through which children make sense of their world. It offers opportunities to explore some aspects of culture that might be impossible in their everyday life. It is through such fantasy that children come to develop a greater sense of meaning and purpose about their own lives. (Bettelheim, 1976). So by structuring learning in play, we are also facilitating active engagement in fantasy and activity that would not otherwise be possible. Crawford (1982) acknowledges, the fundamental motivation for playing games is a desire to learn:

> Games are thus the most ancient and time-honored vehicle for education. They are the original educational technology, the natural one, having received the seal of approval of natural selection. We don't see mother lions lecturing cubs at the chalkboard; we don't see senior lions writing their memoirs for posterity. In light of this, the question, 'Can games have educational value?' becomes absurd. It is not games but schools that are the newfangled notion, the untested fad, the violator of tradition. Game-playing is a vital educational function for any creature capable of learning.
>
> (Crawford, 1982, p. 16)

But Vygotsky also reminds us that this process is not necessarily inherent in children. It arises from, and is developed by, culturally informed action. We suggest that by using digital gaming technology, children can create developmental environments that support them to do what might seem beyond them, thus unifying the process of learning and developing. Digital-based play encourages children to try new things alongside doing things that are familiar to them. In other words, they are pushing themselves forward, expanding their knowledge base and learning as a result. Very young children do this constantly and we encourage it, through speaking, reading, drawing, etc. Introducing games into the arena allows for children to reshape and transform environments. The computer or console becomes a tool that helps produce results through activity in much the same way as other forms of play, as Emily explains:

> In RPG (Role Playing Games) like *Runescape* if you want better equipment then you are going to have work at making stuff – swords, armour, fishing food and stuff like that. But you can't just do anything, you need to know what people want and at what price to sell it at. Also, you don't want to make too much of one thing – or what everyone else is making – 'cos then people don't want to buy your goods. I made a lot of Runescape gold doing this. It makes you feel good 'cos I am never good at this stuff in class but I think it's easier to use your imagination on here. In school you have to do it like your teacher wants.
>
> Emily (14)

Digital games also offer new possibilities beyond the traditional play-based contexts:

> You can't play this game on your own, you have to learn to get on with people and to develop new skills that help everyone in your group not just what is good for yourself.
>
> Nathan (13)

Good games are challenging – I don't mean hard, I mean you have to think. You know, really think! Not just about how to solve immediate problems like how to get to the next level, but you also have to think long term. That sword looks very tasty now, buuuutt … should I wait and save for something better? Should I help that guy now so that later in the game he might help me? You have to learn to think beyond the immediate problem! That's what this taught me.

Vikkii (14)

The above quotes from two young online gamers illustrate that playing digital games is a complex process involving a range of both short- and long-term strategies. Games need to be *learnt* and for the dedicated this is a considered and deliberate process in which short-term individual and emotional responses/pleasures often need to be put aside for long-term success. In this context, learning might be conceived as a *social* activity. It occurs not just through diegetic engagement with the game narrative but more significantly within, and through, the interaction with other players. Interactions between players is a fundamental feature of all online games (Ashton, 2009; Wright *et al.*, 2002) and such interpersonal communication is particularly important to child development since 'Learning awakens a variety of internal developmental processes that are able to operate only when the child is interacting with people in his environment and in cooperation with his peers' (Vygotsky, 1978, p. 90).

In online gaming, success relies as much on collaborative skill as it does on individual ability. Learning how to play the game well – being a 'skilled' player – is obviously important. Digital games might be regarded as effective learning systems since one of their central functions is to teach users to competently engage with its game play (Gee, 2007). One of the things that we have found fascinating as teachers is the way that some young people seemingly excel at the rigours of playing a game with friends but struggle with areas of the curriculum that draw on intrinsically similar skills and knowledge.[3] The Zone of Proximal Development (ZPD)[4] is arguably a factor here since critical functions 'can be most effectively developed through the creative function' (Burn and Durran, 2007, p. 108) but so too is the context in which such development takes place. Digital gaming might therefore be seen as a socially constructed medium offering better access to the ZPD. The nature of the participation in a game may allow those students who face obstacles (such as low self-esteem, lack of support, lack of confidence, fear of failure) to explore new territories, take chances, and endeavour to meet new challenges and potentially attain higher levels of success in a safe environment in which they feel less likely to fail and be openly judged.

Digital games and 'flow'

The popularity of digital games is a significant factor in their potential to offer learning opportunities in the classroom. Yet good digital games also represent 'microworlds' that provide immersive arenas within which play – and hence learning – can take place (De Freitas, 2006). Csikszentmihalyi (1975, 1990) put forward the concept of 'flow', which he identified as the complete engagement in an activity. Flow encompasses many characteristics:

- A challenging activity that requires skills: This requires a fine balance: too high a challenge will produce anxiety; too easy an activity will produce boredom (Pearce and Artemesia, 2009).
- Clear goals and feedback: Good, immediate feedback allows the individual to know they have succeeded. This is a defining feature of all games – they are often regarded as 'rule-based' systems (Caillois, 1961).
- Concentration on the task at hand: When one is thoroughly absorbed.
- A sense of control.
- Loss of self-consciousness: The individual feels s/he is merging with the activity.

Lets us consider how flow might work when using digital games in the classroom. In a study involving 32 schools across Scotland, Miller and Robertson (2008) demonstrate how children's skill and enthusiasm for mathematics could be significantly increased by using the Nintendo game *Dr. Kawashima's Brain Training* for just 30 minutes a day. They identified improvements in pupils' attitude to school: truanting and lateness dropped, children began to take a more supportive interest in the performance of peers and the pupils regarded themselves as 'smarter' as a result of using the game. We see here how aspects of flow might impact on the success of the children in this study. Did those children who made the most improvement do so because they felt more comfortable in the task they were performing? Are they less self-conscious, maybe feeling more confident in their own abilities? They are immersed in an activity in which, to some extent, they are anonymous. The awareness of others and what they are doing and achieving is less evident and, therefore, less intimidating. This may see them pushing themselves further than they would normally feel confident doing in a regular mathematics lesson and also enjoying it more.

The participants in the above study were already familiar with the Nintendo console. It was popular and we suspect provided a welcome break from 'normal' lessons.[5] It is perhaps of little surprise then that the children responded so positively, since learning is seen to flourish where the cultivation of passionate interest was a primary educational goal. Here is a similar example from our work with an English class:

> Yeah, I couldn't do the poetry and stuff it was just dull. But then I started to talk to my mentor about COD[6] and what it was like to fight in those games. This got me thinking about some of the stuff that the war poets wrote about and I went back and read them again. It made English come alive for once, I even had a go writing something about HALO which I put up on the school blog.
>
> Tyrone (14)

> I kept a diary of all my *Monster Hunter* quests. I wrote in that book everyday for two terms, it was actually quite good fun [laughs].
>
> Kyle (13)

Enjoyment is a central theme of this approach. Gee and Hayes (2009) extend flow in their discussions of 'affinity spaces' to identify arenas in which young people congregate around common passions. This positivity can then be directed to facilitate curriculum-based learning. The enthusiasm with which Tyrone and Kyle approached war games provided them with a doorway to an enjoyment of lessons that they had not experienced before and for Tyrone it gave him the confidence to try something new.

> ## Task 9.2 **Ethics, barriers and educational benefits**
>
> Think about introducing digital games into an area of your curriculum. What might be the educational benefits to your students? What might be some of the obstacles to using them in class? Can you think of any ethical or safety concerns? How might these be overcome? What about pupils who have no interest in gaming?

USING ON-LINE DIGITAL GAMES EDUCATIONALLY

Up until now we have been talking very generally about the educational benefits of digital games. In the second half of this chapter we want to consider some practical examples of how these might be used as a tool for learning. It is worth pointing out from the start that we are not asking you to devote all your lessons in school to the playing of computer games. Although this might be appropriate in some settings, there are many reasons why this might not be practical or desirable in your classroom. Games can still provide a focus for learning when they are not played in school.[7] Indeed it might be argued that to attempt to simulate in the classroom what is intrinsically an out-of-school leisure activity might have a de-focusing effect if tasks are over-directed, as one class warns us:

> It started off as fun, you know, a way to feel like you weren't doing work, but when we got to the end I found I was getting bored. It's not like your own space its just more school innit.
>
> Jacob (13)

> Mr P kept getting us to do things – finish this level, get that quest done – but he didn't realise that it wasn't the way that I played the game. I would rather he had left me alone to play it at home.
>
> Graham (12)

One teacher told us that he had found from bitter experience that 'game-playing is best left to the bedroom and class time better devoted to discussions and tasks that drew on pupils' game-playing experiences'. This is not to say that short game-sequences shouldn't form part of lessons (indeed it would be a shame if they didn't) or that game play cannot be adequately undertaken in the classroom (we have seen instances where it has formed a really effective and focused learning task) but caution about how you would manage pupil use of game technology, or resistance to the idea of playing games *in school,* need not be a barrier to explore how it might contribute to teaching and learning more generally.

HUNTING MONSTERS

In keeping with a cross-curricula agenda perhaps the easiest way to introduce games technology into the classroom is to use the texts themselves as a focus for more established areas of the curriculum. We noted earlier how the first-person war simulator *Call of Duty* was used to encourage young men to become more engaged in the English curriculum. Activision's *Call of Duty: Modern Warfare* is at the time of writing one of the most popular games franchise, particularly amongst boys. Closely mirroring world events, the series offers sophisticated narratives involving complex characters, utilising a range of narrative devices and perspectives. We can see direct parallels between such narratives and those of traditional literature (Harushimana, 2008). Similar games such as Kaos Studio's *Homefront* (written by *Apocalypse Now* writer John Milius) and Bethesda's *Elder Scrolls* franchise offer equally well-developed narratives. Blizzard's *World of Warcraft* and Jagex *Runescape* (perhaps some of the most popular online role playing games amongst young people) draw on Tolkienesque narratives and settings. This inter-textuality represents an aspect of 'trans-media storytelling' (Jenkins, 2004) in which narratives interact across a range of platforms and media. Since you can 'apply all those classic themes we have come to love in the English department: gender roles, class struggle, treatment of children, guest–host relationships, etc., to any video game story' (Hidey 2006: NP) such texts offer a wealth of opportunity to explore a range of traditional literary forms.

> I played the Strike at Karkand level in *Battlefield 2* and then for homework I had to make comparisons between that and a memory written by a soldier in the war. 'Cos I play the game it helped the words on the page come alive – I knew what it was like to have bullets flying over your head [laughs].
>
> Justine (14)

> I was playing *Dawn of War*, we had to imagine what qualities the leader of the Space Marines would have, so why his men were loyal, what campaigns he had fought in, why he could be kind but ruthless at the same time.
>
> Harry (13)

We can see again here how using a pupil's ordinary and everyday gaming experience is used to ground aspects of literacy. One of the most interesting projects we observed in this respect was the use of the Capcom game *Monster Hunter* with a group of Key Stage 3 students in an after-school 'booster' club. *Monster Hunter Freedom* is a fantasy action role-playing game in which players band together to hunt mythical monsters. It offers over 400 missions, 1,500 weapons and 2,000 armour sets, with trade and commerce options being an integral aspect of game-play. The narrative is complex and immersive, requiring that players not only engage with the diegesis but also develop their in-game characters and are thus rewarded for expressions of 'social' and 'cooperative' modes of play.

The teachers set a range of learning tasks that focused on literacy. These included:

■ A diary to track their 'monster hunting' activities. This task was designed to boost creative writing. The pupils were encouraged to imagine that their in-game activities were real and the diary was a journal of their adventures. As well as recording 'factual' information about each hunt, children were also asked to comment on the roles and character of each member of their party, how they felt during a particular adventure or what they hoped to achieve in the future. Because of the immersive nature and longevity of the game the journal represented a large piece of work. This not only had the effect of helping the pupils to become more focused on their work but also acted as a resource with which teachers could work with children over a sustained period identifying areas where their work had improved.

- Media literacy. One of the most popular aspects of the project was producing news reports about various 'hunt' activities. Pupils were encouraged to produce newspaper front pages – including screenshot photographs and interviews with 'stars' or witnesses – and to write scripts for radio and television reports. This encouraged appropriate use of language and other media/multi-modal skills.

- Recruiting a 'Monster Squad'. One of the interesting dimensions of game-play is that *Monster Hunter* encourages hunters to team up in order to slay the largest beasts. The pupils organised themselves into formal arrangements called guilds and clans. Each had its own particular identity and competition between them was lively. Teachers encouraged each guild to build its own separate identity and to develop materials to 'persuade' other members to join. This task was designed to encourage language development – particularly persuasive and creative modes – and key skills in design.

Throughout the project, teachers drew parallels between the virtual narrative and 'real-world' texts. The young people were also required to read examples from literature as a means of helping to further stimulate their work. Despite having an after-school slot, the project was popular and the participants spoke positively about their achievements:

> As you get further on it gets harder. More and bigger monsters, you know. Then you need the best, equipped hunters and the most experienced ones. We designed some recruitment posters and leaflets to put online to get people to join our clan. I used some of them for my English coursework. My teacher was well surprised.
>
> Lance (13)

> I kept a diary of all my adventures. I used to do it every night. Only time I ever did that, could never do my homework, but this was different 'cos I was interested.
>
> Si (13)

> The games are really just like books, but books that you can live in yourself … which I think helped me understand things when we had to read in class. I would pretend the character was one in a game that I controlled. It helped me to think through why they might have done things like that, or why things happened the way they did. It's just more interesting than words on a page!
>
> Emily (13)

As Emily shows us, the novelty of a more accessible form of narrative is clearly a factor in the ease with which these pupils transferred game-based skills to their studies. Digital games have traditionally been caught in a tension between narratology (games as 'stories') and ludology (games as formal rule-based systems or 'simulations'). Most modern games – *Monster Hunter* included – allow players to modify levels of difficulty and other aspects of the game environment (such as characters and equipment), all of which help stimulate an insight into the ways that simulations are constructed. But it would be wrong to simply regard digital games as simulations of the 'real world'. Parker (2004) suggests that the 'realism' of games lies not in the ability to simulate the material world as an aesthetic, but in its accurate re-creation of material social processes.

In this respect, games also offer the possibility to develop transferable life-skills. One 'monster hunter' tells us:

> I am like the trader on here. I get the stuff and then sell it to the others [laughs] – it's like a business. But it taught me to know the value of things. So, like, if you price something too high then no one buys, you are gonna be left with loads of stuff that no one wants. Then you are well out of pocket and can't afford more stuff to sell … I know it don't seem much, but us kids don't get the chance to do this sorta thing … made me feel grown or something. It also helped with my maths [laughs] who would'a believed that!
>
> Jordan (13)

One of the benefits of digital technology is that it affords pupils the opportunity to experience and experiment with many of the institutions and structures of the 'adult' world (Crowe, 2011). These are often not available elsewhere in the lives of young people. Compared with many aspects of the school environment, digital play represents a 'safe' arena in which to engage in or 'test out' 'worldly' practices, reflecting the wider ICT theme of independent learning:

> My worker, helped me see how some of the stuff I did on here could help me in school. It seems obvious now, but no one gave us the chance before.
>
> Jon (13)

But they also teach interpersonal skills and teamwork. One thing the 'monster hunters' soon realised was that working as a reliable member of a group was key to in-game success:

> I had never thought much about this before, just done my own thing, you know. But if you are part of a clan you gotta be reliable, you know, punctual, do what you say you will, that sort of thing. If you have arranged a hunt the others in your party are relying on you to be there, and you lose kudos if you let them down.
>
> Lance (13)

What was perhaps more surprising was that staff noticed a similar commitment begin to seep into their attitude to school – the group seemed more committed to their studies, punctuality increased, inter-personal skills appeared to increase. Perhaps we should not be surprised since it is often the way that students *feel* about their learning experience that affects their engagement with their studies, and this need not be based on how they are *actually* performing (Zhang *et al.*, 2005). As we noted earlier in the chapter, Miller and Robertson (2008) made similar observations in their study. It appears that the affinity and commitment generated by a digital game is a potent motivating factor:

> All kids want is to be interested. Once I got interested, and my teachers were interested in me, and in what I was good at, life was sweet.
>
> Manni (13)

Task 9.3 **Class tasks related to concepts in gaming**

Try some of these easy tasks with your pupils:

■ You have created an avatar. Explain why you have chosen to create him/her in the way that you have. What characteristics have you chosen and why? In the character of your avatar, describe yourself, pointing out those things you are pleased your creator added and anything you wish was different and why.
■ Pupils work collaboratively to create a storyline for their preferred game.
■ When playing online games pupils make constant decisions in order to reach new levels and these often involve careful strategic planning. Ask more experienced gamers to teach other members of the class (or teachers) how they did what they did. Get them to explain their reasoning, let them be the teacher and show off their skills.
■ Ask each pupil how they best like to communicate with others, and get them to explain why. How do they communicate with others whilst playing a game? How do they introduce themselves to others online? Get them to keep diaries, to log their interactions at home.

SUMMARY

In this chapter we have tried to show you some of the possibilities that games might offer you in terms of classroom practice and show you how this might be supported by theories of learning and child development. The *Monster Hunter* project shows what can be achieved when teachers take an interest in the contemporary experiences of young people, and then attempt to incorporate those technology-based experiences into their teaching and learning. Of course, hunting fictional digital monsters is not going to replace literacy, numeracy or any other area of the school curriculum. But it does provide another arena through which the curriculum can be delivered. Sometimes there are unforeseen benefits:

> One thing this taught me is that if you want anything good it takes time and a lot of hard work. I never learnt that in school!
>
> Mike (13)

It is easy to dismiss digital games as lazy forms of popular entertainment, but to do so would be to miss out on novel modes of pupil engagement. Similarly, fears and prejudices about digital games (the digital world in general, we suspect) often get in the way of innovative practice in this area. Although many might question what game technology is doing *to* our children, a more pertinent question for you as an education practitioner might be 'What are our children doing *with* all this technology and how can I use this as a way of helping them learn?'

NOTES

1 Massive multi-player online role playing games.
2 Massive multi-player online.
3 For example, Games Workshop's tabletop series *Warhammer* and *Warhammer 40k* often require complex mathematical calculations, yet our observations of players suggests that success in these games can exist independent of pupil school-based numeracy score. If they occurred, mistakes were laughed off as being 'just part of the game' (Jordan, 12).
4 'The distance between the actual development level as determined by independent problem solving, and the level of potential development as determined through problem solving under guidance or in collaboration with more capable peers' *(*Vygotsky, 1978, p. 86).
5 Miller and Robertson acknowledge that one of the reasons that lateness reduced was that the Nintendo sessions were scheduled for first period in the morning.
6 *COD* (Call of Duty) and *HALO* are popular console-based first-person war simulations.
7 A practical problem associated with home-based gaming is that not all of your pupils will be playing the same title or be at the same stage in the game. Teaching needs to be focused around broad learning themes rather than specific texts. The popularity of individual titles moves rapidly, and by adopting this approach you will be ensuring the longevity of your schemes of work.

REFERENCES

Ashton, D. (2009) 'Interactions, delegations and online digital games players in communities of practice', *Participations Journal of Audience and Reception Studies* 6(1), May. Available at: http://www.participations.org/documents/ashton.pdf (accessed 1 November 2011).

Bettelheim, B. (1976) *The Uses of Enchantment: The Meaning and Importance of Fairy Tales*, London: Thames and Hudson.

Byron, T. (2010) *Do We Have Safer Children in a Digital World? A Review of Progress Since the 2008 Byron Review*, DCSF Publications.

Caillois, R. (1961) *Man, Play and Games*, New York: Schocken Books.

Crawford, C. (1982) *The Art of Computer Game Design*. Available at: http://pdf.textfiles.com/books/cgd-crawford.pdf (accessed 14 May 2013).

Crowe, N. (2011) '"It's like my life but more, and better!" Playing with the Cathaby Shark Girls: MMORPGs, young people and fantasy-based social play', *International Journal of Adolescence and Youth* 16: 201–23.

Csikszentmihalyi, M. (1975) *Beyond Boredom and Anxiety: Experiencing Flow in Work and Play*, San Francisco: Jossey-Bass.

——(1990) *Flow: The Psychology of Optimal Experience*, New York: Harper and Row.

Davies, B. (2005) 'Youth work: a manifesto for our times', *Youth and Policy* 88(1): 23.

de Freitas, S. (2006) *Learning in Immersive Worlds:: A Review of Game-Based Learning,* JISC E-Learning Programme.

Gee, J.P. (2003) *What Video Games Have to Teach Us About Learning and Literacy*, New York: Palgrave Macmillan.

——(2007) *Good Video Games and Good Learning: Collected Essays on Video Games, Learning, and Literacy*, New York: Peter Lang.

Gee, J.P. and Hayes, E. (2009) *Public Pedagogy through Video Games*. Available at: http://www.gamebasedlearning.org.uk/content/view/59/ (accessed 3 February 2011).

Greenwald, S. and Rosner, D. (2003) Are we distance educating our students to death? Some reflections on the educational assumptions of distance learning', *Radical Pedagogy.*

Harushimana, I. (2008) 'Literacy through gaming: the influence of videogames on the writings of high school freshman males', *Journal of Literacy and Technology* 9(2) August pp. 34–35.

Hidey, D. (2006) Stop laughing: evaluating video game fan fiction'. Available at: http://www.thebottomlineonline.org/home/index.cfm?event=displayArticlePrinterFriendly&uStory_id=28920688-f745-42fa-9ceb-1aea36155d2f (accessed 12 January 2011).

Hoskins, B. and Fredriksson, U. (2008) *Learning to Learn: What Is It and Can It Be Measured?*, JRC, European Commission Document.

Jenkins, H. (2004) 'Game design as narrative architecture', in N. Wardrip-Fruin and P. Harrigan (eds), *New Media as Story, Performance and Game*, Cambridge, MA: MIT Press, pp. 118–30.

Livingstone, S. and Bober, M. (2005) *UK Children Go Online: Final Report of Key Project Findings*, London: Economic and Social Research Council.

Mezirow, J. (2000) *Learning as Transformation: Critical Perspectives on a Theory in Progress*, San Francisco: Jossey Bass.

Miller, D. and Robertson, D. (2008) *Using Dr Kawashima's Brain Training in Primary Classrooms: A Randomised Controlled Study: A Summary for the BBC*. Available at: http://ltsblogs.org.uk/consolarium/files/2008/09/lts-dr-kawashima-trial-summary.pdf (accessed 1 January 2012).

OFCOM (2011) *Children and Parents: Media Use and Attitudes Report*. Available at: http://stakeholders.ofcom.org.uk/binaries/research/media-literacy/oct2011/Children_and_parents.pdf (accessed 14 November 2011).

Pearce, C. and Artemesia (2009) *Communities of Play: Emergent Cultures In Multiplayer Games And Virtual Worlds*, Cambridge, MA: MIT Press.

Postman, N. (1996) *The Disappearance of Childhood*, London: Vintage.

Prensky, M. (2001) 'Digital natives, digital immigrants', *On the Horizon* 9 (5 October).

PricewaterhouseCoopers (2010) 'Social multi-player gamers named as UK technology's hottest prospect', press release, 19 October. Available at: http://www.ukmediacentre.pwc.com/News-Releases/Social-multi-player-gamers-named-as-UK-technology-s-hottest-prospect-f46.aspx (accessed 24 October 2010).

Raine, L. and Horrigan, J. (2005) *A Decade of Adoption: How the Internet Has Woven Itself into American Family Life*, Washington DC: PEW Internet and Family Life.

Squire, K. (2005) 'Changing the game: what happens when video games enter the classroom', *Innovate: Online Journal of Education*, August/September. Available at: http://www.innovateonline.info (accessed 14 September 2010).

Taylor, T.L. (2006) *Play Between Worlds: Exploring On-line Gaming Culture*, Cambridge, MA: MIT Press.

Vygotsky, L. (1933) 'Play and its role in the mental development of the child', *Voprosy psikhologii*, 1966, No. 6. Translated: Catherine Mulholland; transcription/markup: Nate Schmolze. Available at: http://www.marxists.org/archive/vygotsky/works/1933/play.htm (accessed 3 December 2011).

——(1978) 'Interaction between learning and development', in M. Cole, V. John-Steiner, S. Scribner and E. Souberman (eds), *Mind in Society: The Development of Higher Psychological Processes*, Cambridge, MA: Harvard University Press.

Wright, T., Boria, E. and Breidenbach, P. (2002) 'Creative player actions in FPS online video games: playing Counter-strike', *International Journal of Computer Game Research* 2(2). Available at: http://www.gamestudies.org (accessed 23 January 2011).

Zhang, W., Perris, K. and Yeung, L. (2005) 'Online tutorial support in open and distance learning: students' perceptions', *British Journal of Educational Technology* 36(5): 789–804.

MAKING THE MOVING IMAGE: TEACHING AND LEARNING WITH DIGITAL VIDEO PRODUCTION

Andrew Burn and James Durran

INTRODUCTION: WHAT IS DIGITAL VIDEO?

Digital video (DV) is familiar to most people as a recording format, available on a wide variety of digital cameras, but also incorporated into other devices such as mobile phones. Informal use of digital video has exploded in the first decade of the twentieth century. Many uses are quite familiar, such as family uses to record holidays, weddings, school plays and other significant events. Other uses are more novel, such as the creation of short films for a bewildering variety of purposes, for exhibition on YouTube. Such purposes include parodies of films, adverts and music video; film sequences exported from online video games; films carrying political, religious or social messages; instruction videos; animations of all varieties.

Nevertheless, it would be wrong to think that everybody (or even all young people) is constructing elaborately edited films for these kinds of purpose. The evidence seems to show that those involved in any meaningful way in such activities are a minority, albeit a substantial and growing minority (Burn *et al.*, 2010).

There is a good case, then, for schools to help students to learn this important skill of the digital age. It can be seen as a form of extended literacy, and recent research has given detailed accounts of what moving image literacy might be like (e.g. Potter, 2008).

At the same time, the moving image can be seen as a form of expression useful in all areas of the curriculum. We will give examples later of how digital video filming and editing can offer new ways for students to construct their understanding of subjects as diverse as science and history.

Critically, the general idea of digital video also encompasses the practice of *digital video editing*, and it is here that the real revolution for schools has taken place. Digital editing uses a computer with software that displays the raw footage, the edited version, and a timeline on which the assembled edit is represented (Figure 10.1). As an increasing number of schools are realising, it is now both relatively simple and affordable for students to shoot their own film on digital camcorders, mobile phones or even webcams,

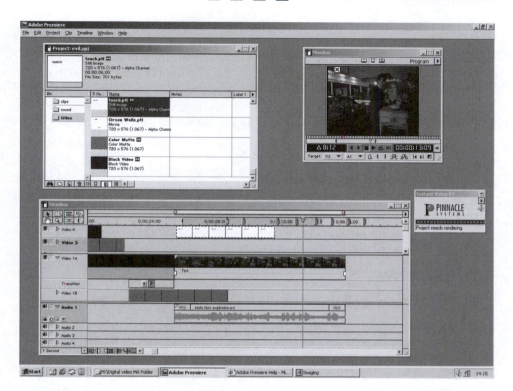

■ **Figure 10.1** The editing interface of Adobe Premiere Pro

and edit it on the school's computers. Though there are some residual practical issues here, the real question then becomes, 'How might students learn what they need to learn in my subject through the medium of the moving image, alongside the more traditional modes of reading, writing and number; or as part of curriculum areas already involved in forms of making in other media, such as Art, or Design Technology?'

The immediate benefit for learning of the digital medium, as all the early studies pointed out, was that the edited video could be constantly reworked (Reid *et al.*, 2002). Instead of being made all in one go, with no room for mistakes, as was basically the case with analogue editing, the new medium allows students to draft and redraft their edit, with limitless room for peer or teacher advice on each version.

The first decade of the twenty-first century saw a rapid expansion in the use of DV in schools. Teachers began to use this new medium with pupils to make videos in a wide range of curriculum contexts, and increasingly with younger children; though at the time of writing, this spread is still quite patchy, especially in the primary sector, and we are only beginning to understand how video can serve different learning needs in different curriculum contexts. In some ways, DV can be seen as a 'Cinderella' medium: in recent preoccupation with the internet, it has almost come to seem an old technology, in spite of the relatively modest uses of its potential by many schools.

The question of how digital video production – filming and editing – can be used in schools is a big one, and this chapter will address the main questions and possible solutions. For reasons of space, it will not also attempt to consider the wider question of how digital video sources, either in the form of DVD or of downloaded movie files from the internet, might be used in classrooms, though this is a related issue which teachers might like to consider. It will also not consider the use of DV in specialist media education and media studies programmes. Teachers in these fields should look for more specialised accounts of media education in general and media production in particular, perhaps beginning with our own book, *Media Literacy in Schools* (Burn and Durran, 2007), which contains three chapters giving specific examples of digital video use: making animations, making adverts, and making film trailers.

This chapter will ask, and try to answer, four key questions:

■ What do we know about digital video so far?
■ Why would video be useful in learning contexts as far apart as, say, PE and Geography?
■ What do we have to know to use video in teaching?
■ How can we tell what kinds of hardware and software to get, with an increasing array of kit on the market, and what principles should guide our choice?

OBJECTIVES

Readers of this chapter should gain four understandings of DV. They should:

■ gain an overview of the existing research about DV in teaching and learning;
■ have an opportunity to map this against the curriculum of their specialist subject;
■ become acquainted with an example of the use of DV in the broad area of their subject field;
■ have an opportunity to consider how DV might assist in wider, whole-school questions about teaching and learning.

WHAT DO WE KNOW SO FAR?

Digital video was taken up first by specialists in media education who already valued students' production of their own video work, and had previously taught them to film and edit using analogue editing equipment, editing videotape across two or three video-recorders. Accounts of DV in the classroom (Buckingham *et al.*, 1995; Burn and Durran, 1998) described secondary students making short videos such as trailers for films or pop videos. The opportunity to actually edit their own short videos gave students a practical understanding of how the moving image is put together, as well as how it tells a story, or sells a commercial product. These studies also emphasised a question of profound cultural significance: that the moving image, produced as cinema for a century and television for half a century by powerful industries, had positioned the population at large as audiences, able to *receive* these new media, which changed their cultural landscape forever, but not able to *make* their own moving image productions, with certain exceptions such as the use of domestic cine-cameras. The advent of new digital production technologies has, for the first time, allowed ordinary people (in this case, school students) to become producers as well as audiences of media texts. If we think of the moving image as a literacy, it has been, for a century, a literacy that only consisted of *reading*. Now, finally, the *writing* has arrived.

This version of media literacy, though it might seem obvious and logical, is in fact exceptional in international terms. Though the term media literacy is often invoked as a desirable critical skill for future citizens by many governments across the world, from Taiwan to the UK, this almost always means the development of critical *reading* skills – the ability to *interpret* media texts. The UK government's media regulator, OFCOM, has a media literacy unit which also promotes this view of media literacy; but it has developed it further to include the importance of production: media literate people should, in its definition, be able to *access*, *understand* and *create*.

At the turn of the century, studies by the British Film Institute (Parker, 1999, 2002) looked at how making films could help primary school children to imagine the visual aspects of stories better, and improve this and other aspects of their writing. Again, there is an obvious literacy emphasis here, arguing that conceptions of literacy need to be widened to include digital media production; but also that children's development in print literacy is related to and affected by their experience of representation on the moving image.

A series of studies by teachers, working with the BFI, Cambridge University, and the London Institute of Education from 2000 to 2004, explored DV both in media education and in different curriculum contexts. The first of these studies (Burn *et al.*, 2001) suggested that digital editing was seen by the teachers in three ways. First, it was a creative process, which involved students making aesthetic choices about how to represent themselves and their world. Second, it was a social process, in which students took different roles, collaborated with each other, and drew on their cultural experience of film and television to make sense of this new medium. These processes can be seen as an example of situated learning (Lave and Wenger), in which children learn from their peers, especially if the situation is appropriately structured by the teacher, and peer learning is integrated with instructional processes. Third, this study also developed the idea of a moving image 'literacy', which involved using a 'language' of the moving image with its own 'grammar' of shots, transitions, soundtrack, titles and so on.

In 2002 the British Educational Communication Technologies Agency (BECTA) ran a pilot study of DV in a wide range of curriculum contexts, both primary and secondary. The evaluation of this project (Reid *et al.*, 2002) found that much of the best work by students was produced where the teacher had a clear idea of how the moving image worked, both technically and conceptually, and communicated this to students.

This study also clarified the benefits of the digital medium: that it was *iterative* (the edit developed through successive versions); it provided *feedback* (the developing edit could be immediately viewed, informing the next iteration); it *integrated* different digital technologies (digital audio compositions, graphic designs, or text could be imported from other applications); and it could be *distributed* in much more versatile ways – in multimedia formats on the internet, on DVD, as projected video in a cinema, on television at broadcast quality. The growing potential here centres on the forms of online distribution that the rise of social media and the participatory internet have made possible. Online resources for the exhibition of moving image work, such as YouTube and Vimeo, have made it possible for schools to break out of the limited possibilities for display previously available, and show their films to worldwide audiences, opening them up to critical commentary.

In summary, then, we can say some things about successful DV work in schools with some confidence:

1   It is a practical way for children to understand the nature of the powerful media of film and television in their lives.

2   It has the potential to change the cultural relation of children to the media of the moving image, making them producers as well as audiences.

3   It can be a valuable accompaniment to literacy work, showing how ideas and narratives can be transformed from print to film, and vice versa.

4   It is a creative activity, requiring aesthetic judgement and many kinds of compositional effort (visual composition, control of time and rhythm, manipulation of sound and music).

5   It is a social activity, in two senses: it is often collaborative; and it draws on students' own media cultures.

6   It can be seen as (and taught as) a kind of literacy, with its own language.

7   It is best taught by teachers who have some understanding of this 'language'.

8   It is a fluid, flexible medium, ideally suited for learning, providing *iteration, feedback, integration* and versatile *distribution*.

One thing can be added, which emerges from the research story so far. The first is that teachers overwhelmingly report the motivating power of DV – the ability to control the moving image when children's biggest experience of it by far is as an audience of film and TV, can be a powerful experience for them.

Task 10.1 Identify opportunities for DV production in the curriculum

The only real value of such research is in its capacity to inform future classroom practice. Readers might like, then, to try the following task: Look at the curriculum for your subject across one Key Stage. Highlight any curricular requirements (either nationally prescribed or emphasised by your own department) that could benefit from the use of DV production work. Next to any highlighted areas, write in the number(s) of the relevant benefit of DV from the list above.

WHY WOULD WE USE VIDEO IN DIFFERENT SUBJECTS?

In this section, some possible uses of DV are sketched in different curriculum areas. These are all intended only as examples, to raise possibilities and principles. Schools will want to consider for themselves how the moving image, as well as other audio-visual and digital media, are used as part of the rapidly expanding array of communication technologies available to teachers and children. The argument of this chapter is that this consideration should begin by thinking what needs to be taught, and how the moving image can serve that need, rather than beginning from the technology, as we are often tempted to do.

Narrative

Much of children's experience of television and film from an early age is narrative. They know that stories can be told in pictures and words, both in books and in films. They have an extensive, if unconscious, understanding of the conventions of the moving image – how it frames places and people; how it chops up time and reassembles it, speeding it up, slowing it down, splitting it between present, past (flashback, or *analepsis*) and future (flashforward, or *prolepsis*).

Wherever narrative is used in the curriculum, video will always provide an alternative mode to explore it. So, for instance, it could be used to tell stories from history, from myth, from literature or from the contemporary world. In the classroom, this might appear as children making videos of key scenes from *Oliver Twist*, perhaps, looking carefully at the language of Dickens' book for clues about which character to focus on, what details of the workhouse to show in close-up, how to angle the camera to make the workhouse master look threatening and Oliver look vulnerable.

DV also offers a halfway house between the analysis and production of media texts. One of us, for example, has used it to study *Romeo and Juliet* with Year 8, by importing a collection of clips from Baz Luhrmann's film into Microsoft's Windows Moviemaker, giving students the relevant bit of script from the play, and asking them to edit together a sequence to go with the script. This activity prompts close critical attention both to Shakespeare's words and to the film-text; but it is also a creative and disciplined piece of production work, requiring an understanding of the editing process, and the importance of juxtaposition, duration, tempo and music (see Burn and Durran, 2006, for a more detailed account).

Narrative appears in curious places – many pieces of music have a narrative quality, either because they tell a story themselves (*Peter and the Wolf*), or because they are often used to accompany filmic narratives (*Ride of the Valkyries*; *Carmina Burana*). Also, because video editing is a time-based medium, it has much in common with music, and can be used to expand students' understanding and practical experience of rhythm, tempo and duration. One school developed a Year 9 music project based on the music of horror films, which have often used more avant-garde musical styles than other mainstream genres, because of their usefully disorientating effects! In this project, students had to compose their own music for a short sequence of the film, and then edit it onto the sequence.

Narrative is also, importantly, about dialogue. A simple use of film narrative in foreign languages is to take short clips from English movies that use particular repertoires, such as meetings-and-greetings, and ask students to do their own dubbing. This requires them to translate the dialogue, practise speaking it in an appropriate voice and accent (and attempting to lip-sync with the actors in the film), recording the voices, and editing the new soundtrack.

Documentary

Documentary films are widely used in classrooms as accessible and engaging sources of information. What DV offers is the possibility of students making their own documentary film. This allows all the benefits of active, practical learning, and also encourages students to consider profound questions about how truth is constructed and contested. In considering how events and ideas are represented through the selection and combination of elements, and through the use of different forms of address, they should have the chance to learn that the apparently factual basis of documentary and historical fact is actually highly mediated, manipulated, and sometimes distorted.

This could apply, for instance, to a history lesson, in which video is used to interview medieval serfs and villains about their life in a feudal manor, interspersed with footage showing them about their daily work, and contrasted with an interview with the lord of the manor. The class could make quite specific decisions about how to represent the different interests of the lord or the peasants, through the juxtaposition of their points of view, through the scripting of their words, even in quite direct ways, such as through the use of a voiceover commentary.

Similarly, one school turned its annual Geography field-trip into a documentary-making session. GCSE students studying coastal erosion on the North Norfolk coast filmed examples of the eroded coastline, of the coastal defence systems, and interviewed local council officers and local people in Cromer about the issue. This allowed them to put opposing views side by side, about, for instance, who should be liable to pay for coastal defences. In this way they were able to explore the politics of the issue as well as visually representing the physical processes of erosion and defence structures like timber groynes and gabion cages.

Another school used the documentary genre to make a video of a French daytrip, in which the emphasis was on particular language repertoires. The different parts of the day were filmed, such as a visit to a French baker, and his explanation of the baking process, along with a question-and-answer session. These were then edited together with a voiceover commentary in French.

Some documentary sub-genres relate specifically to domains of subject content. In PE, for instance, it might be interesting to explore how matches are conventionally analysed in sports television. The genre of the match report, with its selected footage of the match, its use of slow motion to emphasise and clarify key moments, its discussions between sporting pundits, and its interviews with players and managers, is easily imitated by students in the context of the school match, or even practice session. One school also uses DV to analyse and improve targeted skills in team sports. Students film each other practising the skills, then edit the footage with a critical commentary, using slow-motion, repeated sequences and freeze-frames to emphasise particular movements, errors and successes.

Similarly, all the sciences have their place in television in popular science programmes, from David Attenborough's natural history documentaries to Robert Winston's ponderings on the wonders of human biology. Though the high-quality camerawork or computer-generated imagery of these programmes are difficult to imitate in schools, other aspects are not, in particular what is arguably their greatest asset – the use of a charismatic presenter, who, in the role of expert, presents much of the information to camera, in close-up. Perhaps the most valuable aspect of this kind of approach to science is not so much as a technical exercise, but rather as a way of exploring what science means to people and what makes it interesting. This kind of televisual presentation is a long way from the neutral, objective tone of the conventional written science report. For that very reason, it allows some discussion of the place of such objective reporting in science, and how presentations of popular science serve a different purpose, making room for a more subjective experience, for enthusiasm, imagination, even fantasy.

Animation

Children bring an extensive knowledge of animation to school, and it makes sense to recognise this experience. But animation is a tool often used to represent abstract ideas also, not least in science and maths. Distance learning models of education, such as Open University television broadcasts, have been using this technique for many years, to give the abstract ideas of maths and science concrete form. One group of schools has used computer animation software in Maths to represent ideas of space, and how to calculate the area or volume of different shapes. So they would ask children to show how a kite shape or a parallelogram are made up of simpler triangles and rectangles, by animating the shape so that it broke up and reformed, revealing the simpler shapes and the key to calculating its area. To explain the principles at work, the children also used voiceovers, and on-screen text. They were able to consolidate their learning by inventing ways to make newly acquired ideas visually concrete. This package was the cheap 'edutainment' software, *The Complete Animator*, which produces an AVI movie file as its outcome. This in turn can be edited further in a digital editing package, allowing for voice tracks, music, titling and re-editing. Alternatively, animation of this kind can be carried out in Macromedia's *Flash* animation software, which many schools possess as part of the Adobe suite.

Another form of animation is 'claymation', or stop-frame animation using plasticine models. One department of Design Technology has built a project round this form of animation as part of a Year 9 course in Design (construction). Students had to construct small sets for their animation, build the models from plasticine with a pliable aluminium wire armature, film the animation, record the vocal track, and edit the whole thing. The time-consuming part of this is the filming, which uses a stop-frame setting on the digital camcorder, filming four frames a second (this is slow compared with the standard 24 frames per second of film; but it can be speeded up in the editing process). After each frame, the models are adjusted slightly, so that the illusion of movement is built up frame-by-frame. Here, the model-making and set-building were obviously central to the curriculum.

Yet another school incorporated animation in a Year 7 Art project. Students researched African folktales, storyboarded them, and drew pictures for each frame, which they then filmed, again using the stop-frame setting. In this case, visual design was the central curriculum concern.

Another project asked Year 7 students to make animations of volcanic processes. Previously, classes have made papier-mâché models of volcanoes; animation, however, offers a way actually to show geomorphological processes happening in compressed time, rather than just implying them from a static representation. Students used the software Stop Motion Pro on laptop computers, with ordinary, focusing webcams. The software allows them to capture single frames, 15 per second; to review captured frames running as a film, at any point; and to delete unwanted frames as often as necessary. The webcams do not offer the picture quality of a digital video camera, but are affordable, very easy to use and take up little space on desktops.

Each group of three students works on a different aspect of volcanic activity – composite cone formation, plate tectonic movement, the creation of ash layers and so on. They work to a given 'script', which they time and visualise as a moving image, sketching 'key' frames for the start, for the end and for one interim point in their animation. At this point the convergence of disciplines is particularly apparent: the consideration of image and representation is inseparable from the consideration of geomorphological processes. Specialist verbal language, such as 'pyroclastic' or 'transverse', has to be translated into an accessible visual language. And more everyday terms, such as 'flow', 'eruption' or 'cone', have to be represented in their specialist meanings.

Finally, a further possibility for animation is 3-D animation made in virtual spaces. This grew out of gaming culture, which developed a form of film known as *machinima* – film made in virtual worlds or game worlds (see Burn, 2009). One school has recently made films with Year 7 using the 3-D animation software Moviestorm. They built virtual sets, designed virtual characters, plotted their moves and dialogue, and created individual shots with a wide range of camera angles and movements. The advantage of such software is that it allows students to experiment very quickly with different camera positions, lighting and many other features of moving image production in ways that would not be possible with physical cameras.

Task 10.2 **Planning lessons using DV**

Take one class that you teach, or are about to start teaching. Choose one topic or project that could benefit from the use of DV, using or adapting the examples given above. Plan a lesson or sequence of lessons, thinking through what kinds of learning DV could promote, and how you would set up these opportunities. (NB: you might like to read the following section also, before trying this activity.)

WHAT DO TEACHERS NEED TO KNOW?

Two things are important – an understanding of how the 'language' of the moving image works; and a grasp of the technology (see the next section).

DV is, in some ways, different from other ICTs. If we teach word-processing, spreadsheets, or presentational devices such as PowerPoint, these have no important references to children's lives or cultural experience. Teaching with video, on the other hand, uses a medium that is saturated with culture, a form of entertainment of which almost all children will have extensive and profound experience. Furthermore, these media have developed through half a century of television and a century of cinema, and have long and complex histories. Students' parents and grandparents will also be familiar with different parts of these histories. Teachers need to help students to make explicit the largely implicit knowledge they have gained as members of these viewing cultures. The following points are basic ones that can easily be taught to classes.

Planning

Students should plan the shape and detail of their video carefully, shot by shot. This can be done by making a shot list, which just describes each shot, or by making a storyboard. In either case, what needs to be planned is how the shot will be filmed. Students should be encouraged to film what they will need for the final edit, not to film long, rambling, unplanned sequences thinking that they can edit these down later. A good discipline, especially where time is short, is to ask them to 'edit in camera' – to film the shots as close as possible to their vision of the final edit. The editing can then concentrate on reworking, developing soundtracks and rhythm, and other post-production decisions.

It is at this point that students' own media experience can be explored. They will have extensive knowledge of what the genres they are imitating look like – it is worth analysing examples in class, to find out what they know about their structures, visual styles, detailed conventions. They will have concrete ideas about what kind of voice a newsreader uses, or how a conversation can be filmed, or what the key elements of a music video are.

At the same time, it can be difficult for them to plan shots if they have never really used a camera in this way. Ideally, they should have a chance to try constructing different kinds of shot, before trying a storyboard, so that they can understand clearly what a shot is, and realise that a frame on the storyboard represents a shot. Younger children often use frames of a storyboard to represent much bigger structures, such as a whole scene, which then has to be broken down.

As well as planning the filming and editing, students should plan for other aspects of the film. Recent work in this field has observed that the moving image is a *multimodal* form – it incorporates several modes of communication, such as language, gesture, music, visual design, lighting, costume. It is very easy to neglect some of these. So, if students are using speech, they may need to plan it carefully, script it if appropriate, and practise it. If the video involves drama or role-play, this mode deserves as much attention as filming and editing. It can be developed carefully, stopping to refine it, to deepen the quality of the drama, to explore motivation, to model physical aspects of the drama, to explore alternative ways of presenting the dramatic content or narrative. Similarly, music needs to be thought about, chosen carefully, even maybe made specifically for the project, if the students have those skills.

Filming

■ **Framing**: shots need to be framed carefully. This will take into consideration the establishing shot, which shows the whole scene, and lets the viewer know where everything is before the sequence moves into closer shots. It will also include shot distance: whether to show people or objects in long shot (the whole person), medium shot (perhaps waist-up) or close-up (most frequently a face, or head and shoulders).

■ **Camera angle**: the angle, conventionally, signifies power. A level angle will signify neutral power – that is, the subject of the shot is neither more nor less powerful than the viewer. A low angle shot will signify power (the subject is more powerful than the viewer). A high angle shot will signify weakness (the subject is weaker than the viewer). In schools, it is particularly important to think about the filming of children. It is all too easy for taller people (older students or adults) to film younger children from a slightly high angle, unintentionally reinforcing a sense of them as relatively powerless.

■ **Camera movement**: the most important movements are pan (side to side), tilt (up and down), track (the whole camera moves, traditionally on tracks, to follow the subject). These movements take place with the camera on a tripod, which should generally be encouraged with young film-makers, to produce steady, stable shots. Tracking, however, can be done with a handheld camera, with care; or with a homemade 'dolly', such as a wooden triangle to hold the tripod, with castors at each corner.

■ **Zoom**: The other movement is the lens movement of the zoom. This should be used sparingly – in television journalism, for instance, it is almost never used. When the BBC used a crash-zoom (a rapid zoom in and out) in coverage of the Queen's Diamond Jubilee pageant, they received complaints from viewers about its jarring effect.

■ **Sound**: the natural sound that comes with the shot, especially dialogue, needs to be as good as possible, so if an integral microphone on the camera is used, it needs to be fairly close to the speaking subject. It is better to use an external microphone if possible. It is also a good idea to re-record the dialogue just with the speaker talking close to the camera. This second audio track can be very useful for parts where the dialogue is unclear; even for a whole sequence in a piece of drama.

■ **Continuity**: this is a conventional method of filming and editing typical of mainstream film and television drama. The idea is to film events in fragmented pieces in such a way that they can be edited together to show the relationships between elements in a situation, allowing the viewer to grasp these relationships. The most familiar example is the shot-reverse shot structure often used to film a conversation. The film wants to show each speaker in turn, to allow them to fill the frame, to keep changing the point of view, and to show each speaker as they are seen by their interlocutor. A little reflection with students will show why a simple two shot, with both speakers shown in profile simultaneously, is not a satisfactory representation of a conversation. In the shot-reverse shot, there is usually not two cameras, as is often supposed; nor does the camera change position between each line of the dialogue. Instead, the whole conversation is filmed from one point of view, and then performed again, filmed from the other point of view. The alternating shots are then edited together; and other options appear, such as cutting the soundtrack from one speaker into the reaction shot from the other.

- **180 degree rule**: The other continuity convention typically observed in the shot-reverse shot is the 180 degree rule. This means that an imaginary line is drawn on one side of the actors, and the camera never crosses this line. Therefore, the shot is on the same side for each speaker, so that each speaker occupies the space we expect them to occupy, their gaze apparently directed at the other speaker, avoiding any disorientation for the viewer. There are many other continuity 'rules', all developed to create the illusion of a complete and coherent space through shots which are actually carefully planned and fragmented, not 'continuous' in reality at all. There is no space here to elaborate – teachers who want to go further with these ideas can find useful guides, most comprehensively in Bordwell and Thompson's *Film Art* (2001), though there are plenty of simple guides on the internet.

Editing

- **Assemble editing**: this refers to the practice of assembling all the shots in the right order on the timeline of the editing software. In fact, it will usually mean two other procedures first – chopping up the footage into relevant chunks, if it has all been imported as one long sequence; and then trimming each shot to get rid of unwanted footage at the beginning and end. All of these procedures can be done by simple, intuitive drag and drop movements of the cursor in most editing software. However, this is not just a technical process. Deciding how much information a shot needs to contain can be complex. Students will usually err on the side of too much information, resulting in shots which are too long, and which labour the point. Giving strict constraints about length can often be very productive.

- **Audio**: it can be tempting to leave extra audio tracks until the end. However, it is a better idea to lay down extra audio early. This might be music, in which case the rhythm and duration of sections of the music may determine the length and cutting of the visual track. Or it might be a voiceover commentary, in which case, again, the length of spoken segments may determine how much visual footage is needed.

- **Transitions**: the default transition is the cut, where one shot stops and the next immediately begins. The next most common is probably the dissolve, where one shot dissolves into the next. It is also common for sequences to fade in from black, and fade out again at the end. There are many other transitions, which beginners will want to play with; but they quickly realise that these can look confusing and inappropriate unless they are used for a specific meaning, or are conventional in the genre, such as the use of wipes in sports television. The important principle is to discuss with them why they want a particular transition, such as a dissolve to signify the passing of time.

- **Colour**: the most common colour effect, perhaps, is black-and-white, which can signify a particular artistic style, or can suggest a gritty, bleak, documentary approach. Other effects may be useful for specific reasons, such as producing bizarre effects in a pop video.
- **Speed**: slow motion is often useful for emphasis, or for producing a dreamlike effect. Examples might be a key moment in a football match; a turning point in a drama; an action of historical importance in a documentary. Speeded up film is less common.

Exhibition

When the students' videos are completed, the other affordance of the digital medium comes into play – that they are very flexible in terms of exhibition, so offer opportunities well beyond showing the video to the class. A popular option is to project them in a bigger venue, such as a school hall. Some schools even build partnerships with local arts cinemas, which can screen work when the cinema is not being used for commercial screenings.

The learning opportunity here is to encourage students to think about audience, a key concept in media education. Real audiences, such as younger children, students in a partner or twinned school, parents and governors will all require different forms of address, different levels of sophistication, different cultural styles. These are valuable lessons for students to learn.

WHAT KINDS OF HARDWARE AND SOFTWARE TO GET

This involves decisions that are about both learning principles and about hard practical considerations. Try discussing the following points with colleagues to establish the principles important to you.

Task 10.3 **Choosing cameras and editing software**

Discuss the principles below to consider your choices of cameras and editing software:

Cameras

Digital camcorders are becoming increasingly affordable. Here are some important principles to evaluate different products.

- You need to decide the balance between quality and quantity. The same amount of money could buy you one camera or six: the question is whether you need very high quality of lens or functionality, or whether it is more important to have a camera for each of six groups of five students in a group of thirty, possibly even considering webcams with audio, as in the volcanoes animation project described above. You may even want to consider letting students use video functions on their mobile phones.
- DV is still a commonly used format at the time of writing. It comes in tape cassettes, most commonly in a small size (mini-DV). This needs to be transferred to the computer using a high-speed cable such as USB. However, many cameras have solid state storage, and may even have USB connectors to plug directly into the computer.

- Cameras are increasingly available in very compact sizes. These may be more expensive, and are not necessarily 'child-friendly'. They are more easily lost or stolen, and the smaller controls are sometimes less visible and harder for younger children to use, especially if they have problems with fine motor skills.
- Many cameras have flip-out LCD viewfinder screens. The learning advantage of these is that a group of students can all see the shot that is being composed. The practical disadvantage is that they use up battery power more quickly.
- Finally: invest in tripods, spare batteries, and well-padded bags, budget permitting.

Editing software

Again, there are an increasing number of packages on offer. These are key points to consider.

- **What do you want to teach?** If students need only to learn the basics, and they need to do this quickly, then a simple, intuitive package is best. Apple's i-movie and Microsoft's Moviemaker are the software that come 'bundled' with computers for no additional cost. They will enable students to see the basic structure of a timeline, to learn the basic procedures of drag and drop editing, and to add at least one extra audio-track. Apple's iMovie is now available as an app for the iPhone. On the other hand, if you want them to learn about more complex editing, how to layer graphic and video tracks, how to edit multiple audio tracks, something more sophisticated is needed, such as Adobe Premiere, or Apple's Final Cut Pro. These packages are better suited to older students, and to curriculum contexts that can spare more time for the editing process. They are also more expensive.
- **What experience do the teachers who will use the software have?** If they have little or no experience, and little time for training, then again one of the simpler, cheaper packages should be adopted. Using the more complex tools suggested above would need careful planning for teachers to become comfortable with them. This may involve a series of structured training courses, ideally in the school, leading soon into the first classroom use. Alternatively, it may mean providing a laptop with the software for the teacher to take away and play with.

DV IN THE WHOLE-SCHOOL CONTEXT

Finally, it may be worth considering the value of digital video in the context of whole-school work. Three particular areas are especially relevant.

Learning styles

All schools have invested effort in exploring how the traditional learning regimes of print literacy, still dominant in many subjects, can be expanded. They know that many students are more comfortable learning in a visual way, or through physical activity, or through practical problem-solving. Digital video is a valuable addition to the range of styles on offer – it allows students to represent their ideas visually, but also dramatically, orally and musically. Learning Support departments may find DV a useful tool to widen the expressive range of students with identified print literacy problems. Furthermore, as we have seen, DV offers a mode of communication embedded in rich audio-visual traditions that are important elements in the cultural landscapes of young people.

ICT

Digital video editing is, of course, an ICT tool, employing many generic features common to presentational and graphic design software. It has an obvious place in programmes of work (both discrete and cross-curricular) that aim to teach generic skills of multimedia design, and digital video is often an important component of CD-ROMs and web pages. As well as teaching discrete courses, ICT departments invariably have a whole-school coordinating role. If this includes DV, then student progression in digital video-making can be planned coherently across the curriculum and the age range, and resources can be acquired and deployed cost-effectively.

Literacy

A good deal of the research on DV in school has seen it as a form of literacy. Video editing is, arguably, a writing-like form – it is composed of horizontal segments which are sequenced and connected in ways which construct the meaning of each part and the whole. Students can be encouraged to think about how this process happens, how a cut between a close-up and a long shot operates like a preposition of place in language, how the moving image handles narrative time, how it structures dialogue, develops characters, represents thoughts, describes places, conveys emotion, constructs arguments; and how it does these things differently from language. At the level of the whole text, film and television have text-types and genres in much the same way as print texts, and their functions and structures will be both similar to and instructively different from their print-based cousins. Students' conceptual grasp of the nature and purpose of genre could and should embrace the variety of digital television channels, the local multiplex and the shelves of the video store as well as the local or school library.

SUMMARY

This chapter has proposed a number of rationales for the use of DV production technologies across the curriculum. Central among these are: the cultural benefits for students of becoming producers as well as consumers of the moving image; the extension of literate practices beyond print and into audio-visual media; the benefits of collaborative learning; and the development of a wider set of creative competencies in the use of ICTs.

The key question for teachers is to think, then, where their own subject requires students to use traditional modes of representation, and how these might be augmented, or even replaced, by the moving image. Forms of print literacy are still overwhelmingly dominant across the curriculum, disproportionately so when we consider how texts in the world at large are moving rapidly towards complex multimodal electronic formats. Of course, the moving image is not always the best medium for any given purpose; but where narrative and documentary modes are most valuable, moving image media come into their own.

The increasing mismatch between forms of representation used in the school and those used outside the school walls is one important reason why the use of digital video as a powerful, creative and motivating tool in different curriculum areas is of growing interest to teachers. It harnesses a medium with an extensive cultural history, and the making of video is a natural extension of the many uses of video resources that all curriculum areas have routinely used for years. Making video, as well as being a satisfying and creative way to handle ideas, helps students to relate school learning and ICT procedures to the (increasingly digital) media cultures of their home and leisure lives.

REFERENCES

Bordwell, D. and Thompson, K. (2001) *Film Art: An Introduction* (sixth edition), New York: McGraw-Hill.

Buckingham, D. (2003) *Media Education: Literacy, Learning and Contemporary Culture*, Cambridge: Polity.

Buckingham, D., Grahame, J. and Sefton-Green, J. (1995) *Making Media: Practical Production in Media Education*, London: English & Media Centre.

Burn, A. (2009) *Making New Media: Creative Production and Digital Literacies*, New York: Peter Lang.

Burn, A. and Durran, J. (1998) 'Going non-linear' *Trac* 2, Winter: 114–18.

——(2006) 'Digital anatomies: analysis as production in media education', in D. Buckingham and R. Willett (eds), *Digital Generations*, New York: Lawrence Erlbaum.

——(2007) *Media Literacy in School: Practice, Production, Progression*, London: Paul Chapman.

Burn, A., Brindley, S., Durran, J., Kelsall, C., Sweetlove, J. and Tuohey, C. (2001) 'The rush of images: a research report on a study of digital editing and the moving image', *English in Education* 35 (2), Summer: 34–47.

Burn, A., Buckingham, D., Parry, B. and Powell, M. (2010) 'Minding the gaps: teachers' cultures, students' cultures', in D. Alvermann (ed.), *Adolescents' Online Literacies: Connecting Classrooms, Media, and Paradigms*, New York: Peter Lang.

Parker, D. (1999) 'You've read the book, now make the film: moving image media, print literacy and narrative', *English in Education* 33: 24–35.

——(2002) 'Show us a story: an overview of recent research and resource development work at the British Film Institute', *English in Education* 36: 38–45.

Potter, J. (2008) 'The locative narrative: Katie and Aroti – "This is where we always used to sit"', *Media Education Journal* 44, December: 18–23.

Reid, M., Parker, D. and Burn, A. (2002) *Evaluation Report of the BECTA Digital Video Pilot Project*. Available at: http://eprints.ioe.ac.uk/4253/ (accessed 14 May 2013).

ICT AND ASSESSMENT

Kevin Burden and James Shea

INTRODUCTION

This chapter considers issues surrounding the use of ICT to aid and support assessment of all subjects in the secondary curriculum. It presents two perspectives written by each author and integrates these into a holistic narrative that places pedagogical considerations at the centre of any decisions you make associated with assessment and ICT. You should be able to engage with the debate around formal assessment and technology at the end of this chapter, but also you should be able to deploy technology based assessment to assist your teaching even if the formal assessment of your area does not utilise technological developments. As you will discover, assessment *for* learning is just as important as assessment *of* learning. In the current dynamic, fast moving era, assessment has to evolve to ensure it is not left behind by developments in pedagogy and technology.

Assessment has been a strong feature of curriculum and pedagogical design for many years but in the last decade it has taken on far greater significance as researchers like Black and Wiliam have identified its value as a powerful tool for learning:

> the term 'assessment' refers to all those activities undertaken by teachers, *and by their pupils in assessing themselves*, which provide information to be used as feedback to modify the teaching and learning activities in which they are engaged. *Such assessment becomes 'formative assessment' when the evidence is actually used to adapt the teaching work to meet the needs.*
>
> (Black and Wiliam, 1998, p. 80)

The impact of Black and Wiliam's 1998 paper 'Inside the Black Box' was such that assessment became more fully embedded at institutional levels, such as through England's OfSTED (Office for Standards in Education) inspections rather than just at the level of teaching. OfSTED drew from Black and Wiliam's work that the assessment *for* learning was as important as assessment *of* learning in their focus on how the teacher or pupil knows that progress and learning has taken place in the lesson. We see, then, a direct emphasis from researchers and governments through institutions like OfSTED that best practice in assessment is a clear focus for teachers and for learners. At the same time, technology has evolved rapidly to a point where computers, mobile devices and other technology tools are capable of supporting, enhancing and in some cases transforming traditional approaches to assessment, and this forms the focus for this chapter.

OBJECTIVES

By the end of this chapter you should have an awareness of important issues concerning:

■ the impact of ICT on the curriculum and pedagogy;
■ the impact of ICT for assessment;
■ computer based and online assessment;
■ the affordances of technology in supporting assessment for learning.

THE IMPACT OF ICT ON THE CURRICULUM AND PEDAGOGY

In this section, we look at the impact of ICT on subjects outside of computing lessons. In order to do this, it is important to consider how technology interacts with and motivates pupils outside school as well as inside the traditional classroom.

Increased motivation of pupils

At a very basic level, ICT has the ability to change the nature of a pupil's work. Scruffy handwriting is rendered legible, crossing out and redrafting of text becomes standardised and the pupil can create their text in the style used in formal publications. You will find that many of your pupils prefer to present their work through ICT instead of scribing by hand. However, is the content of the expressed ideas different because of the use of ICT? Did the pupil respond differently because they expressed their ideas assisted by technology? Powers *et al.* (1994) found that as word processing entered the education mainstream so the recipients of typed work had higher expectations of it than that of handwritten work. Pupils, therefore, may have different perceptions of the assessment of typed work to handwritten work. A similar shift in expectations can be seen at the level of web based e-portfolios (see also Chapter 17). Pupils and assessors are no longer expecting the simple presentation of work but are also expecting reflection on the construction of the work (Pimentel, 2010).

Task 11.1 **Reviewing modes of assessment**

Consider the forms of assessment experienced by a particular year group in your school in the course of a year. To what extent are e-portfolios and other forms of assessment using digital tools employed? Compare your findings with that of a colleague in a different subject area or school. What improvements and changes do you consider might be adopted to improve the learning experience of the pupil?

This requirement for reflection on tasks to be included is a change in assessment mode as the work itself is no longer sufficient. The dialogic conversation around the construction of the work is emerging as a component of assessment processes as educators apply concepts from Black and Wiliam (1998) into the assessment process in particular, the idea that the pupil and teacher must be overtly aware of how the work is constructed against the expectations of the assessment criteria.

To assess whether a pupil understands a topic some teachers are turning to digital texts – both in use as a teaching tool and as an end product for pupils to create. For example, writing for Futurelab, Hague and Williamson cite a Cambridge school in which computer games are approached in a similar way to a novel:

> The approach taken to studying computer games during the lessons is to focus on both the 'critical consumption' of games and the 'creative production' of games. For the critical component of the course, pupils study how the computer games industry operates, how games are marketed to particular audiences and how the design of a game influences the ways in which players engage with it. Pupils also study how character, genre and narrative are created and sustained through design choices and the interplay of images, sounds and action.
>
> (Hague and Williamson, 2009, p. 7)

Thus practitioners are developing assessment, which brings into the school domain the learner's outside interaction with digital texts with a view to developing transferable skills and connections with traditional study materials. This dialogic exchange between a pupil's outside digital life and their school life is beginning to attract further research. Bulfin and North (2007), for example, have posited that assessment of pupils through information and communication technologies is capable of capturing a wider range of assessment opportunities than traditional methods, which are limited to the work undertaken in school settings:

> young people's engagement with language, learning and technology might be characterised as a dialogic negotiation of a complex range of texts and practices that flow across and between school, home and other spaces.
>
> (Bulfin and North, 2007, p. 1)

We are seeing, then, that at an assessment level it is becoming harder to extract that learning which is just undertaken in the classroom as notions of space and classroom are eroded by the introduction of virtual spaces and virtual learning as well as ICT based expression of ideas through hyperlinked three-dimensional texts.

THE IMPACT OF ICT ON PEDAGOGY

Here, the chapter explores how traditional teaching methods are fusing with and being reinforced by technology. It shows how dialogic pedagogies are being embraced and adapted to reinforce learning in the classroom.

Construction of knowledge and understanding

Whilst it might be fair to think that ICT is pushing education into new and innovative areas, at the same time it is reinforcing traditional models of teaching. The concept of constructivism, for example, can be seen as enhanced by the impact of ICT on curriculum delivery. The idea that teachers and pupils engage in a construction of learning and development of knowledge is reinforced by the use of technology. VLEs or MLEs (virtual or managed learning environments) are built around Assessment for Learning principles with peer- and self-assessment embedded into assessed tasks. Tasks can be undertaken and presented en masse with the teacher and other pupils taking in turns to play the Vygotskian role of the 'learned other'. There is a limit here to the success of this approach in supporting learning, however, if those engaged do not understand how to apply these principles. Ravenscroft (2001) explored the contrast between human and computer based dialogic tutoring in his work on Vygotsky's 'Learned Other' but found many weaknesses as computer based tutors' responses lacked 'any clear pedagogic principles' (p. 144). Adams (2011) picks up this issue and develops it to look at other online groups which the pupil belongs to: 'This creation of the differing "domains of knowledge" (Solomon 1987) presents a key difficulty for education: how is it that we are to bring these together?' (Adams, 2011, pp. 27–8).

For Adams (2011), pupils are engaged in a range of knowledge and assessment online domains with the school 'domain' often sitting in isolation and in opposition to the other knowledge domains. The 'voice' of the teacher and school based education will merely sit alongside and in opposition to other voices accessible by the pupil through ICT. For example, a pupil might download an app onto their smartphone that gives assessment advice in opposition to that which their teacher asserts. Adams, therefore, proposes that new learning is being undertaken through the deployment of ICT in pedagogy rather than just 'as a means by which teacher activity (and thus by inference pupil learning) might be enhanced' (2011, p. 30).

To summarise this area, you need to see beyond the teacher using ICT to enhance the learning and assessment of the pupil: the teacher needs to set the agenda for learning and assessment and to be a conduit or a 'learned other' who helps the pupil make sense of the range of pedagogical opportunities over and beyond that which the teacher offers. At the same time, a teacher needs to create a domain of knowledge through the VLE through which the pupils can enter into a constructivist relationship with each other and the teacher to develop their knowledge and understanding of the curriculum *and* pedagogy.

Task 11.2 **Assessment opportunities through the VLE**

Review the ways in which the VLE is used to support assessment in your subject area for a particular year group and compare this with a different year group in your subject area or a similar year group from another subject area. To what extent does the VLE support opportunities for interaction between pupils? To what extent might these exchanges form part of the assessed work of pupils in your subject area?

THE IMPACT OF ICT ON ASSESSMENT

All organisations that need to assess people – from the driving theory test to the new universal benefits system in the United Kingdom – are starting to realise that computer based assessment can offer logistical help but at the same time creates new challenges. This section addresses the challenges faced by an educational system in England that is struggling to assess ICT and assess *with* ICT and compares it with its international competitors.

Separating out ICT from computer science

A curriculum needs to be taught before it can be assessed. Schools expect that teachers will integrate appropriate use of ICT into their subject work. In England, the onus on teaching computer science is the domain of ICT departments, but the deployment of digital technologies in a cross-curricular way is expected across all subjects within the school curriculum. Pupils' skills and knowledge in the use of digital technologies still need to be assessed to ensure pupils develop key skills for their future. The assessment of such skills, however, is likely to be the responsibility of the regular subject teacher. Pupils should be expected to make choices, to use their initiative and to apply and use ICT in a range of concepts and for a range of purposes. For a subject teacher to make an assessment, they must be aware of how ICT might be used in their subject area. For example, if a pupil offers a blog as an element of original writing for the English Language coursework, a teacher must be aware of where that work sits in the field of blogging and whether it is within the boundaries of forms and conventions of blogging. Whilst the isolated and time short examination room has little to recommend it in the modern world, in ICT terms there is frequently an expectation of delivery in a short time span – whether this is a blog, a tweeting service or an app.

The contrast of the isolation of the examination room really stands out here as remote from the pupil experience, as the modern pupil frequently belongs to a range of special interest groups or affinity spaces (Gee, 2004) within which members collaborate in the construction of knowledge and products.

If you remove 'school' from your thinking and think about the processes an individual in modern society might follow in completing an intellectual task there is a sequence they follow in terms of problem solving. They may post in their networking sites – Facebook or Linked-in, for example – and ask for help, advice and links. They may tweet to a specialist who they follow to ask them for help and advice. They may create an online space, such as Google docs or a wiki, where they could work with a group on the problem. They might hold online meetings with interested others. And this process could apply to a whole range of commercial or non-commercial activities: from an app design team, to a protest in the real world against an issue. The activity or product is immaterial – the process is important. Yet, in the English examination room none of this occurs. Pupils still handwrite essay responses using the same assessment types as in Victorian times.

In Denmark, computers have been allowed in the examination room for the last ten years. In 2011, the Danes piloted the use of allowing access to the internet in examinations. According to the Danish Minister for Education, Bertel Haarder, 'The internet is indispensable, including in the exam situation. I'm sure that it would be a matter of very few years when most European countries will be on the same line' (cited in Jordan, 2009).

Thus there is an increasing tension between the assessment styles employed by examination bodies who are struggling to come to terms with technological advances and the ways pupils work: collaborating using digital technologies as part of their learning in ways that mirror ways of working in the modern workplaces.

COMPUTER BASED AND ONLINE ASSESSMENT

In this section, the current state of online and computer based assessment is summarised and the potential future direction for England's educational system is explored by looking at the tension raised by the increased use of PISA (Programme for International Pupil Assessment) table rankings.

Moving from now to the future

Online summative assessment naturally starts at a point where it tries to duplicate the current paper based examination. For example, one UK examination board, AQA has commissioned pilots of flash-based science tests in which pupils draw graphs and push interactive elements together as a form of online testing. The examination boards are not likely to see an issue with replacing the expensive and sustainability-poor shipping of millions of exam papers by lorry to scanning centres to be scanned and made available online for the examiners. However, to replace current examinations, schools would have to deal with the logistics of enabling entire year groups to sit computer based examinations at the same time. This would seem to be impractical. Using online assessment could be replacing one set of difficult logistics with another. The Danish system mentioned earlier simply used mobile computing in the form of laptops. Technicians, having built temporary 'assessment' rooms, managed the environment whilst teachers built tests that did not require secrecy and blanket timed release. The pupils were able to enter in smaller groups and then had to tackle tasks which relied on a range of information that they could research. The differentiation, thus, came from the quality of their research skills.

There are examinations in England which are at the level of GCSEs and which have surmounted these problems. ASDAN (http://www.asdan.org.uk) is a national charity that offers a suite of qualifications worth half a GCSE each. If a pupil takes the ASDAN literacy and numeracy online assessments they can boost their GCSE score for entry onto Level 3 courses such as A levels or the International Baccalaureate. Pupils can take the test at any time, the examination changes each time it is sat and there is immediate feedback on whether the examination has been passed or not. This, then, is the current frontier of online assessment at the level of secondary education in England. The reason for these limits is not hard to ascertain: without human input there is a limit to how well artificial intelligence can cope with the assessment regime. Whilst online assessments can cope with multiple choice formats, the concept of subjective assessment is beyond current artificial intelligences.

In Scotland, a pilot of online assessment as part of the National Qualifications Programme (Ashton and Wood, 2006) met problems in Maths where normally a pupil who arrives at the wrong answer can gain a partial credit for the working out. The problem was eventually addressed through having a 'steps approach' whereby pupils entered values into separate boxes as part of the journey of their working out. A conclusion of the study therefore was 'in order to have a reliable and valid measure of pupil performance in Mathematics the assessment system and questions must enable issues such as partial credit to be taken into account' (p. 128).

Much of this work stems from the drive from ATC21S (Assessment of Teaching of 21st Century Skills available at http://www.atcs21.org) who are a cross international group with a shared aim of driving assessment into the twenty-first century. This focus on online assessment is being led by Finland and Singapore as leaders of the international PISA tables from OECD (the Organisation for Economic Co-operation and Development). ATC21S have developed a test for PISA which measures soft skills of collaboration and communication. They have approached this problem by creating an enormous online cloud network. Thus pupils have access to the cloud during the assessment and work in pairs. They have to communicate and collaborate effectively during the assessment period and this is measured by the system and fed into the range of data held by PISA about each country's cohort of pupils. The impact is likely to increase as successive international governments – not least the UK government – place great store in PISA rankings. This leaves England's assessment strategy with a dilemma – to increase a country's PISA table rankings will mean embracing modern assessment methods and ensuring pupils are taught and assessed in a way that enhances the PISA ranking. However, at the same time, it seems the Department of Education in England is even more committed to the traditional handwritten examination room. The two targets are incongruous and counter-productive and it will take a bold Department of Education to embrace the change needed to bring England into line with other leading countries in the world for ICT based assessment.

THE USE OF TECHNOLOGY TO SUPPORT ASSESSMENT FOR LEARNING

Assessment for learning

Recent research in the area of ICT indicates how computers are more frequently used to support the process of summative assessment and that more work is therefore required to understand and develop the potential of ICT to support formative assessment skills and processes (Luckin *et al.*, 2012). This section explores the theory and practice of formative assessment and the various ways by which technology can support it.

Pachler *et al.* define formative assessment with ICT as:

> the iterative process of gathering and analysing information about student learning by teachers as well as learners and of evaluating it in relation to prior achievement and attainment of intended, as well as unintended learning outcomes, in a way that allows the teacher or student to adjust the learning trajectory.
>
> (Pachler *et al.*, 2009, p. 1)

This definition captures the sense in which ICT enables both teachers and pupils to collect and analyse information, sometimes more effectively than through traditional approaches, thereby helping them to make more informed choices and judgements about further steps in the learning cycle. The actual method of assessment, however, may be less critical than what is done with the data which is collected:

> What is key is not how we assess but what we do with the data we generate as a result of interventions which can be supported by technologies.
>
> (Pachler *et al.*, 2009, p. 8)

In this sense the distinction between formative and summative assessment techniques is somewhat blurred since it is the purpose, rather than the technique itself, that distinguishes between these two forms, leading Wiliam to conclude that 'rather than thinking in terms of "formative assessment", it might be more appropriate to think in terms of how assessment can be used "formatively"' (2009, p. 18).

Assessment data become formative in nature when they are used by teachers, pupils or both to provide feedback and feed-forward information which is used to modify the teaching and learning activities which they are involved in (Black and Wiliam, 1998). Black and Wiliam (2009) identify five different stages in using assessment data for formative purposes which include:

1   engineering effective classroom discussion, questions, and learning tasks that elicit evidence of learning;
2   providing feedback that moves learners forward;
3   clarifying and sharing learning intentions and criteria for success;
4   activating students as owners of their own learning; and
5   activating students as instructional resources for one another.

In each of these stages or phases it is possible to recognise a role for technology but this should be a worthwhile and appropriate role rather than simply using technology for its own sake. Technology is not intrinsically formative in nature and as a teacher you will need to be aware of the affordances and the constraints of different ICTs in order to judge when it will be appropriate and efficacious to use them. This judgement is also contingent upon the specific context in which the assessment will be undertaken:

> No assessment technology is in itself formative, but almost any technology can be used in a formative way – if the right conditions are set in place.
>
> (Pachler *et al.*, 2009, p. 2)

Pachler *et al.* (2009) envisage 'moments of contingency' which are points in time that enable learners to think in other ways about the activity, serving as a mirror to reflect their thinking processes, thereby enabling them to reflect and effect personal change:

> Moments of contingency contain within them the scope for learners' understanding to be 'otherwise'. The technology itself does not create these moments; they are dependent on teachers' and learners' actions. But for technology to perform formatively, it needs to acknowledge and support these moments.
>
> (Pachler *et al.*, 2009, p. 2)

'Moments of contingency' may be recognised by teachers as those occasions when pupils and teachers gain an insight into the complex processes that underpin cognitive activity, when the proverbial 'penny drops' or it becomes more obvious what is required to improve performance. In order to activate and exploit these moments teachers need to be aware of the specific affordances of individual technologies.

Pedagogical affordances of technology to support Assessment for Learning

In the context of this chapter the term affordances is used to denote those specific features and attributes of the technology that add value to the processes of formative assessment, above and beyond what could be achieved through traditional approaches. Pachler *et al.* have identified five generic affordances or features of digital technologies (ICTs) that add value to the traditional approaches to assessment.

1   Speed: ICT and technology in general accelerates many of the processes associated with learning such as providing more rapid feedback to the learners or teacher (e.g. through voting devices), which enables the pupil to move more rapidly through the activity.
2   Storage: technology has the capacity to store and access huge amounts of data that would otherwise be impossible to hold by any single person. This can enable learners

to identify patterns and trends that would be undistinguishable in other ways (e.g. through mind-mapping or analytics software).

3   Processing: ICT technologies are capable of analysing responses automatically and providing feedback to learners in various ways as they undertake the task (e.g. instructional software like 'Successmaker', which analyses a learner's performance and adjust the difficulty of further tasks accordingly).

4   Communication: ICT supports rapid communication and sharing of ideas between learners in ways that can be captured (e.g. podcasts) and analysed by the learner whilst they undertake an activity.

5   Construction and representation: ICT technologies allow learners to build and represent their concepts and ideas in different formats, making them more intelligible and clearer. In so doing technology can simplify processes helping learning to detect patterns or to examine their own thinking process, which become more transparent (e.g. through the use of screen recording technology to capture and record a complicated process). In addition, technology allows learners to change ideas quickly, unlike paper and pen exercises, which are often fixed (e.g. a wiki in which learners continually add and modify their representations of a topic).

(Pachler *et al.*, 2009, p. 4)

Case studies

It was noted previously how technology such as computers is not inherently formative in nature but can be used to support formative forms of assessment. This necessitates imagination and creativity on the part of the teacher who needs to be aware of the various pedagogical affordances of a particular technology, as covered in the section above. Three case studies of technology used to support formative assessment are covered in this section. These are mobile technologies (e.g. phones and tablet computers); simulations and serious games; and electronic feedback devices.

Task 11.3 Formative assessment opportunities and pedagogical affordances of technologies

Select *one* of the following technologies covered in this section and consider how you might use it to provide formative feedback for pupils. Refer to the list of features identified by Black and Wiliam and consider which of these are available through the use of the technology you have selected.

MOBILE TECHNOLOGIES

Mobile technologies such as personal phones and tablet computers are becoming increasingly common in secondary schools representing a significant shift from 'tethered' technologies such as desk-top computers which are fixed in particular rooms and spaces (Traxler, 2010), to portable and ubiquitous technologies that move with the pupils, providing 'just in time' access to technology rather than 'just in case' (Kearney *et al.*, 2012). These technologies are frequently equipped with sophisticated applications and software which enable pupils to capture, record and share aspects of their own learning, such as a camera tool, video recorder and audio device. These tools and software can be used to support many of the processes of formative assessment identified by Black and

Wiliam (see section above) based on affordances such as 'storage', 'communication' and 'construction and representation' identified by Pachler *et al.* (2009).

A number of studies and reports have identified the value of using video recordings to encourage learners to reflect upon and identify areas for improvement in their own practice, particularly in vocational or practical subjects such as learning a skill or competence (Kong, 2010). In many of these cases the use of video or audio recordings allows the learner to review their own practice at their own pace, thereby enabling them to self-assess and diagnose their own performance without the need for a third party such as the teacher:

> It was found that video browsing prompted learner–teachers to make more reflective notes, and that they were more deeply reflective about discipline, classroom management, and professional teaching knowledge.
>
> (Kong, 2010, p. 42)

With the growing availability of mobile technologies in schools, teachers and pupils now have access to technologies that facilitate the spontaneous capture and recording of performance and other processes such as an experiment in a science laboratory or a technique in an art lesson. The ubiquity and portability of such technologies also liberates the learner from purely classroom based recordings, since it is quite feasible for them to record and annotate their ideas and reflections during a field trip or out of school activity, to be used later for reflection and analysis.

Closely associated with these activities is the opportunity to use portable technologies as a means of explanation and analysis through the use of screen recording software such as 'Screen Chomp' or 'Explain Everything'. These kinds of applications allow the user to record and annotate (both orally and with additional written annotations) any activity occurring on the device. Thus teachers are able to personalise the feedback they offer students by including voice comments and other marks (e.g. highlighting a piece of written work) that are richer and more diagnostic than purely written feedback. An evaluation of tablet computers across Scotland (Burden *et al.*, 2012) concluded that these kinds of applications and tools offered great potential to customise the feedback provided by teachers. More significantly in the context of assessment for learning, they shift the responsibility from the teacher to the learner providing mechanisms for greater self-assessment and collaborative peer assessment as one teacher in the study reported:

> before I would have maybe sent a worksheet home and they would just complete it and send it back to me. But if I put the worksheet on 'Screen Chomp', then they can do the worksheet on 'Screen Chomp' but record themselves while they do it, and explain what they are doing to me, so I can see where their understanding is, and I can see any points that they are not understanding. And I can also, when I am marking it when I am talking to the children after, I will be able to give them more direct and targeted feedback because I will know exactly where they have gone wrong with things. I think that has been a big change in being able to do that.
>
> (Burden *et al.*, 2012, p. 99)

SIMULATIONS AND SERIOUS GAMES

Simulations and serious games (defined as games with a clear educational purpose) are valuable pedagogical approaches in contexts where it would be too risky or even dangerous to undertake the actual activity (e.g. exploring a nuclear reactor or flying a plane), too time consuming or slow (e.g. waiting to watch a plant grow in a biology lesson) or simply too expensive (Winkley *et al.,* 2010). Although it may not have been the primary purpose of such activities, formative and diagnostic feedback is frequently a by-product of simulations and serious games enabling the learner to rapidly improve or adapt their behaviours and performance. In this sense simulations and serious games usually incorporate a high level of embedded feedback that is formative in nature, although this can sometimes be so implicit learners need additional help in identifying it (Winkley *et al.*, 2010).

One example that is currently attracting attention and interest amongst educators (Luckin *et al.*, 2012) is ARIS, a serious game that enables teachers and pupils to design their own scenarios and challenges which are played out on a mobile device in the space of a building (e.g. a school or museum) or outdoor site (e.g. a historical site). Currently ARIS has been used to construct a variety of scenario based games, including a historical investigation, a scavenger hunt, a citizen journalism game and a Spanish language development game (see http://davidgagnon.wordpress.com/2010/01/23/mobile-learning/).

In each of these examples learners are provided with ongoing, real-time feedback about their performance which enables them to self-assess and modify their strategies and actions as they move further through the exercise. It is envisaged this type of formative feedback will be seen as a key factor in future developments of the software and in similar activities undertaken by other software developers.

Simulation and games based software like this are beginning to influence the design of some summative assessment activities such as the Cambridge Assessment Geography iGCSE Simulated Field Work. Unlike traditional examinations, pupils participate in a virtual geography field trip which forms the basis of their final assessment, also providing formative assessment opportunities along the way. Students have access to virtual tools that mimic those they would find in the real world (e.g. a compass) and are required to demonstrate their mastery of these tools during the simulation. Although this is mainly a summative use of technology, it is conceivable such practices will encourage schools and teachers to develop similar formative assessment activities as they prepare pupils for such examinations and software like ARIS makes this entirely feasible at this point in time.

ELECTRONIC FEEDBACK DEVICES

Electronic feedback devices, or voting devices as they are often termed, have been around some time, usually associated with technologies like the interactive whiteboards (e.g. ActiveVote). These proprietary devices enable the teacher to collect simple feedback from the class such as multiple choice questions or simple preference data (e.g. yes/no answers) which they can use as summative evidence or as formative data to inform their future planning (feed-forward advice). Until recently this proprietary technology was relatively expensive and often tied to specific makes of interactive whiteboard. More recently developments with mobile technologies such as the personal phone, and web based systems, have enabled pupils to use their own personal devices to provide feedback (see, for example, apps like Socrative). These technologies often include the provision for more open-ended, free text answers which allow the exchange of much richer assessment data between pupil and teacher, and between pupils themselves. With the growth and popularity of social networks and Web 2.0 technologies, applications like Twitter, Todays

Meet and TextWall all serve similar purposes in enabling pupils to ask questions, offer suggestions and gain feedback on their performance in a formative manner, which can be both diagnostic and iterative in nature.

Task 11.4 **Assessment for Learning and digital technologies**

Review assessment practice in your school in the light of the advice on Assessment for Learning above and the affordances of digital technologies.

Make notes about what you consider to be the practice that is most effective in supporting pupil learning in your subject area and implement and test out your ideas as opportunities present themselves.

SUMMARY

Recent developments in digital technologies and software support more extended, flexible and personalised forms of assessment that would not be previously possible in the analogue world. They offer tremendous opportunities to support both summative and formative forms of assessment that can be used by both teachers and pupils.

There are many constraints on schools and teachers in the adoption of new practices, but you will find that you have many opportunities within your own classroom and the resources available to you and your students to use digital technologies to support effective assessment practice.

REFERENCES

Adams, P. (2011) 'ICT and pedagogy: opportunities missed?', *Education 3–13*, 39(1): 21–33.

Ashton, H. and Wood, C. (2006) 'Use of online assessment to enhance teaching and learning: the PASS-IT project', *European Educational Research Journal* 5(2): 122–30.

Black, P. and Wiliam, D. (1998) *Inside the Black Box: Raising Standards through Classroom Assessment*, London: School of Education, King's College London.

——(2009) 'Developing the theory of formative assessment', *Educational Assessment, Evaluation and Accountability* 21(1): 5–31.

Bulfin, S. and North, S. (2007) 'Negotiating digital literacy practices across school and home: case studies of young people in Australia', *Language and Education: An International Journal* 21(3): 247–63. Available at: http://0-search.ebscohost.com.brum.beds.ac.uk/login.aspx?direct=true&db=ufh&AN=25492589&authtype=shib&site=eds-live&scope=site (accessed 23 March 2011).

Burden, K., Hopkins, P., Male, T. and Martin, T. (2012) *iPad Scotland Evaluation*, University of Hull. Available from https://xmascotland.wufoo.eu/forms/scottish-mobile-personal-device-evaluation-2012/ (accessed 10 December 2012).

Gee, J.P. (2004) *Situated Language and Learning: A Critique of Traditional Schooling*, New York: Routledge.

Hague, C. and Williamson, B. (2009) *Digital Participation, Digital Literacy, and School Subjects*, Slough: Futurelab.

Jordan, J. (2009) 'Danish pupils use web in exams', BBC News. Available at: http://news.bbc.co.uk/1/hi/education/8341886.stm (accessed 10 December 2012).

Kearney, M., Schuck, S., Burden, K. and Aubusson, P. (2012) 'Viewing mobile learning from a pedagogical perspective', *Research in Learning and Technology* 20: 1–17.

Kong, S.C. (2010) 'Using a web-enabled video system to support student–teachers' self-reflection in teaching practice', *Computers and Education* 55: 1772–82.

Luckin, R., Bligh, B., Manches, A., Ainsworth, S., Crook, C. and Noss, R. (2012) *Decoding Learning: The Proof, Promise and Potential of Digital Education*, Nesta: London. Available at: http://www.nesta.org.uk/press_releases/assets/features/decoding_learning_the_proof_promise_and_potential_of_digital_education (accessed 10 December 2012).

Nielson (2009) 'Global places and networked faces', 9 March. Available at: http://blog.nielsen.com/nielsenwire/wp-content/uploads/2009/03/nielsen_globalfaces_mar09.pdf (accessed 10 December 2012).

Pachler, N., Mellar, H., Daly, C., Mor, Y., Wiliam, D. and Laurillard, D. (2009) *Scoping a Vision For Formative E-Assessment: A Project Report for JISC Version 2.0*, London: Institute for Education. Available at: http://www.jisc.ac.uk/publications/reports/2009/feasstfinalreport.aspx (accessed 10 December 2012).

Pimentel, J.M. (2010) 'High school teachers' perceptions of eportfolios and classroom practice: a single-case study', Unpublished Ed.D. thesis, Johnson and Wales University.

Powers, D., Fowles, M., Farnum, M. and Ramsey, P. (1994) 'Will they think less of my handwritten essay if others word process theirs? Effects on essay scores of intermingling handwritten and word-processed essays', *Journal of Educational Measurement* 31(3): 220–33.

Ravenscroft, A. (2001) 'Designing e-learning interactions in the 21st century: revisiting and rethinking the role of theory', *European Journal of Education* 36(2): 133–56.

Wiliam, D. (2009) 'Dylan Wiliam's observation at the July 2009 practical enquiry day'. Available at http://purl.org/planet/Groups.FormativeEAssessment/3July (accessed 10 December 2012).

Winkley, J., Wrightson, C., Merritt, R., Mitchell, T. and Roads, M. (2010) *Final Report: A Landscape Review of E-assessment: A Review of the Current Landscape of E-Assessment, Containing a Cross-Partner Analysis of Evidence, and Recommendations For Actions'*, AlphaPlus Consultancy Ltd for Becta (Coventry: UK). Available at: http://www.alphaplusconsultancy.co.uk/pdf/Becta%20-%20E-assessment%20Landscape%20review%20-%20Report%20Final.pdf (accessed 10 December 2012).

12

FOSTERING AN INTERNATIONAL DIMENSION AND GLOBAL CITIZENSHIP IN SECONDARY EDUCATION WITH DIGITAL TECHNOLOGIES

Ana Redondo

INTRODUCTION

As early as the 1960s, Marshall McLuhan (1962, 1964) coined the phrase the 'Global Village' to describe the impact of technology on real-time communication and, in turn, on how people from around the world are involved with and interconnected to one another leading to new socio-cultural structures as well as increased diversity as well as, at the same time, responsibilities.

Another phenomenon characterising all spheres of life in the twenty-first century, including education, is globalisation, which tends to describe the processes attendant to international integration. In the world of education, globalisation has tended to manifest itself in the form of international comparisons and league tables, such as PISA and TIMMS, as well as policy borrowing. For example, the foreword to the 2010 White Paper 'The importance of teaching' (DfE, 2010) by the Prime Minister, the Deputy Prime Minister and the Secretary of State for Education are littered with references to other countries, in particular Finland and South Korea.

There exists, therefore, a clear need for society to prepare young people for life in a tightly technologically, politically, financially, economically, ecologically, linguistically and culturally interwoven world. One key mechanism for the preparation of young people for life in society is the school curriculum, which is why, very often, curricular reform is a very political affair rather than a task mainly for educators. At the time of writing, England is experiencing a lot of change in education policy following the election of a new government, which is trying to make its mark on society through education policy including curricular reform. It is very likely that the role of an international dimension and global citizenship in the new curriculum will be rather different to the one the global dimension plays at the moment as one cutting across various subjects. It seems rather likely that the current attempts to achieve at least some linkages across subjects will be further weakened but, instead, for certain elements around a global dimension, whatever it will be taken to mean, to feature within subject curricula, which are expected to be characterised by local variability (see http://www.globaldimension.org.uk/pages/8444; http://www.education.gov.uk/schools/teachingandlearning/curriculum).

Task 12.1 Exploring the international dimension and global citizenship in your school

By asking key colleagues from subject departments across the school, collect examples of the coverage of the international dimension and global citizenship across the school. Then, try to categorise the examples: what picture emerges? What are the key themes? Which are the key departments? What global teaching resources are in use? What gaps, if any, do you think your data shows? And, what role do digital technologies play in current provision?

In the literature a number of key terms are being used to describe the phenomena discussed in this chapter. The title of this chapter aims to capture related discourses (internationalisation, globalisation) as well as different emphases with the term 'dimension' focusing more on institutional considerations and 'citizenship' more on individuals and their dispositions, values, attitudes, skills, knowledge and understanding. For a discussion of the related discourses in the specialist literature, see for example Knight (2004), who discussed the evolution of the term 'internationalisation'. One definition he rehearses is that provided by van der Wende (1997), who saw internationalisation as 'any systematic effort aimed at making … education responsive to the requirements and challenges related to the globalisation of societies, economy and labour markets' (p. 18). Another term to be found in the literature is that of education for democratic citizenship (see, e.g. Osler and Starkey, 2005).

OBJECTIVES

By the end of this chapter you should have developed an understanding of:

■ the role of the global citizenship in secondary school curricula in general and in your subject in particular;
■ the contribution of digital technologies to the teaching and learning of global citizenship.

THE NATURE AND ROLE OF THE CURRICULUM

In view of curricular uncertainty, rather than discuss the current status of the global issues in the curriculum, let us explore some general issues around curriculum planning with reference to global citizenship and an international dimension. Before we do so, let us just note what value the UK government ascribed to the global dimension in the curriculum in the mid-2000s:

> young people are given opportunities to: critically examine their own values and attitudes; appreciate the similarities between peoples everywhere, and value diversity; understand the global context of their local lives; and develop skills that will enable them to combat injustice, prejudice and discrimination. Such knowledge, skills and understanding enable young people to make informed decisions about playing an active role in the global community.
>
> (DfES, 2005, p. 3)

What seems to be of key concern is the extent to which an exploration of 'otherness' enables young people to relativise their own life-worlds with a view to becoming more tolerant, aware and empathetic of other people and how they live as well as better able to reflect on key issues affecting their everyday lives. In a later section the document identifies this as a key concept and calls it 'interdependence'.

Curriculum developers face the challenge of how to reflect the dynamic inherent in an ever increasing complexity of, and rapid transformation in the world in a set of curricular statements around knowledge, skills and understanding. The fragmentation inherent in globalisation as well as the processes of individualisation inherent in neo-liberal views of the world make it next to impossible to get any sort of agreement on what might constitute a canon to be transmitted to and appropriated by the new generation. In addition, in most countries, including the UK, there exist strong political forces that emphasise the importance of the nation state, few more explicitly than the 2012 *Teachers' Standards* for England (DfE, 2012), which, among many other things, require of teachers to uphold public trust in the profession by 'not undermining fundamental British values' (p. 10). Indeed, as Kress (2000, p. 134) rightly points out in the current societal context of instability, 'reproduction is no longer a plausible metaphor for institutional education and its curricula'. In its place, Kress proposes the metaphor of 'design: curriculum as a design for the future' which he sees linked to notions such as creativity, innovation and adaptability. This idea has, indeed, become very prevalent in research and development work in the field of technology-enhanced teaching and learning:

> the systematic study of designing, developing and evaluating educational interventions (such as programs, teaching-learning strategies and materials, products and systems) as solutions for complex problems in educational practice, which also aims at advancing our knowledge about the characteristics of these interventions and the processes of designing and developing them.
>
> (Plomp, 2007, p. 13)

One central feature of design for Kress is the notion of 'agency', the ability of an individual to act in and on the world. And, for him, this emphasis on creative, individual agency necessitates a very different curriculum to that first conceptualised in the nineteenth century, particularly in relation to the learners' role in knowledge construction and the range of semiotic resources available to them.

KEY CONCEPTS OF GLOBAL CITIZENSHIP

In their study of 'worldly pedagogy', i.e. pedagogy that positively addresses differences across nations and cultures, Fanghanel and Cousin (2012) draw on the work of Carter, who distinguishes three meanings of global citizenship:

firstly, in a neoliberal view, the citizen is a consumer with individual rights and the emphasis is on must-haves and entitlement; secondly, a concept of citizenship based on the liberal nineteenth century view which emphasises a political role within a nation, highlighting rights as well as duties, and notions of social responsibility and universal democratic values; thirdly, a view of the citizen as an activist, being engaged in global economic debates, green issues, social justice, world poverty, etc., briefly as an agenda addressing the failings of neoliberalism … which focuses on agentic and local 'indigenous' manifestations and local responses to structural flows inherent in 'globalisation from above'.

(Fanghanel and Cousin, 2012, p. 41)

All three perspectives delineated by Carter can be seen to map well onto technology-related discourses: research, for example by Pachler *et al.* (2010), has developed the notion of the 'mobile complex', in which fragmentation, provisionality and individualisation are key characteristics of current socio-cultural transformations. Also, sustainability has become an important theme in debates about technology use in educational context in educational institutions in the UK as well as in development education. From an ecological perspective this includes concerns about energy as well as about the raw materials needed for the production of technological devices. It also involves questions of a pedagogical nature, for example how to ensure sustainability and equity in a context of the much discussed digital divide: how can we ensure all learners have equal access to appropriate devices and relevant infrastructure (wireless networks, data plans etc.) inside and outside of school? Traxler (2010), for example, discusses the ethical dimension of teaching and learning with educational technology, in his case mobile devices, and lists the following challenges: sustainability, scalability (or transferability), equity, inclusion, opportunity and embedding. And, there is of course the issue of agency afforded by digital technologies and the digital literacy required to make the best possible use of it to effectively find and critically engage with the digital artefacts and services available online and how related skills, knowledge and understanding map onto more traditional educational resources and processes. Ever since Prensky coined the term 'digital native' back in 2001, a not always particularly critical debate has ensued about the technological skills new generations of learners bring with them when they enter formal education and what the implications are for education and educational reform (for a critical discussion see, e.g. Bennett *et al.*, 2008). One social trend, which is difficult to refute, relates to the potential for participation through social networking and the production of cultural artefacts through digital technologies making it possible for schools to play an active role in social transformation by engaging with the potential of digital technologies, for example by adding a level of reflexivity onto the use of digital technologies not normally in evidence in their everyday use. With social mobility remaining a key function for formal education, a strong focus on digital technologies can be seen to contribute considerably to a number of variables often identified as contributory to social mobility, such as economic, cultural and social capital (see, e.g. Bourdieu, 1984).

In an influential document the UK government delineates eight key concepts underlying the idea of a global dimension in the curriculum (DfES, 2005, p. 12):

■ global citizenship;
■ conflict resolution;
■ social justice;

- values and perceptions;
- sustainable development;
- interdependence;
- human rights; and
- diversity.

For the purposes of this chapter we will look at two of them in more detail here: global citizenship and interdependence.

Global citizenship

Gaining the knowledge, skills and understanding of concepts and institutions necessary to become informed, active, responsible citizens:

- developing skills to evaluate information and different points of view on global issues through the media and other sources;
- learning about institutions, declarations and conventions and the role of groups, NGOs and governments in global issues;
- developing an understanding of how and where key decisions are made;
- appreciating that young people's views and concerns matter and are listened to;
- how to take responsible action that can influence and affect global issues;
- appreciating the global context of local and national issues and decisions at a personal and societal level, understanding the roles of language, place, arts, religion in own and others' identity.

Interdependence

Understanding how people, places, economies and environments are all inextricably interrelated, and that choices and events have repercussions on a global scale:

- understanding the impact of globalisation and that choices made have consequences at different levels, from personal to global;
- appreciating the links between the lives of others and children's and young people's own lives;
- understanding the influence that diverse cultures and ideas (political, social, religious, economic, legal, technological and scientific) have on each other and appreciating the complexity of interdependence;
- understanding how the world is a global community, and what it means to be a citizen;
- understanding how actions, choices and decisions taken in the UK can impact positively or negatively on the quality of life of people in other countries.

DfES, 2005, p. 12

Learning and Teaching Scotland (2011, p. 10) conceptualise global citizenship as a recognition of our responsibility towards each other and the wider world and they offer the circular chart in Figure 12.1 as a visual representation of their approach.

Task 12.2 **Mapping key concepts of global citizenship**

Read DfES (2005) and look in particular at pages 12 and 13. Choose two key concepts described there and consider how the learning outcomes identified against them map onto your specialist subject. For example, how could you contribute towards pupils' understanding of the impact of globalisation through your teaching of modern foreign languages?

   In a second step, consider how digital technologies could be used to support you.

Task 12.3 **The role of technology in education for global citizenship**

Consider how technology can be mapped onto Oxfam's model. What technologies can be used and how? What particular affordances could they bring to supporting the skills the model is trying to foster? Redraw the model showing the contribution of digital technology.

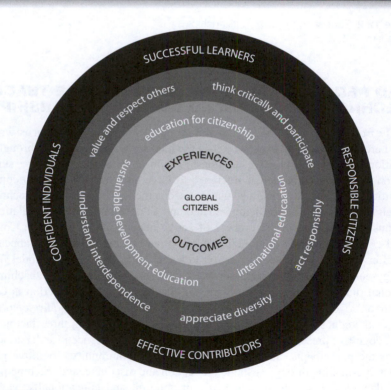

■ **Figure 12.1** Learning for life
Source: LTScotland, 2011, p. 10.

In their guidance for teachers, Oxfam (2008) offer a number of useful practical examples for the classroom. In addition, they put forward a conceptual map for education for global citizenship (see Figure 12.2). It is very interesting to note that technology does not feature explicitly in Oxfam's thinking.

Figure 12.2 Education for global citizenship
Source: Oxfam 2008, p. 3.

BROAD PEDAGOGICAL APPROACHES TO THE TEACHING OF TECHNOLOGY-ENHANCED GLOBAL CITIZENSHIP

One study from the growing body of literature on global citizenship that is worthy of mention here is that by Hoskins *et al.* (2012), which shows that learning through social participation has a strong positive relationship with citizenship knowledge, skills and dispositions. They make particular reference to Lave and Wenger's (1991) concept of communities of practice, which is also widely used in the literature on digital technologies and which explains learning as being situated and as developing through relationships, interactions and conflicts in the process of active negotiation of meaning. Computer-mediated communication in conjunction with online communities would appear to be able to offer useful affordances in relation to social participation. One model from the technology-enhanced learning literature that can be used to support the teaching of an international dimension and global citizenship through social participation is Garrison and Anderson's Community of Inquiry model (http://communitiesofinquiry.com/model), which sees the educational experience influenced by the following three factors: social presence, cognitive presence and teaching presence. Social presence is understood by the authors as the participants' ability to identify with the community; cognitive presence about meaning-making through sustained reflection and discourse; and teaching presence as the pedagogical fostering of personally meaningful and educationally worthwhile learning outcomes. Key processes for Garrison and Anderson are a triggering event leading to perception, exploration leading to deliberation, integration leading to conception and resolution feeding into action.

Task 12.4 **Applying the community of inquiry model to global citizenship**

Consider how Garrison and Anderson's community of inquiry model could be used to develop a computer-mediated communication-based intervention focusing on one of the eight key concepts listed on pages 177 and 178.

Another important pedagogical practice supporting the development of global citizenship is the provision of opportunities for debating and discussing contested/controversial issues (see, e.g. Osler and Starkey, 2005, p. 36). This approach is discussed in detail in a companion title to this book (Huddleston and Rowe, 2003) which, drawing on the work of Neil Mercer (1995), distinguishes disputational, cumulative and exploratory talk with the latter, exploratory talk, being considered particularly valuable as it encourages speakers to engage critically but constructively with each other's ideas. Huddleston and Rowe call their approach a 'public discourse' approach (p. 121). Again, no explicit role is envisaged in the model for technology yet, clearly, social networking tools such as blogs or podcasts offer ample potential to support public discourse.

In addition to public discourse, participation in sustainable global partnerships linked to collaborative curriculum projects can be seen to be an important pedagogical approach to fostering global citizenship as they, for example, enable learners to make links between personal/local and international/global perspectives on issues as well as require of learners to reflect on their own attitudes and values and compare them to those of others. Again, this is an approach digital technologies can meaningfully support. The British Council, for example, runs Schools Online (http://schoolsonline.britishcouncil.org/partner-with-a-school), which offers a partnership database with more than 40,000 schools and colleges from all over the world interested in starting a school partnership. An alternative is ePals (http://www.epals.com), a learning community of teachers and students from over 200 countries, ideas for classroom projects and related resources, collaboration tools including a number of teacher communities, including one on global citizens and a teacher resource library. Another service is eTwinning (http://www.etwinning.net), an online community for schools in Europe.

Task 12.5 **Using technology to support a 'public discourse' model**

Consider how social networking technologies can be used to support a public discourse approach to the teaching of global citizenship. What social networking tools can be used and how? What are their relative advantages and disadvantages in terms of speaking in class versus writing for a semi-private or public audience and in an interconnected way? As a stimulus, read the following blog post: http://mbdoneducation.blogspot.co.uk/2012/07/what-are-you-writing-for.html. For guidance on teaching controversial issues, see Oxfam 2006.

> ### Task 12.6 **Planning an online collaborative curriculum project**
>
> Exploring the resources available on the Schools Online, ePals and eTwinning websites, list the key issues involved in setting up and carrying out an online collaborative curriculum project. Then, develop a project outline in the field of global citizenship following the models available on the ePals website: offer a short description of the concept, outline among other things the intended outcomes as well as the key project elements and specify the intended target group as well as the technologies to be used.

Digital video-based ethnography can be mentioned here. This is an approach exemplified well in a paper by Beers (2001) in the context of foreign language pedagogy in relation to the theme of intercultural sensitivity and tolerance. Beer identifies four key skills required to carry out an ethnographic project: thick observation, thick interpretation, thick comparison and thick description. The basic tasks for learners in this approach is to produce a digital portfolio of still photographs or video shorts individually or in groups on their interpretation of cultural artefacts or phenomena of their choice using the video recording functions of their mobile phones and open them up for critique, for example through uploading them to an online repository. For details on working with digital video, see Burn and Durran in this volume. This approach focuses in particular on the concept of identity as through the artefacts produced and students are given opportunities to explore how they understand the world they live in and what agency they have on it. It also builds on new perspectives on literacy discussed by Pachler, Böck and Adami, also in this volume.

A further approach that could be adopted to develop technology-enhanced global citizenship is Service Learning, which is designed to allow students to apply what they have learnt in school in real life as well as to complement what is learnt in school with experiential knowledge and contextualisation from real life. Grim (2010) provides a useful summary of some of the literature on service learning. The use of mobile devices, in particular smartphone, lends itself particularly well to capture critical incidents related to service learning and given their 'convergence' (Pachler *et al.*, 2010), both in terms of multi-functionality as well as connectivity to the internet, enable the bridging of the world outside the classroom with that in it synchronously or asynchronously. Apps such as Audioboo, Animoto, Qik or Ustream allow for the production and/or streaming of digital audio and video artefacts for journaling. Grim's study inter alia shows that service learning can impact positively on students' civic commitment and fosters the connection of the intellectual and the personal.

SUMMARY

This chapter has explored the rationale behind the introduction of an international dimension and global citizenship in the secondary curriculum and attempted to get you to consider how to integrate some related key concepts into your subject teaching using digital technologies. The chapter has shown how approaches promoted by the UK government as well as NGOs tend not to afford much emphasis on technology-enhanced learning. Through the activities featured in the chapter you have been encouraged to explore how the affordances of digital technologies can be applied meaningfully to developing the young people in our care into citizens who have a heightened sense of responsibility for others, which they use as a moral compass for their actions in everyday life.

RESOURCES

British Council Link and Partnerships (http://www.britishcouncil.org/schoolpartnerships-about-us-our-work-international-dimension.htm)

Global Dimension (http://www.globaldimension.org.uk)

Oxfam Teacher Support: The Global Dimension (http://www.oxfam.org.uk/education/teachersupport/global_dimension)

REFERENCES

Beers, M. (2001) 'A media-based approach to developing ethnographic skills for second language teaching and learning', *ZIF* 6(1). Available at: http://zif.spz.tu-darmstadt.de/jg-06-2/beitrag/beers2.htm (accessed 14 May 2013).

Bennett, S., Maton, K. and Kervin, L. (2008) 'The "digital natives" debate: a critical review of the evidence', *British Journal of Educational Technology* 39(5): 775–86.

Bourdieu, P. (1984) *Distinction: A Social Critique of the Judgement of Taste*, London: Routledge.

DfE (2010) *The Importance of Teaching: The Schools White Paper 2010*, London: DfE.

——(2012) *Teachers' Standards*, London: DfE.

DfES (2005) *Developing the Global Dimension in the School Curriculum*, London: DfE. Available at: http://www.globaldimension.org.uk/uploadedFiles/AboutUs/gdw_developing_the_global_dimension.pdf (accessed 14 May 2013).

Fanghanel, J. and Cousin, G. (2012) '"Worldly" pedagogy: a way of conceptualising teaching towards global citizenship', *Teaching in Higher Education* 17(1): 39–50.

Grim, F. (2010) 'Giving authentic opportunities to second language learners: a look at a French Service-Learning project', *Foreign Language Annals* 43(4): 605–23.

Hoskins, B., Janmaat, J. and Villalba, E. (2012) 'Learning citizenship through social participation outside and inside school: an international, multilevel study of young people's learning of citizenship', *British Educational Research Journal* 38(3): 419–46.

Huddleston, T. and Rowe, D. (2003) 'Citizenship and the role of language', in L. Gearon (ed.) *Learning To Teach Citizenship in the Secondary School: A Companion to School Experience*, London: RoutledgeFalmer, pp. 111–30.

Knight, J. (2004) 'Internationalization remodelled: definition, approaches, and rationales', *Journal of Studies in International Education 8(1)*: 5–29

Kress, G. (2000) 'A curriculum for the future', *Cambridge Journal of Education* 30(1): 133–45.

Lave, J. and Wenger, E. (1991) *Situated Learning: Legitimate Peripheral Participation?*, Cambridge: Cambridge University Press.

Learning and Teaching Scotland (2011) *Developing Global Citizens Within Curriculum for Excellence*. Available at: http://www.LTScotland.org.uk/globalcitizenship (accessed 14 May 2013).

McLuhan, M. (1962) *The Gutenberg Galaxy*, London: Routledge & Kegan Paul.

——(1964) *Understanding Media*, New York: Mentor.

Mercer, N. (1995) *The Guided Construction of Knowledge: Talk Amongst Teachers and Learners*, Clevedon: Multilingual Matters.

Osler, A. and Starkey, H. (2005) 'Education for democratic citizenship: a review of research, policy and practice 1995–2005', *Bera Professional User Review*. Available at: http://www.bera.ac.uk/system/files/oslerstarkeyberareview2005.pdf (accessed 14 May 2013).

Oxfam (2006) *Teaching Controversial Issues*. Global Citizenship Guides. Available at: http://www.oxfam.org.uk/education/teachersupport/cpd/controversial/ (accessed 14 May 2013).

——(2008) *Getting Started With Global Citizenship: A Guide For New Teachers*. Available at: http://www.oxfam.org.uk/education/teachersupport/cpd/ (accessed 14 May 2013).

Pachler, N., Bachmair, B. and Cook, J. (2010) *Mobile Learning: Structure, Agency, Practices*, New York: Springer.

Plomp, T. (2007) 'Educational design research: an introduction', in T. Plomp and N. Nieveen (eds), *An Introduction to Educational Design Research*, Enschede: Netherlands Institute For Curriculum Development. Available at: http://www.slo.nl/downloads/2009/Introduction_20to_20education_20design_20research.pdf/ (accessed 14 May 2013).

Prensky, M. (2001) 'Digital natives, digital immigrants', *On the Horizon* 9(5): 1–6.

——(2001) 'Digital natives, digital immigrants, part II: do they really think differently?', *On the Horizon* 9(6): 1–6.

Traxler, J. (2010) 'Sustaining mobile learning and its institutions', *International Journal of Mobile and Blended Learning* 2(4): 58–65.

van der Wende, M. (1997) 'Missing links: the relationship between national policies for internationalisation and those for higher education in general', in T. Kalvermark and M. van der Wende (eds), *National Policies For the Internationalisation of Higher Education in Europe*, Stockholm: Hogskoleverket Studies, National Agency for Higher Education, pp. 10–31.

MOBILE LEARNING: STRATEGIES FOR PLANNING AND IMPLEMENTING LEARNING WITH MOBILE DEVICES IN SECONDARY SCHOOL CONTEXTS

Judith Seipold, Norbert Pachler, Ben Bachmair and Beat Döbeli Honegger

INTRODUCTION

As the history of mobile learning, which extends to more than a decade by now, has taught us, that banning digital mobile devices such as mobile phones, tablets, mp3 players etc. from classrooms and school yards is not the only option available to deal with these new technologies in school contexts. In fact, in order to be able to make use of the potentials inherent in the use of technologies which originate in learners' everyday lifeworlds and that are originally designed for entertainment, communication and networking, it is necessary to scrutinise opportunities and the learning experiences that the use of mobile technologies offer to learners. In this chapter we critically discuss both aspects and aim to build a bridge between learners' media use in everyday life and school learning with mobile devices. This includes:

- a definition of what learning with mobile devices means;
- an illustration of how learners are using mobile devices in their everyday life including some usage data;
- a problematisation of the mobile phone ban in school contexts including ethical issues and issues such as e-safety;
- guidelines for planning and implementing mobile learning in school, including a discussion of how the use of mobile devices might be linked to learning objectives and how they can be used for situated learning;
- guidelines for evaluating mobile apps;
- a discussion of assessment of mobile learning.

ISSUES IN MOBILE LEARNING

Working definition of mobile learning

Task 13.1 **Your definition of mobile learning**

What do you associate with the term 'mobile learning'? What is your working definition? What examples of mobile learning are you familiar with? What technologies (hardware and software) do you associate with mobile learning?

Now, read through this first section of the chapter. How does your definition compare with that proposed in this chapter? In what way is it similar or different?

We consider it unproductive to limit a discussion of mobile learning to aspects of technology; our concern with mobile learning is not one of technological fetishisation, i.e. we don't view mobile devices as the new panacea and remedy for various educational challenges, such as underachievement or demotivation. In part this is the case because technologies change, often quite rapidly, and, therefore there is the danger of perpetual obsolescence and of constant change in order to stand still. Predominantly, though, it is the case because it is not the technology itself that impacts on teaching and learning but what teachers and learners do with it; i.e. just introducing computational devices into a classroom without appropriate professional development for teachers on how to use them is likely to have disruptive rather than positive effects. For this reason our focus is on pedagogical practice.

The affordances of mobility in mobile learning are important for us because they potentially turn users' everyday lifeworlds into learning contexts by supporting processes of meaning-making in and of the world at all times and in all locations. In other words, the portability of mobile devices and their attendant ubiquity, i.e. the fact that they are readily available and accepted in most social situations, coupled with their multifunctionality, means that they potentially are available any time and anywhere. In particular, we consider mobile devices to be valuable because they enable the user not only the generation of content but also the construction of learning contexts. A key feature in this regard is their convergence: on the one hand, mobile devices combine a myriad of functions in one place and, importantly, in the palm of the user's hand; on the other, internet connectivity, through telephony or wireless, allows users to link local information, artefacts and people with distributed social and information networks thereby bridging the resources available in the here and now with those available at a distance.

As convergent tools, mobile technologies also allow for complex networking activities distributed across time and place. This affordance also makes them attractive teaching and learning tools. What is particularly striking is their potential for social interactivity, information retrieval, processing and exchange as well as context sensitivity and location awareness. The ongoing trend in the reduction of cost of hardware and services as well as in personal ownership and in a growing familiarity with, and personalisation of them allows for more flexible strategies in the implementation of mobile devices in classrooms. Rather than schools purchasing class sets of equipment, we are particularly interested in developing strategies that enable the integration of personally owned devices into school-based teaching and learning. This is not predominantly a question of cost, although it would seem to us to be a more sustainable approach to technology use in schools, but it is mainly about making technology skills and expertise from personal life fruitful for school-based learning.

With the growing popularity of tablets, in particular Apple's iPad, the question begs asking whether the term 'mobile learning' refers mainly to the use of mobile phones, in particular so-called smartphones, or whether tablets also legitimately fall into the category of mobile learning. Practical examples, for instance the work carried out by Fraser Speirs at the Cedars School in Scotland (http://cedars.inverclyde.sch.uk), the Projektschule Goldau in Switzerland (http://www.projektschule-goldau.ch) or work carried out by Kevin Burden and colleges in the north-east of England (http://www.mymobile-project. eu/spip.php?rubrique11#Hull and http://www.mymobile-project.eu/spip.php?rubrique11 #vHull) suggest that iPads but also other devices such as iPods can be used very effectively and in interesting ways in classrooms in particular if the school has a wireless network that allows for connectivity and, therefore, convergence with resources that are not co-located. In addition, the growing popularity of so-called apps, be they explicitly educational or not, suggests to us that a broader definition of mobile learning, namely one that includes tablet devices, is appropriate as these devices, unlike laptops or stand-alone personal computers, have a degree of portability that allows them to be used easily in a wide range of contexts and locations and makes them more or less ubiquitously available – a key element of our definition of mobility.

Central aspects in our conceptualisation of mobile learning are structures, agency and cultural practices (see Pachler *et al.*, 2010):

■　Structures, for example, are features of mass communication and everyday life, such as learning environment, home, school, peers, leisure time as well as social milieus. Learners navigate within these structures but they can also produce structures, which is an important and emancipating aspect. Orientating oneself within structures is as important as it is to provide orientation.

■　Agency means the ability to act in and on the world with all available structures and to appropriate these structures. Part of this is that each individual has a subjective perspective on the world. This indicates that agency is affected by subjectivity and that – as a consequence – appropriation and learning are first of all and always subjectively meaningful. The aim is for school learning to moderate between subjective perspectives of the learner and objective requirements of school. In a context where the relevance of school-based learning is increasingly being questioned by young people, this seems to us to be a particularly important aspect.

■ In some areas young people develop routines (which we call 'cultural practices'). These routines enable young people to act confidently and safely in situations and within structures. Here it becomes necessary to acknowledge, for example the organisation of everyday life, networking, media reception and production or investigation competences of the learners in relation to curricular requirements and to make them available for school learning. The media habits of young people, for example in relation to digital game playing, fall into this category.

As can be seen above, engagement with media is an intentional activity, which is also dependent on the social and cultural situation of learners and use. These aspects are important for learning and teaching (with digital technologies) because they help us understand that learners from different social milieus and backgrounds have different availability of technologies, attitudes towards learning (with them), availability of information, etc.

To summarise our working definition of mobile learning, from an educational perspective, mobile devices are attractive to us for engaging with, and for mediating the world around us as well as for communicating in and with it (see Kress and Pachler, 2007). In our view, mobile learning is the didactic response to the changes in culture, media structures and habits and learning of children and young people, and it takes seriously the new and dominant media culture of everyday life that has to be understood as being individualised, mobile and convergent, as well as the increasing relevance of informal learning and decreasing reach of school-based learning. An important educational task for us, therefore, is the assimilation of learning in informal contexts of everyday life in which students act as naive native experts. Also, mobile devices lend themselves to situated learning, which is often militated against by the fossilised practices of schools. Mobile devices support the notion of learning as meaning-making and they bring into play the lifeworlds of students and create contexts that lend themselves to replacing the passive transfer of knowledge, which can be in the foreground in the approaches to teaching and learning in schools.

Use of mobile technologies in everyday life

The aims of using mobile technologies in everyday life can – in very general terms – be described as the organisation of users' everyday lifeworlds. Young people are using their mobile devices – which they start to own at a very young age, as Figure 13.1 indicates – at any time of the day, as soon as they get up, during breakfast, on their way to school or work, during breaks, when meeting friends, after school, during dinner and when going to bed. In doing so, they use the devices for conversation, entertainment for information retrieval, for media production, distribution of content and to share music, videos and photos (see Figure 13.2). Conversation is often done in writing via text messaging, instant messaging and email, but also using the telephony function of the devices. For entertainment purposes young people are using functions that enable the listening to music, radio, and to look at photos and watch videos on the go. Information retrieval via news services or by accessing the internet is another important use aspect.

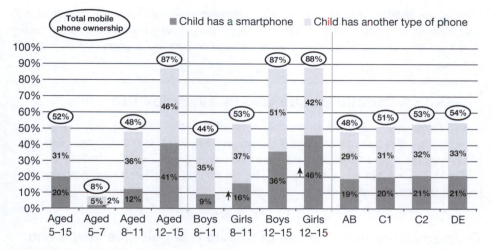

Figure 13.1 Smartphone and mobile phone ownership
Source: Ofcom, 2011, p. 18.

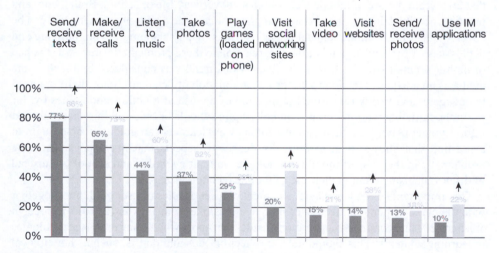

Figure 13.2 Mobile phone activities carried out at least once a week
Source: Ofcom, 2011, p. 43.

Self-generated artefacts such as photos, films, texts, programmes, games, etc. as well as artefacts that were downloaded from the internet or exchanged with others, are re-distributed for instance using Bluetooth or free cloud storage services.

As already mentioned earlier, mobile devices are not stand-alone but convergent media. Contemporary mobile devices allow instant access to functions and functionalities of the internet and especially the so-called Web 2.0 with its social networks, blogs, video and photo platforms and portals, etc. Thus, the use of mobile technologies can increasingly only be distinguished from internet use through time and place independent use.

But mobile technologies are not only tools for (more or less explicit) participation. Also, they need to be considered as being tools to regulate emotions, to manage social relations and to interact with others. Furthermore, mobile devices are style and prestige objects, are used to distinguish oneself from others, for self-expression and identity construction. By using ringtones and other applications young people confine themselves or demonstrate their affiliation to persons, groups of persons or scenes or they want to provoke.

Task 13.2 **Mobile phone use in everyday life**

Invite one of your classes to compile a list of (a) when and why they use mobile technologies in everyday life and (b) when and why they don't use them. Also, ask learners (c) if and how they are using convergent technologies to retrieve and distribute contents and information. This list can then be used as recommended rules and tools when working with mobile devices in the classroom.

Problematisation of the use of mobile technologies inside and outside school

Practice-based research on mobile learning from the last decade provides ample evidence that neither ignoring nor hyping mobile devices is an adequate way of dealing with issues that arise from the use of mobile technologies in everyday life or school. Both theory and practice identified this early and started to pragmatically deal with phenomena that can be covered under the headline 'ethical issues', such as 'happy slapping', cyber bullying and debt issues. A first and arguably affective reaction to these problematic areas was the ban of mobile technologies from schools. Even if this trend was considered by much of the media as an adequate reaction to things like a violation of personal rights, there is a need to engage in a critically reflective examination of the use of mobile technologies by, for example, initiating working groups on bullying in schools or by providing materials that inform young people and their parents. In this way, learners can gradually be brought to a position that allows them to critically deal with aspects that may appear as being problematic in their use of mobile technologies in their everyday and school life instead of disenfranchising them in their use of mobile technologies.

One important strategy is the development of a set of rules or user guidelines together with the class. Experts in the area of mobile ethics like John Traxler (2010) and Jocelyn Wishart (2011) recommend negotiation on rules that apply when using mobile technologies in learning contexts. This should help to reflect on 'dos and don'ts' such as how to deal with contents produced by others (copyright) or photo and film material of other people (right to one's own image), or how to protect oneself from cyber bullying (e-safety), etc. By referring to mechanisms like 'user generated ethics' (Traxler, 2010) learners are invited to think about their own mobile use and the mobile use of their classmates, and to collaboratively find solutions for areas that might appear as being problematic. Also, when learners start not only to be consumers but also producers of digital media, they have another view on copyright that can be discussed in class. Experiences from several projects show that students not only develop tougher rules than teachers but they also accept them better (Döbeli Honegger and Neff, 2011).

Besides aspects that affect personal rights and other ethical dimensions it is also necessary to provide orientation regarding using and caring about hardware and software, and how this affects your attitude – also towards other people around you. The class of Christian Neff, a teacher at the Goldau School in Switzerland, has developed the following guidelines for the use of iPod touches in his Year 5 primary class (translated in part here from German):

General:

- I look after my iPod touch and make sure I don't drop it.
- I won't delete any content and the teacher and parents are allowed to check my device at any time.
- I can be proud of my iPod touch but shouldn't boast about it.
- I won't use the iPod touch to denigrate others.
- The iPod touch should not get wet or dirty. I won't use it outdoors when it rains and normally use it with a cover and with clean hands.
- When I lend my device to someone, I'll stay with that person and make sure they don't use any programs which incur costs.
- I will use the iPod touch in meaningful ways and won't play around with it.
- At school I will only use the iPod touch during class time. Before or after school I'll leave it in my pocket or satchel. During break time it will stay in the classroom.
- I know that using free apps can incur costs and won't, therefore, ever give personal information or credit card details.

E-mail:

- I start with an address and finish with a greeting and will write in an appropriate manner.
- I won't send unnecessary mails.
- I won't send any pornographic, sexual or violent images/videos.
- If I receive an e-mail that contains inappropriate content, I delete it and inform my teacher or my parents.
- If I receive e-mails from a suspicious, unknown sender, I won't open it. If I want to open it anyway, I ask the teacher for permission.

Task 13.3 **Developing guidelines for mobile device use**

Sketch out some ideas for items to include in guidelines for mobile device use with a class you teach. Also, draft a concept on how to discuss ethical issues with your class by means of 'learner generated ethics'.

Task 13.4 **E-safety**

Read the following NFER research report by Helen Aston and Bernadetta Brzyska (2012):

Protecting Children Online: Teachers' Perspectives on eSafety (available at http://tiny.cc//nfer) and the recent (2010) OFSTED report Safe Use of New Technologies (available at http://tiny.cc/ofsted). Then, put together a presentation for your head of department and the senior management team about the benefits of mobile phone use and how you will pre-empt concerns around e-safety.

Guidelines for planning mobile learning in school

Planning learning with mobile devices in the classroom requires good preparation in order to make the most of it and to provide a basis for learners and teachers to make mobile learning sustainable, scalable and transferable. Over the last decade many researchers and teachers have created checklists that can help with project planning (see, e.g., Bachmair *et al.*, 2011; Seipold, 2012a; Kukulska-Hulme and Traxler, 2005). Here, we do not provide such a checklist but, rather, discuss our approach of putting the learner and his or her everyday lifeworld and school-based agency, cultural practices and structures in the foreground to support learners in the process of meaning-making, be it inside or outside school. The following guidelines are referring to this approach.

In earlier work, we defined 'focal points' (see e.g. Bachmair *et al.*, 2011) that can be seen to represent educational and didactic options in the form of guidelines and combine them with the breadth of available mobile applications. They are by means of the mobile phone:

■ integrate informal learning;
■ set up episodes of situated learning;
■ generate learning and media contexts;
■ construct conversational bridges;
■ support students as experts of media use in everyday life within the school;
■ set up responsive contexts for development and learning.

Behind these focal points for planning mobile learning activities sit a number of important conceptual and theoretical considerations. They have been developed in the context of a project entitled MyMobile: Mobiles Lernen mit dem Handy and are discussed in detail in a book published in 2011 in German. The book includes some 50 scenarios for mobile device use in school. Material relating to the project, including practical examples and ideas for the use of mobile can be accessed on the website of Medien+Bildung.com at http://medienundbildung.com/mymobile/material as well as that of the Projektschule Goldau at http://www.projektschule-goldau.ch/permalink/category/unterrichtsidee (text in German). The scenarios include literacy and numeracy related activities, versions of treasure hunts, photo and video safaris, etc.

Besides the quite specific and detailed focal points, we want to provide planning guidelines in order to motivate teachers and other practitioners to critically engage with considerations about learners' structures, agency and cultural practices, and to provide incentives that allow for them to be brought in relation to school learning in order to foster sustainable learning. The following scheme for planning mobile learning in schools is based on Seipold 2011 and 2012a, and draws on the 'focal points' mentioned above.

REFER TO LEARNERS' STRUCTURES, AGENCY AND CULTURAL PRACTICES

As we noted above, mobile technologies and their functions lend themselves particularly well to communication, entertainment and consumption. This means that at face value they more easily map onto the practices of learners' everyday lives outside of school rather than those of school. However, this doesn't mean that the use of these devices, their functions and their contents in these contexts is un-reflected. On the contrary, everyday life use of technologies is always intentional. The everyday use – e.g. making appointments with friends, using the calendar function of the mobile phone or accessing the internet with its social networks – indicates that users deliberately use the devices to communicate, structure, organise and order, plan, network, furnish information, assess, evaluate and produce. In the process they perform different roles such as friends, managers, producers, journalists, reviewers, etc. The challenge is to acknowledge such activities taking place in everyday life and attendant skills as competences with relevance for school-based learning and thus to relate school and everyday life meaningfully to each other. This can be realised for example, by considering within which structures young people are acting, which structures they are constructing, which competences they are establishing in this process and which routines they are developing in the process (see the socio-cultural ecology model by Pachler *et al.*, 2010).

APPROPRIATION MECHANISMS AND USE OF RESOURCES TELL TEACHERS ABOUT WHAT LEARNERS CONSIDER TO BE (RELEVANT FOR) LEARNING

When talking about learners' structures, agency and cultural practices it is necessary to consider their appropriation mechanisms as well. We use the term appropriation here, by which we mean the internalisation of cultural products – in our case artefacts accessed with and produced by mobile devices – and their externalisation of what is in their inner world (see, e.g. Pachler *et al.*, 2010 and Pachler *et al.*, 2013), as we want to emphasise the fact that 'learning' can be described in terms other than those related to school and assessment. Also, by referring to appropriation we point to the fact that learning also takes place outside school and that it is often not even recognised as 'learning' but rather as a hobby (see, e.g. Vavoula, 2009) or personal interest. However, when looking at how learners deal with mobile technologies for meaning-making or learning inside or outside school we can see that they use resources such as materials, tools, communication structures that they deem adequate for specific learning/meaning-making situations or, to put it another way, to generate contexts for learning. Learners are normally very flexible in the use of different information sources, functions of their devices and strategies to communicate. Having a careful look at these mechanisms and strategies, you can learn a lot about what learners consider to be relevant for their learning/appropriation; and you will learn that there are many more resources available for learning and meaning-making than those provided and hosted by school.

Parameters for teaching and learning at the interface between formal and informal learning

Structures, agency and practices of mobile device use in everyday life are often very informal and seemingly stand in opposition to formalised school-based learning. This means that there exist tensions, and that these tensions need to be discovered and used productively instead of mobile devices being banned from classrooms and learning processes. The following four parameters developed by the London Mobile Learning Group (http://www.londonmobilelearning.net) (see, e.g. Bachmair *et al.*, 2011 or Pachler *et al.*, 2012) acknowledge these tensions and also aim to acknowledge the learners' media use, content preferences, styles, expertise, competences, knowledge and so on which they bring to school from their everyday life. The parameters assume an understanding of mobile phones as global cultural resources within individualised, mobile and convergent mass communication. As such mobile phones and other mobile devices function as resources for learning in formal and informal contexts. Therefore, they can be seen to offer different possibilities for assimilating international youth culture and media habits, consisting of structures, agency and cultural practices with specific learning potentials, into school – or, in more general terms, different ways of dealing with mobile technologies that are more or less close to or removed from school or everyday life.

Parameter A:
Learning sets
Pole: Practices of the school – Pole: Practices of mobile devices

Parameter B:
Relationship to the object of learning
Pole: Mimetic reproduction – Pole: Personal reconstruction

Parameter C:
Institutional emphasis on expertise
Pole: School curriculum – Pole: Personal expertise

Parameter D:
Modes of representation
Pole: Discrete (mono media, mono modal) – Pole: Convergent

For an application of the parameters, see, e.g., Pachler *et al.*, 2010, pp. 297–314.

CONSIDER WHICH APPROACH OF IMPLEMENTING MOBILE LEARNING MEETS CURRENT CURRICULAR REQUIREMENTS

When using mobile devices in the classroom it is necessary to think about how, when and why they are going to be used in the learning process. It is possible to distinguish mainly two approaches of the implementation of mobile learning practice (see, e.g. Seipold 2012b; Pachler *et al.*, 2012) which address different infrastructural and didactic requirements and opportunities:

■ **Top-down approach** (also known as 1:1 computing): often mobile devices are implemented into learning contexts from top to bottom which means they are set up in relation to already existing teaching and learning structures. This happens often within big projects that have large budgets. In such projects, whole grades, years or even schools are provided with mobile devices such as iPads. A benefit of this approach is that learners who are structurally disadvantaged are not excluded because all learners own the same devices through which equal opportunities are ensured. From a usability perspective it is easier for teachers to manage such 1:1 projects when all learners use the same devices and programmes and therefore also generate data that is compatible with the other devices. Challenges extend especially to two aspects: first, it may be possible that technologies now have to be used in situations that didn't require the use of technologies before and that learners and teachers need to adjust their teaching and learning process to the requirements of technology and infrastructure. This can result in excessive demands. Second: because tools from everyday life can now be used in school contexts, conflicts might arise; this could happen because learners often are not allowed to use the mobile devices the way they are used to using them in their everyday lives and how the use corresponds to their patterns of use or usage preferences, their agency and their cultural practices.

■ **Bottom-up approach:** the bottom-up approach (also known as BYOD: bring your own device) takes account of available resources such as devices and know-how of learners and teachers. This is cost-saving because no devices have to be supplied. Besides, learners are confident with their devices and can revert to their routines, competences and knowledge when using them. Such projects benefit also from a range of resources originating from the everyday life of learners. If they get the opportunity to work in a self-directed manner when using mobile technologies, contents and other resources supporting their creativity, learners often build exciting connections between school and everyday life – and at the same time the outcomes are still re-usable and assessable in school categories. However, one needs to take into consideration that some learners don't own mobile devices, or that they have only old models at their disposal which don't have all the features that new devices boast. In this case learning groups can be recommended. The cost question still exists in relation to the internet or connection cost. And finally, the diversity of devices and models can be a challenge, which, on the other hand, can be considered in advance when planning carefully.

CASE STUDY: IPADS AT THE CEDARS SCHOOL

by Fraser Speirs (http://speirs.org/blog/tag/theipadproject)
Across Scotland's state schools the average pupil:computer ratio is 3.2:1. A quarter of our pupils attend schools run by authorities whose pupil:computer ratios hover around 5:1.

In the lives of most professionals, the person:computer ratio is easily 1:2 – a laptop and a smartphone are part of the uniform of business in 2011. Add in a tablet or a desktop computer and it's more like three computers per person.

One computer between three in schools, three computers per person in business. Something's wrong with this picture.

I work as Head of Computing and IT at Cedars School of Excellence, a small independent school in Greenock. In late 2009 we were faced with a problem: our teachers wanted to use technology in the classroom but we didn't have enough computers to satisfy the demand. At the time, our pupil:computer ratio was just about 4:1, our provision split between desktop computers and laptops.

We met to discuss how we could improve the situation. Our options were clear: buy more laptops or look for an alternative. One option was simply to buy more laptops. Our other option was the iPod touch. Unlike a laptop, the sub-£200 price of that device made it something we could provide for every pupil. Teachers had concerns at the time about the device size and software capabilities.

About a month after we met and agreed to look into a 1:1 iPod touch program, Apple announced the iPad. We arranged to have one shipped from the US on launch day and it was obvious to us within the first hour of use that this was the future of school computers. By June, we completed the planning for a 1:1 rollout. In July we signed a lease with Apple and in August we became, to our knowledge, the first school in the world to deploy an iPad to every pupil.

The impact has been tremendous. Pupils and parents are wholeheartedly behind the scheme. Inverclyde is not a rich area and few parents send their children to Cedars out of pocket change. They save and sacrifice other luxuries to do the best for their children yet not one parent has complained that our iPad program is a frivolous waste of resources.

School now looks a lot more like the real world of 2012: the internet is constantly available. Information flows through email and the cloud. Digital calendars have replaced homework diaries.

People ask me how many hours a week the pupils use the iPad. That's impossible to answer. We no longer have a meaningful distinction between 'ICT lessons' and 'ordinary lessons'. Every lesson is an ICT lesson and every ICT lesson is an ordinary lesson. There is no longer a barrier to using technology during a lesson. There's no cart to wheel in, no charger to find and no boot-up and log-in. It's just 'slide to unlock' and suddenly it's a lesson using technology.

The kind of cross-curricular work that the Scottish curriculum emphasises is now easy to organise. Pupils have their work from every subject with them in every class. The Art department wants to illustrate a poem that was done in English? It's on the iPad. Maths wants to do some teaching based on data gathered in Science? That data is on the iPad.

I ask you to consider this: my youngest daughter, Beth, started Primary 1 last August. She won't leave school until the summer of 2025. If universities as we know them still exist by that time, she'll be job-hunting as a graduate in the year 2029. The last year in which I didn't have exclusive use of at least one computer was 1995.

Can we continue another twenty years with this disparity between the way IT is used in schools and the way it's used in society? Can we even wait another ten? Can we prepare children for the year 2030 with the same level of access to IT as I had 35 years prior?

Task 13.5 **Differing approaches to the implementation of mobile learning**

Discuss the case study by Fraser Speirs in relation to the distinction we make above about bottom-up and top-down approaches. Which category does it fall into? What key issues arise from it in relation to our characterisation of the categories? And, how does the case study relate to our conceptualisation of mobile learning around structures, agency and cultural practices?

LINKING THE USE OF MOBILE DEVICES TO LEARNING OBJECTIVES

From our perspective mobile devices are one component of the ecology of resources available to teachers. Therefore, as with other resources, such as course books, the question arises how they map onto learning objectives specified in schemes and units of work as well as lesson plans. Just as with the deployment of other resources, it is learning objectives that should drive the use of mobile devices, not the technology; i.e. the approach we advocate is one of mapping the affordances and functionalities of mobile devices onto learning objectives. As a result, teachers are often inclined to look for subject and age specific apps covering precisely aspects of the (prescribed) curriculum. The blog EdTechTeacher offers a useful post at http://edtechteacher.org/index.php/teaching-technology/mobile-technology-apps/ipad-as which lists apps in relation to learning objectives. For example, if the intended learning focus is on creating digital stories, a specific range of apps will be relevant (see also http://www.diigo.com/user/servusuk/digitalstorytelling). For a more detailed discussion of apps, see the section 'evaluating apps' below.

Task 13.6 **Mapping the affordances of mobile devices onto learning objectives**

Read through the EdTechTeacher blogpost on iPad apps and learning objectives. Download some of the free apps and explore ways of using them to augment some of your pedagogical approaches.

MEDIATE BETWEEN EVERYDAY LIFE AND SCHOOL/INFORMAL AND FORMAL

As we mentioned already in the parameter section above, transforming informal structures, agency and cultural practices into formalised ones requires us to address certain tensions and contradictions. In practice, it means that as teachers we need to help learners transform informal resources so that they fit into formal school learning. This can be achieved by what we call 'scaffolded structuration' in the process of meaning-making/learning. The aim is to allow learners to position themselves as individuals in mass communication processes and in so doing to position themselves in learning contexts. To achieve this it is necessary to provide spaces where, and tools with which learners can interact in discursive and communicative ways to negotiate common meanings and discuss perceptions, notions, etc. And, it is necessary to find ways to support situated learning and thus to acknowledge that different learners have different socio-cultural contexts and thus experiences, goals and resources (see http://www.medienundbildung.com/mymobile for details and examples that are based on the premise of teacher-led instruction interspersed with media-based episodes of student-centred activities). In general terms, we would recommend the following points to handle the transition between formal and informal learning contexts:

- contextualise naive activities and allow for reflection and reasons/give incentives for reflection;
- frame situative experiences from everyday life within the categories and demands of school and curriculum;

- guide learners from uncertainty, coincidence and serendipity to scheduling and measurability, i.e. from more or less un-stable to plan-able aspects;
- reconceptualise unintended and spontaneous everyday activities in terms of school-based learning.

Or, to put it differently, this transformation can be initialised (see Seipold *et al.*, 2010) e.g. by:

- allowing learners to be fans and experts;
- allowing learners to collect and exchange things they are a fan or expert of;
- negotiate rules, e.g. for the use of technologies for learning in the classroom – or times and rules for referring to being a fan, expert, collector, etc.

PROJECT PLANNING AND CATEGORIES FOR THE SCALABILITY AND TRANSFERABILITY OF PROJECTS

In addition to the educational and didactic aspects, there are a number of logistical issues to be considered when planning learner-centred mobile device use. Here is a short list of items that should be helpful in setting up a project plan (see e.g. Seipold, 2012):

- outline aims and concept, including implementation plan, teaching focus, research focus (if any), sustainability measures;
- address decision makers: head of school, administration, parents, teachers;
- calculate infrastructure cost: mobile technology, financing, network, convergent technologies;
- consider usage and target groups: training strategies, rules and regulations, mobility within school and outside, ethic dimensions, data privacy;
- outline a detailed project and time schedule for your project.

To allow for scalability and transferability, and thus for others to adopt your mobile learning concept for their own purposes, we recommend the following dimensions that should be addressed in a public project description (see, e.g. MoLeaP – the mobile learning projects data base to which projects can be submitted according to the following categories; http://www.moleap.net):

- general project data;
- context/rationale;
- approaches to teaching and learning;
- technologies and requirements;
- project outcomes;
- lessons learnt/issues emerging;
- recommendations and future possibilities;
- replicability and transferability.

Task 13.7 **Writing a project plan**

Write a detailed project plan by considering the dimension given above. Be as clear as possible when defining aims, objectives and goals that refer to both the needs and demands of the curriculum and the learners' structures, agency and cultural practices.

Then, design a scenario in which learners are using the mobile devices and other convergent technologies they have at their disposition. Provide spaces for self-organised learning in which learners cooperate in groups and in which they access resources that are relevant for learning from their point of view (this might also include digital resources from outside school).

Evaluating apps

As our discussion of learning objectives has already started to show, software programs specifically developed for mobile devices, so-called apps, are of great importance in the use of mobile devices for teaching and learning. A whole host of such applications are available. Teachers wanting to use mobile devices successfully in their practice invariably need to invest time in identifying and evaluating apps. As with other educational technology, the evaluation should be systematic and carried out on the basis of a set of relevant criteria. One useful set of criteria is offered by Tony Vincent, the author of the 'Learning in Hand' blog. In a post entitled 'Ways to evaluate educational apps' (available at http://learninginhand.com/blog/ways-to-evaluate-educational-apps.html) Vincent inter alia delineates the following criteria: relevance, customisation, feedback, thinking skills, engagement and sharing. He also offers the following educational app evaluation checklist:

■ Use of app is relevant to the purpose and student needs.
■ Help or tutorial is available in the app.
■ Content is appropriate for the student.
■ Information is error-free, factual, and reliable.
■ Content can be exported, copied, or printed.
■ App's settings and/or content can be customised.
■ Customised content can be transferred to other devices.
■ History is kept of student use of the app.
■ Design of app is functional and visually stimulating.
■ Student can exit app at any time without losing progress.
■ Works with accessibility options like VoiceOver and Speak Selection.
■ App is free of charge.
■ No in-app purchases are necessary for intended use of app.
■ App loads quickly and does not crash.
■ App contains no advertising.
■ App has been updated in the last 6 months.
■ App promotes creativity and imagination.
■ App provides opportunities to use higher order thinking skills.
■ App promotes collaboration and idea sharing.
■ App provides useful feedback.

> ## Task 13.8 **Familiarising yourself with mobile apps**
>
> One of the authors of this chapter maintains a comprehensive list of social bookmarks. One key tag relates to apps and can be accessed at http://www.diigo.com/user/servusuk/apps.
>
> At the time of writing some 1,000 links about mobile apps have been bookmarked. Another useful source for educational apps is I Education Apps Review (IEAR) at http://www.iear.org/iear/, a website that offers regular reviews of software with educational potential.
>
> Explore these two online resources and evaluate some of the apps using Tony Vincent's evaluation tools (or one you have developed yourself). On the basis of your results, what are your top 10 apps?

Assessment

Assessment is an integral part of teaching and learning. Therefore, it is important to ask yourself what actual learning takes place in classrooms in which mobile devices are used. The key to the assessment of mobile learning, as could be seen earlier, is for teachers to articulate a clear set of intended learning outcomes against which the affordances of mobile devices are matched. Just as with other teaching activities, these objectives should be challenging but manageable and achievable, measurable, motivating, incremental, etc. Importantly, the use of mobile devices should add value and not be burdensome or time consuming.

One aspect of mobile devices we want to stress in relation to assessment is their potential to collect and capture multimodal artefacts created by and/or accessed with mobile devices in a so-called mobile portfolio. Images and videos captured with mobile devices lend themselves particularly well to fostering reflecting about learning processes and outcomes. For example, an image of board work or a short recording of an episode of group work can be used for individual reflection and self-regulation in private with the learner seeking to understand what s/he needs to do in order to bridge the gap between where their current achievement and attainment is, and where they should be; they can equally be shared through projection on the whiteboard (using software such as Reflection) and become the stimulus for class discussion. This use of mobile devices for assessment has been researched in the context of higher education students (see, e.g. Coulby and Davies, 2011 and Coulby *et al.*, 2011) who have found evidence in support of portfolio-based approaches in reflecting. In the domain specific discourse this process is sometimes referred to as 'curation' (see, e.g. Potter, 2009), which can be seen to be different from aggregation as it is not just about collecting and sharing of artefacts but also about personalisation and contextualisation.

Task 13.9 **Using mobile devices for professional development**

In order to harness functionality of mobile devices for professional development purposes you should subscribe to and regularly read some blogs on the topic of mobile learning.

Here are three blogs to get you started:

- http://www.freetech4teachers.com
- http://www.schrockguide.net (start with the guide to iPads in the classroom at http://www.schrockguide.net/ipads-in-the-classroom.html)
- http://learninginhand.com

In due course you may even want to start your own blog to share your experiences with others.

Task 13.10 **Designing an assessment strategy**

Conceptualise an assessment strategy according to the points raised in the section on assessment, taking into account the assessment policy of your placement school demands.

SUMMARY AND KEY POINTS

In this chapter we have provided an overview of key issues in the use of mobile devices for teaching and learning in a school context. We have stressed the importance of not viewing mobile devices as the new panacea of technology-enhanced teaching and learning. Instead, we have tried to show how the increasing normalisation of mobile devices in the everyday lifeworlds of students creates the needs for schools and teachers to go beyond viewing them as a disruptive force and instead recognising their potential and affordances to add value to the students' educational experience.

FURTHER READING

Hartnell-Young, E. and Heym, N. (2008) *How Mobile Phones Help Learning In Secondary Schools. A Report to Becta*, Nottingham: University of Nottingham. Available at: http://schools.becta. org.uk/upload-dir/downloads/page_documents/research/lsri_report.pdf (accessed 30 August 2012).

Ito, M., Horst, H., Bittanti, M., Boyd, D., Herr-Stephenson, B., Lange, P., Pascoe, C. and Robinson, L. (2008) *Living and Learning with New Media: Summary of Findings from the Digital Youth Project*, Chicago: MacArthur Foundation. Available at: http://www.itofisher.com/mito/weblog/2008/11/living_and_learning_with_new_m.html (accessed 30 August 2012).

Johnson, L., Adams, Becker, S., Cummins, M., Estrada, V., Freeman, A. and Ludgate, H. (2013) *NMC Horizon Report: 2012 K-12 Edition*, Austin, Texas: The New Media Consortium. Available at: http://www.nmc.org/pdf/2013-horizon-report-K12.pdf (accessed 21 June 2013).

Shore, R. (2008) *The Power of Pow! Wham! Children, Digital Media and Our Nation's Future: Three Challenges for the Coming Decade*, New York: The Joan Ganz Cooney Center at Sesame Workshop. Available at: http://joanganzcooneycenter.org/upload_kits/cooney_challenge_advance_1_.pdf (accessed 30 August 2012).

Shuler, C. (2009) *Pockets of Potential: Using Mobile Technologies to Promote Children's Learning*, The Joan Ganz Cooney Center at Sesame Workshop. Available at: http://joanganzcooneycenter.org/upload_kits/pockets_of_potential_1_.pdf (accessed 30 August 2012).

REFERENCES

Aston, H. and Brzyska, B. (2012) *Protecting Children Online: Teachers' Perspectives on eSafety*. Available at: http://www.nfer.ac.uk/nfer/publications/95001/95001.pdf (accessed 30 August 2012).

Bachmair, B. and Pachler, N. (2013) 'Composition and appropriation in a culture characterised by provisionality.' Böck, M. and Pachler, N. (eds) *Multimodality and Social Semiosis: Communication, Meaning-Making and Learning in the Work of Gunther Kress*. New York: Routledge, pp. 211–220.

Bachmair, B., Pachler, N. and Cook, J. (2011) *Parameters and Focal Points For Planning and Evaluation of Mobile Learning*. Available at: http://www.londonmobilelearning.net/downloads/Parameter_flyer.pdf (accessed 30 August 2012).

Coulby, C. and Davies, N. (2011) 'Leading by the hand: exploring the factors affecting individual student engagement with self-directed mobile assessment', *MedienPädagogik, Zeitschrift für Theorie und Praxis der Medienbildung* (19. Special Issue – Mobile Learning in Widening Contexts: Concepts and Cases). Available at: http://www.medienpaed.com/zs/content/view/325/82/ (accessed 30 August 2012).

Coulby, C., Laxton, J., Boomer, S. and Davies, N. (2011) 'Mobile technology and assessment: a case study from the ALPS programme', in N. Pachler, C. Pimmer and J. Seipold (eds), *Work-based Mobile Learning: Concepts and Cases* (pp. 51–70), Oxford, Bern, Berlin, Bruxelles, Frankfurt am Main, New York, Wien: Peter Lang.

Döbeli Honegger, B. and Neff, C. (2011) 'Personal smartphones in primary school: devices for a PLE?', *International Journal of Virtual and Personal Learning Environments* 2 (4). Available at: http://beat.doebe.li/publications/2010-doebeli-honegger-neff-smartphones-in-primary-school.pdf (accessed 30 August 2012).

Friedrich, K., Ranieri, M., Pachler, N. and Theux, P. de (eds) (2012) *The 'My Mobile' Handbook: Guidelines and Scenarios For Mobile Learning in Adult Education*. Available at: http://www.mymobile-project.eu/IMG/pdf/Handbook_web.pdf (accessed 14 May 2013).

Kress, G. and Pachler, N. (2007) 'Thinking about the 'm' in m-learning', in N. Pachler (ed.), *Occasional Papers in Work-based Learning: Vol. 1. Mobile Learning – Towards a Research Agenda* (pp. 7–32), London: WLE Centre. Available at: http://www.wlecentre.ac.uk/cms/files/occasionalpapers/mobilelearning_pachler_2007.pdf (accessed 30 August 2012).

Kukulska-Hulme, A. and Traxler, J. (eds) (2005) *The Open and Flexible Learning Series. Mobile Learning: A Handbook for Educators and Trainers* (new edition), London, New York: Routledge. Available at: http://books.google.com/books?id=Io5A5JfrI7EC (accessed 30 August 2012).

Ofsted (2010) *The Safe Use of New Technologies*. Available at: http://www.ofsted.gov.uk/sites/default/files/documents/surveys-and-good-practice/t/The%20safe%20use%20of%20new%20technologies.pdf (accessed 30 August 2012).

Pachler, N., Bachmair, B. and Cook, J. (2010) *Mobile Learning: Structures, Agency, Practices,* New York: Springer. Available at: http://www.springerlink.com/content/v65pt8/ (accessed 30 August 2012).

——(2013) 'A socio-cultural frame for mobile learning', in Z. Berge and L. Muilenburg (eds), *Handbook of Mobile Learning*, New York: Routledge, pp. 35–46.

Pachler, N., Cook, J. and Bachmair, B. (2010) 'Appropriation of mobile cultural resources for learning', *International Journal of Mobile and Blended Learning* 2(1): 1–21, reprinted in Parsons, D. (ed.) (2012) *Refining Current Practices in Mobile and Blended Learning: New Applications*, Hershey, PA: IGI Global, pp. 10–30.

Pachler, N., Seipold, J. and Bachmair, B. (2012) 'Mobile learning: some theoretical and practical considerations', in K. Friedrich, M. Ranieri, N. Pachler and P. de Theux (eds), *The 'My Mobile' Handbook: Guidelines and Scenarios For Mobile Learning in Adult Education* (pp. 11–16). Available at: http://www.mymobile-project.eu/IMG/pdf/Handbook_Considerations.pdf.

Potter, J. (2009) *Curating the Self: Media Literacy and Identity in Digital Video Production by Young Learners*. Available at: http://www.scribd.com/doc/22605066/Curating-the-Self-PhD-Thesis-2009-by-John-Potter (accessed 30 August 2012).

Seipold, J. (2011) 'Planung von Mobilem Lernen im Unterricht: Hinweise und Beispiele für die Praxis', *Computer + Unterricht - Lernen und lehren mit digitalen Medien* (84. Spezial Lernen. Themenschwerpunkt betreut von: Fromme, Johannes; Biermann, Ralf; Unger, Alexander), 49–51.

——(2012) *Mobiles Lernen: Analyse des Wissenschaftsprozesses der britischen und deutschsprachigen medienpädagogischen und erziehungswissenschaftlichen Mobile Learning-Diskussion*. Available at http://nbn-resolving.de/urn:nbn:de:hebis:34-2012121242324.

——(2012a, January) *Learning with Mobile Technologies: Teaching Approaches and Systematic Change Management Issues*, BETT2012 conference, London. Available at: http://www.slideshare.net/KlausR/presenation-bett2012-judith-seipold (accessed 30 August 2012).

Seipold, J., Rummler, K. and Rasche, J. (2010) 'Medienbildung im Spannungsfeld alltäglicher Handlungsmuster und Unterrichtsstrukturen', in B. Bachmair (ed.), *Medienbildung in neuen Kulturräumen. Die deutschsprachige und britische Diskussion* (pp. 227–241). Wiesbaden: VS Verlag für Sozialwissenschaften. Available at: http://springerlink.com/content/h56426/ (accessed 30 August 2012).

Speirs, F. (no date) *The iPad Project*. Available at: http://speirs.org/blog/tag/theipadproject.

Traxler, J. (2010) *Doing it Right! Methods, Ethics and Hearing the Learner Voice*. Online Beitrag bei ELESIG & HEEthicsWeb2.0 joint event. Available at: http://wlv.academia.edu/JohnTraxler/Talks/15764/Doing_it_Right_Methods_Ethics_and_Hearing_the_Learner_Voice (accessed 30 August 2012).

Vavoula, G. (2009) 'Issues and requirements for mobile learning research', in G. Vavoula, N. Pachler and A. Kukulska-Hulme (eds), *Researching Mobile Learning: Frameworks, Tools and Research Designs* (pp. 339–349), Oxford: Peter Lang.

Wishart, J. (2011) 'Ethical concerns relevant to researching work based mobile learning', in N. Pachler, C. Pimmer and J. Seipold (eds), *Work-based Mobile Learning: Concepts and Cases* (pp. 305–331), Oxford, Bern, Berlin, Bruxelles, Frankfurt am Main, New York, Wien: Peter Lang.

URLS

apps – Norbert Pachler on Diigo. Available at: http://www.diigo.com/user/servusuk/apps (accessed 30 August 2012).

Cedars School of Excellence. Available at: http://cedars.inverclyde.sch.uk/ (accessed 30 August 2012).

digitalstorrytelling – Norbert Pachler on Diigo. Available at: http://www.diigo.com/user/servusuk/digitalstorytelling (accessed 30 August 2012).

Free Technology for Teachers. Available at: http://www.freetech4teachers.com/ (accessed 30 August 2012).

I Education Apps Review. Available at: http://www.iear.org/iear/ (accessed 30 August 2012).

iPad As… Available at: http://edtechteacher.org/index.php/teaching-technology/mobile-technology-apps/ipad-as (accessed 30 August 2012).

iPads in the Classroom. Kathy Schrock's Guide to Everything. Available at: http://www.schrockguide.net/ipads-in-the-classroom.html (accessed 30 August 2012).

Kathy Schrock's Guide to Everything. Available at: http://www.schrockguide.net (accessed 30 August 2012).

London Mobile Learning Group – LMLG. Available at: http://www.londonmobilelearning.net (accessed 30 August 2012).

Medien+bildung.com: Material. Available at: http://medienundbildung.com/mymobile/material (accessed 30 August 2012).

MoLeaP – The Mobile Learning Project Database. Available at: http://www.moleap.net (accessed 30 August 2012).

MyMobile – Conference. Available at: http://www.mymobile-project.eu/spip.php?rubrique11#Hull (accessed 30 August 2012).

Ofcom (2011) *Children and Parents: Media Use and Attitudes Report*. Available at: http://stakeholders.ofcom.org.uk/binaries/research/media-literacy/oct2011/Children_and_parents.pdf.

Projektschule Goldau. Available at: http://www.projektschule-goldau.ch (accessed 30 August 2012).

Tony Vincent's Learning in Hand – Home. Available at: http://learninginhand.com (accessed 30 August 2012).

Tony Vincent's Learning in Hand – Blog – 'Ways to Evaluate Educational Apps'. Available at: http://learninginhand.com/blog/ways-to-evaluate-educational-apps.html (accessed 30 August 2012).

Unterrichtsidee – Projektschule Goldau. Available at: http://www.projektschule-goldau.ch/permalink/category/unterrichtsidee (accessed 30 August 2012).

WHOLE-SCHOOL APPROACHES: INTEGRATING ICT ACROSS THE CURRICULUM

Lawrence Williams, Lorian Mead, Lloyd Mead and Marilyn Leask

INTRODUCTION

Many of the chapters in this book focus on what you, as a teacher, might do in your own classroom. However, research (OECD, 2001; Kington *et al.,* 2001, 2002) into the role of ICT in whole-school improvement illustrates the value gained for pupils and teachers when there is a whole-school integrated approach to the use of ICT. This chapter provides examples of such approaches.

The pace of technological development is such that the world many children face outside school demands ICT competence. E-commerce (electronic commerce) is growing, with business transactions on the web and jobs related to this form of technology rapidly increasing. The distinction between the TV and the computer is increasingly blurred as both items offer both functions. Network literacy, i.e. the capacity to use information and communication technologies appropriately to communicate and to access information, is an important basic competence for all young people. We suggest that network literacy is a vital extension of the ability to read and write. Cross-curricular projects such as those suggested here also support the ongoing professional development of teachers who can use the opportunity to share ideas and practice from their different discipline areas.

Increasingly, teachers are competent in the use of ICT in their subject but given the range of possibilities for creating different learning opportunities using different forms of digital technologies, a planned whole-school approach offers both an integrated experience to pupils but also supports teachers in becoming familiar with the forms of ICT most appropriate for their subject, knowing that other teachers will be offering pupils other complementary experiences.

You may wish to adopt some of the practices described here but be in a school where attitudes of staff appear unchangeable. In some countries, such as parts of Australia, staff apply to a central government body for a teaching post, they are then allocated to a school and are likely to be transferred around the system. In these schools we have observed more similarities in practice between schools than differences. In the UK, because individual schools appoint staff who may then never work anywhere else, between-school variation seems to be stronger. So teachers in the UK may find transferring to another school enables them to find a work environment that more closely matches their educational philosophy.

In any case, it will be many years before the knowledge recorded and presented in this book is embedded in the professional knowledge of the majority of teachers in the UK. It is of course not just attitudes that need to change. In the introduction we discuss some of the hurdles that have to be overcome if we are to integrate ICT use into the curriculum.

Where staff work together, supporting one another in experimentation and change, the acquisition of skills and knowledge is easier. In this chapter, we chart the progress of development in one school over a seven-year period.

The projects described in this chapter, involving as they do staff from departments across the school, provide opportunities for teachers to learn together about the various technologies and to build new practices together. We suggest that undertaking such activities promotes attitudinal change and training through an experiential model which is coupled with just-in-time learning, i.e. you learn just what you need to achieve your current goal, rather than undertaking a block of training in which you try to learn everything at once.

OBJECTIVES

By the end of this chapter you should have considered:

■ how the school ethos and the school's philosophy of learning can support the development of ICT across the curriculum;
■ possible learning outcomes for pupils and staff where a number of departments collaborate in undertaking cross-curricular ICT projects;
■ whether ICT projects involving staff from a range of departments are feasible in your context.

SCHOOL ETHOS AND CHANGE

Many studies of schools that were early adopters of new ways of working using digital technologies to support the curriculum, school administration and the professional lives of teachers, identified the importance of a supportive, collaborative school ethos (Watson, 1997 Wasser *et al.* 1998). In schools where a few people are seen to be the holders of knowledge about ICT, there is no shared body of professional knowledge about the use of ICT and when the individuals leave the knowledge leaves with them. Understanding the ethos of your school helps you understand what change is possible and how it might be achieved.

In the case study that follows, you will see how at Holy Cross Convent School, staff skills and expertise were built up over a period of years through collaborative work across departments. Lawrence Williams, who was the Director of Studies from Holy Cross Convent School in Surrey for many years, describes how the school's philosophy of learning supported the development of a whole-school approach to the use of digital technologies that took place over a period of several years and emerged from practice in several projects. In the first part of his contribution he looks briefly at what sort of curriculum we need for the twenty-first century and how we prepare pupils to become active participants in a highly technological world.

Task 14.1 **Is the ethos in your school supportive of change?**

We suggest you consider the ethos in your school. To what extent are the staff working together in considering the role digital technologies can play in the experience of pupils at the school? What factors are supporting collaboration? What are the constraints? What is the quality of technical support? This was found in early research into the adoption of ICT in schools (Leask and Wilder, 1996; Leask, 2002) to be a critical factor in aiding or hindering whole-school development. What digital resources are available? What are widely used? What is the skill base of staff and who appears to be interested in using digital technologies in new ways?

The model of cross-curricular projects supported by ICT, developed from a project embracing English and Dance, which widened to include Music and Drama, and eventually covered every aspect of the school curriculum, through the Caribbean Project. Further projects with organisations outside the school refined and developed their skills still more.

KNOWLEDGE AS A SEAMLESS FABRIC: DEVELOPING A MODEL OF AN INTEGRATED CURRICULUM SUPPORTED BY ICT

This section has three main aims: first, to show how one school made a steady and continuous development in its use of ICT across the curriculum; second, to outline some specific examples of our practice; third, to suggest a cross-curricular model of working which not only uses ICT to support all aspects of the curriculum, but attempts to unify that curriculum, by opening windows between subjects, while retaining the integrity of individual subject specialisms. See Chapter 6 for worldwide links to examples of school ICT projects.

The school's philosophy of learning

The model that Lawrence developed at Holy Cross is based on a philosophical position that regards knowledge as a seamless fabric. The school built on the integrated approach of the local primary schools (ages 5 to 11 years). Cribb makes the following point:

> We do not experience the world separated into ingredients. If we want to understand or change it, we must be able to integrate different forms of knowledge.
>
> (Cribb, 1995, pp. 78–81)

Holy Cross School started, then, from this belief that children learn better when links are made between different subjects, and that digital technologies provide teachers with an immensely powerful set of tools, which enable teachers to develop a model of learning which serves this purpose.

The model developed in response to a number of challenges that faced the school over a period of years, and by adopting a positive stance in each case, the staff was able to turn problems into solutions, and thereby advance the learning of the pupils.

The first problem concerned the restricting effect that the English National Curriculum was having on the development of Expressive Arts in the school. Dance and Drama were reduced in curriculum time to a risible amount. The second problem was how to teach a programme of English Literature designed by a government committee. I'm sure you can imagine the result! Accordingly, staff devised the system shown in Figure 14.1.

The second project was also the solution to two problems:

■ How do you teach a Shakespeare play meaningfully to 13-year-olds?
■ How do you develop the use of the new digital camera, which we had purchased as a result of the success of the Dance Project?

The solution was to unite the two (see Figure 14.2).

Dance and Drama were concentrated into useful, practical blocks of time. Then, in English, we studied the particular literary extracts.highlighting the metaphors and similes in the text. Next, we went to the Dance Studio and explored how these images could be set to music, illustrating the effects which Shakespeare and other writers had created. We recorded these dance performances onto video tape, exported digitised still images into our desk-top publishing program, and word-processed articles about the performances. in the role of newspaper reporters. The quality of the finished work was astonishing. By using the desk-top environment to unite English and Dance, new standards of achievement were set.

As pupils commented:

'When I first heard that we were going to have dance lessons during English, I thought to myself, "What has dance to do with English?" Now I can see that dance is another way of expressing yourself. It also becomes useful in explaining the poem and making it become alive.'

'Putting the poem into dance helped the poem actually come alive. It wasn't a poem to me – it was a real situation.' and

'I learnt things in dance that I had never thought about before.'

I find these perceptions astonishing for pupils aged thirteen.
The computer had led us to a new way of approaching learning. This was an exciting beginning.

■ **Figure 14.1** Project 1 – Integrating Dance, Drama and English through the use of ICT.

Our main aim was to develop an understanding of 'Romeo and Juliet', as was required for a national test. This would then expand into a study of 'West Side Story' and Prokofiev's 'Romeo and Juliet', so that we could build on the earlier dance work. We planned to produce a dance assessment, a drama assessment and a word-processed English Literature assessment as well as developing our understanding of how the digital camera could be usefully deployed as a supporting tool for drama.

The advantage of the digital camera is that images can be fed directly into a monitor and viewed instantly. This has obvious applications in drama. The pupils prepared the text, chose a scene to dramatise, and then selected a moment from their performances to 'freeze frame'. Two images were taken with the camera, and these two images could be discussed immediately in class with regards to their visual effectiveness. By moving from, say picture three to four, and then back again, a useful and otherwise impossible comparison could be made. Of course, since the image was digitised, it could now be imported back into the desk-top, and word-processed text could be added. This was done with a prepared page of four frames available on the school network – to save time and effort – a quotation was added below the picture, a summary of the scene followed this, and an in-role response finished the assignment. Once again, the response of the pupils was staggering. The sensitivity of the writing was amazing, and it was clearly the integration of the various elements of the process which had brought this about. This marked another step in our journey. (Chapter 7 provides detailed guidance about the use of digital video in your classroom.)

■ **Figure 14.2** Project 2 – *Romeo and Juliet*: integrating Music, Drama, Dance and English through the use of ICT.

The next problem arose out of a school inspection. The school was highly praised for its work, and was named as one of the most improved in the UK, but (and there is always a 'but') the inspectors suggested that we should more actively celebrate the cultural diversity of the pupils. We took this challenge seriously, and embarked on what was to prove to be a turning point in the academic success of the school, the Caribbean Project (see Figure 14.3).

Such was the impact of the Caribbean Project across a variety of learning outcomes, that we decided to take a further step. There were two faults in the Caribbean Project work. One was that too many children had a tendency to produce work that contained elements that, though well researched and stunningly presented, were copied from books or downloaded, with little evidence of some of it having actually passed through the brain. Second, scientific work was poorly represented.

So, the next project was designed to solve these two problems. Lawrence realised that he had, in fact, created the curriculum model inside out. However, by restructuring the model, these two problems could be solved simultaneously. Instead of an Expressive Arts based project, with science and technology added on, as it were, we would start, instead, with solid scientific content and ensure that the pupils word-processed their own experiments, undertaken in the laboratories, and create the Light Project (see Figure 14.4).

This was to be a detailed study of every aspect of Caribbean life, studied across the whole curriculum, and using as many IT tools as possible (to develop skills) – word-processing, desk-top publishing, spreadsheets, databases, clip art, scanned images, digital camera work, draw files, graphics packages – and would be completed in a single school term by all of the lower school (some 400 pupils). Each Department contributed ideas appropriate to its own needs in meeting the requirements of the National Curriculum, and the pupils moved from subject to subject, building on their knowledge of the topic.

It is important to note that there was no pressure for Departments to contribute particular amounts of time or resources, only that which arises naturally out of existing schemes of work. Looking back at the scale of this project, it was clearly complete madness on my part, and my only defence is that the pupils and staff made it completely successful in every way. I was grateful for this. The creative energy which it released was colossal. **The learning outcomes went far beyond what we expected.** Pupils visited libraries, consulted CD-ROMs, searched the internet, went to travel agents for brochures, telephoned Trinidad (I was relieved to learn that they had parental permission to do this). They danced to the music which they had recorded onto audio tape, took photographs of the dances with the digital camera, imported the images into the desk-top, and added word-processed comment. They used their IT lessons (once a week), time before school, lunch time, time after school (often until 6 o'clock), their computers at home, where possible, and simply poured information into their project folders. An outline of aims was given, but this was completely ignored as they sailed graciously past every assessment marker devised. The finished folders were of such a high standard, displaying knowledge, skill and creative energy that colleagues from colleges and universities in the UK and the USA asked to borrow them. They were used to support a Race Relations Conference, because of the harmonious multi-cultural dimension they gave to the school. Again, the use of various digital technologies to create the folders had proved a triumph.

■ **Figure 14.3** Project 3 – the Caribbean Project: using ICT to unite subjects across the curriculum around a theme

The project was therefore initiated by the Science Department with Year 8. The topics covered would have cropped up in the syllabus later in the year, but they were brought together in the Autumn Term. The topics included the following:

- The eclipse of the sun and the partial eclipse
- How to view a partial eclipse with a pin-hole camera
- Colour and colour chemistry
- Fibre optic light and cable
- Neon lighting and gas discharge lamps
- Holograms
- Shadows / shadow theatres
- Camouflage
- Radiation
- Reflection
- Refraction
- Lenses
- Photosynthesis
- Fuels
- The changing seasons
- Light detectors

In Drama, by now a familiar partner in all our work, the pupils improvised short scenes on the theme of good and evil (light and darkness). The Drama teacher used the digital camera to take a picture of a freeze-frame from the play, which the pupils then imported into the computer. They then wrote up what the play was about underneath the picture. Although the picture would only be printed in black and white in their project folders (colour printing is horribly expensive!) the pupils discussed what colour of light could be used in the staging of their performances. Red was seen as an appropriate colour for evil and anger, and white or blue was thought to represent goodness and 'calmness'. Some pupils word-processed a play to go with their Science Shadow Theatre. The moral dimension of the characters in the plays was broadened in the Religious Studies lessons into moral and spiritual aspects of good and evil. The symbolism of light and dark recurs throughout the Bible and the liturgy, so the pupils studied this, too, and presented attractive work as part of the Light Project.

When the Art Department started working on the project the pupils already had a far greater understanding of colour, light and shadow than would normally be expected. The subject was infinite when it came to painting and drawing. In English, they spent two double periods in the computer room. They scanned through a slide-show of 100 high quality images installed on the network, and chose the one they most liked to write a poem about light on. They then printed the poem together with the picture. A student teacher was helping with this lesson, and was amazed to see how easy they found it to write something which would have been quite abstract as a normal classroom task. Obviously the finished product gave them a great deal of satisfaction, and they proudly showed her their work the following day. They also used a graphics package to create decorative 'light' vocabulary, and explored the uses of the thesaurus to find more words. Some groups did the same in French.

Later in the term, new music software was deployed on the school network, a music keyboard was added (for faster input). and the pupils were soon able to write both the words and the music for some Christmas songs to do with light, using the pentatonic scale – required for the National Curriculum in Music.

In Mathematics, they studied enlargement, reflection, and mirror images. In Technology, they made circuits, created stained glass mirror effects, and used computer-aided design to make T-shirts with computer-embroidered candles on them. In Geography, they studied the Sun, the seasons, and starlight using CD-ROMs. A group that went to Germany returned and wrote about the Christmas lights they had seen there. The project culminated in a beautiful Advent Service in the Church, with carols, dance, and drama, all linked to the theme of Light, and a fitting conclusion to a busy and successful term's work.

Pupils' comments included the following:

'I like using computers. It gives me more confidence.'

'It made me go to the library more than I normally do ... I didn't use to stay in the computer room after school, but now I do.'

'I could use a lot of resources on the computer. Talk to other people.'

'I really understand science better now, and enjoy it more.'

'I enjoyed doing this project. and I find the research to be fun, as there are so many different sources of information, and it was inspiring.'

'It showed how different subjects can be linked up.'

■ **Figure 14.4** Project 4 – the Light Project: using ICT to unite subjects across the curriculum around concepts from the science curriculum

Clearly a wide variety of learning outcomes was being achieved. Grades achieved by pupils were higher than expected.

Next steps at Holy Cross School

From this success, we decided to develop another project, centred this time on Japan, for our Year 9 pupils, and drawing together all of the experience outlined here. Each Department would contribute as much as is appropriate to the topic, as shown on the curriculum model used for the Light Project. We aimed to use the model this time, however, to target specific teaching departments, so that staff training needs could be met. For example, Science teachers wished to develop their skills in data logging, and the Art Department wanted to use a new graphics package for computer-controlled calligraphy work. I wanted to experiment with sending music files in midi format to Japan, so that the accuracy of our attempts to write Japanese music could be monitored at source! The model for integrating the curriculum and ICT outlined above can thus be used as a professional development tool, as well as for inspiring the pupils (see Figure 14.5).

Spurred on by this success, the next move was to see if Music could be added as another dimension to our work over the internet. Accordingly, the school set out to collaborate with a school in Japan – Ikeda Junior High School, Osaka. Coupled into a whole Year Group project (Year 9) using IT across the curriculum. and incorporating an Open Day with Performing Arts productions (integrating music. dance, drama and IT) the school sent Ikeda JHS some simple specifications for music to be performed on the actual day. This was accompanied by explorations of the technical difficulties of collaborating in this way.

Having thus established a successful pattern of working, the students at Ikeda JHS set about writing some Japanese-style fanfares to introduce the Open Day.

The whole project brought Holy Cross staff and pupils, and the work of Ikeda pupils together in a day of vibrant collaboration. On the Open Day, the school welcomed a small Japanese vocal group, who sang a number of Japanese songs, and performed a traditional dance. The girls from Year 9 then took up the theme in a series of integrated music/dance/drama/martial arts performances. in which they explored various aspects of Japanese life and culture.

This was all carried out against a colourful background of art, textile, and pottery displays, and included a range of Project Folders produced during Information Technology lessons, which showed the girls of the school using and integrating up to sixteen different IT tools. These included desk-top publishing programs, word-processors, databases and spreadsheets, flat-bed scanners, clip art, digitalcameras, CD-ROMs, files from the internet, files from the school's intranet, art packages. graphics programs, and music software.

■ **Figure 14.5** Project 5 – Japan Project: using email, image files, and music files to support pupil learning

Mrs Watson, the Head Teacher at the time, commented,

> We see our many international links as small steps towards world peace. If our children can grow up with an understanding of people from different cultures across the world, they will find no need to engage in conflict with them, when they are older. We see the internet, used creatively, as a powerful tool for spreading peace and harmony in the world. Today marks one more step forward towards that goal.

CONCLUSIONS FROM THESE PROJECTS

We have found that the stimulus of using ICT to develop our curriculum has had a quite astonishing effect on the motivation of pupils across the whole school. There is a real sense of purpose to all of the related curricular activities. Our belief is that, like any new technology, ICT is neither intrinsically useful nor interesting. However, our experience shows us very clearly that, used creatively, ICT tools open up new audiences, bring together new partners in learning, and stimulate pupils to reach ever-increasing high standards in their work. We owe it to our students, therefore, to approach these opportunities with all of our skill and imagination.

GUIDELINES FOR THOSE WANTING TO DEVELOP WHOLE-SCHOOL APPROACHES

On the basis of the experience of projects within Holy Cross, the following points may provide useful guidance to others following in our steps.

- **Confidence** Approach this model of work with confidence. The model works extremely effectively, and has considerable educational research supporting it.
- **Enthusiasm** No-one will follow you if you are half-hearted in your leadership.
- **Build a team** Begin by working in small ways with people who share your vision. This might, at first, be just one colleague in a different subject area. Expand the team as your success grows. This may take months or years. Be sensible in your expectations concerning change. At Holy Cross this process took nearly three years.
- **Keep others informed** If you want more equipment, resources or time, then let people know of early successes, so that they are encouraged to support your work.
- **Display good work** Publish your pupils' success by displaying their work prominently everywhere (not just in the computer rooms). Give copies to your senior management team.
- **Work within the right framework** Don't do *anything* that distorts good practice, or distracts others from their own responsibilities. Let others work with you to develop their own skills, and meet their own agendas, within your overall framework.
- **The framework** Create a framework (an outline, a set of goals, a set of tasks) and then let the pupils have freedom to explore for themselves. They will *always* surprise you by exceeding your most ambitious expectations!
- **Above all, keep focused** on the learning outcomes to be achieved by the pupils. Ask yourself *why* you are using a computer. If the answer is not convincing, use a pencil!

The work undertaken at Holy Cross provides examples of the learning outcomes, the constraints and the excitement engendered in pupils by integrated ICT projects. In the following activity, we suggest you consider the approach taken by Holy Cross and think about whether it would work in your context.

Clearly there are many opportunities for developing pupils' ICT capabilities in a whole range of subject areas. How the school tackles this challenge is a responsibility of management and teachers wishing to work across curriculum will no doubt need to convince appropriate managers within the school.

Task 14.2 **Identifying ICT opportunities across the curriculum**

Consider how ICT is integrated into the curriculum in your current school. Read through the curriculum documents for your subject area together with any relevant school documents to identify how ICT relates to your specific area. Make notes about how you feel that ICT could be used to support teaching and learning in your subject area. Now consider other subject areas. What opportunities for cross-curricular work might arise between your subject area and other areas? If appropriate, discuss these ideas with other colleagues and perhaps start with planning small projects.

PROJECTS WITH OTHERS IN THE COMMUNITY

Following the success of the integrated ways of working described above, staff and students at the school worked with staff and students with learning disabilities at a local further education college and occupational therapists on three projects: one on healthy eating, one on keeping safe and one creating interactive games for the whiteboard. All use ICT tools in different ways, all require the active engagement of people of all abilities, especially those with learning disabilities, and all involve a visual learning element.

Healthy eating project

The first project centred on healthy eating, using visual learning techniques, and utilising a range of ICT tools to draw together several local agencies. This was achieved by devising a series of practical activities through which all the participants could share and develop their different knowledge and expertise. The content focus of the project was on healthy eating recipes produced for, and by, people with learning disabilities. The planning stage is an extremely important aspect of any community project, and so it is described here in detail and the aims and objectives of each of the groups in turn are given in Table 14.1.

■ **Table 14.1** Healthy eating project: aims and objectives of the different participants

Occupational Therapy Group

Aims
■ To support processes by which people with learning disabilities are active and equal participants in the project.
■ To link with the wider community, sharing knowledge and understanding of the work of occupational therapists (OTs).
■ To be involved in the development of accessible resources (web and paper-based) that support people with learning disabilities in leading healthy lifestyles.

Objectives
■ To develop resources that can be used by OTs and their clients, in the development of healthy eating/cooking skills. These would be in a range of visual learning formats that meet the needs of adults with learning disabilities.
■ To support the work of local schools and colleges through a series of educational visits, providing consultation about activity analysis, healthy eating, and the impact of learning disabilities on occupational participation.
■ To use the healthy eating resources in the work of OTs.
■ To contribute to a written final report of the project, which will be of use to other groups within the NHS, and beyond.

The Holy Cross School

Aims
■ To learn about the work of occupational therapists, and the role they play in the community (citizenship).
■ To develop AS and A2 Level Health and Social Care knowledge and skills in healthy eating, communication skills, and visual learning.
■ To widen the knowledge base of visual learning, and to support the NAACE Visual Learning Project through the publication of relevant aspects on the MirandaNet website.

Objectives
■ To create a series of recipes in different visual learning formats.
■ To create a set of web pages to publish these recipes.
■ To contribute student evaluations to the final written report of the project.

The Further Education College

Aims
■ For the further education (FE) college students to collaborate, as consultants, with students and teachers in another educational institution, and to share their experiences of learning disabilities.
■ To increase their knowledge about healthy eating.

Objectives
■ To understand their role in the process.
■ To pilot the draft visual learning resources, by trialling the recipes created.
■ To provide constructive feedback on the visual learning resources.
■ To contribute student evaluations to the final written report.

Project development

Occupational therapists (OTs) wanted materials about healthy eating skills for people with learning disabilities and approached the school to set up a joint project. The first step of the project was a series of visits to the school, by OTs with the Year 12 AS Health and Social Care students. These visits supported the work of the Holy Cross AS students, as well as widening the knowledge of the OT group regarding school Health and Social Care course requirements.

The tutor from the FE college, brought a group of his students with learning disabilities to act as consultants on the project. They spent a morning at Holy Cross, working on the project planning alongside the school's AS Level group. Prior to engaging in any project activity, the college students gave consent to participating in the project. During the visit to Holy Cross, the college students presented their views on how draft content could be improved. The draft content was posted on the college's accessible website. (Several of the college students were visually impaired so accessibility was an important part of the design of the materials.) The purpose of this session, for the FE students, was to provide expertise on accessible information formats for the designers from the Holy Cross students. In addition, the visit to Holy Cross was intended to give college students a positive and concrete experience, which could be used to reinforce their understanding of their role in the project. Photos were taken during the visit, to reinforce the learning process. The visit and the photos supported the FE staff in reinforcing the project aims for the students.

The information and expertise both in learning disabilities and healthy eating, gained from the OTs and from the college students, was then passed down to a group of Year 9 Holy Cross students, who stayed behind on several Mondays after school to work on the project. Their task was to cook a series of healthy meals using the design brief that was given, and to record the whole process with a digital camera, so that the food recipes would be in an accessible format for people with learning disabilities.

Following the Year 9 cooking and photography work, the images of the cooking process were added into PowerPoint files, each file containing a recipe.

Then, the project moved down the school year groups again, this time into Holy Cross Year 8 work, where two students added text and symbols. These PowerPoint files were sent electronically to the FE college, where they were trialled by the students with learning disabilities on the Preparation for Vocational Skills course.

The FE students were supported in their purchase of the ingredients from local shops by their teacher. Once in the kitchen, the students worked through the recipes. Some of the students were able to problem-solve around missing steps that came up in the recipes, whilst others needed further prompts. The college students were keen and able to work through the recipes, and had a meal at the end, which they reported to have enjoyed eating. The FE students were then asked for their comments. They were encouraged to record their feedback using IT tools. All students completed this activity when it was provided as a choice to complete during their tutorial time.

One college student, Rachel, recorded, '... and I enjoy making it and I did it all by myself and I would like to do it again and, and I put my own spices in with food and it is nice and I did it right and I do it different at home'.

The comments from the FE students were then compiled and the final files agreed. Finally, the recipes were emailed to the NHS OT department, who have started to identify service users who might adapt them in their work.

Keeping safe project

PROJECT PLANNING

A project planning meeting with all three partners – OTs, school and FE college staff – was undertaken in September. The OTs stated their interest in commissioning the DVD, and outlined their need for training resources for adults with learning disabilities that could be used to provide positive visual images in order to reinforce skill development in keeping safe. The inclusion of people with learning disabilities in the development of the DVD was an integral component of the project. Table 14.2 sets out the aims and objectives of the different participants.

■ **Table 14.2** Keeping safe project: aims and objectives

Aims

- To commission and develop a DVD about keeping safe.
- To continue the development of links between the National Health Service, secondary education, and further education.
- To build on the success of the healthy eating project.

Objectives

Occupational Therapists

- To commission a DVD about keeping safe for OTs to use to support their work in the local area.
- To use the DVD for training purposes to use alongside existing resources.
- To promote the involvement of people with learning disabilities as partners within service development work.

Holy Cross School

- Academic: To meet the needs of students studying AS Level Media in three units of their course:
  - work experience;
  - making a video;
  - presentation skills.
- Citizenship: To provide AS Level and Year 9 students with the opportunity to use their ICT skills in support of the project of benefit to the wider community.
- To develop baseline knowledge of the principles of accessible information for people with learning disabilities.
- To build stronger cross-agency links (now called Community Cohesion).

Further Education College

- For students to be provided with the opportunity to participate in a socially inclusive project.
- For students to participate actively in the making of a positively presented film about keeping themselves safe, in a variety of social contexts.
- To fulfil a unit in the City and Guilds course qualification.

All the college students had a learning disability, with an entry 1 or 2 in Numeracy and Literacy Skills.

Script development

The outline for the DVD was developed and a list of key components for each scene was developed to balance the needs of the occupational therapy service with the interests and abilities of the college students. For example, some scenes were non-verbal and some voice-overs were incorporated. The outline provided by the OTs was specific to their own service needs, but it had sufficient flexibility to enable the college students to be creative, and to use their own knowledge and experiences. This flexibility was incorporated to enable maximum participation in the project from students with learning disabilities who had a range of learning and verbal abilities.

Project development

The college students did their planning throughout the first half of the autumn term. This initially involved a wider discussion about keeping safe based on the individual experiences of the students. Once the topic had been introduced and students had familiarised themselves with areas of promoting personal safety the project was introduced as an opportunity to further support their learning. At this stage information was given to the students that when it came to filming they could choose whether to opt in. Accessible video consent forms were used to support students to make informed choices.

The students then considered the components of the project and through topic work considered the props the script would need, potential locations in addition to practising role-playing a range of scenarios. The students took it in turns to act out the different scenarios, and to try out different roles in order to see who felt comfortable at acting, and who the best actor for the part might be. This was done through the students appraising each other's performances, until it was agreed who would be taking which part. As different students did the acting, different interpretations of how to be safe arose. This, in itself, led to useful further discussion about ways to keep safe.

Preliminary filming at the college

The filming took place at the college and gave all involved a chance to get to know each other, and to demonstrate their acting skills. The college students acted through the different scenarios in a familiar setting, so that they felt comfortable. A few weeks later, the students were able to watch the film, and this was a chance to review and reinforce their work around keeping safe.

Preliminary filming at the school

The students then went to the school to see the community setting where the final filming would take place. This visit aimed to familiarise college students with the locations for the final filming in addition to meeting the school students again.

Final filming

On day one of final filming college students arrived at the school and were asked whether they were feeling confident and a final check was made as to whether they wanted to go ahead with the filming.

School students gave a demonstration of the professional equipment that had been hired for the final filming. College students gave an overview of the scenes that had been rehearsed, and 'walked through' some scenes so that the positioning of the cameras could be finalised. Scenes were then filmed and often small differences would occur during the 1–2 minute clips, which resulted in the need for each clip to be filmed at least three times.

On day two of the final filming the school students paid a return visit to the college to film the 'shop scene'. We had two actors to buy food from a shop. This took at least five takes, due to other things happening in the shop!

After the filming

The Year 9 Technology/ICT students at Holy Cross created PowerPoint slides of similar scenarios to the keeping safe project. These files were then used at the college to reinforce the learning steps around students keeping themselves, their property and possessions safe.

Although not all the students are in the filmed scenes, the whole group took an active part in the perusal of the scripts, and made amendments, or provided props and scenery. The making of the film has kept an important topic fresh in the students' minds, with continual reminders.

CONCLUSION

Through taking part in the project, college students were given the opportunity to participate in a multi-agency project of which they were key partners. All those with acting roles stated that they really enjoyed taking part in the filming and working with the group of students from the school. These lessons involved a better level of engagement than other lessons the students participated in. This could be due to the students being able to have visual feedback of their own performance and other students being able to contribute their feedback also. This led to broad discussions about students' personal experiences and students were given positive feedback from their peers when they were making safe choices. It was also noted and of interest to the tutor that in this academic year fewer students lost personal items, including college passes, than in the seven previous years of teaching experience at the college.

SUMMARY

There are a number of other projects and initiatives integrating the use of ICT into a range of curriculum areas and in which groups of teachers from different subject areas are working together. Building the resources on the school intranet is an important way of drawing on the varied expertise of staff and creating an environment where planning time can be reduced. Staff interviewed for the English case studies in the OECD ICT and whole school improvement project (Kington et al., 2001) said that considerable time was saved by such shared working once staff had their own laptops which gave them access to the network and resources when they were planning.

Teachers with whom we work have explored the possibilities of virtual field trips and virtual factory tours (in preparation for work experience) and working in collaboration with colleagues in other countries. The EU e-twinning programme is recommended for anyone wanting to do projects with other schools across the EU (see http://www. etwinning.net/en/pub/index.htm). Clearly, many opportunities exist with respect to school exchanges visits. Aspects of school exchanges that could be included are pre-visit preparation, communications during a visit, e.g. letters home, and post-visit review.

Developing content for the school website provides opportunities for collaborative, integrated work across subject areas and not just between teachers. Different year groups, for example, could be given responsibility for maintaining aspects of the school site (e.g. the annual drama production) and this responsibility could be passed on year after year. This work could involve tasks focused around particular sets of learning outcomes. These sorts of possibilities highlight the need for a school to adopt policies covering the use of the internet.

ACKNOWLEDGEMENTS

The authors would also like to acknowledge the support they have received throughout the projects from: Jim Power, Board Lead for Clinical Services, Long Term Care, Your Healthcare, and all those working in specialist health care, Occupational Therapy Service for People with Learning Disabilities, and from Zeina Ekuban, Catering Tutor, and Peggy Freyne, Learning Assistant, Lambeth College

Several of these cross-agency projects were published, each separately, in the *Journal of Assistive Technologies*. We are grateful to the editor, Dr Chris Abbott, King's College, London, for his continuous support, encouragement, and guidance, and also for permission to reproduce some of the material:

Healthy Eating project published by the *Journal of Assistive Technologies* 3(1), March 2009.

Keeping Safe project published by the *Journal of Assistive Technologies* 4(2), June 2010.

REFERENCES

Cribb, A. (1995) 'Philosophy of education: a few questions', *Educational Issues: A Reader*, London: King's College.

Gillmon, E. (1998) *Building Teachers' ICT Skills: The Problem and a Framework for the Solution*, London: Technology Colleges Trust.

Kington, A., Harris, S. and Leask, M. (2002) 'Innovative practice using ICT in schools: findings from two case studies', *Management in Education* 16(1): 31–5.

Kington, A., Harris, S., Lee, B. and Leask, M. (2001) 'Information and communications technology and whole school improvement: case studies of organisational change', paper reporting outcomes of the UK case studies for the OECD ICT and Whole School Improvement research project, BERA, September.

Leask, M. (2002) *The New Opportunities Fund ICT Training for Teachers and School Librarians: Progress Review and Lessons Learned Through the Central Quality Assurance Process in England*, London: Teacher Training Agency. Available at: http://www.teach-ttaa.gov.uk (accessed 14 May 2013).

Leask, M. and Wilder, P. (1996) *Project Connect Evaluation Report*, Bedford: De Montfort University.

OECD (2001) Case studies of innovative schools use of ICT are listed on the OECD website. Available at: http://www.oecd.org/home (accessed 14 May 2013). Searching the site for 'ICT and whole-school improvement' brings up the studies.

Wasser, J., McNamara, E. and Grant, C. (1998) 'Electronic networks and systemic school reform: understanding the diverse roles and functions of telecommunications in a changing school environment', paper presented at the American Educational Research Association Conference, San Diego, USA, April. Available at: http://www.scre.ac.uk/bera (via the web links button) (accessed 14 May 2013).

Watson, D. (1997) 'A positional good: change and IT', paper presented at the British Educational Research Association Conference, York, September.

LINKING SCHOOL WITH HOME USE

Ana Redondo and Gareth Whyte

INTRODUCTION

Recent advances in information and communications technology (ICT), in particular the use of virtual learning environments (VLE) and mobile devices make new things possible; this is as true for the so-called 'real world' as it is for education. As access to new technologies grows outside schools, particularly in homes, and as more and more learning resources become available in digital form, the role and function of school as the best place of learning are being called into question.

OBJECTIVES

By the end of this chapter you should have an awareness of:

- issues concerning the increase of computer use in the home/outside school;
- how new technologies might be used to support home-based learning;
- what schools can do to maximise the potential of ICT for home-based learning.

THE PROLIFERATION OF ICT AND ITS IMPLICATIONS

Work by Lewin *et al.* (2003, p. 45) commissioned by the DfES (see also Comber *et al.,* 2002; Somekh *et al.,* 2002a; Somekh *et al.,* 2002b; DfES 2009) stresses the breadth of computer-based activities that are happening in many homes, allowing young people, and their parents, to access specialist information and knowledge relevant to their own interests to an extent and in a way that has not previously been possible (see also Hennessey *et al.,* 2010; Younie and Leask, 2013). Together with the advent of more portable technology such as smart phones and tablet computers, these technologies considerably challenge teachers and schools among other things in their role as gatekeepers. Lewin *et al.* posit that schools generally fail to draw upon these experiences of knowledge creation outside school.

> Rather than technologies having any impact on transforming knowledge in the majority of schools, the traditional structures of curriculum and pedagogy were colonizing technologies and directing students' energies in schools to doing 'more of the same more efficiently'.
>
> (Lewin *et al.*, 2003, p. 45)

Whilst subject to transformation, the role of the teacher does not become redundant with the proliferation of 'edutainment' nor, indeed, more overtly instructional applications. Suggestions that the coherence teachers provide to the learning process will, in the foreseeable future, become less important can be seen to be misguided. Nevertheless, there exists a clear move in the world outside school towards self-directed, autonomous learning and knowledge creation which requires learners to identify their own goals and plan and structure their learning that sits ill-at-ease with practices and curricula in schools that have not responded to the opportunities offered by digital technologies to enhance learning.

> Pedagogy is no longer merely a process of teacher–student interaction, but a complex process of interaction between teacher, student, peers, family and technology.
>
> (Lewin *et al.*, 2003, p. 28)

Currently prevailing notions of schools as institutions and places of learning need to be seen as having social and historical functions, amongst others as repositories and transmitters of knowledge (Hutchinson, 1996, p. iv). In view of the increasing ease of access to information through new technologies as well as the expansion of our knowledge bases, the so-called information explosion, the idea of 'virtual schooling' is no longer inconceivable.

David Hargreaves, for instance, argues that if we want to make conceptions such as 'the learning society' or 'lifelong education' a reality,

> [the] traditional 'education system' must be replaced by *polymorphic* provision – an infinite variety of multiple forms of teaching and learning. Future generations will look back on our current sharp disjunction between life and education and our confusion of education with schooling as a barrier blocking a – perhaps the – road to the learning society.
>
> (Hargreaves, 1997, p. 11)

From a teacher's, rather than a policy maker's perspective, proclamations about an 'infinite variety of ... forms of teaching and learning' are, often quite rightly, bound up with concerns about the impact on personal professional practice. Not only in terms of pedagogical challenges and implications – and of course these do exist – but also in relation to workload. Anybody with experience in technology-enhanced teaching and learning will know about the complexities involved and the increased amount of teacher time required. From a teacher's, as well as a school's, perspective there will be concerns about the professional development implications of familiarisation and appropriation of ever-changing technologies and the psychological challenge in working in environments in which young people often show less inhibition and a greater knowledge and skills base than their teachers.

In the context of ICT use for increased home–school links the issue of (a lack of) familiarity on the part of parents with new technologies also comes into play. In England in 2006 the government launched a Computers for Pupils scheme (Lynch *et al.*, 2010) and a £300 million initiative called the Home Access Scheme in 2009 to provide the poorest families in England with computer and broadband access. This latter scheme had a short life but was seen to be effective in the independent evaluation report (SQW, 2011). The scheme reached '4.5% of England's six million households with children' (p. 91). It was closed by the incoming government in 2010 part way through implementation (for details see http://www.direct.gov.uk/NI1/Newsroom/DG_183990).

A survey conducted by the Office for National Statistics in August 2011 suggests a critical mass in home computer use has been achieved:

■ 90 per cent of households had access to a computer in the home, up from 81 per cent in the 2002 survey.
■ 71 per cent of households had access to the internet at home, up from 68 per cent in 2002.
■ 98 per cent of 5- to 18-year-olds used computers at home, school or elsewhere, with 92 per cent using them at school and 75 per cent using them at home.
■ 84 per cent of 5- to 18-year-olds used the internet at home, school or elsewhere, with 71 per cent using it at school and 56 per cent using it at home.
■ Young people of all ages used computers at home for a wider range of activities than in 2001.

An OFCOM survey reports a similar dramatic increase of home ownership of ICT and the use of the internet over the period 2008–10 (OFCOM, 2011):

■ 90 per cent of households have access to at least one computer.
■ 91 per cent of pupils can access the internet at home.

In view of these statistics and the transformational potential of ICT discussed earlier, schools in the UK are now in a position to use digital technologies to communicate with parents and the wider community to involve them in the learning process.

New technologies have the potential for fundamentally changing home–school relationships not only by enabling better access to information but also by providing tools for knowledge creation and participation in new cultural practices. Nevertheless, there is a real danger of new technologies increasing the gap for young people without ready access to computers and other technology at home, for example, for reasons of social deprivation. In addition to differences in the amount of computer use in the home, there are differences in the extent to which computers at home are used to enhance learning and help with homework.

Use of computers in the home: a comparison between primary and secondary pupils

A study by DFES (2009) reporting research on home use suggests that primary school pupils tend to use computers less for school work at home than secondary. Table 15.1 summarises some of these differences in use.

■ **Table 15.1** Differences in home computer use between primary and secondary pupils

	Write homework	Find information on the internet	Revise for tests
Primary	46%	35%	31%
Secondary	83%	43%	45%

Source: DfES, 2009.

The digital divide

The surveys above show there is still a 'digital divide' between 'haves' and 'have nots'. An article in the *Guardian* (28 December 2010) suggested there were at that time over 1 million people without computer access at home and 2 million without internet access. Clearly schools need to make provision for equal opportunities in terms of the differential of computer access by learners not only across the social divide but also by gender and ethnic background. In schools with a high population of poorer children, for example, these issues may be particularly pronounced, according to a survey carried out in 2010 by the Office for National Statistics which found in the 10 per cent richest households in the country 98 per cent have at least one computer and 97 per cent have internet connection. In contrast, in the 10 per cent poorest families only 38 per cent have computers and only 30 per cent have an internet connection.

This is, of course, not to ignore some of the seemingly more encouraging evidence. According to a survey commissioned by BT as long ago as 1998, the use of computers at home seems to increase fathers' involvement with their children's school-related work:

> 16 per cent of dads with home computers were involved with their children's home learning, compared with just 9 per cent of fathers relying on traditional homework resources. Computers and the internet provide men with the opportunity and incentive to interact more with their children, BT suggests.
>
> (*Guardian*, 13 January 1998)

When considering such evidence it is important to remember that home-based use of ICT to support learning is a growing market with considerable commercial importance. Publicity material is inherently characterised by vested interests and it is often not possible to make informed judgements about the validity and reliability of the research carried out by service providers.

Significantly, there are many pupils who have a strong preference for using ICT at home (see, e.g. Furlong *et al.,* 2000; Sutherland *et al.,* 2000; Hennessey *et al.,* 2010; Younie and Leask, 2013) due to enhanced hardware and software availability as well as increased access, choice and agency. Schools and teachers ignore the resulting ICT capability of pupils at their peril.

TYPES OF HOME AND SCHOOL USE OF ICT

The DfES-funded research carried out by Lewin *et al.* (2003, p. 34) identifies a number of what the researchers call 'special initiatives' to develop links between home and school including:

■ virtual classrooms;
■ homework guidance on the web;
■ emailing parents;
■ emailing homework to teachers;
■ home access to school servers;
■ online tutoring;
■ parental access to school attendance registers via the internet; and
■ online conferencing for parents and school governors.

Many schools are still a long way from taking advantage of these opportunities. Clearly digital technologies can play a crucial role at the interface between home and schools. There are many research reports commissioned by the now defunct UK government agency BECTA that provide details of the use of specific digital technologies to link home and school. Many can be found on the Digital Education Resource Archive site at http://www.dera.ioe.ac.uk. Effective practices identified as well as email include:

■ a resource-rich or interactive school website linked to mobile technologies (phones, tablets);
■ online learning/virtual school;
■ student, parent and community use of school-based ICT facilities;
■ loan and subsidy schemes, including portable ICT schemes;
■ local TV – locally produced educational content on TV networks;
■ community intranets; and
■ additional online resources of use to parents and pupils.

The use of apps and tablets, particularly iPads, forms a new focus for research at the time of writing.

Task 15.1 **Establishing patterns of home computer use**

Carry out a survey amongst your classes to establish prevailing patterns of computer use at home and on the move amongst your pupils. What are the implications of your findings for the work you ask your pupils to do in the class and away from school?

THE ROLE OF HOMEWORK

One obvious opportunity of linking home and school use of ICT is through ICT-enhanced homework. Pupils often find homework a chore. Encouraging the use of ICT for homework purposes is one way of capitalising on the motivational potential of new technologies. Equity of access is an important issue here and schools must ensure that strategies are in place to enable those pupils who have not got access to ICT at home to enhance their classroom-based learning as well as their more fortunate peers who have. This can be done, for instance, through lunchtime or after-school ICT/homework clubs.

Findings by Comber *et al.* (2002, p. 31) suggest that teachers tend to encourage, rather than require, internet use for homework because of concerns over equity of access. Yet, there are real advantages to be had by students being able to access their schoolwork from home for continuation, extension and refinement (see Lewin *et al.*, 2003, p. 39). Homework can supplement and/or differentiate what happens in the classroom and it can reinforce or consolidate work carried out in school.

Homework, in a sense, can be seen as the space between school-based and out-of-school learning, where teacher- and curriculum-specified tasks meet a learner-defined curriculum and culture. A report of emerging findings from the evaluation of the impact of ICT on pupil attainment (Harrison *et al.,* 2001, p. 5) uses the concept of a 'socially contextualised integrated model of learning' to explain this interrelationship.

Pupils can benefit from the attention given to them by 'significant others', e.g. their parents/guardians at home or ICT/homework club supervisors in school, as well as make use of reference material which might not be available during lessons.

Competition for access to computers is likely to be less fierce at home as well as in ICT/homework clubs, i.e. the user–hardware ratio is bound to be better than during normal classwork and will continue to improve as we move to a model of individual machines. In 2003, according to OFSTED (2004), the average number of pupils per computer in secondary schools was 5.4; however, in 2009, according to BECTA, this had dropped to 4.2.

Computer-supported work outside the classroom still causes anxieties in certain quarters, traditionally in relation to spelling and handwriting but more recently in relation to plagiarism. In order to ameliorate some of these anxieties it is important that explicit assessment criteria are used that recognise the work done using ICT but at the same time do not disadvantage those pupils unable to use ICT.

Task 15.2 **Integrating ICT use into homework tasks**

1 Examine your current scheme-of-work for one class you are teaching with a view to how ICT resources could be used to supplement homework tasks.
2 Also, what ICT-based revision material do you know of for your subject area? Talk to colleagues in your department, get in touch with your subject association and look out for subject-specific software catalogues as well as reviews in the educational press for ideas. See, for example:
   ■ BBC Learning at http://www.bbc.co.uk/learning;
   ■ BBC Bitesize Revision at http://www.bbc.co.uk/schools/gcsebitesize;
   ■ Channel 4's Homework High at http://www.channel4.com/homework;
   ■ S-cool at http://www.s-cool.co.uk.

OFFERING ADVICE TO PARENTS ABOUT EFFECTIVE ICT USE

A key consideration for schools in relation to home-based ICT use for learning is the provision of guidance on e-safety, when, where and how to use computers. Ever since the internet emerged, there has been a lot of hype about its potential dangers:

> Child porn, adult porn, instructions on how to make bombs, how to engage in autoeroticism ..., the finer points of glue-sniffing, rants against the black and Jewish world conspiracy and why we should all have the freedom to carry guns are just

some of the Net's offerings that have been whipping up a frenzy of paranoia, moral outrage, medium-level concern in the media and, consequently, among parents and teachers.

The simple, rather banal fact is that the internet is only as bad and as good as society itself.

(Klein, 1995, p. 20)

These potential dangers and the anxieties parents might have need to be taken seriously if progress can be made in terms of ICT use within and outside school. As far as ICT-enabled work within school is concerned, the adoption of an acceptable use policy such as the one suggested by Naace, the ICT association, seems imperative (see http://www.naace.co.uk/512). Guidelines for ICT use outside school are also available online. The government Think You Know website (http://www.thinkuknow.co.uk) provides some useful advice. Many local authorities and other bodies provide advice on e-safety.

Advice is also available from a number of other websites, including government-sponsored ones. Schools might wish to develop these guidelines, tailor them to their local needs and disseminate them to parents.

A different type of support can come in the form of open days or open evenings during which pupils can demonstrate what they have learnt, what equipment there is available at school and what software is used by subject departments. But also, events like these can be used to offer parents and the wider community training in (basic) ICT skills in the hope that this will bridge the fear barrier for some parents and facilitate them working with their children on ICT-based work. The fact that there are lots of benefits to be had from pupils learning with their parents or even from teaching their parents is well known. Once parents see how proficient their children are and what motivational effect ICT might have on them, it is likely that they are going to be positively disposed towards ICT use in school.

Schools might consider providing parents with suggestions about what software would be beneficial in supplementing school-based work in various subject areas. Experience suggests that it is preferable to discourage parents from purchasing software that forms an integral part of a department's scheme-of-work as use outside school of such core applications might take some of the excitement out of their use in school. Also, the fun element of learning through computers at home might be diminished in that way. Teachers could concentrate on recommending supplementary as well as revision material. Parents, could, for instance be directed to vetted web-based revision and supplementary material (see Task 15.1, page 225).

Apart from technical considerations, schools might consider discussing with parents some of the most pertinent pedagogical implications of ICT use such as the tensions between presentation versus content, i.e. 'not all that glitters is gold', the dangers of plagiarism or the importance of fostering pupils' research skills, etc.

One area parents, as well as pupils, tend to be particularly interested in is advice and guidance concerning examination periods, particularly during the study leave period in preparation for GCSEs and A-level examinations. Again, ICT-based materials are available, such as guidance on exam stress or study skills.

Also, parents could be in touch with relevant organisations, such as the Parent Information Network (PIN), an independent national support membership organisation that aims to help parents support children using computers.

THE ROLE OF A SCHOOL VIRTUAL LEARNING ENVIRONMENT

According to a report by Geoff Minshull (2004, p. 4) Direct Learn Training on behalf of BECTA, the definition of a VLE is that it is a single piece of software that brings together a variety of different tools and functions, notably:

- content management and delivery;
- communications;
- assessment;
- tracking;
- administrative tools, which may include links to other systems, notably management information systems.

As we have noted above, together with email, school virtual learning environments are particularly potent in linking home to school use. The use of web technology for VLEs means that the system can be accessed anywhere, not just in school or at home; this development together with the rapid development of portable devices mean the school VLE can become the 'any time any where' learning model that teachers and students are starting to demand.

According to the Harnessing Technology Review by BECTA in 2009 the number of primary schools that have a VLE have gone from 11 per cent in 2006 to 40 per cent in 2009. The number of secondary schools that have a VLE in place has gone from 46 per cent in 2006 to 79 per cent in 2009.

There are two main roles of a VLE. One is to strengthen the contact of the school with home for the student and teachers by utilising features such as real time chat and online discussions with other students where students can use these facilities to build on existing knowledge and create new ideas even if they are unable to be present in the classroom.

Parents may be granted access to a range of information using the VLE depending on the chosen VLE, ranging from traditional school website information such as school announcements and holiday schedules, to attainment information, report cards and due dates for assignments and tests, again strengthening the home–school link.

Task 15.3 **School virtual learning environments**

Find out whether your school has a VLE:

- View the site and consider what its aims and purposes are. What type of material can be found on it: curriculum-related links, publicity material, information about the local area? Who is the target audience: pupils, parents, teachers, the wider public?
- Find out about its management and production. Who is responsible for creating it? Who is updating it? What curriculum areas are contributing?
- Find out how you could make your own contribution, preferably in conjunction with one of the classes you teach.

The other major role of the school VLE is to support pupils in a personalised way by using the VLE to provide high-quality learning materials in and out of the classroom. This enables students to learn and to work at an independent pace, with differentiated learning materials in an environment they feel comfortable in. All of this together is a key factor in raising attainment.

SUMMARY

In this chapter we have attempted to demonstrate how ICT can meaningfully be used for bridging the gap between school and home learning. Communicating with pupils and parents through the school VLE, for instance informing them about school events or even allowing pupils to submit homework, etc., nevertheless remains problematic as it can easily represent extra workload for already very busy professionals.

In concluding, we want to refer to Thomas *et al.* (1998, pp. 149–50) who voice a note of caution when they point out, on the basis of their experience of working for a big distance-learning provider, that certain prerequisites for successful, large-scale internet-based teaching are necessary:

- a culture *of supported* learning;
- recognition of cost;
- integration of technology with the administrative infrastructure, as well as with teaching practice;
- transformation of practices (both teaching and administrative) to take advantage of technology in order to provide needed functions, rather than superficial translation of existing practices.

REFERENCES

Becta (2008) *Extending Opportunity. Final Report of the Minister's Taskforce on Home Access to Technology*, London: Becta. Available at: http://dera.ioe.ac.uk/8285/1/home_access_report.pdf (accessed 23 June 2013).

——(2009) *Harnessing Technology Review 2008: The Role of Technology and its Impact on Education*, Coventry: Becta. Available at: http://dera.ioe.ac.uk/1423/1/becta_2008_htreview_report.pdf (accessed 23 June 2013).

Bradbrook, G., Alvi, I., Disher, J. and Lloyd, H. (2008). *Meeting their Potential: the Role of Education and Technology in Overcoming Disadvantage and Disaffection in Young People.* Coventry: Becta. Available at: http://dera.ioe.ac.uk/1657/1/becta_2008_meetingtheirpotential_report.pdf (accessed 23 June 2013).

Comber, C., Watling, R., Lawson, T., Cavendish, S., McEune, R. and Paterson, F. (2002) *Learning at Home and School: Case Studies,* ImpaCT2, ICT in Schools Research and Evaluation Series No. 8, London: DfES/Becta. Available at: http://dera.ioe.ac.uk/1574/1/becta_2002_ImpaCT2_Strand3_report.pdf (accessed 23 June 2013).

Davies, C., Carter, A., Cranmer, S., Eynon, R., Furlong, J., Good, J., Hjorth, I.A., Lee, S., Malmberg, L. and Holmes, W. (2008) *The learner and their context – Interim report: Benefits of ICT use outside formal education*, Coventry: Becta. Available at: http://dera.ioe.ac.uk/1524/1/becta_2009_learner_context_interim.pdf (accessed 23 June 2013).

Davies, S. (1998) 'More than just a prospectus', *TES Friday,* l0 July: 15.

Department for Education, (2011) *Evaluation of the Home Access Program: Final Report*, Available at: http://www.sqw.co.uk/file_download/361 (accessed 14 October 2012).

Furlong, J., Furlong, R., Facer, K. and Sutherland, R. (2000) 'The national grid for learning: a curriculum without walls?', *Cambridge Journal of Education* 30: 91–110.

Hargreaves, D. (1997) 'A road to the learning society', *School Leadership and Management* 17(1): 9–21.

Harrison, C., Cavendish, S., Comber, C., Fisher, T., Harrison, A., Haw, A., Haw, K., Lewin, C., McFarlane, A., Mavers, D., Scrimshaw, P., Somekh, B. and Walling, R. (2001) *ImpaCT2: Emerging Findings from the Evaluation of the Impact of ICT on Pupil Attainment*, Research and Evaluation Series No. 1, London: DfES/Becta. Available at: http://dera.ioe.ac.uk/1575/1/becta_2002_ImpaCT2_ngfl_report.pdf (accessed 23 June 2013).

Hayward, B., Ally, C., Pearson, S. and Martin, C. (2003) *Young People and ICT 2002: Findings from a survey conducted in Autumn 2002*, London: DfES/Becta. Available at: http://dera.ioe.ac.uk/1646/1/becta_2002_youngpeoplesuse_report_queensprinter.pdf (accessed 23 June 2013).

Hutchinson, C. (1996) 'Snares in the charmed circle', *Times Higher Educational Supplement* 12 April: iv–v.

Klein, R. (1995) 'Naughty toys and dirty pictures', *TES Computers Update,* 20 October: 20–1.

Lewin, O., Mavers, D. and Somekh, B. (2003) 'Broadening access to the curriculum through using technology to link home and school: a critical analysis of reforms intended to improve students' educational attainment', *The Curriculum Journal* 14(1): 23–53.

Lynch, S., Bielby, G., Judkis, M., Rudd, P. and Benton, T. (2010) *Evaluation of the Computers for Pupils Initiative: Final Report*. Available at: http://www.dera.ioe.ac.uk/1543/1/becta_2010_cfpevaluation_report (accessed 14 October 2012)

Millard, E. (1997) 'New technologies, old inequalities: variations found in the use of computers by pupils at home with implications for the school curriculum'. Available at: http://www.leeds.ac.uk/educol/documents/000000362.htm (accessed 14 October 2012).

Minshull, G. (2004) 'VLEs: beyond the fringe and into the mainstream', proceedings of the 2004 online conference from BECTA. Available at: http://www.directlearn.co.uk/downloads/VLEs%20-%20into%20the%20mainstream.pdf (accessed 14 October 2012).

Morris, D. (2010) 'E-confidence or incompetence: are teachers ready to teach in the 21st century?' *World Journal on Educational Technology*, 2(2) 141–154. Available at: http://www.world-education-center.org/index.php/wjet/article/viewArticle/180 (accessed 23 June 2013).

OFCom (2011) *Communications Market Report: UK*. Available at: http://stakeholders.ofcom.org.uk/market-data-research/market-data*communications-market-reports/cmr11/ (accessed 14 October 2012).

OFSTED (2004) *ICT in Schools: The Impact of Government Initiatives Five Years On*, London: OFSTED. Available at: http://www.ofsted.gov.uk/publications/index.cfm?fuseaction= pubs.displayfilc&id=3652&typc = pdf (accessed 14 October 2012).

——(2009) *Virtual Learning Environments: An Evaluation of Their Development in a Sample of Education Settings*, London: OFSTED. Available at: http://www.ofsted.gov.uk/resources/virtual-learning-environments-evaluation-of-their-development-sample-of-educational-settings (accessed 14 October 2012).

Shepherd, S. (2010) 'No web access at home for 2m poor pupils, warns charity', *Guardian*, 28 December.

Somekh, B., Mavers, D. and Lewin, C. (2002a) *Using ICT to Enhance Home–School Links: An Evaluation of Current Practice in England,* ICT in Schools Research and Evaluation Series No. 4, London: DfES/Becta. Available at: http://dera.ioe.ac.uk/4725/2/ngflseries_hsl1.pdf (accessed 23 June 2013).

Somekh, B., Lewin, O., Mavers, D., Fisher, T., Harrison, O., Haw, K., Lunzer, E., McFarlane, A. and Scrimshaw, R. (2002b) *Pupils' and Teachers' Perceptions of ICT in the Home, School and Community: ImpaCT2,* ICT Schools Research and Evaluation Series No. 9, London: DfES/

Becta. Available at: http://dera.ioe.ac.uk/1573/1/becta_2022_ImpaCT2_strand2_report.pdf (accessed 23 June 2013).

SQW in partnership with Ipsos Mori and London Knowledge Lab (2011) *Evaluation of the Home Access Programme: Final Report*, London: Department for Education. Research Report DFE-RR132. Available at: http://www.sqw.co.uk/file_download/361 (accessed 14 October 2012).

Sutherland, R., Facer, K., Furlong, R. and Furlong, J. (2000) 'A new environment for education? The computer in the home', *Computers and Education* 34: 195–212.

Thomas, R., Carswell, L., Price, B. and Petre, M. (1998) 'A holistic approach to supporting distance learning using the internet: transformation, not translation', *British Journal of Educational Technology* 29(2): 149–61.

TEACHING AND LEARNING WITH ICT: OVERCOMING THE CHALLENGES OF BEING A TWENTY-FIRST CENTURY TEACHER

David Morris and Michele Burns

INTRODUCTION

Drawing upon and considering recent research and political change, this chapter identifies the implications of what it means to be a teacher in the twenty-first century. It also provides advice on how to overcome some of the challenges you may face, including teaching pupils who may have a firmer grasp of technology than yourself. According to the General Teaching Council for England (GTCE), 'The use of ICT and keeping abreast with its application and potential to contribute to work in the classroom' is 'an important focus' for teachers when 'seeking professional development opportunities' (Poet *et al.*, 2010, p. 4). Although most teachers are enthusiastic about using ICT to support the teaching of the curriculum, the British Educational Technology Association (Becta)'s recent *Harnessing Technology School Survey* indicates that even those new to the profession would still need continuing professional development (CPD) in using ICT in the classroom (Becta, 2010a). Whilst you no longer need to take the ICT skills test to gain Qualified Teacher Status (QTS) and even though the current government has axed Becta and the GTCE, the expectation, from both employers and the pupils you teach, is that you are a competent user of ICT.

You may have been an ICT industry professional but this does not necessarily mean that you will be a great teacher of ICT. The current political debate on teaching ICT (Gove, 2012) suggests a shift away from ICT application based learning towards developing pupils' innovation in programming skills and you may need to consider how you will incorporate this into your teaching. Auditing your developing ICT needs and completing the tasks in this chapter should not only help you to see yourself as a learner, but also help you understand how to improve pupils' learning experiences using ICT. Guidance is provided on how to include pupils' use of technology to broaden the range of ICT(s) you use to support teaching and learning, as well as ensuring pupils' e-safety in doing so.

OVERVIEW

At the end of this chapter you should be able to:

■ incorporate pupils' own experiences of ICT in your subject area;
■ enable pupils' effective engagement with teaching and learning including addressing current government curriculum initiatives in ICT;
■ confidently use a wider range of ICT(s) including more recent technologies.

Check the requirements for your course to see which relate to this unit.

CURRENT ISSUES IN ICT

Knowledge shift

In the early 1990s information was accessed via an encyclopaedia or a visit to the library, whereas now you "Google it". For your pupils, exchanging and sharing information this way is second nature; Table 16.1 illustrates the context of such technological evolution. It is, therefore, not surprising that pupils have learnt to use technologies confidently, including the wide range of powerful ICT devices they currently own (e.g. tablets and mobile phones). As you will see from Table 16.1, technological change is rapid. Your pupils are likely to take technological change for granted and you, as their teacher, need to adapt to this change.

According to Prensky (2001) your pupils are 'digital natives' and although you may be a 'digital native' yourself (if you were born after 1980) there is evidence to suggest that in the context of the twenty-first century the way you and your pupils engage with ICT may be different. A three-year study in the United States involving over 2,000 student teachers found that, statistically, there is no significant difference in terms of ICT competence across age groups, although learning behaviours between 'natives' and 'immigrants' may vary (Guo *et al.*, 2008, p. 252). This might manifest itself in alternative ways, and may relate to inclinations towards different uses of Web 2.0 technologies; for example, *The Spire Project* shows that people's use of Facebook falls significantly after the age of 24 (White, 2007, p. 4).

Evidence of this 'cultural gap' may exist in Secondary Schools whereby pupils have turned to Web 2.0 technologies to 'communicate, share and learn informally using knowledge systems their elders [teachers] can barely understand' (Williams, 2008, p. 213). The landscape is changing, however, with senior leaders in schools claiming that 36 per cent of secondary pupils are encouraged to use Wikis to support learning, although the figures for instant messaging and social networking are considerably lower at 13 and 11 per cent respectively (Becta, 2010a, p. 35).

Many of the pupils you teach, however, may be submerged in a technology-rich environment where they can 'select and appropriate technologies to their own personal learning needs', which potentially has 'profound implications for the way in which educational institutions design and support learning activities' (Conole *et al.*, 2008, p. 511). Some teachers, however, feel threatened because they find themselves in situations where the pupil is more knowledgeable than they are (Condie *et al.*, 2005 and 2007; OFSTED, 2009). Seeking advice from pupils should be encouraged because it can be beneficial in 'building relationships and breaking down barriers' and can provide a catalyst in terms of encouraging pupils and teachers to work together in new ways (Cardinal Newman Catholic School and Brighton and Hove LA, 2006, p. 2).

■ **Table 16.1** Significant developments in technology, 1998–2007

Pupils' D.O.B	Secondary School entry	Pupils' age	Significant technological developments
1989	2000	18	Modem is the most common household connection; first UK person has broadband. Nintendo GameBoy released.
1990	2001	17	Sega Mega Drive and IMDb internet movie database launched.
1991	2002	16	World Wide Web released by Tim Berners Lee.
1992	2003	15	The Internet Society formed. The Internet Engineering Task Force operates under its guidance.
1993	2004	14	The internet carries 1% of information through two-way telecommunications.
1994	2005	13	Mobile network Orange created. Amazon founded in USA.
1995	2006	12	Windows 95 released (even consumers without home computers bought copies!). Alta Vista, the first major search engine launched.
1996	2007	11	Google Beta and Hotmail (free web-based e-mail) launched.
1997	2008	10	First online internet banking service introduced by Nationwide Building Society. Yahoo Babel Fish automatic translation launched.
1998	2009	9	The National Grid for Learning (NGfL) launched by the (Labour) government.
1999	2010	8	Dreamcast 128-bit video game console released by Sega. Napster peer-to-peer file sharing begins.
2000	2011	7	Wikipedia born. Dot-com bubble bursts.
2001	2012	6	Nintendo Gamecube introduced. iPod line released by Apple.
2002	2013	5	Nanodrive (Millipede project) announced by IBM, on the size of a coin. Introduction of Microsoft Tablet PC operating system.
2003	2014	4	Chip-and-pin cards issued throughout the UK. Skype voice calls begin. iTunes Store created.
2004	2015	3	O'Reilly Media Web 2.0 conference featuring Facebook (social networking) launched. Flickr image hosting begins.
2005	2016	2	Launch of Nintendo DS and YouTube video sharing. Google Earth virtual globe arrives.
2006	2017	1	Twitter microblogging launched.
2007	2018	R	Google Maps Street View introduced. More than 97% of all telecommunications carried over the internet.

Although Becta's 2010 *School Survey* indicates that 'over three-quarters (77 per cent) of Secondary School ICT coordinators reported that either most or all of the teaching staff at their school were enthusiastic users of ICT in delivering the school curriculum' (Becta, 2010a, p. 36), research suggests that most teachers' use of ICT applications is limited to only a few types (Becta, 2008; Cox and Marshall, 2007). This landscape remains largely unchanged. Even though teachers are 'generally enthusiastic' about using ICT, there are still gaps in teachers' knowledge and skills and that 'most would benefit from further training in the use of ICT' as well as being given 'further development' in order to use 'most technological devices to their full potential' (Becta, 2010a, p. 37).

Returning to the 'digital natives' debate, however, there is research that questions the reality of such a digital divide. Li and Ranieri (2010) contest that pupils may be less digitally skilful when it comes to using ICT in an educational setting, and that pupils' use of 'digital technologies' may vary and may often be 'unspectacular' (Selwyn, 2009, p. 364). Bennett and Matton (2010, p. 322) claim that there is also a 'significant lack of consensus' as to the effects that new and emerging technologies have on pupils. There are also issues of access to technologies that may be restricted by socio-economic factors such as class, gender and geography (Bennett *et al.*, 2008; Selwyn, 2009) and pupils' skill levels may subsequently be prone to vary (Bennett and Matton, 2010). Pupils' aptitudes are subsequently unlikely to be 'uniform' (Bennett *et al.,* 2008) and their use of the internet and Web 2.0 technologies may subsequently be passive in simply receiving information as opposed to being active in creating online content (Selwyn, 2009).

To conclude, your main consideration here is to think about how you can capitalise on the diversity of your pupils' knowledge, experiences and preferences for ICTs and how you may be able to incorporate these in order to make lessons more engaging. However, resistance remains in many schools regarding the use of pupils' own devices, such as mobile phones and social networking sites, so before completing any tasks you are advised to consult your tutor before planning lessons that may involve the use of these.

Becoming a twenty-first century teacher

Following on from the 'knowledge revolution' at the end of the previous millennium, you will invariably face challenges teaching in the twenty-first century. This is not only because you cannot predict the social or economic trends in education (Robinson, 2010) but also because the changes to the National Curriculum (Gove, 2012) may determine the impact your practice has in the classroom. The problems of teaching in the twenty-first century may range from a withdrawal of funding and resourcing for previous Building Schools for the Future (BSF) initiatives, to how pupils engage with the information they find online. A widespread misconception that you need to be aware of is your pupils' unshaken trust in information accessed via the internet. You are advised to watch the following video clip that presents a case study highlighting how important it is for pupils to vet the source and reliability of information accessed from the internet (Green, 2006): http://www.teachfind.com/teachers-tv/secondary-ict-web-literacy.

It may also be useful to consider your pupils' developing needs alongside your own. Auditing the ways in which you and your school use ICT can provide a useful starting point from which to create your own development plan. Research suggests that there is a correlation between institutions where there is good subject knowledge and where ICT skills are systematically audited, although such 'audits of staff needs' are rare (OFSTED, 2009, p. 25).

Task 16.1 **Auditing and building upon your ICT skills**

Make a list of the ICTs you feel competent in using to support learning and teaching.

1 Which ones could you use in your classroom?
2 Can any of them be used to:
   ▪ expedite administrative tasks?
   ▪ create learning resources?
   ▪ foster independent learning?
   ▪ generate lessons plans that you can modify in the future?
   ▪ instantly allow you to personalise learning?
   ▪ cater for different learning styles?
   ▪ engage and motivate your pupils?
   ▪ make assessment for learning more effective?
   ▪ support learning outside of the classroom?
3 Choosing one or two of the above as areas for development, formulate an action plan that is SMART – your targets need to be specific, measurable, achievable, realistic and time-specific. Your targets should also enable you to:
   ▪ review your progress;
   ▪ evaluate the impact this has had on your classroom practice;
   ▪ further develop your knowledge and skills (see Figure 16.1).

Action Plan

Area for Action	Target	How I will achieve it	By (date)	Review/Further action
Assessment and record keeping using a spreadsheet	Use conditional formatting to track grades/marks (as discussed with tutor)	Use Help function in Excel. Refer to handout emailed by tutor	12-11-12	Completed. Develop use of further functions
Assessment and record keeping using a spreadsheet	Apply use of IF and COUNT IF to track pupil progress	Handout from tutor	19-11-12	

▪ **Figure 16.1** Creating an action plan

Your pupils use technology as part of their daily life and increasingly expect to use it for learning in school, but how does this align with you as their teacher? Teaching in the twenty-first century requires that you are a learner yourself – adapting your previous skills and knowledge as new technologies emerge. You know when to use technology and when other strategies are more appropriate. You need to constantly review how you use technology to support your wider professional role and how you incorporate your ICT skills into your classroom practice.

MAKING EFFECTIVE USE OF ICT

Surveying pupils' use of ICT

When planning lessons it can be useful to know what technologies the pupils in your school are using. A survey of pupils in Key Stages 3 and 4 at The Sandon School was undertaken whereby pupils were asked about the technologies they use. The survey was offered to all Key Stage 3 and Key Stage 4 pupils via a link on the school's VLE (virtual learning environment). Responses were collated via spreadsheet software and the 'randomise' function was used to select a sample of 100 responses from each of the Key Stage subgroups representing 36 per cent and 40 per cent of responses. The survey results are shown in Table 16.2.

The first six rows of the table provide, effectively, a benchmark of pupils' use of ICT inside and outside of school. Given that 100 per cent of pupils use a mobile phone as an organiser, an interesting question for you might be: How can this skill be incorporated and utilised in school to facilitate teaching and learning?

The table also illustrates a clear division between Key Stages 3 and 4 and consideration must be given as to why. Possible reasons may include social and financial factors such as older pupils having more income and more opportunities for purchasing technologies but may also include pupils' social autonomy and increased peer influence.

■ **Table 16.2** Pupils' social use of ICT

	Key Stage 3 50 pupils	Key Stage 4 50 pupils	Key Stage 3 Percentage	Key Stage 4 Percentage
Mobile telephone – SMS	50	50	100%	100%
Mobile telephone – camera	50	50	100%	100%
Mobile telephone – organiser	50	50	100%	100%
Social networking website	50	50	100%	100%
Blog	50	50	100%	100%
Digital camera	50	50	100%	100%
Games console	42	49	84%	98%
Digital video camera	30	50	60%	100%
MP3 player	27	48	54%	96%
Laptop	21	42	42%	84%
Handheld gaming console	19	31	38%	62%
Microphones	13	32	26%	64%
Handheld computing device	13	24	26%	48%
Graphics tablet	7	12	14%	24%
Podcast	6	13	12%	26%
Digital photograph frame	5	9	10%	18%
Projector	2	6	4%	12%
e-book reader	2	5	4%	10%
3D digital camera	0	0	0%	0%

How could you use your pupils' experience and knowledge of these technologies in your lessons? The first steps involve implementing a survey to determine usage. There is a free online survey tool called Survey Monkey, which is intuitive to use and can be found at http://www.surveymonkey.com. Here, you can generate online surveys in minutes, and view the results graphically and in real time. Consider if the results of your survey match those found above and, in doing so, consider the socio-economic demographic. The Sandon School is a Maths and Computing Academy with 1,200 pupils ranging from 11 to 18 years and is larger than the average Secondary School. The school's website can be viewed here: http://www.sandon.essex.sch.uk. In this instance, the pupils who undertook the survey were keen to know why we were interested in their use of technologies and also keen to talk about how and what they used. Clearly opportunities exist for pupils to share, lead and facilitate teaching and learning.

Task 16.2 **Surveying and critical appraisal of findings**

In your school conduct a similar survey as above using Survey Monkey as suggested or other appropriate methods.

Analyse findings by identifying any differences or similarities within your school and provide an explanation as to the possible reasons why this may be the case. In doing so, you may wish to consider using additional data available to you, e.g. Raise Online, OFSTED reports (http://www.ofsted.gov.uk/inspection-reports/find-inspection-report/provider/ELS/115379) and internal school data, in order to provide a rationale to analyse the conclusions. Details of any Secondary School's performance can be found at: http://www.education.gov.uk/performancetables/schools_09.shtml.

1 Using the suggested further reading at the end of this chapter as your starting point, although you may wish to research more widely, write an appraisal of how the most common and most widely used technologies by pupils may be integrated to support teaching and learning in your subject area. This should be approximately 1,000 words.

2 Choosing up to three technologies from your survey, write a further 500–750 word rationale explaining why you consider a particular technology (e.g. the mobile phone) to be advantageous to teaching and learning in your school. The intended audience for this proposal should be your tutor initially, and possibly the school's leadership team. In your proposal outline the key objectives for the delivery of a unit of work, making reference to the relevant aspects of the National Curriculum and/or your school's schemes of work.

You should aim to make your appraisal critical by supporting your rationale and arguments with reference to relevant theory and literature.

You could extend the task with the agreement of your school and, bearing in mind any suggested changes you are advised to make, evaluate the impact of the unit of work by considering the following:

■ learning outcomes;
■ levels of pupil engagement;
■ levels of pupil attainment;
■ any issues relating to functionality or e-safety.

Using newer technologies

A hardware peripheral is a device that operates separately from the computer's central processing unit (CPU) but is connected to it temporarily. There are a wide range of ICT peripherals that can be used in the classroom to support learning and whilst some schools are well resourced, a more familiar story is that peripherals are used only by the school's ICT champions and are otherwise left to gather dust. This can be due to a lack of realisation that tools such as digital cameras, video recorders and visualisers can save a teacher time as once the technology is mastered it has the potential to make lessons more interesting and lead to effective pupil learning. For example, digital cameras are a useful technology to record out of school events such as a geography field trip or cultural celebrations. Research (Smith *et al.,* 2008) indicates that there still exists some reluctance to incorporate digital cameras into lessons, possibly due to a lack of know-how and confidence with accessing images captured immediately whilst teaching a lesson and then incorporating the images into the lesson. A Modern Languages teacher at The Sandon School, with minimal ICT training, confidently uses her digital camera during lessons to take photographs of the pupils for a French vocabulary task using the context of a dating agency database and instantly uses the projected digital images for pupils to indicate hair colour and so on. She felt that the time spent learning how to use the camera and upload the images to the computer in her classroom was saved in subsequent, lessons as time spent planning and resourcing was reduced, and the pupils were motivated in managing tasks.

Peripherals include mainly input and output devices. An input device allows a user to enter data into a computer and, once processed, the data output is presented in an intelligible format. Input devices can be both manual, such as a keyboard or a mouse, and automatic, such as a barcode reader or a sensor. Examples of output devices include a monitor or a printer.

1　A wireless mouse allows the teacher to move around a classroom freely whilst manipulating displayed materials. This is a good use of technology to support classroom management and allows the teacher to perform other tasks such as monitoring and assessing pupils' progress during the lesson. Pupils are also encouraged to engage in lessons by taking control of the mouse, for example, by demonstrating and sharing knowledge with their peers.

2　A visualiser is a digital camera linked to a computer and enables the teacher to display items in real time. This is particularly useful if a pupil has created exemplary work that can be easily illustrated to a whole class by holding their exercise book under the visualiser for immediate display. It is also excellent for demonstrating detailed 'workings out' as in mathematics lessons and can be a powerful tool for enhancing understanding.

3　Voting technologies allow instant feedback to questions by the whole class or groups and provides an immediate graphical display of responses in percentages or numbers. The technology usually needs specific software to be loaded onto the teacher's computer and a set of small input devices that are remotely connected to the computer. These devices have numeric/alphabetic display choices, are easy to use and are an excellent method of posing questions to a class. Personal, social and health education (PSHE) teachers may find this effective when teaching sensitive subject material such as drug use and abortion choices as the tool allows immediate and anonymous responses from pupils.

4   Handheld Universal Serial Bus (USB) video cameras are ideal for both pupil and teacher use in the classroom partly because they are simple to operate as they are small, cable-free and robust but also because the quality of both video and audio recording is excellent and it is easy to transfer recordings to a computer for editing and sharing without additional software. These can be used as a method of observation for assessment of pupils creating blogs and reviews as evidence for GCSE coursework.

5   USB microphones are also easy to operate and go beyond the initial novelty factor of having the ability to record and edit voices by giving pupils the opportunity to engage fully and concentrate entirely on their opinions and preserve real-time conversations. Uses include recording pupils discussing their emotions when viewing artwork, explaining how a mathematical problem was solved or revising for an examination using material recorded in lessons.

6   Tablets are handheld devices used like a mouse to control actions on screen. They can be used by pupils using their fingers to draw, or using a rubber tipped pen to take notes or annotate a digital e-book. Many pupils are familiar with the use of such tablets for gaming purposes, thus many are more knowledgeable than their teachers and this pupil know-how can be a good foundation for peer learning in lessons. There are many applications known as 'apps' that allow pupils to revise subject material, turn their tablet into a musical keyboard to play, or read e-books. Given Michael Gove's (2012) emphasis on the need to teach pupils programming skills, it is worth considering involving pupils in creating their own android phone applications. This may be dependent upon yourself and your pupils developing and sharing the required skills and 'know how' in order to achieve this.

7   Monitoring software for classrooms is useful as it gives teachers control of the classroom technology. Teachers can monitor the applications and websites being accessed in real time, share files, seize computer control for demonstrations and send messages to individuals or groups of pupils. The initial mastering of the monitoring software may be daunting, but once grasped, this tool can transform a lesson.

Some schools recognise pupils' confidence and aptitude with technology use and through actively valuing their input, promote pupil involvement for the planning and delivering of both part and whole lessons. As the research outlined earlier shows, this shared responsibility for ICT use and learning demonstrates how pupils and teachers can take joint ownership for the deployment of these ICTs in the classroom.

E-safety across the curriculum

E-safety principles and rules must be shared with, and understood by pupils because the term 'e-safety' encompasses a wide range of potential dangers. It is important that you consider the following whenever pupils use ICT in your lessons:

■   ensuring that your own e-safety training is current;
■   understanding your school's e-safety policies and sanctions, including guidelines for pupils;
■   planning tasks to ensure that computer-based learning is combined with discussion or kinaesthetic activities;
■   using monitoring software for 'real time' supervision allowing immediate intervention as appropriate;

■   The use of a 'walled garden', meaning a controlled environment that restricts pupils' access to specific online content.

Pupils are unlikely to stray from their ICT task if given clear learning objectives and achievable goals and are motivated by the activity they undertake, although some pupils still make poor choices. Always make sure that you report any incident to your tutor.

Task 16.3 **Using new technologies**

In your setting, select a technology you are not familiar with which could be used to support teaching and/or learning and which could be one of the above. For this technology:

■   Identify whether it is an input or output device.
■   Establish if the technology is easy to use and/or access where you will be teaching. Will you be able to learn how to use it independently or will you need help and/or technical support?
■   What are the implications for pupils using this ICT, e.g. will they need to be shown how to use it?
■   Identify three expected learning outcomes that will have impact on your teaching and learning.

Once you have completed the above, undertake the following.

Using this and/or other chapters in this book, create a lesson plan or sequence of plans that incorporate the use of this technology within your subject area. Following the lesson/sequence of lessons, evaluate the success of the ICT(s). You may want to consider the following:

■   the level of pupils' enjoyment/motivation using the technology;
■   the level of individuals' progress made during the lesson(s);
■   whether any new learning was accelerated by the use of ICT;
■   if there were any advantages/disadvantages in using this ICT to support teaching and learning.

Create a simple feedback survey* for pupils to complete following the lesson(s) based on:

■   I felt more engaged in this lesson than if we had not been using ICT.
■   I feel I learned more in this lesson because I was using ICT.
■   The use of ICT made no difference to what I learned.

Using this feedback repeat this process using another new technology that is available to you in your setting.

You could also share this experience and the benefits with a colleague and jointly plan an INSET session in consultation with your tutor.

*You may wish to use pupil voting system technology if available in your school.

Pupils can be made aware of the dangers of using the internet by accessing online resources including the Child Exploitation and Online Protection Centre (CEOP) website 'thinkuknow' (http://www.thinkuknow.co.uk).

Other websites that provide pupils with an opportunity to assess their knowledge of internet safety include:

BBC's internet safety: http://www.bbc.co.uk/cbbc/help/web/staysafe.

McAfee internet security: http://us.mcafee.com/en-us/landingpages/quiz_kids.asp.

SUMMARY

Having read this chapter, you should now be able to incorporate a wider range of technologies into your teaching. You may also have benefited from auditing both your own and your pupils' ongoing needs as an integral part of your classroom practice. You should be able to identify how different technologies can be used effectively to support learning and teaching, but most importantly how new and emerging technologies can motivate pupils in your subject area. You can now consider appropriate methods to measure the impact of pupils' use of technologies in your classroom. You may now know how to evaluate the effects of adopting such strategies and will have shared the benefits of these ideas with colleagues and possibly senior leaders in your school. You will, through completing the tasks in this chapter, be on the way to transforming your practice and becoming a teacher for the twenty-first century.

FURTHER READING

Carrington, V. and Robinson, M. (2009) *Digital Literacies: Social Learning and Classroom Practices*, London: Sage.
    At times, this book reads as a series of case studies. It presents scenarios of the pupils you may be teaching and how they use ICT outside of school as well as the kind of staffroom debates you may be having. The book also offers suggestions, like the one you are reading here, as to how to integrate technologies as part of your classroom practice. It also provides some sound further reading along the way.

Nielsen, L., Webb, W. and Prensky, M. (2011) *Teaching Generation Text: Using Cell Phones to Enhance Learning*, San Francisco: Wiley.
    Marc Prensky – alluded to earlier in this chapter – is the founder of the term 'Digital Natives' and 'Digital Immigrants' although there is some debate as to the validity of his arguments. This book focuses on ways to incorporate the use of mobile phones in the classroom. Although the suggested teaching activities relate to strands of the US national curriculum, it offers useful advice and presents lesson plans where mobile technology can be used, for example to support the teaching of science.

Prensky, M. (2010) *Teaching Digital Natives: Partnering for Real Learning*, London: Sage.
    Stephen Heppell's foreword recognises the contribution Marc Prensky has made to revolutionising the pedagogical ways in which technology can drive educational practice in the twenty-first century. The beauty of this book is that it boldly outlines why pupils are dissatisfied with the current educational system. It considers themes such as collaborative learning as well as taking into consideration pupils' interests to motivate learning. The book's main ideas also translate well in practical suggestions for teachers.

Richardson, W. (2009) *Blogs, Wikis, Podcasts, and Other Powerful Web Tools For Classrooms* **(2nd edition), London: Sage.**

> This book is used by Initial Teacher Training programmes, so it may already be known to you. It provides both a background to the birth of the internet and useful guidelines on how to use a range of technologies in the classroom, including live streaming, really simple syndication (RSS) feeds and Flickr, and how these technologies can be used to transform teaching and learning.

Selwyn, S. (2009) 'The digital native – myth and reality', *Aslib Proceedings: New Information Perspectives,* **61(4): 364–79.**

> This journal article contains an analysis of the 'Digital Natives' debate that may help you in developing your arguments and line of questioning that is required at M Level because it will hopefully encourage you to challenge your own and others' assumption as to how pupils may engage with technology in the classroom.

REFERENCES

Becta (2008) *Harnessing Technology Review 2008: The Role of Technology and its Impact on Education: Full Report*, Coventry: Becta. Available at: http://dera.ioe.ac.uk/1423/1/becta_2008_htreview_report.pdf (accessed 5 January 2012).

——(2010a) *Harnessing Technology School Survey: 2010*, Coventry: Becta. Available at: http://dera.ioe.ac.uk/1544/1/becta_2010_htss_report.pdf (accessed 5 January 2012).

——(2010b) *21st Century Teacher: Are You Ready to Meet the Challenge?* Coventry: Becta. Available at: http://webarchive.nationalarchives.gov.uk/20101102103654/publications.becta.org.uk/display.cfm?resID=41521 (accessed 5 January 2012).

Bennett, S. and Maton, K. (2010) 'Beyond the "digital natives" debate: towards a more nuanced understanding of students' technology experiences', *Journal of Computer Assisted Learning* 26: 321–31.

Bennett, S., Maton, K. and Kervin, L. (2008) 'The "digital natives" debate: A critical review of the evidence', *British Journal of Educational Technology* 39(5): 775–86.

Cardinal Newman Catholic School and Brighton and Hove LA (2006) *Rolling Out ICT in a Secondary School: Learning and Teaching Using ICT. Hands On Support Primary Case Study.* Available at: http://www.teachernet.gov.uk/docbank/index.cfm?id=9486 (accessed 15 January 2009).

Carrington, V. and Robinson, M. (2009) *Digital Literacies: Social Learning and Classroom Practices*, London: Sage.

Condie, R., Munro, B., Muir, D. and Collins, R. (2005) *The Impact of ICT Initiatives in Scottish Schools: Phase 3*, Edinburgh: SEED. Available at: http://www.scotland.gov.uk/Publications/2005/09/14111116/11170 (accessed 5 January 2012).

Condie, R. and Munro, B. with Seagraves, L. and Kenesson, S. (2007) *The Impact of ICT in Schools: A Landscape Review*, Coventry: Becta. Available at: http://dera.ioe.ac.uk/view/organisations/becta.html (accessed 5 January 2012).

Conole, G., de Laat, M., Dillon, T. and Darby, J. (2008) 'Disruptive technologies, pedagogical innovation: what's new? Findings from an in-depth study of students' use and perception of technology', *Computers and Education* 50: 511–24.

Cox, M. and Marshall, G. (2007) 'Effects of ICT: do we know what we should know?', *Education and Information Technologies* 12(2): 59–70.

Gove, M. (2012) http://www.education.gov.uk/inthenews/speeches/a00201868/michael-gove-speech-at-the-bett-show-2012 (accessed 6 February 2012).

Green, J. (2006) *Secondary ICT: Web Literacy*. Available at: http://www.teachfind.com/teachers-tv/secondary-ict-web-literacy (accessed 6 February 2012).

Guo, R., Dobson, T. and Petrina, S. (2008) 'Digital natives, digital immigrants: an analysis of age and ICT competency in teacher education', *Journal of Educational Computing Research* 38(3): 235–54.

Guzetti, B.J., Ellit, K. and Welsch, D. (2010) *DIY Media in the Classroom: New Literacies Across Content Areas*, New York: Teachers College Press.

Hennessy, S., Deaney, R. and Ruthven, K. (2005) 'Emerging teacher strategies for mediating "Technology-integrated Instructional Conversations": a socio-cultural perspective', *The Curriculum Journal* 16(3): 265–92.

Li, Y. and Ranieri, M. (2010) 'Are "digital natives" really digitally competent? A study on Chinese teenagers', *British Journal of Educational Technology* 4(6): 1029–42.

OFSTED (2009) *The Importance of ICT: Information and Communication Technology in Primary and Secondary Schools, 2005/2008*, London: Ofsted. Reference no: 070035. Available at: http://www.ofsted.gov.uk/resources/importance-of-ict-information-and-communication-technology-primary-and-secondary-schools-20052008 (accessed 5 January 2012).

Poet, H., Rudd, P. and Smith, R. (2010) *How Teachers Approach Practice Improvement*, London: General Teaching Council for England (GTC). Available at: http://www.gtce.org.uk/documents/publicationpdfs/teach_survey10practice.pdf (accessed 5 January 2012).

Prensky, M. (2001) 'Digital natives, digital immigrants', *On the Horizon*, 9(5).

——(2010) *Teaching Digital Natives: Partnering for Real Learning*, London: Sage.

Robinson, K. (2010) Royal Society for the Encouragement of Arts, Manufactures and Commerce [RSA] Animate, *Changing Education Paradigms*. Available at: http://www.youtube.com/watch?v=zDZFcDGpL4U (accessed 5 January 2012).

Selwyn, S. (2009) 'The digital native: myth and reality', *Aslib Proceedings: New Information Perspectives* 61 (4): 364–79.

Smith, P., Rudd, P. and Coghlan, M. (2008) *Harnessing Technology Schools Survey 2008: Report 2 – Data*, Coventry: Becta. Available at: http://www.nfer.ac.uk/nfer/publications/TSV02/TSV02_home.cfm?publicationID=11&title=Harnessing%20Technology:%20schools%20survey%202008.%20Report%202:%20data (accessed 12 February 2012).

Richardson, W. (2009) *Blogs, Wikis, Podcasts, and Other Powerful Web Tools for Classrooms* (2nd edition) London: Sage.

White, D. (2007) *Results and analysis of the Web 2.0 services survey undertaken by the SPIRE project*, Oxford: University of Oxford. Available at: http://spire.conted.ox.ac.uk/ (accessed 5 January 2012).

Williams, P. (2008) 'Leading schools in the digital age: a clash of cultures', *School Leadership and Management* 28(3): 213–18.

USING ICT IN THE CLASSROOM AND FOR ADMINISTRATION

Marilyn Leask and Gareth Whyte

INTRODUCTION

The other chapters in this book provide ideas and advice across a wide range of contexts, which you may wish to refer back to as your experience in education develops.

This chapter returns to the fundamentals of the individual teacher's practice – maximising the learning of the individual pupil in an era where technology enhanced learning is changing the way teaching and learning is undertaken.

In the 2005 edition of this book we quoted a head teacher at an innovative school in the UK where by 2000 all teachers were issued with laptops and ICT use was integrated across the curriculum.

> Every student needs a grandparent linking them to the past and a PC to take them into the future.
>
> (Head teacher in Leask and Kington, 2001)

OBJECTIVES

By the end of this chapter, you should:

- have considered how through your teaching you are going to ensure your pupils are equipped with the concepts, attitudes, skills and knowledge necessary to function in a digital world;
- be able to audit resources in the home and school environment where you are teaching and review your current skill base and knowledge base of the pupils;
- know what questions to ask to establish whole school and departmental ICT policy and practice, including administrative systems and management information systems in use;
- have an understanding of e-safety.

But in just a few years, the young people from this school were in a world where the notion of having a personal PC was outdated. The home and work environment has been transformed by the explosion of low cost mobile digital devices with functions once provided by typewriters, cameras, tape recorders, record players, telephones, pagers, and giving access to services and products that once required visits to job centres, council offices, book stores, music shops, and in fact all the shops once found in high streets.

So your pupils can expect to live and work in environments where familiarity with technologies and mobile devices with functions such as those listed above is taken for granted and a high level of skill is expected. As a teacher, regardless of your subject, you have responsibilities to prepare your pupils for this future.

YOUR RESPONSIBILITY TO YOUR PUPILS

In the UK there can be few occupations now that are unaffected by ICT. Regardless of the level of skill required for the job, records are kept on computer, equipment and supplies ordered on the internet, online filing of tax returns is expected; online ordering of prescriptions from the doctor is standard. However, integrating appropriate forms of e-learning into the learning environment remains a major challenge for many teachers.

'If someone is learning in a way that uses information and communication technologies (ICTs), they are using e-learning' (Department for Education and Skills, 2003, B: 6). In this Department for Education and Skills (DFES) consultation paper on how to achieve a unified approach to e-learning across England, the DFES called on all involved in education to ensure that the benefits of e-learning are available to all learners, not just those in innovative institutions with innovative teachers.

This challenge involves you directly as you make decisions about the teaching strategies and learning approaches that are employed with the pupils for whom you are responsible. Ways in which you use digital technologies in your teaching, preparation and administration provide models of e-learning for pupils that help prepare them for the uncertain future. Writing in 1993 when personal computers were becoming widespread but before internet, mobile phone and digital video technologies were widely available, Papert identifies the future as being one of constant change in the workplace, and this change applies to the workplace of teachers as well as the pupils:

> Not very long ago, and in many parts of the world even today, young people would learn skills that they would use in their work throughout life. Today in industrial countries, most people are doing jobs that did not exist when they were born.
>
> (Papert, 1993, p. vii)

During your teaching career you can expect that digital technologies will be used to make schooling more individualised with assessment strategies and teaching styles increasingly being adapted to include individualised resources, learning and assessment opportunities. Ways of providing teachers with appropriate data about individual pupils' attainment are being improved and you can expect to be held accountable at the individual pupil level for your use of such data in planning your teaching.

So in deciding what to teach and how to teach it you as the teacher are preparing pupils for a future that the pupils themselves will make by building on the foundation that parents, teachers and society have laid for them.

Papert (1993, p. vii) makes the point that:

The most important skills in determining a person's life pattern have already become the ability to learn new skills, to taking on new concepts, to assess new situations, to deal with the unexpected. The competitive ability is the ability to learn.

Task 17.1 **Building lifelong learning skills in your pupils**

Review the ideas in the other chapters in this book, consider and make notes about how, through your teaching, you are going to ensure your pupils are equipped with the concepts, attitudes, skills and knowledge necessary to function in a digital world. Talk with other teachers about this issue and build up a file of best practice to guide your work as a teacher. We suggest you return to this annually and review whether you are achieving these goals.

What you are able to do within your classroom will depend to some extent on the school in which you are teaching. In the United Kingdom (UK) there was substantial investment in digital technologies infrastructure, hardware and software over a sustained period from the mid-1990s (Department for Education and Employment, 1995). Free training was provided for teachers in the UK in the use of ICT in their subject areas during the period 1999 to 2003 (Leask, 2002) and a rolling programme of providing laptops to teachers was developed along with investment in online materials and access to software (see Younie and Leask, 2013).

The Office for Standards in Education (OFSTED) reports on ICT (available at www. ofsted.gov.uk and www.ofsted.gov.uk/resources/subject-professional-development-materials-ict) indicate that pupils in technology rich environments achieve on average higher grades than other pupils when allowances are made for home background and access. However, UK schools take very individual positions with respect to the provision of digital technologies to support technology enhanced learning and many schools struggle to maintain ICT resources for a number of reasons: the lack of expert knowledge by decision makers or financial constraints in comparison with commercial organisations.

AUDITING YOUR ENVIRONMENT

All teachers trained in the UK are expected to be digitally literate but you will need to regularly assess new opportunities in your subject area as new digital technologies become available. You need to assess your own needs for knowledge in your subject areas and for professional development and, if you are a new teacher, discuss them with your mentor in your induction year in order to develop a plan for your on-going professional development. An online digital creativity and literacy resource designed to upskill teachers and lecturers can be found on the Education Communities website (www. educationcommunities.org) by searching for 'digital literacy and creativity'.

Task 17.2 **Planning your personal development**

Review your needs by going through the materials on the digital literacy and creativity community on the Education Communities website (www. educationcommunities.org/c/157123/home.do?id=157123&x=149&y=13). Make a plan for your personal development and ensure you keep up to date.

As well as drawing on support from staff in your own school you may find advice and support is available from your subject association and that an annual conference provides you with the opportunity to find out about new approaches. In the UK, NAACE is a professional association and a community of educators, technologists and policymakers who share a vision for the role of technology in education and can be found at: www. naace.co.uk. Mirandanet is a network for innovative educators who share ideas about next practice and is open to all to join at: www.mirandanet.ac.uk.

It may also be possible for you to observe another teacher using technology with classes similar to your own. Over a period of time, you should build up a bank of ideas and resources to support the use of digital technologies in your teaching.

Various sites offering support resources for teachers in particular countries are as follows: In England: the Excellence Gateway (www.excellencegateway.org.uk), and the Department for Education (www.education.gov.uk/schools).

- In Scotland: Education Scotland (www.educationscotland.gov.uk).
- In Northern Ireland: the Northern Ireland Curriculum (www.nicurriculum.org.uk/).
- In Wales: the National Grid For Learning (www.ngfl-cymru.org.uk).

SCHOOL AND DEPARTMENT RESOURCE AUDIT

What ICT resources are available in your school? The availability and use of ICT in schools varies considerably so in each school in which you teach you need to audit resources before undertaking detailed planning for schemes of work and lesson plans. Table 17.1 provides an example of an audit tool, which you could use to give an overview of the resources available to you and how you can access them.

Familiarity with computer-based equipment comes with experience and you are unlikely to gain this if you're restricted to using such equipment during the school day. Research (Leask and Younie, 2002) shows that the ethos of schools where ICT is most embedded in classroom and general professional practices is likely to be supportive and collaborative. Ideally ICT expertise should be held by staff within all departments and not just concentrated in the ICT department, so that the 'just-in-time' learning of individual staff trying out new methods of working with ICT can be supported. Tasks 17.3 and 17.4 suggest ways of auditing the resources of your school.

Task 17.3 **Auditing the ICT available in your subject area**

Using the audit table in Table 17.1 find out how to access different forms of digital technologies to support your area of the curriculum.

Your department may have a budget for buying resources that you may be able to use. Consider using pupils to help you find and evaluate such material for your teaching programme. Find out if your school has facilities for multimedia production and see what has been produced so far; plan to incorporate the resources available into your teaching over time. Some schools will run projects across the school, as described in Chapter 14 of this volume – find out if this is done in your school.

■ **Table 17.1** Auditing school and department resources: ICT audit tool.

ICT Type	Person responsible for maintenance and booking	Booking procedure	Availability	Your training or practice requirements	Notes: e.g. access codes, locations of keys, passwords, pupil access, problem solving notes
Mobile technologies for teachers					
Mobile technologies for pupils					
PCs for teacher use					
PCs for student use					
Visualisers					
Scanners					
Data projector					
Interactive whiteboard					
Printers					
Digital cameras					
Virtual learning environment					
Departmental website					
Audio resources					
Subject specific ICT such as digital microscopes					
Management information systems					
Other					
Other					
Other					
Other					

AUDITING HOME ACCESS AND THE SKILL AND KNOWLEDGE OF PUPILS

Successful teaching and learning is more likely to occur when the teacher builds on what the children already know. In the case of ICT you are likely to find pupils in your class that have access to family members with top of the range ICT resources. Such access is not necessarily directly related to income. Some refugee families and other immigrants prioritise ICT equipment at home as a means of keeping in touch with friends and relatives in the countries left behind. Local communities that are mono-cultural and on low incomes may lack access to the local problem-solving skills held within a community that facilitates home access and enables families to keep the technology working. Some schools acknowledge this and take on the role of providing ICT support for the local community, sometimes in conjunction with local colleges.

Clearly identifying the skills and knowledge base of pupils is a necessary prerequisite to using ICT in the classroom. A brief pupil questionnaire asking pupils about their experience with and access to the different forms of technology you wish to use is probably the quickest and easiest way to identify this knowledge and skill base. Questions you might pose include:

■ What ICT resources do you have at home that you are allowed to use?
■ Which of the following resources can you use now and which do you need training to use? (You need to provide a list of those relevant to your classroom and context.)

As well as the technical skills your pupils may need, skills in critical evaluation are particularly important where electronic information sources are to be used, so the pupils are able to evaluate the quality of information that they are receiving. These skills in critical evaluation must be taught. This is discussed later in this chapter.

Gaining an overview of the kind of ICT related projects which have been done in your department and other departments in the school in previous years gives you an understanding of what is accepted practice in your school. Some schools have extremely high expectations about the level of ICT use in the work of departments; other schools may not be able to support the level of practice you would wish to achieve personally. Variations between schools and departments in the ICT policy and practice are huge. In schools using ICT effectively, you can expect to find a school wide virtual learning environment (VLE) packed with high-quality electronic resources and schemes of work, which you should expect to use and add to.

SCHOOL AND DEPARTMENT ICT POLICY AND PRACTICE – E-SAFETY

You need to be aware of the cyber context that pupils experience beyond the classroom. Check whether the school has a policy giving teachers and pupils guidance about appropriate online behaviour within and beyond the school and ensure you know the appropriate actions to take if anyone experiences cyber-bullying, whether a teacher or a pupil. In some cases, police involvement may be required. In the UK under the 2012 Freedoms Bill there is an amendment to the Protection from Harassment Act which covers cyber-harassment, social networks, emails and stalking. See also Maple and Short (2012) for research on the impact of cyber-stalking.

In your classroom, you need to ensure that e-safety ground rules are established for working with ICT, for example for internet and e-mail use. Inappropriate use needs to be defined, e.g. no bullying e-mails, no downloads of copyright material. Pupils need to be aware that records are kept of the sites they visit and the e-mails they send. When people store their files in their user area they need to be aware of security issues and that interfering with other people's files is a serious offence. We've found young pupils are not as careful to keep the passwords private as older pupils.

Pupils need to be made aware that their digital footprints cannot be erased, that everything they access can be monitored and potentially checked, that what they do could lead to significant damage to their personal reputation perhaps years into the future, that material downloaded or sent from computers to other students and members of the community can be tracked.

Task 17.4 **Auditing school and department ICT policy and practice**

As well as knowing what resources are available to support technology enhanced learning and how you can access them, you need to know about school and department policy and practice about the use of resources. You may wish to:

- Check the procedures governing pupil access to ICT resources.
- Find out about department ICT policies, including policies on posting lesson plans and homework on the school VLE or department website for out-of-school access by pupils and parents.
- Ask about the kinds of ICT related work the pupils readily undertake in your department and across departments, e.g. production of podcasts following visits or field trips, international collaborations with other schools using e-mail or video conferencing, links with the EU E-Twinning initiative.
- Review the resources available on the department shared area or VLE and find out how you can contribute to building a shared professional resource.
- Check what the processes for monitoring, recording, analysing and reporting pupil achievement are. Different schools will use different systems but management information systems will be in place to handle data and to give you feedback about individual pupils' achievement over time.

ADMINISTRATION, INCLUDING PUPIL ACHIEVEMENT TRACKING

As research has been done into how digital technologies can benefit education, a priority has become developing ways in which the technology could support teachers in their administration, including planning, monitoring pupil achievement and record keeping. Best practice is that teachers are provided with a school laptop to manage the administration necessary for their work. This ensures the separation of personal and professional files. You can expect the following practices:

- Lesson plans and schemes of work worksheets are stored and shared electronically where once hardcopies would be kept in filing cabinets, perhaps never shared or used until they become increasingly dogeared before having to be reproduced over again. Electronic versions should be easily accessible to all teachers and easily adaptable to different pupil's needs.

■ Syllabi and supporting materials are available as downloadable files on the websites of examination boards as this makes teachers' planning of courses leading to national examinations much easier than was previously the case.

■ Electronic Mark Brooks created though, for example, spreadsheet software which allow the production of graphs showing pupil progress over time with the touch of a button so that individual pupil data is easily available to the teacher. When schools make effective use of management information systems, data on the individual pupils can be used to compare their performance across subjects and throughout their school career. The data can be mapped against the expected outcomes. Evidence from the OECD ICT and whole school improvement project (OECD, 2002) suggests that a pupil can be motivated when this type of data is discussed with them as individuals.

■ Individual contact by e-mail with pupils and parents is part of the work of some teachers but this has to be managed carefully because of work overload implications for the teacher. In addition some schools have policies about the procedures to be followed for home–school communication.

TEACHING AND LEARNING USING DIGITAL TECHNOLOGIES – THE MOVE TO PERSONALISATION

The digital technologies now available are an extension of the types of technologies that have been available for decades (video, audio, computer technologies), and the understanding developed through the research on computer-based education and media studies provides a solid foundation for the on-going development of pedagogy which uses new forms of ICT to aid teaching and learning. Major pedagogical changes that can be expected are those focusing on personalisation of learning supported by digital technologies. The cheapness of ICT, including that which gives low cost access to schools with expert knowledge and communities around the world, provides scope for the individualisation of the curriculum.

THE ROLE OF THE TEACHER

How does the availability of digital technologies affect the role of the teacher? The vision of the teacher-less learner sitting in front of a computer screen is prevalent but as knowledge of how effective learning is supported by ICT has developed so has a new role for teachers developed – as e-learning mentors providing individual support at the time the learners need it. This support is very time intensive and as mentioned above you need to consider your workload carefully if there are elements of e-mentoring within it (e.g. feedback on drafts, which are submitted electronically, providing individual helpline via e-mail). It is advisable to focus this support on targeted groups for short periods of time, at least at the beginning, until you get a sense of how much time you have available for this work.

In contrast, the time taken to post advance lesson plans and homework on the department or school VLE clearly is a sound investment. Teachers report gains in pupil learning as pupils are more easily able to revisit lessons in which they may have had difficulties or which they missed, and they may also see the progression that is planned for their learning as well as the relevance of the homework linking in with the overall learning programme.

Those who believe the interaction with material is an important part of learning find ICT offers pupils tremendous opportunities to explore the world and undertake projects under the teacher's guidance. Daily contact can be made with pupils, schools and communities around the world, collaborative history, art and science projects can provide immediate insights into the life experiences and environments of others. Experts in different fields can sometimes be involved in such projects through contact via e-mail or, for example, video conferencing, which can be easily managed via free software, which at the time of writing includes Skype or Google groups.

ACTIVE LEARNING APPROACHES

Active learning plays a central role in most lesson plans that integrate ICT, i.e. where the approach to lesson planning is underpinned by activity learning theory (learning by doing) as opposed to acquisition learning theory (learning through acquisition of facts). Those whose view of teaching is that the pupils passively receive knowledge from the teacher have a limited view of how technology enhanced learning can be used in the classroom. This view is based on limited understanding of learning theory – the acquisition of knowledge is the endpoint.

Capel *et al.* (2013) identify dimensions of active learning which include: meaningful learning, giving a sense of ownership, personal involvement in learning, valuing of pupil ideas, problem-solving, questioning, incorporating talking debate, resource-based learning, collaboration with other learners and negotiation over content and focus on learning. Teaching sessions using ICT can be structured to include active learning approaches. In designing lessons that incorporate pupils' use of ICT, teachers apply the same principles that they use when planning all lessons.

Depending on the required outcomes, pupils may work as individuals, in groups or teams and on the same or different tasks. Your lesson objectives, which indicate the outcomes you desire any teaching strategies used to achieve, may for example include problem-solving, group work, planning research, analysis and reporting skills. Approaches to learning that can be adapted to the teaching environment using ICT include independent pupil-centred learning, enquiry or active learning, cooperative or collaborative learning.

Internet research projects can be designed so they require active interaction with data collected; e.g. where e-mail or Skype links are made with other schools pupils could be collecting, sharing and analysing data rather than simply writing to each other. Such E-Pal or Skype based activities, whilst useful on one level, are more likely to be sustained if they are linked with collaborative projects, e.g. pupils could be directed to produce a report with their E-pal on, for example, an aspect of their local area such as population characteristics, occupations and so on. In carefully constructed situations ICT can be used to provide opportunities to develop high-level cognitive skills. Table 17.2 provides further examples.

■ **Table 17.2** Examples of the opportunities available through ICT.

■ Pupil presentations of work as webpages, podcasts or PowerPoint presentations – developing creativity as well as skills.
■ Resource-based learning – information retrieval from the internet, and other media sources.
■ Partnerships with experts and networking with individuals and institutions around the world – through e-mail links, video conferencing and E-Twinning.
■ Virtual environments – you can "stroll" through art galleries around the world or take virtual field trips linking the experience with direct questions to pupils in schools living in such environments.
■ Access to services: health and careers advice, information about revision guides online and subject specific sites.

DEVELOPING PUPIL SKILLS IN CRITICAL EVALUATION

The internet in particular contains information from sources that have not undergone the degree of scrutiny and quality assurance that traditional published paper-based sources have. Pupils all too often perceive what is on the internet as fact. It is particularly important that pupils learn to critically evaluate information they find on the internet. They need to routinely consider questions such as:

■ Who is providing the information?
■ What do they hope to achieve by providing this information?
■ Are they in a position to provide accurate information?
■ In what way might the information be biased or inaccurate?

Pupils must be made aware that information on the internet is produced for particular purposes, as is that in the press and on television, to which they are exposed daily, so it may be unreliable or biased. While some providers may have education as a priority, other providers want to sell products or to influence recipients' thinking.

Plagiarism takes on new directions as pupils can now access huge amounts of information from the internet straight into their assignments. Pupils need to be alerted to the unacceptability of including text written by others in their work unless they attribute the source of such text. When referencing internet sources pupils should state the internet address together with the date and time of access as well as any other identifying features.

CLASSROOM MANAGEMENT ISSUES

Management of limited ICT resources so that all pupils are treated equally requires careful planning. Arrangements for computer access in classrooms vary considerably, from hubs (i.e. groups of computers in an open area serving groups of classrooms giving pupils access during all lessons), to mobile devices which might need to be booked, or computer suites available on a much more restricted basis.

The use of the internet in the classroom poses a number of challenges. In secondary schools, if it's used for resource-based learning, pupils may take longer than traditional teaching methods of around an hour to achieve useful results, even if the teacher directs their search to some extent. Logging onto the school network and logging off often takes a significant amount of lesson time and there will often be one or two people who experience difficulty (e.g. their password doesn't seem to work), which can disrupt the lesson.

The problem with speed of access to internet sites may hinder the use of the internet during lessons in some schools. Downloading files from different internet sites in advance of lessons is one solution that some teachers propose, however there is something intrinsically motivating for a learner to have access to an open-ended resource. The open-ended nature of the internet as a resource does mean that the path of learning is less predictable and some teachers may find this difficult to manage. Many schools have resource centres that pupils can access outside of class time. Where all pupils can access the internet outside of lessons, it may be appropriate to set internet-based homework. Traditional library searches can sometimes be quicker and yield more high-quality information than internet searches and those should be normally included in such work as well.

CONFRONTING TECHNOPHOBIA

Whatever your own feelings about the use of ICT, as a professional you have a responsibility to the pupils you teach to prepare them for the future. It is not uncommon for teachers and some pupils to feel out of their depth when it comes to the use of ICT. As with any teaching and learning situation, the problems need to be identified and strategies put in place to remedy them.

Not being familiar with ICT is hardly an option for teachers working in the twenty-first century. At a fundamental level ICT allows you to use time much more effectively, from administration, the keeping of up-to-date records and in the searching for information related to subject areas. The quality and quantity of the work of those not able to use such ICT will be increasingly seen to be unacceptably limited. Take, for example, the art teacher. Why should pupils be limited to examining printed or pre-recorded material about artefacts from different cultures when with the use of the internet, they can roam the galleries and museums of the world, incorporating directly into their own projects images of what they find? In the case of science teachers teaching about space, why not use the latest video streaming from NASA?

SUMMARY

Using ICT in the classroom does not ensure that the most effective learning takes place; so many other factors come into play. What we are suggesting is that using digital technologies is an integral part of the learning experience of pupils in the twenty-first century and you are responsible for ensuring that such opportunities are provided for your pupils. To ensure you are addressing their needs, you should review your teaching strategies regularly and be ready to assimilate new methods of proven worth into your teaching.

In the first year of your teaching, you are likely to be very busy getting to know the school and the pupils and developing and consolidating your teaching skills. The texts that follow in the further reading section below provide useful material for you to draw on when you have time to reflect and when you're extending your work using ICT.

FURTHER READING

Kennewell, S. (2007) *A Practical Guide to Teaching ICT in the Secondary School,* London: Routledge.
> A workbook designed to support student and experienced teachers using ICT in the classroom, focusing on managing the class and learning environment.

McKeown, S. and McGlashon, A. (2012) *Brilliant Ideas for Using ICT in the Inclusive Classroom,* London: Routledge.
> A book full of interesting ideas and practical suggestions for using ICT to enhance pupil learning.

NATIONAL CONFERENCES AND EXHIBITIONS

The British Education and Training Technologies (BETT) exhibition takes place over several days including Saturday each January: free tickets are available for teachers. This is a huge exhibition, which includes software and hardware suppliers and publishers. There is considerable focus on software and other resources to support each subject area, including special educational needs software. See www.bettshow.com for further details.

REFERENCES

Capel, S., Leask, M. and Turner, T. (2013) *Learning to Teach in the Secondary School: A Companion to School Experience*, Abingdon: Routledge/Taylor & Francis.

Department for Education and Employment (1995) *Superhighways for Education,* London: HMSO.

Department for Education and Skills (2003) *Towards a Unified E-learning Strategy*, London: DFES.

Leask, M. (2002) *The New Opportunities Fund ICT Training for Teachers and School Librarians: Progress Review and Lessons Learned Through the Central Quality Assurance Process in England,* London: Teacher Training Agency.

Leask, M. and Kington, A. (2001) *A Case Study of ICT and School Improvement at Greenfield College, England. Integrating ICT into Teachers' Practice*, A case study undertaken for the OECD (2002) ICT for Whole School Improvement Project.

Maple, C. and Short, E. (2012) *Cyberstalking in the United Kingdom: An Analysis of the ECHO Pilot Survey 2011*, Bedford: University of Bedfordshire, National Institute for Cyberstalking Research with the Crown Prosecution Service.

OECD (2002) *ICT for Whole School Improvement Project*, Paris: OECD.

Papert, S. (1993) *The Children's Machine: Rethinking School in the Age of the Computer,* New York: Basic Books.

Younie, S. and Leask, M. (2013) *Teaching with Technologies,* Maidenhead: Open University Press.

INDEX